DIGITAL SOLDIERS

DIGITAL SOLDIERS

THE EVOLUTION OF HIGH-TECH WEAPONRY AND
TOMORROW'S BRAVE NEW BATTLEFIELD

•

James F. Dunnigan

ST. MARTIN'S PRESS
NEW YORK

PUBLISHED BY THOMAS DUNNE BOOKS
An imprint of St. Martin's Press

Book design by Ellen R. Sasahara

Library of Congress Cataloging-in-Publication Data

Dunnigan, James F.
    Digital soldiers: the evolution of high-tech weaponry and tomorrow's brave new
battlefield / by James F. Dunnigan.
        p.   cm.
    Includes index.
    ISBN 0–312–14588–8
    1. Weapons systems—Technological innovations.   2. Military-industrial
complex.   3. Armed Forces and mass media.   I. Title.
UF500.D87   1996
355'.07—dc20   96–18924

First edition: October 1996

10 9 8 7 6 5 4 3 2 1

To

STERLING STREET HART

(1943–1995)

Soldier, scholar, author, father, husband, and good friend

Contents

Tables

Acknowledgments

Thanks to Steve Patrick, Al Nofi, Trent Telenko, Doug Hughes, Scott Rosenthal, William Gross, Kurt Aldag, Shawn Coyne, and Adam Goldberger, who all provided invaluable comments, criticisms, and corrections to the manuscript.

Introduction

B EFORE WE GET started with page after page of fascinating detail and in-numerable facts, let us partake of some introductory items. These make the book easier to use, especially if you are short on time, or knowledge of matters military.

Ten-Minute Version of This Book

THERE'S A LOT of good stuff in this book. A whole book's worth, in fact. But there is a center, a bundle of ideas on which everything in the book hangs. Here I'll give you the central ideas. In short, so to speak, a ten-minute version of the book.

• Weapons-technology development has historically been slow. Centuries would pass before a new weapon appeared. Now, radically new weapons appear every decade.

• Weapons technology will only win some kinds of wars. High-tech weapons weren't much help in places like Somalia or Vietnam, where leadership and diplomacy were more important.

• Weapons have always been less decisive than the skill of the troops. This has been true throughout history and is still true today.

• Money is the key factor; without it you cannot have better weapons or well-trained troops. Poor nations can make the most of a meager budget, but unless a wealthier nation really goes to sleep, money will talk louder than good intentions.

• Defense budgets have historically been a major source of political power and corruption.

• The enemy often has the same technology you have, because these days just about everything's for sale and information travels quickly and easily.

• Trillions of dollars have been spent on space satellites and ICBMs. Fortunately, the former have been put to work a lot, for warlike and peaceful purposes, while the ICBMs have not been used.

• The L. L. Bean advantage. Commercially developed camping equipment has given U.S., and other Western infantry, a combat edge. Little is made of this advantage, nor many others that make wide use of civilian equipment.

• What is happening with all the changes in warfare because of technology is not new, it's just happening faster than it ever has before.

• Military technology saves lives, up to a point, but you can rarely afford to buy as much as you would like.

• There is now a virtually endless list of new military technologies that you can buy.

• Robots are taking over, faster than you think. But in most cases the robots don't look like what you assume a robot should look like.

• Information warfare, the latest military buzzword, is less than it appears. It's old wine in new bottles, and is pushed aggressively as a means to market proposals to research and study the new threat and then study it some more, and more.

• There's nothing new with the problems of developing new weapons and getting them to work on the battlefield. There is still a lot of trial and error, and lots of surprises when you actually use the new item in combat for the first time.

• There are plenty of examples of how to, or how not to, get new weapons from the bright-idea stage to combat-ready status. But there is little sense of history in weapons development, so there is a lot of making the same mistakes over and over again. Then again, even if some of the potential errors are known, there's often little that can be done. This is especially true with the political aspects of what gets built, and the way the media treat the weapons-development process.

• A new weapon, no matter how wonderful its prospects and how hassle-free its development, will be savaged in the media. Bad news is good (salable) news. Even if you have to make up some gory details.

• The new forms of "techno-war" are the continuation of a five-century trend in new military technology invented and continually led by European nations, a development picked up and carried forward by the United States for most of this century. As more nations industrialize, they adopt this form of fighting, but never as successfully as the European and American leaders.

• There is another revolution in warfare coming on. The last one involved mechanization. It began in World War I (1914–18) with the use of tanks, trucks, and aircraft. This revolution matured during World War II (1939–45). This trend continued to develop into the 1980s, when the next revolution, featuring computers and robots, began to appear. Revolutions in warfare usually appear during major wars. This one is likely to sneak in during a period of relative peace.

• The new revolution in warfare comes with a revolution in defense spending and weapons building. Never before has there been so much money for weapons, nor so much technology available for their development and construction. This has changed the ways in which weapons are bought and built. Defense budgets have become political footballs, the weapons spending seen as another form of political patronage. The troops don't always get the weapons they need, but they usually do get the ones that are most politically useful.

• The mass media and public relations have also become major elements in creating a new military technology. The media move the public to urge politicians to do this or that. Public relations (PR) moves the media in this direction or that. Soldiers have, over the decades since World War II, become increasingly adept at playing the PR game, if only in self-defense at times.

• While there has been no major war since World War II, the cold war served as an excuse to do the kind of weapons development usually only seen during a major shooting war.

• Digital infantry is not developing into grunts wearing space suits, but rather more effective communications so the infantry at the front can make better use of the high-tech armored vehicles, aircraft, and robots that still serve mainly to "support" the ground troops.

• The moves toward this new revolution in warfare have been gradual during the last thirty years, but constant. Advances in electronics have brought us better sensors (such as thermal gun sights that can see through smoke and darkness) and much better communications. The better sensors make missiles more deadly. More powerful computers give missiles the ability to think for themselves. This results in deadly robots, of which there are several in use already. More technology has brought about miniaturization. Putting the equivalent of a laptop computer in a soldier's helmet is already in the prototype stage.

• While attention has concentrated on massive new technology for ships and aircraft, the technology has slipped into everything. This has been the true revolution in warfare. The World War II soldier may look like the 1996 version, but the technology available to the modern infantryman makes an enormous difference in that soldier's effectiveness, and his ability to survive, and win, on the battlefield. The change has been so gradual that you have to take a close look at the 1945 and 1996 grunt to appreciate the differences.

• To a certain extent, the fascination with upgrading the traditionally high-tech warships and combat aircraft has left insufficient money to take advantage of technology that can help the low-tech infantry and support (supply, maintenance, etc.) services. It's easier to get money for the ships and airplanes, but these have become so expensive that we can, literally, not afford many of them anymore.

• All the new technology has come with costs other than fiscal. These high-tech gadgets require a lot more support (supplies, technicians) than their predecessors. In World War II, about a quarter of the troops got within the sound of battle. Today, it's down to about 10 percent. The other 90 percent are moving supplies, fixing things, and generally "supporting" the handful of people doing the actual fighting.

• New technology not only makes the fighting troops more deadly, but also makes them a lot faster. "Speed is life" not only for jet fighters, but also for anyone going in harm's way against an armed enemy. Everything moves a lot faster, and combat goes on around the clock.

• The revolution in warfare has also made it easier to run things. Until quite recently, commanders prepared for battle by making a lot of plans, and then expecting their well-trained subordinates to improvise successfully once the fighting began. As the ancient saying went "No battle plan survives the first contact with the enemy." This is no longer the case. Today commanders can see live radar and TV images of how their troops are doing, and give orders to the troops on their computer screens.

• The enormous sums spent on new technology for ships and bombers have made these vehicles the first to be replaced by robotic versions, somewhat to the consternation of the air force and navy commanders.

• Guided missiles are typical of those weapons that began as seemingly impossible dreams and combat failures. But the pressure of the cold war kept the money, and development, coming. Thus, eventually, the impossible dreams became practical reality. After three or four decades and billions of dollars, the missiles work.

• One of the stranger offshoots of high-tech weapons has been those called "nonlethal." Weapons of this sort have long been available, but only recently has it been suggested that they be used in large quantities to achieve a relatively "bloodless" battle.

Glossary

ALTHOUGH I HAVE tried to write this book in plain English, some military jargon is unavoidable. Therefore I provide a glossary of the military terms you will encounter, and what they mean in plain English.

AGM—U.S. prefix for an air-to-ground missile (as in "AGM-12").

AIM—U.S. prefix for an air-to-air missile (as in "AIM-4").

Airedale—Military slang for naval pilots (who fly from aircraft carriers) and also the ground crew that service the aircraft.

ATGM—Anti-Tank Guided Missile. A guided missile for attacking tanks, obviously, but also used against other targets, like buildings or bunkers. Fired from the ground, vehicles of all types, and aircraft.

AWACS—Air Warning and Control System aircraft. Four-engine aircraft with large radars, operators, and electronic equipment to spot enemy and friendly aircraft and control the latter.

Bubblehead—Military slang for a sailor who serves in submarines.

CEP—Circular Error Probable. Used to define missile/bomb/shell accuracy. The distance from the point the missile is being aimed at in which 50 percent of the missiles fired will fall. CEP can be calculated with a computer or, more realistically, with actual testing of the weapon.

Data Links—Usually used to mean a radio signal between a missile and a human controller.

Deck Ape—Military slang for a sailor who mostly does maintenance away from the high-tech gear.

Digital Battlefield—A concept in which all the communications equipment can talk the same language; namely the 0's and 1's of computer and CD-ROM language.

Dogface—Military slang for an army infantryman.

FDC—Fire Direction Center. An American World War II innovation that could, in extreme cases, tie together hundreds of artillery pieces and scores of FOs (forward observers.) The FOs at the front could radio back a request for artillery fire, and their position, and within minutes have hundreds of shells pounding the targets in front of them. FDCs are now used at all levels.

Fleet Train—Supply ships that refuel and otherwise replenish warships at sea (called underway replenishment or UNREP).

Footslogger—Military slang for infantryman.

Force XXI—U.S. Army plan for figuring out and implementing new techniques for twenty-first-century warfare.

Forward Observer (FO)—An artillery specialist who goes with the frontline infantry and armored troops. Sometimes the FOs fly in aircraft or helicopters. The FO has a radio linked with the local FDC and knows the techniques of measuring the amount and type of artillery fire needed to deal with enemy targets they have in view. Sometimes combat troops are trained in FO techniques so they can call in fire themselves. FOs can also call in helicopter gunships. The air force has its own FOs to call in heavier air force bombers.

Front line—Usually a line of trenches, but can also be just a line of armored vehicles and infantry, that denotes the area where your troops are in contact with, or very close to, the enemy. Also called MLR (Main Line of Resistance), FEBA (Forward Edge of Battle Area), or FLOT (Forward Line Own Troops.) To the combat troops, it's always "the front."

Gentleman of the Earth—Military slang for infantryman.

GIB—"Guy in Back," the weapons-system operator in the rear seat of a two-seat combat aircraft.

GNP—gross national product. The total wealth produced by a nation in a year. How we keep track of the wealth-producing ability of a nation.

GPS—Global Positioning System. A series of space satellites put into orbit during the 1980s. Anyone with a palm-sized receiver for the satellite signals knows exactly where they are (within about one hundred feet.)

Groundpounder—Military slang for infantryman.

Grunt—Military slang for infantryman.

HEAT—High-Explosive Anti Tank, a form of antitank missile or shell warhead that, when it hits the target, explodes and forms a superhot jet that burns through armor and, if the jet gets inside the tank, burns whatever is there. Another word for a shaped-charge warhead.

ICBM—Intercontinental ballistic missile (one of those that travel over five thousand miles to nuke a city or a military target).

NCO—noncommissioned officer. A sergeant or petty officer (Navy). An older and more experienced soldier who directly supervises the younger troops.

Nukes—Either nuclear weapons (in their many forms), nuclear submarines, or the sailors that run the reactors on nuclear-powered ships.

Sensors—Electronic equipment used to find things. Radar and sonar are active sensors because they send out electronic signals to detect things. Microphones and heat-detection devices are passive sensors because they do not send out signals (and thus cannot be detected).

SFW—Self-forging weapon. New type of shaped-charge explosive. But instead of creating a stream of superhot gas to melt through armor, SFW creates a stream of very hot metal that is even more effective in going through armor and can do it from a distance away (a hundred meters or more).

Shaped Charge—An explosive warhead that forms a stream of superhot gas that will melt through metal. Depending on the size of the warhead, must detonate a certain number of inches from the target in order to get the most effective penetration of the armor. Commonly called a HEAT warhead.

SLBM—Submarine-launched ballistic missile. Like an ICBM, but fired from a large submarine.

Squid—Military slang for sailors.

Synchronization—U.S. Army term for getting all the weapons systems and units to work together on the battlefield.

Task Force—A group of warships. Also used to describe a temporary ground combat organization.

Treadhead—Military slang for a soldier that serves in tanks.

Wild Weasel—Jet fighter equipped to defeat enemy anti-aircraft defenses.

Zoomie—Military slang for members of the air force. More specifically, air force pilots.

PART I

Preliminaries

1

From Rocks to Electrons

YOU HEAR THEM all the time, blurbs or sound bites on how nifty modern military equipment is and how, if it is unleashed, some situation or another will be made right. This is an easy angle to fall for, as the twentieth century has been one of increasingly numerous and complex weapons. Why, they are no longer merely weapons, but "weapons systems." There is a method to all this hype, but not the one you might imagine. For high tech does not always mean high performance, or even minimal effectiveness. Remember that, because it only gets worse when you take a closer look

What is happening today with high-tech weapons is unique. Never before in history has there been a period where there were so many new weapons in such a short period of time. But there have, obviously, been new weapons over the centuries. For as long as there has been warfare, there have been new weapons. But until the 1800s, the new weapons were slow in coming. Really new weapons or items of military equipment were quite rare. Centuries would go by before anything particularly novel came along. And even then, the tradition-minded fighting man was usually reluctant to adopt the new technology until (and usually because) someone else used it. There were only a handful of technological breakthroughs until about eight hundred years ago, when gunpowder weapons began to appear. Then came a deluge of technology in this century.

Before looking into the avalanche of twentieth-century weapons, it's important to look back at how new weapons were developed in the past. Many of the conditions that have driven, or inhibited, weapons development in the past are still with us. You will better understand the present, and the future, if you have some knowledge of the past.

Weapons Development: The Stone Age

THE FIRST WEAPONS were rocks and clubs. Rocks were chipped to create primitive knives. Then came spears, using stone (flint, usually) heads. Bows were a major advance, using flint-tipped arrows. The sling and clubs fitted with flint were other prehistoric advances in weapons technology. Eventually there was bronze, which came along about six thousand years ago. This metal was an alloy of copper (by itself too soft for effective weapons) and tin. It was a major technological advance, and was propelled into wide use as much because of bronze weapons as for the economic advantages of bronze tools. Even that long ago, warfare gave a boost to technological advances. While bronze had obvious advantages over copper for hunting, food preparation, and construction, it was the fear of "losing the bronze race" that motivated tribes to find out how to make bronze and make a lot of it before warlike neighbors paid an unfriendly visit to show them what the new bronze weapons could do to someone still using copper.

Another such breakthrough didn't take place until some fifteen hundred years later, when iron was discovered. A much harder metal than bronze, its use gave soldiers a significant advantage over bronze-equipped opponents. The "iron race" went on for a century or two in the Middle East until everyone had it. Those that were slow in adopting the new metal were either wiped out or absorbed by iron-outfitted kingdoms. The new metal was not only useful for weapons, but led to the development of many new kinds of armor. Iron weapons dominated the battlefield for over three thousand years. Some seven hundred years ago, gunpowder weapons began to appear, but it wasn't until three hundred years ago that gunpowder displaced iron swords and spears as the primary weapon in most armies.

Military Innovations of the Ancients

JUST BECAUSE IT took so long to get from the discovery of iron to the introduction of gunpowder does not mean that three thousand years went by with little innovation in weapons. There were quite a few new ideas involving missile weapons. Then, as now, missiles were seen as the wave of the future. They were also seen, then as now, as a less dangerous way to attack an opponent. Ancient missiles were usually arrows, or large rocks thrown at fortifications by catapults and similar machines. Several new types of bows were developed during the golden age of iron weapons. Some involved the use of some iron, like the crossbow. Others used no metal at all, like the compound bow favored by the Mongols, or the longbow used by the English yeoman archers in the medieval period. While the bows often used no iron, the arrows did. Later crossbows used an iron bolt, rather than a specially designed wood arrow, and eventually the bow itself had iron parts. All arrows had an iron head, and these varied greatly in their design. One of the more interesting of these is the bodkin arrowhead used by English longbows; it was particularly effective penetrating armor.

There were many other developments during the military Iron Age, but these were tactical and administrative innovations. Some of these were very important. For example, about 2,200 years ago, the Parthians (Iranians living in the Iraq-Iran area) developed full suits of armor for mounted spearmen. They also had mounted archers. The term *Parthian shot* refers to their technique of riding away from an approaching enemy and turning around in the saddle to let off an arrow or two. This organization was almost identical to what the Mongols used 1,500 years later, and similar to the mounted knight developed in western Europe 1,000 years later. The Parthians didn't have the stirrup yet—that came a few centuries later. But they did have the heavy (armored) cavalry that dominated the battlefield for the next 2,000 years. The stirrup helped the later knights stay in the saddle, but the lack of same did not make the Parthian knights that much less effective. Besides, the stirrup was invented by the Chinese to make it easier to get on a horse, not just to make it easier to stay in the saddle. Special saddles had long been used to aid in staying astride the horse.

Another example of innovation during this period was the use of heavy infantry. Originally, infantry tactics had been nothing more than a mass (or mob, depending on the quality of leadership) of stout fellows armed with spears and swords. Most carried shields of metal, wood, hide, or woven material (or combinations thereof) and armor of similar construction to the shield. At various times, armies really got their act together and equipped all the troops with excellent armor and trained them thoroughly. This was more difficult than it sounds, as professional armies were, until a few centuries ago, rather rare. They were too expensive, and enthusiastic amateurs were a lot cheaper and nearly as good as most pros. In such situations, if the amateurs outnumbered the pros by, say, two to one, the amateurs usually won.

But when someone came along and managed to finance a well-trained and -equipped professional army, this was unique and the result was usually a long string of conquests followed by the establishment of yet another empire. Most commonly, these conquering armies were primarily infantry. Horses were expensive to maintain, and their quality was poor, so most professional troops walked. The mounted soldiers were usually nobles who only turned out for an emergency or when the prospects of loot were particularly good. The Assyrians, Greeks, and Romans (to mention the more successful ones) all established large empires with professional infantry armies using unique organization, tactics, and lots of training.

Ancient Inhibitions

YOU WOULD THINK that people would have picked up on the importance of training and attention to tactics. But such was not, and still is not, the case. The reasons for this lapse are rather easy to understand. First, there is the innate conservatism of military men everywhere and for all time. Warfare is a deadly business, and most of those who engage in it want to minimize their risk, rather than maximize their chances of success. In other words, the soldier will avoid combat, or anything else, that might get him killed. No one is going to readily adopt untried new weapons or tactics when he knows that the traditional arms and techniques have worked in the past. Second, there is the problem of experience. Most soldiers fight very little, if at all. Throughout human history there have always been wars or organized armed conflicts ("skirmishes") going on somewhere. But for the individual soldier, on average, there has been very little action. There have always been plenty of armies around, but very few wars for them to participate in. Thus an army, or tribal levy, might go years, or decades, without having a chance to actually get into a battle. Thus there is little opportunity to test new weapons or techniques. Few people, especially soldiers, want to bet their lives on some untried technology or technique. It took a rare, and unique, leader to get new weapons and techniques accepted and tested in combat. Once these new items are seen to work in battle, people are much more willing to accept them. But getting past that first trial has always been a nearly insurmountable task.

Human nature has shown itself to be even more perverse. Even in the face of successful new weapons, many tend to attribute such achievements to "luck," or the result of some grievous error by the loser. In times past, many believed that it was because the gods were mad at the loser and caused the defeat as a form of divine punishment. On the losing side, the people in charge often find it politically expedient to give the enemy credit for successful new ideas. After all, a general, even one who has just lost a battle, would rather blame the gods than his own lack of foresight in properly equipping and training his troops. Often it was simply pride. The losers could not bring themselves to admit that those bums on the other side were better soldiers.

Until a few hundred years ago, new weapons commonly came into military use after having first been tried out while hunting game. Thus there were many other weapons available, and there always had been. While the earliest civilizations came about because of the use of large-scale farming, hunting still brought in a significant proportion of the calories. Along rivers and oceans, fishing was usually the principal form of "hunting." But there was usually land game available. While the poorest people used slings or snares to kill small animals, the nobility were more ambitious. It was common for the rich folks to hunt from horseback. They would use spears or bows. The hunt was considered largely sport by the aristocrats, and also training for war. But even with that, there was enough difference between hunting animals and confronting humans on the battlefield to make the crossover a slow process. Some weapons, of course, were primarily used for warfare. Swords are the best example. Except for finishing off large wounded animals, swords played little part in hunting. Spears were the most common hunting/warfare weapon, and the largest number of troops in an ancient army were spearmen, but these were generally the poorest members of the society and had little practice using spears on large game. The nobles, who could afford to spend days or weeks riding off to unpopulated areas where large game lived, eventually developed the technique of spearing deer, bears, buffalo, or lions from horseback. This was useful practice for doing the same thing to enemy soldiers. This extensive practice made the aristocratic cavalry rather more deadly than the peasant spearman filling the ranks. It wasn't until innovative peoples like the Greeks or Romans developed specialized spears for combat, and diligently trained the troops in their use, that cavalry again had to fear infantry.

Archery, Technology, and Culture

ARCHERY WAS ANOTHER matter. The bow was an ancient weapon, and was favored by peasants for hunting birds and animals that could not be run down on foot. Unfortunately, the average hunting bow was of only marginal use in warfare. Combat troops usually had shields, and often armor. Massed archers had some effect against horsemen, or at least the horses. But many armies, when constantly faced with such archers, would armor their horses too, or see to it that battles began with an archery duel to kill off the enemy archers, or drive them from the battlefield, before sending their cavalry in.

Historically, there have been four types of bows. These are (in order of appearance), the short bow, the longbow, the composite bow, and the crossbow. The short bow is shorter than the longbow, and requires less muscle to pull. We know it was in use at least fifty thousand years ago, and it is still used by many primitive cultures today. The longbow, which is usually at least five feet long and requires a lot more muscle and skill to use, is probably nearly as old as the short bow. Longbows have been found that are over six feet long and require nearly two hundred pounds of pull. Cultures that had a lot of large people, and free time to practice with this larger bow, used the longbow. The longbow had a longer range than the short bow, usually two hundred to four hundred yards, compared to somewhat less than half that for the short bow. The longbow had more penetrating power. With the right kind of metal arrowhead, a longbow could penetrate most kinds of armor and shields at short ranges. In Europe, the Vikings, Germans, and Celts all used the longbow at one time or another. A major disadvantage of the longbow was that in cold weather the bow had a tendency to snap. Short bows would do this too, but not as often because not as much stress was being applied to the wood of the bow.

The longbow required a lot of constant practice to maintain the needed skills. Only those cultures that tolerated, or could afford, a lot of the manpower spending much of their time at war or preparing for it used the longbow on a large scale. Today, there are still tribes in Africa that use the longbow for hunting large game, including elephants. To bring down an elephant you need a powerful longbow and a skilled hunter to operate it.

The composite bow is, unlike the short bow and longbow, more than just a carefully selected and shaped length of wood. Often the same size as the short bow, the composite bow uses pieces of bone and sinew glued to wood to produce a bow that produces the same striking power and range as the longbow, but without requiring nearly as much pull. The composite bow has long been favored by those who hunt, or make war, from horseback. As a hunter's weapon, the composite bow is superb. The composite bow is known to have existed at least five thousand years ago, and probably earlier. The ancient Egyptians made composite bows that were as long as longbows and fired light arrows made of reeds. These Egyptian arrows apparently could be fired over three hundred yards and would land with great force. The composite bow was also less likely to break if used in freezing weather.

Short bows and longbows, although carved out of single logs of wood, often had the characteristics of composite bows if they were carved out of the center of a tree log. The sap-soaked wood at the center of a tree has different characteristics than the wood closer to the bark. Different types of trees have different properties, some species being more suitable for bows than others. While none of these "organic" longbows were as effective as the top-line composite bows, they were much cheaper to make and maintain. The English medieval longbow is an excellent example of the "organic" composite bow. While made from a single log cut from a yew tree, if carefully selected and cured just so, the English longbow was a match for most composite bows of the medieval period.

What armies needed were specialized "heavy" bows for wartime use. The problem with this was that handling a "war bow" required constant practice. While the nobility had the time to do this, you needed a lot of archers to make a difference on the battlefield. The peasants had to work hard just to survive, and provide a surplus for the nobility to live on. The ancient Egyptians, with their wonderfully fertile Nile Valley agriculture, often had the surplus wealth to maintain hundreds, or thousands, of heavy archers. These bowmen, combined with the pharaohs' hundreds of chariots, made Egypt a major military power in the Middle East for thousands of years. But whenever the royal budget could not afford the archers, or civil war diluted their numbers, archery became much less of a decisive element. What was needed was a bow that did not require so much constant training. The answer to this came in the form of the fourth type of bow, the crossbow.

The Star-crossed History of the Crossbow

THE FIRST SOLUTION to the battlefield archery problem was introduced by the Chinese nearly three thousand years ago, when they developed the crossbow. This was a mechanical bow that required skilled artisans to construct it. But once one built it, little skill was needed to use it, and the crossbows could be stored during times of peace and would, if properly cared for, last for decades. The crossbow bolt had tremendous penetrating power. If it didn't go through enemy armor or shields, it gave the enemy soldier on the other end a severe jolt. This did not help enemy morale much. A typical ancient army, with perhaps ten thousand troops, would have an enormous advantage if 10 to 20 percent of those soldiers were equipped with crossbows.

It took the crossbow some five hundred years to reach Europe, and then it was considered a specialized hunting weapon for many centuries. What was missing here was a government that could muster the resources (human and financial) to build enough crossbows to be effective. This didn't happen until the eleventh century. Why did it take so long? We'll never really know. But we can make some educated guesses. The earlier Romans could make crossbows but simply chose not to. Military tactics were fairly primitive in the medieval period, as the armored and mounted knights became more dominant. The knights monopolized military affairs, and they were not keen to mess up their thrilling cavalry charges with a lot of pesky crossbow bolts.

The crossbow was also expensive. In an era when most people were small farmers and a good annual income was a few thousand dollars, a crossbow cost about $250 (in 1990s dollars) and each of the bolts it fired cost approximately $1.25. The crossbowmen themselves cost from five to ten dollars a day, depending on their level of experience and whether they supplied their own weapons. The employer usually supplied the *quarrels* (arrows, or bolts fired) and this could get pretty expensive. A regular bow was a lot cheaper, costing thirty to fifty dollars, with arrows being a bit more expensive at about two dollars each. Crossbows were popular for equipping the garrisons of castles and walled towns. The crossbowman could fire the weapon from protected, if cramped, positions behind the walls. A regular archer would have to stand in a more open position to fire and could more easily get hit by besieging archers. Moreover, the time it took to reload a crossbow (a bolt or two per minute) favored those who were safe behind stone walls. It did not require much skill to do this, thus allowing for untrained (and poorly paid) men to defend the place. Remember that any other kind of bow could fire from a dozen to twenty arrows a minute, about ten times the rate of fire of crossbows. But this sort of archery required a very well trained man pulling a powerful bow.

The Romans, in the fourth century A.D., were using the crossbow, so it's not surprising that the Italians were the biggest users of the weapon throughout the medieval period. Mercenary units of crossbowmen (often numbering in the thousands of troops) served whichever Italian prince would pay them. But the crossbow never caught on as much in the rest of Europe. It wasn't just the expense; mainly it was the approach to warfare and the lack of army commanders who could see, and carry through, effective archery tactics. There were exceptions, especially during the Crusades of the twelfth and thirteenth centuries. But this involved fighting Muslims. There was a feeling in the West that the crossbow was an "unchristian" weapon and the pope unsuccessfully tried to ban its use for Christians fighting Christians.

When firearms were introduced in the 1500s, the crossbow fell from favor and eventually disappeared except for recreational or hunting use. While firearms revolutionized warfare over the next few centuries, it is well to remember that, for all practical purposes, the crossbow provided much the same battlefield firepower as the primitive muskets of the 1500s. You could line up a few thousand crossbowmen in the year 1300, and they would generate the same number of lethal missiles heading for troops a hundred yards away as the same number of musketeers would in the year 1700. Okay, the musket balls had a bit more penetrating power, but the muskets generated all that smoke (which made it more difficult to find the target), and muskets were generally less reliable than crossbows. But there was no reason that a medieval commander could not equip and drill an army of crossbowmen in the battlefield tactics of musketeers, and with the same devastating effect.

Why, then, didn't commanders seize on the crossbow to provide the massed firepower that transformed combat several centuries later? The answer is simple, and frustrating: no one thought of it, and, perhaps more importantly, no one could really afford it. Throughout history it has always been the case that just because something is possible does not mean that someone will do it.

This explains why the Chinese, with a more ancient, better organized, and more advanced civilization, were eclipsed by the Europeans from the 1600s on. People still argue over just what it was with the Europeans that caused them to come out of the period of innovation known as the Renaissance and just keep going in the new-ideas department. Unlike the Chinese, and many ancient societies, the Europeans didn't just think up a lot of new ideas, they enthusiastically went out and put them to use. Then they devised variations and improvements and just kept on going. This simple mental revolution enabled Europe to, literally and figuratively, conquer the world. Many of the older cultures, in places like India, the Middle East, and China, are still trying to catch up. Learning to "think like a European" is not as easy as it seems. Conservatism is an ancient custom in humans and one not easily discarded for the seemingly dangerous world of new and untried (or at least unfamiliar) ideas.

But there was one bunch of medieval Europeans that did adopt musketeer tactics before the guns arrived. And they didn't do it with crossbows, but with an older type of bow.

Intelligent Archery

THE ENGLISH CAME up the concept of a battlefield dominated by firepower in the thirteenth century. They did it not with crossbows (which the English were familiar with), but with longbows. The Celts and Germans had been using longbows for centuries. The Romans had reported running into problems with longbow-equipped German armies. But the longbow was a difficult weapon to master and its popularity waxed and waned. The short bow was always popular, for it was the favored hunting weapon, and when the Normans invaded England in 1066 they brought short bow–equipped troops with them and encountered few longbows. But the longbows were there. When the English king Edward I set about conquering Wales in the thirteenth century, he found the Welsh using the longbow in larger and larger numbers. The Celts in Wales had been familiar with the longbow for as long as anyone could remember. Against the English knights, the Welsh found the longbow to be an ideal weapon. The English eventually prevailed, and Edward I not only conquered the Welsh, but won them over to his side by a combination of carrot (benevolent rule) and stick (many castles and a large garrison). He also hired the Welsh archers for his other wars and paid the longbowmen well, and on time. These last two points cannot be underestimated, as it was common for a noble to shortchange his armed retainers. Edward's attention to timely payment of good wages to the archers, and winning most of his battles, sent the archers home with full purses and good things to say about this English king. Edward I, and his successors, encouraged Welsh and English subjects to take up the longbow. This strategy worked, helped by the Hundred Years War (1337–1453) between France and England. This series of wars provided constant employment for archers, and ample opportunity to get good pay and a chance to get rich from plunder.

The archers were not just ordinary commoners, but largely free farmers. That is, they were not serfs, but men who either leased land from a noble or owned it outright. This was a class of people found throughout Europe, but they were particularly numerous in England. Known as "yeoman farmers," they had the resources to buy longbows, arrows, a sword, some armor, and even a horse. More importantly, as free men, they had the discipline and drive to regularly practice with the longbow. Finally, the yeomen were big men. It required a lot of muscle to muster the 100 to 150 pounds of pull needed to draw an arrow on a longbow. The yeomen farmer was a more successful and better-fed farmer. In an age when a large chunk of the population was always on the verge of starvation, the free farmers were relatively prosperous. They produced more food and consumed more of it. When the mass graves of medieval battlefields are exhumed, it's always easy to pick out the skeletons of yeomen. They are the ones that are taller and have the massive bone structure typical of those who, even today, work with heavy bows or weights all their lives. Even at the time, these archers were often described as *stout* yeomen. And the English king that led a few thousand of them could do whatever he wanted to do in France. For a century, that's just what the English kings did, and the burly yeoman archers were the main reason why.

The yeoman saw regular service as a fighting man in the king's service as making him socially superior to those farmers who didn't serve under arms. For many centuries, the aristocracy had tried to monopolize the profession of arms. There were still hordes of infantry in medieval armies, but increasingly these troops were seen as a rabble that could be squandered in suicidal attacks or left in the lurch. The yeoman archers were treated, and paid, as professional soldiers. This gave the English a more capable and unified army than any of their opponents.

The kings passed laws making archery practice obligatory, but it was the prospect of employment as archers from time to time that kept the yeomen at it. For several centuries, the English yeomen were, along with the Swiss pikemen, the premier foot soldiers of Europe. For three or so months campaigning, a yeoman could pick up three or four thousand dollars in pay, plus that much or more in loot. Since the average yeoman farmer only generated one to three thousand dollars of cash income a year, this "campaign bonus" made the yeoman class even stronger. Much of the new wealth went into buying more land, or improving the land already worked. Many yeomen worked their way into the minor nobility and some went even further over the centuries. All because some of their ancestors were willing to learn how to handle a longbow.

In combat, the longbow was the most fearsome weapon to grace the battlefield until the coming of large musket-equipped armies in the 1600s. Indeed, English officials noted that up through the 1800s, longbows were superior to an equal number of muskets. But the problem was that the archers had to practice constantly, and from a young age—practice was daily, or several times a week. To justify this much effort, there had to be regular employment at good wages. When England ran out of profitable wars in the late 1400s, the demand for archers declined, and so did the diligence of the yeomen for all that practice. Even the English kings soon found that it was easier to equip any old commoner with a musket and give him a few months' training. The musketeers could get off one or two shots a minute, versus over a dozen a minute by a longbowman. Moreover, the longbow had a longer effective range than the muskets. But the golden age of archery, as exemplified by the English longbowman, lasted only about two centuries. It was too expensive to maintain, and was eventually replaced by a less labor-intensive and cheaper technology.

Renaissance and Reason on the Battlefield

THE RENAISSANCE, that period in late medieval Europe when many new ideas, and quite a few old, forgotten ones, came into fashion, also brought a renaissance in military thinking. While artists and architects throughout Europe were creating a multitude of tourist attractions, soldiers were beginning to tinker with gunpowder. In the 1300s, cannons were ever more common battlefield weapons, at the same time that the arts were flourishing elsewhere. But for soldiers, there was far more than just gunpowder happening. Renaissance artists applied their talents to castles, weapons, and armor as well as painting, sculpture, and palaces. Soldiers were equally imaginative in rethinking how they organized, trained, and fought. The traditionalism of soldiers was still there, but there was so much imagination in the air that even conservative warriors were willing to risk all on a new idea. Many of the ideas didn't work, but many others did. Moreover, there began in this period a tradition of experimentation. These same attitudes among nonsoldiers led to the Industrial Revolution, an ongoing string of scientific breakthroughs, and startling new political ideas.

So let us not forget the roots of the digital soldier. They began in the Renaissance, when the likes of Leonardo da Vinci sketched plans for automatic weapons, armored vehicles, and all manner of military gear. Leonardo was not unusual for his time, or the times that followed down to the present.

The Renaissance thinkers often came up with concepts that required more advanced technology than was then available. Moreover, so many new ideas were introduced that it was only a matter of time before a few really good ideas would be organized to create a fighting style that would be difficult to improve on. For example, the Spanish invented the modern regiment (or brigade, as it is sometimes called.) The Spanish called it the *tercio.* It was commanded by a colonel, and the troops were called infantry (from *infanta,* or child). This unit was organized and trained in a regular and disciplined fashion. Not all the troops had firearms; some still used sword and shield, or various types of specialized spears (halberds.) The Spanish were not the only ones innovating. Europe became a cauldron of new ideas, with everyone playing an ongoing game of "can you top this?" Every time one turned around, someone did.

The development of seventeenth-century muskets (as used in our own Revolutionary War) from the thirteenth-century "firepots" was a succession of "can you top this?" challenges taken up by a lot of very ambitious military commanders and weapons makers. The innate conservatism of military men was overcome by increasing technical innovations, and the advantages better weapons gave to those who possessed them.

But more importantly, the Renaissance brought with it a social revolution. Europe entered the Renaissance a very stratified society. A small portion of the population, a few percent, monopolized the profession of arms. The democratic (by ancient standards) armies of Rome and German tribes, where most adult males were armed, had been overwhelmed by these armored and mounted men-at-arms. These knights ruled the population, fought the wars, and maintained their power by personally wielding military power. Crossbows and muskets allowed commoners to fight a knight on equal terms. This threatened the social order, but it had an economic ally. The economy of Europe was changing, as commerce, banking, and manufacturing increasingly were dominated by commoners. During this period, all this economic activity was making cities larger, richer, and more numerous. The commoner citizens of these cities formed their own infantry armies and hired mercenaries. Many of the wars of this period were between the rural aristocracy and the independent-minded cities. The kings and nobles had to either make deals with the commoners or smash their opponents and extinguish the intellectual and social progress under way. In Europe, the knights compromised, and became officers in armies of commoner musketeers, or bureaucrats in ever growing governments. It didn't have to be that way. When Japan faced this development in the 1600s, the nobles decided to outlaw muskets and armed commoners in general. The Japanese knights (the samurai) and the nobles maintained this freeze-frame history for two centuries, until a fleet of American steamships armed with large cannons showed up. The Americans announced they were looking for trade. The Japanese saw what the alternative was and quickly played catch-up in government, industry, and military technology.

Many other great cultures of ancient times, in China, India, and the Middle East, also ignored what was going on in Europe. In these regions, the idea of change for the sake of change never caught on. If someone did try to innovate, he was eventually stomped on, or simply buried in delay and petty opposition by the conservative majority. These regions eventually had to submit to European domination, or undergo a European-style revolution.

It was not preordained that Europe would produce the scientific, social, and military progress after the Renaissance. But it did happen, and *didn't* happen in the rest of the world. Which means that in the future, no such similar progress is a sure thing. But for the moment, the idea of "progress" is still widely accepted. Yet in many parts of society, there is still the ancient opposition to progress and change. The military still contains a lot of people disposed toward keeping things as they are and not risking the unknown consequences of change.

What did give Europe an advantage, which it and America still hold, in this unprecedented explosion of new ideas and acceptance of them was the combination of:

• Rediscovering the "lost" knowledge of the ancients (the Renaissance).

• The fragmented political state of Europe. There were hundreds of independent kingdoms and smaller states. Each was competing with many neighbors. If an original thinker couldn't sell his idea in one place, a neighboring prince would usually be more open to something new.

• Europe had much in the way of new ideas and products coming in from other parts of the world, and the Europeans were more inclined to accept and adopt new things. Such was not the case with India and China, which, for geographical and social reasons, tended to look inward more than outward. The Middle East was also going through a renaissance, but lacked the political diversity of Europe. A handful of empires in the Middle East eventually smothered change, and the entire region stagnated while Europe went forward.

• The political divisions in Europe eventually led to religious divisions, and the new religious ideas often carried with them new concepts of social and political relationships. The other regions of the world did not have this degree of religious ferment. The Protestant movement did not produce one new church, but many, and forced the mainstream Catholic Church to reform.

• The pace and extent of change in Europe made change respectable. Even the conservatives embraced change (if only to better oppose change they didn't agree with). With this, the static nature of human cultures was forever changed.

By the 1600s in Europe, the Renaissance had petered out and things were settling down somewhat. Unfortunately, one of the leftovers of the Renaissance was a multitude of religious arguments. In Europe, the 1600s saw a number of very destructive religious wars. The Thirty Years War (1618–48) was the worst of the lot. These wars were partly caused by the great number of individual states. With no political cohesion in places like Germany and Italy, it didn't take much to get someone fighting, and soon the neighbors were taking sides, and so it went. But even unified nations like France and England were rent by religious antagonisms. All this bad blood made people desperate to win, and survive. Technology was seen as a means to victory and the output of new weapons, or variations on old ones, was staggering. In less than two centuries, armies went from swords and spears to cannons and muskets.

But more than the hardware, there were now a lot more ideas on how to fight. There were training manuals and "how-to" books for officers. There were technical manuals for those who maintained the new technology, and regulations to keep the larger armies and navies functioning in an orderly fashion. Printing presses were in widespread use by 1500, and this had a lot to do with the rapid spread of the new knowledge. Literacy among the upper classes and nobility had become common during this time, and everyone read avidly. There had never been anything like this before. During the previous golden ages of culture, there had been ferments of new thought among the few tens of thousands of literate people with ready access to libraries of hand-copied manuscripts. But in Europe, barely a century after the Renaissance began, printing was invented and spread rapidly to fill an existing and swiftly growing demand for printed versions of all this new (or ancient and rediscovered) knowledge.

When the contending parties wore each other out fighting during the 1600s, they made peace. By 1700, everyone found themselves with very well developed and effective armies and navies. The infantry had muskets and bayonets, there was plenty of artillery, and even the remaining cavalry troops had firearms. Warships depended on cannons, and all this weaponry was supported by government bureaucracies and complicated, but effective, taxation systems. By 1700, one could see what was coming: more government, more tax money to spend, and more military things to spend it on.

The Renaissance and the religious wars were followed by the "Age of Reason." Sort of a Renaissance, Part 2, it was a period of more new ideas and intellectual ferment. Out of this period came, for example, the basic laws and form of government of the United States. The Age of Reason also produced a flood of new military thinking, and the fundamental organization of military units and officer ranks that persists to the present. Perhaps most importantly, this period saw the birth of the Industrial Revolution. Yes, you could say the eighteenth-century brought together all the elements necessary for the current military-industrial complex and the horde of concepts surrounding the concept of the digital soldier. It all had to begin somewhere.

Where Will It End?

WHILE THE FREQUENT appearance of new military technology is a recent development, you can now see that the rate of new military technology being developed has been increasing for over seven hundred years. Until about a century ago, weapons and equipment changed relatively slowly by current standards, but they did change. Before that, weapons and military equipment changed very little for centuries.

The development of military technology has speeded up throughout this century. Each decade of the twentieth century has seen an increased tempo of new weapons development. Part of this was due to the two world wars. Wartime always speeds up the introduction of new weapons. Partly this is because there is a huge demand. An equally important reason for all these new wartime weapons is the chance to instantly test the new ideas. Indeed, during wartime, many new weapons and items of equipment are found wanting on the battlefield and are quietly dropped. You don't hear about those, only about the ones that work.

This century has ended with the most expensive arms race in history. Between the late 1940s and the late 1980s, trillions of dollars was spent just on developing new weapons. This was more than was spent in any war in human history. While the cause of it all, the cold war, is over, the headlong plunge toward even more new military technology continues. While the Soviet/Russian weapons budget has shrunk to a fraction of its cold war size, American spending has declined much less. Other Western nations are also still spending at a large fraction of their cold war levels. In effect, money is still going into new weapons development at more than a third of the cold war rate.

We are still in an era of immense military change. For even though the spending on new weapons has come down, the thinking about how to use all the existing new (and many still untried) weapons has actually increased since the end of the cold war. What has happened in the Western nations is that the large armies and defense budgets common through most of this century have become accepted as the norm. We have gotten used to maintaining our forces on a wartime footing in peacetime. The traditionalist now resists going back to the small military force and slow change in weapons and equipment that were the pattern for thousands of years.

The Holy Grail of post–cold war military affairs has become the digital soldiers. We seek a new standard of technology and tactics for unknown future wars. The question is, What are the questions?

PART II

Press Releases and Promises

The whole concept of the "digital soldier" is part (the large part) promise and part (the small part) performance. For the people who make the high-tech gear, and the legislators who vote to buy it, the promise is more important than the performance. For the troops, performance is everything. But soldiers are trained to take orders, and know from experience that the struggle for survival is aided by making do with what you got.

2

··

How to Sell a
Killer Idea

O NE OF THE MOST important things to remember about weapons and military hardware is that they can be designed, sold, and used for many years without ever being successful, or even used, in combat. There aren't that many wars, especially for the more expensive high-tech equipment. Many weapons in this century have been used for many years, and then retired from service, without ever being put to the test of combat. Naturally, the manufacturers of high-tech military gear are aware of this situation. The only test new gadgets have to undergo is whatever evidence the buyer, or sometimes the seller, comes up with to "prove" the effectiveness of the new item.

Providing weapons for the troops is an ancient undertaking. Surviving records, some thousands of years old, show that the arms business has long been a big business. But until recently, you knew that the weapons you sold would soon be put to use. If what you sold turned out to be defective, you could expect an unpleasant, perhaps fatal, visit from some angry soldiers. This kept the arms merchants honest for a long time. It also kept the developers of new weapons in check. No one was about to push a new weapon that was likely to fail. Such a clinker could also prove fatal for its inventor. Life was rather more rough in the old days, but it did have the advantage of keeping the arms-procurement scandals under some degree of control. It's interesting to note that the Russians during World War II, in one of their many pragmatic acts, sent officers from units to receive new tanks to the tank factory. These officers checked on the quality of the tanks, the same tanks that they would soon be using in combat. It was a very effective system.

Until really large industrial, and government, bureaucracies came along, weapons procurement was a relatively personal business. The contractor would personally buttonhole the aristocrat in need of weapons and make his pitch. Since the generals, until recently, went with their troops to where the fighting was taking place, the task of buying weapons was considered a matter of life or death. The contractor had to assure the general that the weapons would be good and the general, in turn, assured the contractor that a painful death awaited any arms merchant who provided substandard weapons. Even when a king or general used aides to take care of weapons procurement, these were trusted aides who made sure the arms manufacturer knew what was at stake.

Keeping the Merchants of Death Honest

ARMS DEALERS HAD strictly business reasons to deal fairly. In ancient times, weapons were expensive. Medieval English yeoman archers needed hundreds of arrows each for a campaign. They might not use those many-yard-long, iron-tipped arrows, but the arrows had to be available and each arrow cost one to two dollars (depending on type and demand). This in a period where the king needed only about twenty million dollars to run his government in peacetime, and about twice that in wartime. The average commoner family got by on a few thousand dollars a year. So a three-hundred-thousand dollar contract to supply a quarter million arrows was a nice piece of business. It was equal to a five- or ten-billion-dollar contract today. If you wanted to survive to get future contracts, you had to make sure all of those arrows were good. Either that, or be a cousin to the king and engage in a bit of political corruption. But that's another subject we'll deal with further on.

Introducing new weapons was also a personal process. Then, as now, arms makers often offered to make prototypes at their own expense and provide them for use in combat. Such tests did not always work. This was especially the case with early cannons and muskets. But the inventors were risking their own money, and often their lives, when they operated the weapons during battle, so a margin of failure was allowed.

The private development of nearly all new weapons continued until about a century ago. At that point, for many weapons, it became too expensive. Only a government had sufficient cash to risk on new weapons, especially things like warships. While the government also had its own shipyards, it still needed to call on private shipbuilders when the demand for new ships was great. But even today, many smaller new weapons are developed privately, without government money. There are more new ideas than there are government bureaucrats who can make a decision to try something new. So a lot of new weapons and other military equipment will continue to come from nongovernment laboratories.

Over the last two centuries, private companies have noted that it can be quite profitable to build weapons and other military equipment for the government. The key task has become, not actually building the stuff, but getting the contract. As more nations turned to democracy, the ancient tactic of lobbying key aristocrats or government officials no longer did the job as efficiently as before. All those voters had to be convinced, as did the more numerous media outlets. Two centuries ago, the first newspapers began to appear, and a century ago, newspapers were a mass medium that could move public opinion and make governments tremble. If you wanted to deal with the government, you had to deal with its new extension: the mass media.

The Military–Industrial–Public Relations Complex

IN THE TWENTIETH century, public relations (as we know it) was invented and the arms manufacturers were quick to get on the bandwagon. A good public image was very helpful now that there were mass media to feed on this image. The better you looked in the press, the easier it was to get a hearing from government officials, especially those who granted military contracts. During wartime, lots of ads and press releases aimed at the general public were used. There was a war to be won and, by God, look at us do our part by building the tools. It was an easy sell, and a means of building up goodwill to be used after the war. In peacetime, the pitch was more to the procurement professionals in the government and the military. Press releases to the media were always seen as a prime vehicle for getting your message out. New weapons were considered newsworthy, especially if news about them was presented in an exciting way. That wasn't hard to do. Weapons are by their nature exciting, frightening, and, if they are on your side, reassuring.

But then things went wrong. New weapons and military equipment were coming on-line faster and faster. World War II wasn't the first time new weapons were brought from the idea stage to battlefield use in months. This had also happened during World War I and even earlier, in the American Civil War. But the tempo had kept increasing. During World War I, new aircraft were dreamed up, designed, and built in weeks. The tank, a revolutionary weapon, only required a few months of work to perfect, at least by World War I standards. During World War II there were breakthroughs in jet propulsion, shipbuilding, and, as a crowning achievement, nuclear technology. This last item, the atomic bomb project, took three years, but it was an unheard-of scientific and engineering achievement.

While a lot of this R and D (research and development) experience was put to civilian use after the war, there was still a demand for new weapons. Well, there's always a demand for new weapons. Normally, during peacetime, this demand is rather low and can often be ignored with little risk. But the end of World War II was followed a few years later by the beginning of the cold war. This was the third epic military struggle of the twentieth century (after the two world wars). We are still coming to terms with the cold war, for it ended suddenly in 1990. Most people thought the cold war had several decades to go. When it ended, it had already covered two generations—over forty years. People had become used to it, sort of like somber background music for late-twentieth-century life. While the cold war had killed less than 10 percent as many people as World War II, it had cost much more in terms of money. And the money that didn't go into killing and maiming (ammunition, fuel, and medical services) went into dreaming up and procuring new weapons.

The cold war was fought mostly with potential military strength, not actual combat power as used on the battlefield. Potential military strength meant large forces, which the Soviets favored, and the latest technology, which the United States preferred. Both superpowers ended up fielding large forces (four million Soviet troops, two million U.S.), and together they spent trillions of dollars developing new military technology. Most of this new gear never got much of a workout in combat. But these cold war weapons did get a lot of coverage in the media, and not all of it was favorable. Most of the bad press was in the West; the Soviets saw to it that bad news about their weapons never appeared on their side of the Iron Curtain.

There was plenty of bad press for both superpowers on the Western side of the Iron Curtain. For about fifteen years the media went along with the party line on all that weapons development, even though the disasters were piling up. But by the late 1950s, the military had so many ill-conceived new weapons in development that the worst of the lot were being publicly withdrawn with little attempt to hide the reasons why (that is, they didn't work and never would). By the time the Vietnam War came along, and public opinion began to turn against the military, the media found themselves with twenty years of funny business in the procurement area to jump on. And jump they did. The Vietnam War was the worst possible war for digital soldier wanna-bes to get involved in. The press ripped the Pentagon up one side and down the other as the Department of Defense tried to apply high technology to guerrilla war. This was not a situation that makes high tech look good.

The situation was compounded by the military's continued fixation on Europe, and the Soviet Union, even as most of the fighting was going on in Vietnam. The war in Indochina was seen as a sideshow by U.S. generals, a distraction from the real enemy in central Europe. But while the Pentagon's heart might have been in Europe, most of its budget was going to Vietnam. For ten years, all the weapons-development money went to support a war few in (or out of) uniform wanted. When the last American troops left Vietnam in 1975, the military faced an angry nation that was now soured on its military and the cold war. But the cold war would not go away. Even before Ronald Reagan was elected to "strengthen the military," his predecessor, Jimmy

Carter, was pouring more money into more new weapons. What reignited enthusiasm for weapons development was the fact that while most of the U.S. defense budget was going into Vietnam for ten years, the Soviets were spending all theirs on creating and building new weapons.

At the time America went into Vietnam, there wasn't much of an arms race between the United States and the Soviet Union. In the late 1950s and early 1960s, the U.S. defense budget was pretty stable at about $220 billion (1996 dollars). During the same period, the Soviets were still reducing their armed forces, a process they had been doing slowly since the end of World War II. But at the same time America entered Vietnam in a big way, there was a change of leadership in Russia. Nikita Khrushchev was replaced by Leonid Brezhnev. The Soviet armed forces backed this change of leadership, and as payment for this assistance they were given a blank check for the next twenty-five years. This led to an enormous buildup of Soviet military might. This bankrupted the Soviet Union and contributed greatly to its collapse in the late 1980s. But no one knew that outcome during this Soviet buildup. By the late 1960s, American military and political leaders noted the Soviet arms buildup and began to react. The result was a ruinous arms race. It was a golden age for weapons developers and manufacturers.

It was also a golden age for the media and their arch enemies, the public relations crowd. Vietnam had, in America, done away with any great respect for the military. The press was out for blood, even though most voters were basically in favor of the military buildup. On the face of it, one would think that the media triumphed in this period, mainly during the 1980s, when a flood of "expensive weapons that don't work" stories flooded the news. It didn't happen. This deluge of bad press was countered by the equally stout effort by the government and military to justify the expense. The voters decided, and they consistently came down on the side of more money for more weapons.

It was generally a case of each side promoting their own brand of evil and trying to convince as many as possible that their evil was the greater curse upon the nation. The press was pushing the "Military-Industrial Complex Run Amok" angle while the military (and quite a few politicians) went with the "Evil Empire That We Must Protect Ourselves From" position. As battles go, this conflict is worth a book or two itself. But we are only concerned with what impact it all had on the development of new weapons and how those weapons turned out when the industrial, doctrinal, and media dust had settled. The battle was not a lock for the military-industrial side. The media had plenty of ammunition and numerous juicy targets. It could have gone either way. Indeed, the best thing the Evil Empire crowd had going for it was the secretive nature of the Soviet Union. The Russians did not allow reporters to sneak around trying to get at the real facts of the matter. When all was revealed in the early 1990s, it became obvious that the Evil Empire was like the Wizard of Oz, a lot of smoke and noise, but not much in the way of real wizardry.

The general effects of the press release war were to make the manufacturers and users of the new weapons very wary of doing anything that might cast a bad light on their system. This was a very negative thing, because in wartime much of that effort is directed toward making the weapon work. In peacetime, you don't have to worry about battlefield embarrassments. While many people involved in weapons development *are* concerned with the damn thing working well, they have to pay attention to the flacks and their counsel regarding the potential PR problems if tests are held and they are not a resounding success.

One result of the cold war arms buildup is the feeling that more technology for the troops is always a good thing, even if training and readiness have to be sacrificed in the process. Oh, it's not quite that simple. Generals and politicians will both proclaim publicly that it is preferable that the troops be well trained and supplied with sufficient spare parts and resources to keep them combat ready. But the reality is another thing. New weapons, and the vast sums needed to develop and build them, always seem to get more attention than training and readiness. Words are important, but actions speak louder.

What we have is a continuing rush to automate and digitize all aspects of the armed forces. Digitize is the buzzword du jour, and it means computerizing and networking all the weapons and sensors so that all weapons and troops on the battlefield become aware of what everyone else is doing. This is a trend that has been building for over a century, and glimpses of it have been seen ever since World War I, when the first artillery observers went up in tethered balloons, connected to the ground, and directed distant artillery batteries by a telephone. In World War II it was done from aircraft with radios, and one pilot-observer could literally direct the fire of hundreds of guns. In the half century since, there have been more radios, more automated weapons, and more hopes that the "digital battlefield" would arrive. It always has seemed to be just around the corner. But this time it apparently is, for better or for worse.

Each of the different combat services will reach the digital promised land by a different route, and at a different time. The next few chapters show these differences, how they developed, and where they lead.

3

Digital Infantry

T HE FUTURE OF THE digital infantry is a complicated and murky one. But let us look at the background of all this before peeking at the future.

While ground combat during the 1991 Gulf War was able to use a lot of new technology, little of it was of immediate use to the infantry. As has been the case for thousands of years, the infantry during the Gulf War were in the most danger and took the most casualties. For all the laser-guided bombs and satellite reconnaissance, the groundpounders still had to go in with their own weapons and roust the Iraqis out of Kuwait the old-fashioned way. The friendly losses were as low as they were because of training, not high-tech gear. As the Israelis have long observed, they would still have won their wars with the Arabs even if they had exchanged weapons. Most wars we can expect in the future will still feature more American infantry going into harm's way without much succor from fifty-million-dollar aircraft.

The problem is that the infantry have to carry all of their gear and, once the shooting starts, your average groundpounder ("grunt," "dogface," "Gentleman of the Earth," you get the idea) wants to travel light. New technology usually weighs more than it's worth for a foot soldier. But, as a new century dawns, plans are being made for equipping the infantry with gadgets they won't want to leave behind. Or, at least that's what the press releases will have you believe.

Predigital Soldiers

BEFORE TAKING A peek at the promised future, we would do well to take a good look at the present and the immediate past. It is particularly important to keep in mind that the infantry are not alone on the ground. For thousands of years they have been accompanied by men on horseback and other specialists using bows or other mechanical devices to throw objects. The latter two functions have been replaced by tanks and artillery, two items we will cover while explaining why it is so difficult to turn the infantryman into a high-tech warrior.

What we think of as infantry combat—a bunch of helmeted guys wandering around in the open, or in a city, armed with rifles and other portable weapons—is a relatively recent development. In the late nineteenth century, most infantry still marched into combat as they would today for a parade. Everyone was lined up, some drummers were drumming, other fellows were carrying flags, and a few officers on horseback would be there waving swords and urging everyone on.

Eighty years ago, the ancient style of warfare disappeared once and for all. During World War I (1914–18), millions of infantry died advancing in ranks against machine guns and artillery. By the end of that war, the troops were advancing as we think of them today: in small groups, running and dodging from one bit of cover to the next.

It took something as traumatic, and bloody, as World War I to convince the armies of the world that after thousands of years, marching together was no longer practical for the infantry. What replaced the well-organized formations of infantry has yet to be completely sorted out. For not only did the parade-type formations for the infantry change, but so did many other aspects of the typical battle.

For thousands of years, wars were fought as battles or sieges. In this century, this has all changed. In the past, battles were events where two armies would line up, have at it for a few hours or a few days, and then that would be that. Under these circumstances, the troops went into battle carrying their rifle, ammunition, and little else. They could move about easily. Their camp was in the rear, and the survivors would return there after the battle was over. The losers would simply run away, if they managed to avoid capture or death. The twentieth-century battle is an affair that can go on for weeks or months. The infantry have to move around carrying a lot of their gear with them. There is no longer a camp where they can drop their blankets, spare clothing, tents, and other stuff. The "camp" is now wherever the infantry stop and rest in the midst of these interminable battles. The result is infantrymen lugging around fifty to a hundred pounds of gear on their backs. Naturally, the troops drop most of this stuff somewhere the first chance they get, but then they find themselves sleeping in the open without a tent or a sleeping bag. Moreover, under these circumstances there is often no food or clean clothing. The soldiers are thus prone to more illness and disease from living like wild animals.

This dreadful situation was noted as early as World War I. A solution of sorts developed during World War II (1939–45), when more and more troops were assigned to units that had armored vehicles or trucks for all the infantry. In the past, the infantry had always marched to battle, and then kept at it during battle. If ships, and later trains and trucks, were available, these would be used to get the infantry to the area where the fighting was going on. But after that, the troops had to hump it, carrying all their gear on their backs. But by 1945 it was obvious that infantry needed help in hauling all their gear around for these drawn-out battles. The solution was to motorize most of the infantry. Every soldier now had a (thinly) armored vehicle to ride around in. Of course, the grunts were still expected to "dismount" to do most of their fighting. But all their gear was stowed in the vehicle. The armored personnel carrier (APC) or more elaborate infantry fighting vehicle (IFV) became the infantryman's home in the field. They could sleep in, under, or next to it (rigging bits of canvas for additional shelter). In the winter, the vehicle had a heating system that came in handy (at least when it worked). The APCs and IFVs also carried additional weapons. APCs had little beyond one or two machine guns. But IFVs carried small (20mm to 80mm) cannons and antitank missiles. The "mechanized" (APC- or IFV-equipped) infantry were getting pretty high-tech. But there were still infantry that, for a number of reasons, could not take their vehicles with them to the war. These were called "light infantry," and the loads they carried were heavier than ever.

Paratroopers and infantry units meant to be flown to trouble spots quickly were called light infantry. Going by air means leaving the five- to twenty-ton vehicles behind. Every nation has some of these light infantry. Trouble is, these guys still have to lug their gear on their backs. Because they are without vehicles, but possibly fighting infantry that do have APCs and IFVs, the light infantry are pretty heavily armed. The only truly light infantry are those troops that go out for a day or two of patrolling and carry minimal loads (weapons and ammo, a canteen or two, some food, a blanket and waterproof sheet, etc.). Even this light load can weigh thirty to forty pounds, minimum. But it works. In many Third World wars (usually in tropical areas), most of the troops have little but the clothes on their backs, a rifle, and some ammunition. They steal whatever else they need as they go.

That other ancient form of warfare, the siege, is still with us. In fact, it has become much more common. In a classic siege, a smaller group of soldiers inside a fort or walled city is surrounded for weeks or months by a larger force. The besiegers usually dig trenches and erect walls themselves as they wait for the defenders inside the fort or town to run out of food. That's your classic siege. During World War I you had siege lines stretching across continents, with armies laying siege to each other. That's what the vast trench lines of World War I were all about, one army besieging another. Under these conditions, the infantry didn't have to worry much about carrying equipment on their backs. Most of the time, the infantry were improving their trenches or going out a short distance at night on patrol. When there were attacks, it was soon found practical to travel light, because few of these World War I attacks got very far.

World War II, and its abundance of tanks and APCs, cut down on the siege-type operations so common during World War I. The infantry still spent a lot of time in trenches, as that was the safest place to be any time the grunts were within artillery range of the enemy. The rest of the time, the infantry were moving about in trucks, APCs, or, most often, in boxcars or on foot.

The First Digital Soldiers

THE ONLY BITS OF technology to really help the infantryman individually in this century have been the radio and flak jacket. The latter is not really what we would think of as a digital item, but its importance for the infantry has been enormous. We should also remember that "digital soldiers" is a concept that includes all sorts of new technology. It doesn't have to use electrons to qualify, it just has to make the soldier more effective.

At the turn of the century, the telephone was already a useful tool for infantry in siege situations. Via a telephone wire going back to the artillery, infantry could direct the fire of the big guns. This advantage was exploited widely during World War I. In addition to directing the welcome fire of the artillery, the telephone also allowed the frontline troops to let the generals know what was going on up there and whether reinforcements were needed. The telephone was the first really high-tech item to prove useful for the infantry.

This rapid communication had a lot to do with the deadlock of World War I fighting. Until tanks and trucks were introduced, a telephone call would bring reinforcements before the attacking infantry could make any real progress getting through the front line of barbed wire, artillery fire, and trenches filled with infantry.

During World War II, radio technology developed sufficiently so that smaller radios could be carried with the advancing troops. Of course, the infantry equipped with vehicles had radios with them, but the really serious fighting was always done on foot, and American engineers developed the handheld "walkie-talkie." This device, rather larger and heavier than the ones you can buy today in any electronics store, was still quite a breakthrough. Its range might only be a few hundred yards (depending on the terrain), but it could be a real lifesaver as small infantry units tried to coordinate their actions in the chaos of close combat. The more common infantry radio was heavy, often weighing in at over forty pounds, but it could be carried by one man and allowed platoon- (thirty men) and company-size (over one hundred men) units to stay in touch with each other and higher headquarters. These radios took a lot of fog out of infantry combat. It did wonders for troop morale, just to know they were "still in touch."

The flak jacket first appeared during World War II, but only for use by bomber crews as protection against enemy antiaircraft guns (which the Germans called "flak"). Bomber crews flying over Germany often took higher casualties than the infantry, and most of it came from 88mm and 105mm antiaircraft shells exploding near their planes. The jackets, using metal plates, were too heavy for infantry to wear on the battlefield. This had been used in World War I, but only for troops in fortifications. It was simply too much weight (forty to fifty pounds) and too cumbersome for a soldier to move around in. Besides, the earliest flak jackets were for protection from shell fragments, not machine-gun bullets.

After World War II, new, lighter materials were developed for flak jackets, and they became practical for infantrymen to wear. Soldiers had been wearing steel helmets since 1915 to protect their heads from shell fragments; the flak jackets greatly expanded the area protected. Infantry casualties, while still high, were reduced. They would have been reduced a lot more were it not for the vast increase in the volume of firepower on the battlefield. But for the infantryman, any protection was appreciated. The flak jacket was as much a morale booster as it was a form of protection.

In the last thirty years, some new bits of gadgetry have been given to the infantry, but none have dramatically changed the grunts' lifestyle. Some of the more notable bits of high tech for the infantry have been:

• Starlight scopes. Binoculars or telescopes that electronically amplify available light so that whatever you can see in the starlight or moonlight appears to be in daylight. These weigh a few pounds (down from up to ten in the 1960s) and came into use during the Vietnam War. Like most innovations for the infantry, they are too expensive (still over a thousand dollars a unit) and too heavy to equip every man with one. In some special cases, each infantryman can be equipped with a set that appears like a bulky (and heavy) pair of eyeglass-mounted binoculars. But these items cannot be worn for too long under these conditions. Fatigue sets in, the batteries run down, and you have a narrow field of vision that takes getting used to. Eventually, say in ten years, these will be available in a format that looks (and weighs) about the same as a pair of goggles. The troops are already being equipped with goggles, but these are to protect the eyes from sand, small debris on the battlefield, and laser burns. When the going gets hot, the troops still prefer to have their eyes, and field of vision, as unencumbered as possible. But when lying in ambush (a common battlefield job for the infantry) or advancing into enemy-held territory, night is the best time and the ability to see through the darkness is a major advantage. A key advantage of a starlight scope is that it is a "passive sensor" that doesn't broadcast anything the enemy can pick up.

• Individual radios. Ever since the first combat radios appeared early in this century, soldiers have dreamed of having their own lightweight individual set. Technically, it is possible now, and has been for a couple of decades. But, as is often the case with technology, there are some problems. Radios do add weight, and you either put the individual's radio in his helmet or you get complications with components of the radio getting damaged in the heat of the action. There's a lot of action for a groundpounder. Then there are the batteries. This power problem can be solved, to a certain extent, with the newer battery technologies. But all batteries eventually run out of juice, so when the soldier runs out of batteries, he's carrying around a dead radio. The biggest problem is that the radio sends out signals when the soldier is trying to talk to someone. If the enemy is a high-tech opponent, he can pick up these signals and use them against you. There are some ways to get around this, mainly by using burst-type transmissions. With this technique the voice message is compressed (and often scrambled) and then sent out in a short burst that is hard to locate. If you have a squad (up to a dozen troops) or a platoon (up to fifty men) chattering away, there will be enough bursts for an enemy to pick up the location of the troops and start shooting with machine guns or artillery. This sort of response will end more than just the conversations. But individual radio sets are used by some infantry, particularly commandos who are conducting surprise attacks against relatively low-tech opponents (who are not likely to be monitoring the airwaves for individual infantry radios). But widespread use of these radios is still in the future.

• A GPS is a one- or two-pound handheld receiver of satellite signals that tells the user exactly where he is (to within a hundred meters or less). This is not the sort of thing that every soldier needs most of the time. Every small (half dozen or so) group of troops can get away with only one GPS, and through the 1990s that is exactly what has been happening. For most of this century, more and more troops have been moving about in small groups, often out of sight of their fellows, so getting lost has been a growing problem. The GPS changed all that. The GPS receivers are so cheap (a hundred to a thousand dollars) that just about anyone can afford them. A GPS does wonders for the infantry's effectiveness and morale. Already there are GPS units weighing a few ounces and as small as a wristwatch. These are for missile-guidance systems and are expensive. But it won't be too many years before they will be cheap enough to stick in every soldier's helmet, and they will display location and direction of advance information on the soldier's goggles.

• CBW (chemical and biological warfare) suits are much like space suits, except they are not airtight. Rather, they filter the air and are otherwise hot, stuffy, and uncomfortable in warm weather. In hot weather, they can kill or injure you with heat stroke. But they do protect the wearer from most, if not all, chemical and biological weapons. Historically (since 1919) the best protection from chemical and biological weapons has been the ability to use them. Since 1918, no nation has used chemical weapons against an opponent who was able to use them right back. But you can never be sure. So most armies have some of the CBW suits, and often the troops are sent into action wearing them. While the troops appreciate the protection, they are also aware of how tiring it is to wear the suits, even in cool weather, and how much their sight and hearing are limited by the suits. What really bothers the troops who have used these suits is that someone will try to air-condition them and make them a permanent part of the combat uniform. This has been proposed, but is far from being technically feasible.

• CBW detectors. These have been common for several decades. Mainly, they warn of the presence of chemical weapons before said weapons are present in lethal concentrations. In theory, the detectors would provide time for the troops to get their gas masks, and their CBW suits, on and get out of the area. In practice, these devices have proved to be good for morale, as long as they don't give an alert. When the detectors do go off, morale takes a dive and all but the most stalwart troops become more concerned with getting away from the chemical weapons than with continuing the fight. These detectors have gone off more often with false alerts than as real warnings of chemical weapons being present.

• Target designators are sort of like powerful flashlights that allow the user to put a beam of light (initially infrared, but now laser) on a target. A shell, bomb, or rocket then uses the reflection of that light off the target as a means to find the target and destroy it. The first of these target designators appeared in the late 1950s. They weren't all that portable, but could be manhandled to the front. The laser wasn't patented until 1960, and it took over a decade to make laser devices portable. Now they are, and a soldier can carry one around and point it at something he wants a bomber or missile to destroy. Obviously, the laser designator isn't a weapon itself, but merely a means of designating a target. But that's good enough for the infantry, as they know what needs destroying on the battlefield, and as long as they control the laser, they control their fate a little more.

• Drugs are nothing really new on the battlefield. Alcohol has long been used to get the troops in the mood, or help them recover from the stress of battle so they will be ready for another round. Other drugs have been used, but professional-minded troops know that this is a shortsighted approach to enhancing combat performance. Actually, the drugs, especially alcohol, have generally been used as a desperate (and often effective) gambit to get reluctant troops into combat. In the mid-twentieth century, more practical drugs have come into use. Among the more important drugs for the combat soldier have been antibiotics (to prevent minor wounds from becoming infected and killing the soldier), amphetamines (to keep soldiers alert under sleepless and stressful conditions); water-purification chemicals (added to questionable water to prevent intestinal diseases); insect repellent; and tranquilizers (to calm down combat-fatigue cases). There are many more, with new ones appearing each year. Drugs, for the most part, are very portable. Painkillers, first introduced in the mid-nineteenth century, have become more effective in the twentieth. All of these drugs make the infantry soldier more effective and less likely to become a long-term physical or psychological casualty. Not to mention dead. Some of the more recent drug developments are items that will counteract chemical and biological weapons, as well as improvements on the ones already mentioned. The military doesn't tout its extensive use of battlefield drugs, largely because it's a hard sell PR-wise. But the troops know better, and take help wherever they can find it.

• Combat rations are another twentieth-century innovation. Canned food was first developed for military use in the early 1800s. Before that the best you could hope for was salted meat and uncooked grain. Until the last few decades, canned food was about the only decent battlefield chow the troops could get when they were moving or when the fighting was too intense for cooking. But canned food is bulky and heavy. Troops were frequently left with glorified candy bars (often lacking much sugar, but technically very nutritious). Of late, long shelf life meals (MREs, or meals ready to eat) have shown up for the troops. Long used by civilian campers, the MREs promptly became the soldiers' favorite gripe, and MRE was said to really mean "meals rejected by everybody." But under battlefield or field conditions, there is no practical alternative to MREs, and campers continue to enjoy the same chow in the field (and to buy military surplus MREs at bargain prices). As many earlier commanders have noted, "an army travels on its stomach." If you don't feed the troops, they can't, or simply won't, fight.

• Modern field gear. This includes all the stuff a camper needs, from cooking utensils to sleeping bags, and the gear you use to carry it on your back. Field soldiers, tank crews, artillerymen, support troops, and, of course, the infantry, spend a lot of time camping out when there's a war on. This is not only uncomfortable, but quickly becomes unhealthy. Until a hundred or so years ago, you could expect to lose half your troops in eight months of campaigning (not including winter) without having been in combat. Exposure and diseases were the most common causes. A major remedy for these losses is more effective "field gear." Better sleeping bags, tenting, and "webbing" (the belt and harness worn to carry everything) all make a big difference. Not only do losses go down, but morale goes up. It was during Vietnam that the U.S. Army noted troops buying superior civilian camping gear with their own money. The American military has since tried harder to keep up with the advances made by commercial firms developing better gear.

• Portable heavy weapons comprise lightweight launchers for antitank rockets, bunker-buster shells, flamethrowers, and antiaircraft missiles. Firepower, not manpower, dominates the battlefield, whether it be from arrows or artillery shells. Despite all the artillery and aircraft the infantry theoretically have on call, there are often times when neither is readily available. At that point the grunts have to go with what they got and what they got is often not hefty enough to do the job. During World War II, the first "portable artillery" for the infantry was invented: the bazooka. This portable rocket launcher weighed under ten pounds and could destroy a tank (if you got within a hundred yards and hit it from the side or rear). The infantry soon discovered that the bazooka was effective (and safer to use) against enemy bunkers. In the last few decades, more variations on this portable firepower have been developed. There are rocket launchers just for bunkers and guided missiles that bring down aircraft. The downside is that these things have been getting heavier, with the weight of "portable" antiaircraft missile systems growing over twenty pounds. All this stuff adds up if you want to carry a little bit of everything and still be able to move quickly cross-country. While most troops now have a vehicle to ride around in, there are still times when you have to dismount and hike cross-country. It can be said that no good infantry weapon can be too lethal, or too light.

• Electronic locators are a recent development that has been tested for years, and they are only recently entering limited use. What they do is periodically send a hard-to-detect message from infantry and tank platoons back to headquarters. A division commander can look at a computer display that shows a map of the local area and gives accurate locations of the hundred or so combat platoons under his command. A major problem in twentieth-century battles is that of the boss not knowing where all his troops are. The electronic locator solves the problem. Alas, these systems are expensive, and burst transmissions from the locators can still be detected and the broadcasting unit found. Hmm, there are always nagging little problems like this— namely, a shortage of money and an abundance of real or potential problems. Because of the friendly-fire problems in the 1991 Gulf War, more effort was put into getting locator devices to the troops. This has resulted in the development of SABER (Situational Awareness Beacon with Reply), a device that puts IFF (Identification, Friend or Foe), GPS, a computer and radio all in one small box (large cellular phone size). SABER broadcasts a "don't shoot me" signal so that other friendlies know who not to shoot. The basic SABER technology will be used for downed pilots and commandos to identify themselves to friendly aircraft. The computer and GPS in the SABER enable the unit to sort out who is where doing what for each SABER user.

• Field sensors are electronic devices that allow the ground soldier to detect a far-off enemy. During World War II, when radar was first used in combat, the technology was too bulky and crude to be used on the ground against ground targets. But that changed after World War II, and by the 1960s, the first ground radars appeared. By the 1970s, most nations had ground radars that could detect troops up to a kilometer or so away, and vehicles much farther (ten or more kilometers). By the 1980s and '90s, the radars had gotten lighter (under forty pounds) and extended their range somewhat. But these radars were not a cure-all for the problems of keeping an eye on approaching enemy troops at night. Ground radars, like airborne radars, could not see through hills, trees, or buildings. Experienced troops reminded the scientists and engineers that a soldier who has been in action for a while can use his ears to detect oncoming armored vehicles (which make distinctive sounds) even when such vehicles are behind obstacles that radar cannot see through. Moreover, no radar has been developed that can spot infantry crawling toward you through the underbrush. Despite these limitations, the radars have proved useful in keeping an eye on open areas and thus freeing up troops for other tasks.

Electrifying the Infantry

FOR THOUSANDS OF years, the infantry have been doing the dirty work of ground combat. While a lot of technology has been handed to the grunts, it hasn't changed their position at the bottom of the food chain. It all comes down to weight. The agility that makes the individual infantryman so nimble and useful on the battlefield is canceled out if you try to load the poor guy down with all manner of well-meaning but weighty gadgets. But the gadgets do have advantages, if only their numerous disadvantages can be overcome.

There's also a question of costs. In the past, to be useful, infantry were needed in large quantities. For several decades, more and more technicians have been added to armies, while the number of groundpounders has declined. These days, for every combat pilot in, say, the American armed forces, you're going to have only about a dozen infantrymen. While turning a civilian into an experienced pilot costs several million dollars, it normally cost a lot less to produce an effective infantryman. Given that you can still win a war without pilots, but not without infantry, it makes sense to try and improve the quality of your grunts as much as possible.

Training is the key. Always has been, always will be. But training is expensive and not as attractive as new gadgets, even electronic training aids.

This will cause problems. Given a choice between money for training and funding new equipment, most legislators and some officers will go for the gadgets. Training money goes for fuel, transportation, ammunition, and spare parts. Just more spending on the same old stuff. New gadgets require new contracts, often with new, and politically grateful, vendors. New contracts are more profitable, because they require more R and D. So even if training is needed more than new technology, the new gear is more likely to pass muster with lawmakers than is something as mundane as training funds.

Post–cold war conflicts will depend more on the infantry than on tanks or artillery. Post–cold war battles will also be less popular for the industrialized nations, with the voters unwilling to accept many casualties. But infantry combat has always been bloody and new technology can only go so far in limiting the friendly casualties. Indeed, the high-tech approach limits friendly losses by increasing the amount of firepower directed at the opposition. This increases the damage done to the foe, as well as the enemy casualties, and when these show up on TV, they also become a problem. The 1991 Gulf War was an example of this, but the later operations in Somalia and Bosnia are more typical. In neither of these last two operations would digital infantry have changed the situation much if the infantry were not allowed to train intensively and realistically.

The Future of Digital Infantry

THE BASIC JOB and tools of the infantry have not changed much in eighty years. It's still a bunch of fellows in green or brown uniforms, equipped with steel helmets and shovels, armed with rifles and grenades, running around dodging artillery and machine-gun fire while trying to stay out of the way of armored vehicles. All of the gadgets that have been added to the infantryman's knapsack in those eight decades have not made any fundamental changes.

Keep this in mind as you peruse the current barrage of press releases and briefings that tout the coming "digital soldier." Based on past experience, and most likely future technology, you can expect to see:

• Individual GPS. This is already possible, as GPS devices have rapidly become smaller, lighter, and cheaper in the last few years. This will make it very difficult for troops to get lost. Even if several troops have their GPS units put out of action, there will still be several functional ones in each squad (three of which make up an infantry platoon).

• Individual radios. These are already used by some commando-type units in various nations. These have been proven in combat. Despite the potential problems of the enemy listening in or using your radios to locate you, the ability to communicate in city or forest fighting is a major step forward. The troops will appreciate the relief from isolation in combat, although they may curse always having a sergeant or officer in their ear.

• Night-vision goggles. These may be the last of these gadgets to show up, because of the new technologies needed to make these things small enough, light enough, and rugged enough to be practical. But most of the technology is already there, and troops can already "see in the dark" with bulkier night-vision devices. These items are a major advantage against someone who doesn't have them. Operating at night enhances surprise and usually finds fewer civilians to get in the way of all the firepower.

• Information displayed on the goggles (as on a computer screen) via a miniature (pack-of-cigarettes-size) computer carried by the soldier. This will follow as soon as the practical night-vision goggles are perfected. While this is a tricky bit of technology, it has been used for years in combat aircraft (the heads up display, or HUD) and has a track record of reliability and usefulness. The most obvious things to display on the grunt's goggles are directions and fields of fire. The GPS not only tracks its own position, but you can also enter the location of the unit's objective. So the soldier would always have, by touching a switch on his helmet, a symbol popping up before his eyes indicating "This way!" Very handy. There would also be red symbols indicating "Be careful shooting in this direction because there are supposed to be friendlies over there." There would be a small numeric keypad built into the hand-size computer itself, and the helmet radio could receive additional instructions and store them in the computer. You can also get useful stuff like time of day, how many minutes and seconds to some event (like an air strike right in front of you), and a to do list ("Patrol three hundred meters in this direction, then turn right two hundred meters. Start in two hours, forty-six minutes"). Timing and location have always been critical factors on the modern battlefield. As able as modern artillery is, when the gunners are told to put so many shells onto such and such a piece of ground, there's no way of checking at the last minute to make sure some wayward friendly infantryman has not wandered into that place. That's how most friendly-fire casualties occur. Information on the battlefield is not only useful and reassuring, it's often a lifesaver. Again, by giving every soldier a pair of these "smart goggles," you can be assured of each squad having at least one set working most of the time. Troops will still be responding to spoken instructions and hand signals. But the addition of the technology makes it harder for the entire group to get lost or otherwise get out of step with other units.

• Mine and booby-trap detectors. These weapons often cause the majority of casualties in little wars, especially the type of peacekeeping operations that have become so popular in the post–cold war world. Modern mines and booby traps are often made of plastic and contain little or no metal. This makes them extremely hard to detect. But modern sensor technology, again using a lot of microcomputer power, makes it possible to detect even these modern mines. Using "sniffers" to detect trace gases given off by explosives, or imaging sensors to see mines under the dirt, these nasties can be found. Some of these detectors are already in use, although in somewhat crude form. But there will be plenty of opportunity to try them out, with tens of millions of mines left lying around cold war battlefields.

• Individual locators. These can be built into the radio. In addition to letting higher commanders know where you are, they can be used for troops who are wounded and left for the medical troops to take care of. Not everyone's locator would be going off at all times. But on command, one trooper in each squad or platoon would transmit the location signal. This sort of thing will take a lot of the anxiety out of being a company or battalion commander.

• More firepower per soldier. More new weapons that are, pound for pound, deadlier than current ones. Although soldiers today and eighty years ago both carried rifles, the current weapon of choice is not the old bolt-action rifle, but the "assault rifle." These assault rifles, be they AK-47s, M16s, or whatever, could have been manufactured eighty years ago. The generals have always resisted rifles that fire more ammunition more quickly, and for good reason. For while the troops appreciate increased personal firepower, the generals understand better the problems of getting additional ammunition to the troops. But once one army equipped its troops with the automatic weapons (Germans and Russians in World War II), everyone else was compelled to follow suit. It turned out that, while there were some cases of troops with automatic weapons (assault rifles) running out of ammunition, the soldiers proved more practical than the generals thought they could be. That's not uncommon. What is changing is the variety of additional weapons available for the infantryman. Not only are these new weapons portable (twenty pounds and under), but they are increasingly lethal. In 1916, and for some decades thereafter, the only portable weapons for the grunts were mortars. The ones light enough to carry (50mm to 60mm) threw the equivalent of hand grenades several hundred meters. It helped, but not nearly as much as the antitank missiles, bunker-buster rockets, flamethrowers, and antiaircraft missiles now available. There are also more kinds of mines and booby traps, many electronically controlled, that can be thrown into a backpack. In the hands of well-trained troops, this arsenal of special weapons make the footsloggers a lot more lethal than they appear.

• Digitizing the battlefield is doing to the combat zone what has already been done to the offices and factories over the last decade with networked computers. The advantages are obvious: aircraft, tanks, infantry, artillery, etc. can share information and more effectively coordinate their operations. But the reason the buzzword "digital battlefield" has been used is because first one must get everyone to use a common form of communication. This requires replacing a lot of existing equipment with radios that all speak the same digital language and introducing a lot of new stuff (sensors that talk digital to radio equipment). Put simply, by connecting everyone on the same "net," what a tank commander sees through his thermal (heat-sensing) sight can be transmitted to a jet or helicopter overhead, or vice versa. Sharing information over high-speed digital links allows everyone to comprehend the situation quickly and with the same information. This is all rather unprecedented, but is even now technically possible. It's just a matter of doing it. This, from past experience, won't be easy.

• Who is really in charge? Major arguments over how much control higher commanders should have over individual troops continues. As soon as radios were introduced on the battlefield eighty years ago, there arose the problem of generals at the other end of the phone wire trying to tell the very junior officer on the spot what to do. This got worse in Vietnam, where there were helicopters for senior officers to ride around in. Digital soldiers will mean more abundant communications. This will include video capabilities that will allow a general far to the rear to see what the troops on the fighting line see. We know it takes a great deal of self-restraint for said general to refrain from telling the troops exactly what to do. But there are always those that argue for giving the higher commanders more control over troops and units at the front line because said commander is now "better informed" with all this digital communication. This debate will rage on until there's a bit of serious warfare in which to try all of this out.

• More fear of electronic warfare. Electronic warfare followed right on the heels of the first electronic devices (radios) being used in combat. Then, and to this day, it was found quite useful to fill the airwaves with a lot of loud static when you wanted to disrupt the enemy's radio communications. Of course, this disrupted yours too, but you were usually the attacker and had made careful plans for other forms of communication. Your opponent didn't know what you were up to and had a harder time sorting it all out with his radios, which were useless because of all that static.

• Substantial change in tactics to accommodate and exploit all these goodies. A phenomenon unique to the twentieth century is the development of a lot of new weapons between wars. This is followed by a frantic scramble after the next war has begun, as all concerned try to be first to figure out the best way to use the new stuff. This was seen to happen in World War I, World War II, Vietnam, the Russo-Afghan war, the Arab-Israeli wars, and the 1991 Gulf War. It will happen again and it will happen big-time if the next war arrives after a lot of the above weapons and gadgets have been introduced.

This future full of digital soldiers running around with TV sets in their goggles may end up as little more than an opportunity for clever troops to play video games while they're supposed to be working (troops have a long tradition of modifying their equipment for other purposes). But war is a deadly business, and most of the troops will either find a way to turn those goggles into a useful combat tool, or else the battlefield will be littered with them. The troops do have a tendency to simply discard what doesn't work. When it's a matter of life and death, no one hangs on to some general's pet idea.

Despite the smaller budgets in the post–cold war world, a lot of the digital soldier gear will come into use because much of it is off-the-shelf and cheap. This will be a problem for industrialized nations, who tend to think they have the technological edge on the battlefield. When a lot of the new gear is off-the-shelf, anyone can get it. And that's what will happen, because it has already been happening. Anyone can buy a GPS, and a lot of the other stuff can be assembled with some good engineers and money. There will be a lot of digital soldiers running around, with a lot of digital weapons and equipment that may not be known to their opponents.

4

....

Digital Artillery

WHILE THE INFANTRY have not yet gotten a great deal of support directly from high tech, they have received some help by the greatly increased use of digital technology in other areas of ground warfare. Tanks and artillery have been the major recipients of high-tech enhancements in this century. Artillery was always high-tech, from the moment it appeared on the scene in the thirteenth century. For a long time, the technological achievements of artillery were in the areas of metallurgy and chemistry. But in this century the guns began to make use of electronics. The first digital aid for artillery came from the telephone and radio. Just before World War I (1914–18), artillery became accurate enough to fire "by the map" at targets the gunners could not see. Advances in metallurgy, chemistry, and hydraulics brought this about. These developments immediately provided the opportunity for the troops at the front to get in touch with the gunners several miles to the rear in order to provide targeting information. Flag and flare signals were used with some success, but telephone and radio proved to be extremely useful. The use of radio- or telephone-equipped artillery officers at the front, or in balloons or aircraft, made artillery much more effective. These "forward observers" made the front lines a much more lethal place, as artillery fire would now come down as soon as the enemy showed themselves. This usually happened when the enemy attacked, and their infantry were coming out of their trenches.

Calculation, Chemistry, and Registration Fire

THE RADIO AND forward observers did not solve all the problems of getting the distant guns to hit something at the front lines quickly. For some years, each forward observer was in touch with but one group of guns. For best effect, the guns were prepared to aim at a few targets whose location had already been calculated. Yes, calculated. The guns hit targets they could not see by using a lot of trigonometry. The calculations also had to take into account the height of the guns and the target, as well as the direction and distance. It took a while to do the math. Then there was the problem of chemistry. For the trigonometry to work, each of the shells fired had to have a known amount of explosive force sending it out of the gun barrel. While manufacturing was becoming more precise, there were always some minor differences from shell to shell and, especially, from one "lot" (shells made from a specific batch of propellant) to another. Added to the specific characteristics of individual shells, there was also the weather to worry about. If the humidity, barometric pressure, or cloud cover changed, this would have a noticeable effect on the shells' flight. The maps, especially in the days before satellite pictures, were often just inaccurate enough to throw the guns' aim off. Each gun was also just different enough from others of the same model to create more minor inaccuracies. Put in practical terms, shells from different lots, fired under different weather conditions, could land hundreds of meters from the spot they were aimed at according to the map calculations.

All of these problems were solved by "registering" the guns. The registration process involved doing the calculations on the map, having a group of guns elevate and turn their barrels accordingly, and then firing one shell from one gun. The forward observer noted where the shell landed compared to where (looking at his map) it was supposed to land. He then told the gunners how to adjust their next shot ("Right two hundred meters, up fifty meters."). Another shell was fired, and if it landed where it was supposed to, the forward observer told the gunners they were "on target." That registration would still be off if the guns were fired later when the weather had changed, but the difference would not mean much if you were firing a barrage (a dozen or more guns firing many shells each.)

Coordination

AS SEEMINGLY EFFECTIVE as this system was, it had some serious drawbacks. For one thing, one forward observer was only communicating with one group of guns (a battery of four, a battalion of twelve, or several battalions). This was done largely because radios were not widely available and no one had figured out a system for rapidly recalculating the trajectories for a lot of guns in different locations firing at one target.

Right through World War II, the telephone was the preferred form of communication. It was cheaper than radio, could not easily be overheard by the enemy, and could not be jammed by the enemy broadcasting static on the same frequency. Radios were used when the telephone was not practical, such as when the forward observers were in aircraft, or your troops were advancing.

In the 1930s, the United States developed a system for quickly calculating how to hit new targets and how to coordinate the fire of many different artillery battalions spread over a wide area. This was done primarily by having the forward observers send their messages back to a Fire Direction Center (FDC) rather than to a single battery or battalion. The U.S. Army could accomplish this because they had a lot of radios and telephones, and because they worked out all the details on how to make it work in peacetime. The FDC would then do all the calculations and tell the individual gun batteries or battalions where to fire. Through World War II, primitive computers were built that speeded up the task of doing all the trigonometry. American troops were also the most intensive users of radio equipment. The United States pioneered the widespread use of airborne forward observers as well as ground-based "air controllers" to coordinate the use of fighter-bombers with fast-moving armored columns.

By 1945, Japanese and German troops had learned to fear the massive, responsive, and accurate American artillery fire. American infantry built their operations around the capabilities of their artillery. Opponents chided American infantry for being reluctant to rush in and fight at close quarters. This was a macho accusation, as the prudent thing to do was call in the artillery fire, if you had it. American troops usually did, and they sent in the shells instead of the grunts. Shells don't bleed or, more importantly, vote. For over half a century, this world-class artillery capability has been the key element in U.S. ground-combat tactics.

Smart Shells and Electrified Guns

AS EFFECTIVE AS American artillery has been, there have always been strenuous efforts to make the gunners even more effective. Much money and effort has been thrown in this direction, with decidedly mixed results.

After World War II the two major problems were seen as 1) making more efficient use of artillery ammunition, and 2) finding better ways to shut down enemy artillery.

The ammunition problem was, and always has been, the major headache. As powerful as artillery appears, the people on the receiving end are quick to find ways to dilute the explosive effect of all those shells. Historically, the shovel has proved to be a formidable defense. The troops subject to artillery fire know that digging shellproof fortifications is literally a matter of life and death. What it usually comes down to is the artillery trying to put so many shells on the target that even the stoutest fortifications will crumble. Ultimately, the artillery will prevail. But only if there is enough ammunition at hand. There rarely is. Not only does it require enormous transportation resources (ships, trains, and trucks) to move millions of tons of shells, but the supply tends to get tight at the front just when a lot more is needed. Obviously, anything that would make each shell more effective would be an enormous advantage.

The fire-control improvements of the 1930s and 1940s made the guns very accurate, and the extensive use of radio-equipped forward observers made the fire very responsive and timely. There were no big breakthroughs to be found here. But there was room for improvement in finding targets and in what kinds of shells were fired. The introduction of helicopters and better electronic detection devices made it easier to find out where the enemy was, even if he was camouflaged and buried in fortifications. These improvements in detection were gradual. New kinds of cameras could see differences in heat, which made it easy to see where digging had been done and vegetation killed. Even dug-in troops have to use their radios or other devices that emit electronic signals. These transmissions can be detected. If you control the air, as Americans usually do, you can fly around looking for the enemy's hiding places. Once you find out where the enemy is, you can start firing. When the enemy moves, you can hit him again while he's on the road and when he tries to dig in to a new hiding place. When the opposition is dug in, it takes a lot of shells to do damage. When the enemy moves, you don't always get the word right away. While the enemy is moving, you don't have his position at all times. While your opponent is more vulnerable while moving, you have a less precise idea of where he is and have to fire a lot of shells at suspected locations to insure that you will hit something.

Artillerymen had long had one trick that could, if used right, greatly enhance the effectiveness of shells. This was done through the fuze that caused the shell to explode. Modern fuzes were invented in the late 1800s. Affixed to the front of a shell, they caused the shell to explode when it hit something. Soon, the fuzes became more sophisticated, with some having a delay of a fraction of a second. This allowed the shell to bury itself in the target, and then explode. This caused more damage if the enemy was buried in fortifications, or, in naval warfare, if you wanted the shell to explode inside a ship (where it would do more damage). The other new type of fuze was the time fuze. This one exploded a shell a certain number of seconds after the shell was fired. This means that if you did your calculations correctly (more trigonometry and algebra again), the shell would explode over the enemy position. The advantage of this was that more of the shell fragments would hit something. Normally, when a shell exploded upon hitting the ground, many of the fragments promptly buried themselves harmlessly into the ground. The "airburst" not only put more shells to work, but also eliminated a lot of protection for troops on the ground. When troops are shelled, they will jump into a trench, shell hole, or something like that. If the shells are normal, and explode when they hit the ground, the troops in trenches and the like are safe unless a shell lands right on top of them. But an airburst sends fragments straight down. Unless the troops have overhead protection (which most won't have), they will be killed or injured.

Even with improvements in calculation (calculators and computers), time fuzes are tricky to use. Automatic fuze setters speeded up the tedious process of setting the time fuzes, but it still took time. And the target was often a moving one that would not wait.

During World War II a better, but more expensive, solution was found. While radar was a newly introduced item early in World War II, it had been in development over a decade earlier. The principle of radar was simple enough—send out an electronic signal, and then listen for it to be bounced back if it hits something. Do some calculations and, bingo, you know something is out there, and how far away it is. Doing the calculations was the more complicated part of perfecting radar. But early on it was realized that radar could be used in a primitive fashion simply to detect an object right in front of the radar transmitter. It was also realized that the electronic components of the day could be fit into a large (in this case, 127mm, or 5-inch) shell and still leave room for some explosives. Thus equipped, the 127mm gun became an excellent antiaircraft weapon. Before this "radar fuze" came along, using five-inch guns on ships for antiaircraft work was very inefficient. The attacking aircraft would be coming in fast and from all directions. The time it took to calculate where these aircraft might be in a few minutes, and then aim and set the time fuzes, made it difficult to hit the enemy bombers. Often the five-inch guns were simply used like land-based antiaircraft guns, and simply fired a barrage of shells at a predetermined direction and altitude, where the shells would explode and damage any enemy aircraft that happened to be in the area. With the radar fuze, you could simply aim the gun in the general direction of the incoming enemy aircraft and fire. If the shell came close enough for its explosives and fragments to have any effect, the radar in the nose of the shell would detect this closeness and explode.

The smaller (20mm and 40mm) antiaircraft guns operated like machine guns, putting out a stream of shells that allowed the gunner to adjust his aim and eventually hit the target. The longer-range five-inch (127mm) guns and their radar fuzes went after the enemy aircraft before these planes came within range of the 20mm and 40mm weapons. Even farther out you had friendly interceptors. Thus during World War II the U.S. Navy developed a three-layer defense against enemy aircraft that proved invaluable in saving ships, and lives.

The radar fuze was first developed for antiaircraft work in the Pacific, mainly to prevent any of them from falling into enemy hands. The technology in the radar fuze was not all that exotic by World War II standards, so if the Axis got their hands on one, they would have little trouble duplicating it. The radar fuze first entered service, in the Pacific, in early 1943. In the last year of the war, it was used by field artillery and proved very effective.

Because the radar fuze was expensive to build, costing more than the shell it was fitted to, its use was limited. The field-artillery version was different than the naval version, because you wanted the shells to explode at a certain altitude, and the army used different caliber guns (155mm, or six-inch, which was not the same as the naval six-incher/152mm). Of course, not every target needed a radar fuze. Much of the time, artillery was used on fortifications or structures that were blown up more effectively with the old impact fuze.

In the 1960s, work began in earnest on developing new types of "smart" shells. At first, the additional smarts were mainly mechanical. Shells were made that contained a number of smaller explosive devices. So, rather than just landing and exploding, the new shells first came apart and spread their smaller shells (or "bomblets") over a wider area. The bomblets then exploded, and because they spread out first, they greatly increased the chance of damaging someone or something. A truly smart shell was developed that would home in on tanks. This U.S. development, the "Copperhead," was eventually made to work by the 1980s, and was put into service. But only a small number were manufactured because the shell was so expensive. There were, it turned out, many more cheaper ways to destroy tanks.

The most "intelligent" shells were actually just containers for little robot bombs that were popped out of the shell at the right moment. Some of the bomblets thus ejected were basically land mines with a brain—in this case, a special microprocessor (similar to the brain of a personal computer) with very specific instructions on what to do when on the ground. At first the instructions were very simple, as in "Wait for so many hours, explode if anyone steps on you, and then blow yourself up." This little bit of timed suicide was to allow friendly troops to pass through the area. Mines know no friends and attack anyone who comes close. Eventually, the bomblet mines acquired more "intelligence," as well as some sensors so that they could detect targets farther (up to a few hundred meters) away. By the 1990s, the components of the smart bombs were being called "brilliant." Well, perhaps that is overstating it a bit, but by previous standards of weapons intelligence, these bomblets were quite smart. They still couldn't tell friend from foe, so they were still equipped with self-destruct programming in their tiny electronic brains.

The "brilliant" shells were not as expensive as the Copperhead antitank round, mainly because the new bomblets were using off-the-shelf technology. One could go down to an electronics parts store and buy the components to make a smart bomb (less the explosives) for a high school science project.

Weapons designers were dreaming up ways to make these systems more capable, but that meant much more expensive. With the cold war coming to an end just as the first generation of these computer-controlled shells was coming into use, the military made it clear that they had to be cheap or the troops could not afford them.

Like any good weapon, it wasn't just the shell itself that made it effective, but the ways in which it was used. One thing that was readily obvious was that these bomblets were relatively big, and most artillery shells didn't have all that much cargo space for a lot of the bomblets. Thus, larger guns and rockets were, obviously, better weapons to use with the smart shells and their bulky bomblets. Historically, the larger (over 155mm) guns were not used much for day-to-day fighting, but more for the occasional major offensive. But the big guns were, well, big, and if you wanted a lot of smart shells and their smart bomblets, it was easier to use rockets. This was another case of technology and tactics changing together in the face of a new situation.

Artillery rockets were introduced early in World War II by the Russians. Rockets as artillery is nothing new; the Chinese had been doing that over eight hundred years ago, as had the British in the nineteenth century. But improvements in rocket technology (fuel and fire control) had enabled the World War II–era rockets to fill several needs.

First there was the need to provide a lot of firepower on a target in a short period of time. This need was not so obvious, but think about it: When the first shell of barrage lands, what will all the troops in the area do? Exactly, they will all jump into a trench or otherwise remove themselves from all those explosions. A barrage of rockets comes all at once. While a cannon can fire a shell or two per minute, rockets can be fired all at once. Thus a battalion (eighteen guns) of artillery firing, say, ten tons of shells at a target, will find troops in the target area scrambling for shelter, or getting away from the area, after less than a ton of shells has landed. With a battalion (twelve launchers) of rocket launchers, all ten tons of rockets land at once. This makes a big difference in how much damage you do.

Rocket launchers have other advantages, mainly that they are cheaper to build than cannons and are more mobile. But rockets became even more useful once the bomblets were available. The rockets have more room for these "submunitions" not only because rockets can be built bigger, but because their lower speed allows them to be built less robustly than artillery shells. When a cannon fires a shell, it exposes the projectile to enormous stress. Thus over half the weight of most shells is for thick walls, leaving little room to carry things, like submunitions.

These submunition-carrying rockets got their first major combat workout during the 1991 Gulf War. The impact of the "steel rain" on the Iraqis was devastating. The multiple-launch rocket system (MLRS) rockets were carrying the smallest types of bomblets, which spread over a wide area and exploded, filling the air with small steel fragments (the "steel rain"). An area measuring hundreds of meters by hundreds of meters would be hit all at once. Anyone in the open would be wounded or killed without any warning, or opportunity to duck for cover. Iraqi prisoners, who had the good fortune to be in a bunker when these rockets hit, told of coming outside to see nothing but dead or wounded soldiers. And on their heads they could feel the small steel fragments, the ones that had been thrown straight up, falling slowly back to earth like a steel rain.

German troops first encountered the shock of getting hit by hundreds of rockets hitting the ground simultaneously. This first happened in 1941. But those rockets were operated just like large artillery shells. They were loud when they hit and exploded. They were fatal to anyone standing nearby when they went off. But they were much less accurate than modern rockets, and many of the rockets would land far from where they were aimed. You stood a much better chance of surviving a 1941 rocket barrage than a 1991 version.

Keen to exploit what was obviously a good idea for artillery, weapons designers built rockets with a variety of different submunitions. In addition to the steel rain antipersonnel bomblets that tormented the Iraqis, there are similar-size bomblets that act as mines. Some of the mines are designed for people (to blow off feet), while others will work against trucks (blowing off wheels). Heavier bomblet mines will damage or destroy armored vehicles. The latest items are the robotic submunitions, which either turn into guided missiles once released from the rocket, or fall to the ground and search for targets from there. These missiles and smart mines have not yet been tried in combat and it may take a while before technology this fancy gets all the wrinkles worked out. Moreover, the end of the cold war has reduced budgets for such expensive weapons. For the moment there are plenty of "dumb" submunitions to be had and everyone knows they work.

But sometimes the submunitions don't work as intended, and fail in particularly nasty ways. Not all of the bombs and shells explode when they should. Many, up to 10 percent, just sit there until they are found and disposed of, or are accidentally found and tragically detonated by hapless civilians. More reliable self-destruct fuzes cost a lot more. There is still some lethal stuff from the American Civil War lying around, and a lot more from the wars of the twentieth century. Submunitions have increased this problem. Not only does one shell or bomb deliver a hundred more bomblets, but the submunitions are more likely to fail, and then wait years for some kid to play catch with them, and reactivate the detonator. So, where in the past a barrage of several thousand shells and several hundred bombs into a few square miles might have left a hundred or more dud shells and a few dozen dud bombs, a similar attack today will use some half million submunitions and leave over ten thousand duds. Then, and now, many of the duds will be cleared, or degrade into uselessness some years after the battle. The submunitions, being smaller, are harder to find and more likely to be buried and stay hidden. Even today, we have large areas of Afghanistan, Africa, the Falklands, and Kuwait that are considered quite dangerous because of the large number of unexploded submunitions and mines. Progress is never without cost, especially in the area of weapons.

Sons of the Horse Artillery

AFTER A FEW centuries of use and technical development, someone finally realized that it would be useful to have some of your artillery moving as fast as the calvary. This became, in the seventeenth century, the "horse artillery." For over two centuries, these fastmoving, although lighter, guns were always in the thick of the action. Speed was always a weapon, but when combined with the firepower of artillery, the combination was often decisive. Of course, all artillery were hauled by draft animals, including horses. But by using lighter guns and more horses, one got real "horse artillery." But World War I brought an end to cavalry, and horse artillery. Yet within twenty years, the horse artillery was reinvented by mounting the guns in the same kind of chassis used for tanks.

Beginning in World War II, more and more artillery became self-propelled. This brought a lot more technology into play. Most self-propelled (SP) artillery appears, to a casual glance, like a tank with a very large gun. The gun part is correct, as the standard artillery piece has always been a bit larger than the standard tank gun. But self-propelled artillery only look like tanks. SP guns have thin armor, only good for protecting the crew from the fragments of exploding enemy shells. Without all that armor, the SP gun has more space inside. It's still crowded, as the artillery piece takes up more room than a tank gun and the crew of an artillery piece is larger than that of a tank gun. The reasons for this have to do with the differences in technology between artillery and tanks. An artillery piece usually fires at targets that it cannot see; tanks can see their targets. Tanks don't fire their guns that much, but when they do, there is a high probability that the target will get hit. Since tanks fire at targets they can see, they have no need of fancy fuzes that have to be set, or put on the shells. Artillery fires a lot more, and shells can use different types of fuzes. The fuzes have to be screwed into the front of the shells as needed. The larger guns of the artillery take different amounts of propellant for each shell fired. It varies depending on the range to the target and the type of shell fired. In effect, tanks fire a very simplified form of artillery.

The SP guns have to be ready for a much wider array of jobs. Because artillery fires at targets they can't see, they use a more complicated system for aiming. Firing locations are fixed by surveyors using highly accurate mapping techniques, linked to instruments attached to the guns. Calculations are then performed and the gun is turned and elevated in the proper direction. More radios, computers, and more complex fuzes turned artillerymen into technicians. Well, artillerymen were always considered technical sorts, but there was always a lot of heavy lifting and scut work that didn't require much technical skill. But anyone on a gun crew knew that if he learned some of the more complex skills he would do less heavy lifting and get paid more for being around the guns. SP guns added a more complex, tanklike, vehicle. An SP artillery unit could go places that guns towed by trucks could not. Many SP guns existed mainly to keep up with tank units. This meant that SP guns were often used for "direct fire" (the crew could see what they were shooting at) and thus artillerymen had to learn the same firing skills as tank crews used. Direct fire also was more dangerous, for if you could see the target, the target could see you and shoot back.

Once it was proven that SP guns were good at keeping up with tanks, attention turned to taking advantage of this mobility to enable the guns to rapidly get into position and fire accurately at distant targets. This has taken several decades to accomplish and has required a lot of new technology. The principal problem was finding out, quickly and accurately, exactly where the guns were in relation to their target. Remember, modern artillery fire depends on a lot of calculation and knowing exactly where the gun and target are. The location of the target is easy enough; there would be no need for artillery fire if someone didn't already have a target in mind. But an SP gun motoring down a country road somewhere is another matter. The commander of an SP gun unit (usually a battery of four to six guns) would not have an exact idea where he was when he got the order to pull off the road and prepare to fire. Using conventional survey methods, it would take an hour or more to establish the precise position of the guns. Then they could fire. With a GPS (a small receiver of satellite signals), the exact position can be known within minutes and firing can commence a minute or so after that. Actually, further technical refinements have allowed the guns to fire within a few minutes of having received the order. Depending on how quickly the SP guns could be stopped and gotten off the road, and shells put into the chambers, firing could commence without waiting for location to be determined. A GPS can be used continuously, while on the move. Before the guns have even come to a stop, each gunner can enter the location of the target into the fire-control computer. When the guns stop, the gunner presses a button to transfer the current position to the computer and firing can begin. The first round will still be for registration, unless the folks up front want a barrage right away. In that case each gun fires several rounds right away. At that point the SP guns can up and scamper away, before the enemy can calculate their location and shoot back. This is called "counterbattery" fire and is another reason why modern guns are self-propelled and have some armor.

Shooting Back

DEALING WITH THE technical complexity of counterbattery fire has generated a large amount of improvisation and new technology. Because artillery in this century is almost always several miles behind the infantry (and most of the combat), the only weapon that can get at artillery is other artillery. Enemy aircraft are also a threat, but night and bad weather can keep the planes grounded much of the time. Nothing stops enemy counterbattery fire, except your own counterbattery fire.

The one catch with counterbattery fire is that you have to figure out where the enemy guns are before you can shoot at them. Since the artillery is behind the lines, you either get aircraft back there to spot the guns, or use other means. The other means are more common and have long included such simple techniques as watching for the flash (at night) of the enemy guns firing, counting the seconds until you can hear the boom (after seeing the flash), and then calculating the distance (just like you would to determine how far away lightning is). You estimate the direction and then start firing a lot of shells toward where you have a pretty good idea the enemy guns are. This "flash-and-sound ranging" procedure proved fairly effective during the two world wars. If the skies were clear and you controlled them, you could also send aircraft in to confirm the location of the enemy guns.

After World War II, better methods of directing counterbattery fire came into being. Radar was developed that could track the enemy shells in flight and calculate with increasing precision where they were coming from. The first counterbattery radars were relatively crude, as new technology tends to be, but even then they were superior to flash-and-sound ranging. Moreover, the older techniques depended a lot on developing personal skills among the people using the flash-and-sound ranging. Counterbattery radar was mainly technology. It got assembled at the factory, training of the radar operators did not take long, and if the system worked, it worked well. As time went on, these radars worked better and better. From the first crude systems in the 1950s, there developed reliable and accurate radars twenty years later.

The development of counterbattery radar and SP guns created a situation in which different kinds of technology canceled each other out. It worked like this. As the first counterbattery radars appeared, artillery officers quickly realized that they would have to change the way they did business. It was obvious to anyone with a sense of history that in a decade or two, the counterbattery radars would instantly give away the exact location of any artillery that had just fired. Counterbattery fire would, in a few minutes, destroy those guns. Artillery tactics would quickly degenerate to a game of who fires what and when. One side could have a few well dug in (to give the crews a chance of surviving) guns fire in order to draw the counterbattery fire. Then your counterbattery would try and smash their counterbattery guns that had just revealed themselves. This would go on until one side had pretty much wiped out the other side's artillery.

Well, it didn't quite work out like that. There was never a war large enough (with both sides employing a lot of artillery) for the radars to get an extensive workout. When the radars were used from time to time, they often had problems dealing with different models of artillery and new types of shells. But in response to the still very real threat of radar-directed counterbattery fire, it was determined that the only protection was to "shoot and scoot." This meant SP guns getting into firing position, firing several shells per gun very quickly, and then promptly leaving the area before the radar-directed counterbattery fire arrived. Whoever could scoot the fastest would win the artillery battle, because the fast scooter would lose fewer guns to counterbattery fire.

The highest-tech 1990s-type SP gun could get off the road and ready to fire in a few minutes. After firing a few shells, each gun could be on the road again in less than a minute. As fast as this was, it did not confer absolute immunity from radar-directed counterbattery fire. But it did make it unlikely that such lively SP guns would be at much risk.

In theory, the counterbattery radars and SP guns had canceled each other out. But it rarely works out that way. Few nations have the best counterbattery radars and the well-equipped and -trained SP artillery. What usually happens is that an army with older SP guns and feeble counterbattery radar comes up against someone like the United States that has the latest in radars and SP guns. The result is a wipeout. That's what happened during the 1991 Gulf War. The Iraqi artillery was largely of the older towed (by truck) type. The Iraqi guns were dug in, and most were discovered even without benefit of the counterbattery radar. After all, the battlefield was a desert and American forces had air superiority. On the few occasions that undiscovered Iraqis got some shots off, their guns were quickly pinpointed and smothered by artillery or rocket fire. Yet, with all the American superiority in this area, Iraqi artillery was able to get many shots in. Even a wealthy nation like the United States can't have functioning counterbattery radars everywhere on a fast-moving battlefield. That 1991 live-fire exercise in the Persian Gulf showed that a determined opponent can quickly find ways to make high-tech gear substantially lower in performance.

Capable counterbattery radars and well-equipped SP guns are a tremendous advantage in combat. But don't forget the other side of this technical advantage. Both these items are expensive to buy and expensive to maintain. In peacetime, the money to keep all the high-tech gear in tip-top shape is not always available. A common solution is to slap a new coat of paint on everything and issue press releases reminding the taxpayers about what great counterbattery radars and SP guns their tax dollars have bought. Send out some pictures too, so everyone will notice the fresh coat of paint.

But now that these wondrous devices have been out awhile, it's become obvious how one might deal with them. The counterbattery radars are, after all, like any other in that they emit a strong and distinct electronic signal when they are turned on. This can be used to launch a radar homing missile, or a long-range counterbattery attack against the radar itself. Also, the radar signal can be jammed, just like any other signal. Remember, any technical advantage is a wasting asset. Which is why you always have to come up with new ones and hope that they work without too many years of additional effort to debug and perfect them.

The Future of Digital Artillery

THE TRENDS IN artillery lean toward:

• More self-propelled guns. Towed guns are thought useful only for airmobile units that have to bring in everything by aircraft or helicopter, or for units that must operate only in mountains or jungles. What is wanted is more mechanically reliable SP guns, and ammunition vehicles that are armored and can keep up with the guns.

• Liquid propellant. This makes it easier to use the guns, as you don't have to fiddle about with different numbers of propellant bags. You just load the shell, the computer determines how much liquid propellant to squirt in, and ignite, and off goes another round. The liquid-propellant idea has been in the works for several decades. The technology is pretty mature now, but it's expensive to replace all the current guns with new ones now that the cold war is over. But eventually, there will be liquid propellant.

• Better communications. More GPS, more radios and satellite hookups. More use of drone aircraft to spot for the guns. As money becomes available, this stuff will come into use.

• More sophisticated shells. An ongoing project. The submunitions are becoming more sophisticated, and expensive. There are even "stealth" and electronic warfare shells to fool counterbattery radars.

• More counterbattery technology. More powerful radars and computers, plus more rapid communications. It's getting tough to play the artillery game without a major counterbattery capability.

• More sophisticated rockets for the MLRS. The current MLRS normally carries various loads of submunitions. This is unlike the original World War II rockets, which simply carried high-explosive warheads. The original 230mm, 600-pound MLRS rocket is already being supplemented by a larger rocket, the ATACMS (Army Tactical Missile System). This fits into the MLRS container that fires six normal MLRS rockets. The ATACMS has a range of 150 kilometers, versus 40 kilometers for the smaller MLRS rockets. The ATACMS can carry 950 submunitions, versus 688 for the MLRS. But the ATACMS has more space inside and can carry even more capable submunitions. By carrying fewer munitions, the ATACMS can go as far as 240 kilometers. Adding GPS guidance makes an ATACMS rocket accurate to 300 km.

• Link the fire of artillery and MLRS/ATACMS with sensors on J-STARS, UAVs (drone recon aircraft), and ground troops. This is part of the army's "digitization" program. This is something that has been going on for over half a century, since American troops were first able to use their World War II FDCs (Fire Direction Centers). The FDC allowed individual forward observers. But the World War II–era radio links were often unreliable and all the calculations at the FDC had to be done by hand. This took time, unless the math for some targets had been worked out in advance. In the decades after World War II, the radios got more reliable and computers were introduced to speed up the calculations. But the range of the artillery did not improve by much, approximately doubling from the 1940s to the 1980s. But by the 1990s there had been some significant changes. Satellite and digital radio made communications more reliable. More aircraft (both manned and drones) were available to spot targets over a wider area. New rockets and "smart" submunitions were available. Tying it all together are more, and cheaper, computers. In theory, if not in practice, we are at the point where a commander can sit anywhere with a laptop computer/portable satellite dish combo and command units nearby, or halfway around the world. This is what U.S. forces are aiming for. Most other national armed forces are only vaguely aware of these technologies and their implications. But the "laptop general" and his electronic tendrils will change warfare in ways not seen before in military history.

5

Digital Tanks

W HEN ARMORED FIGHTING vehicles (AFVs) were first developed during
World War I, they were the most complex ground-combat systems yet
seen. The first AFVs were called "tanks" (an innocuous term meant to keep
their existence a secret). Armored, with a truck engine and track-laying mechanism like a bulldozer, they were also equipped with machine guns and small
artillery. These were very complex weapons. They broke down a lot, but they
worked often enough to revolutionize warfare.

The primitive tanks of 1918 evolved into rather complex, and much more
reliable, beasts by 1945. Even during World War II, tanks were developing
complexity along the same lines as aircraft. Although AFVs were never
equipped with radar, they did have radios, intercoms for the crew, and increasingly complex fire-control systems for the many weapons they carried.
By the 1990s, tanks were every bit as digital as all but the most complex combat aircraft. Some even had a form of radar and a number of other complex
sensors.

The increasing complexity of tanks was not achieved without a lot of pain.
There are many lessons here for those who would introduce more technology
for the ground-combat troops.

Tanks, unlike artillery, were a mixed blessing for the infantry. As the grunts
like to put it, "tanks draw fire." Tanks are considered prime targets and stand
out rather more distinctly than an infantryman. While tanks are not invulnerable, they are better protected than infantry or the thin-skinned APCs and IFVs
that carry the grunts around. When the enemy decides to throw everything he's
got (artillery, usually) at a bunch of tanks, any infantry in the same neighborhood suffer more than the tanks.

As much as the infantry dislike tanks, these heavily armored behemoths
are the toughest thing on the modern battlefield. Tanks are not indestructible,
but are better able to take a hammering and keep on going. Among the things
tanks are vulnerable to are infantry armed with portable antitank weapons. For

this reason, tanks like to have some friendly infantry in attendance. When the friendly infantry are gone, the tanks find themselves vulnerable to enemy infantry, and retreat or destruction are the two things the now "naked" tanks' crews have to face.

As tough and capable as tanks are, they haven't got the staying power of infantry. Tanks run out of fuel and ammunition a lot faster than infantry. There are also places a tank cannot go, like thick forests and very broken ground. Think of tanks as powerful, but not very bright, beasts that have to be led about the battlefield by infantry. Many tanks even have a telephone attached to their rear, so that the accompanying infantry can literally phone in what the tank should do next.

A Very Short History of Tanks

TANKS WERE ORIGINALLY conceived to assist infantry, but almost immediately, some officers began to imagine what the fast-moving (by World War I standards), armored, and well-armed vehicles could do all by themselves. Unfortunately, tanks did not get enough of a workout in World War I to settle a lot of the arguments over exactly what their potential was. This is not a new problem; it happens every time a new weapon appears. Without the crucible of actual combat, and a lot of it, to settle these arguments, the result is a lot of chasing phantom ideas down dead-end roads. Much wasted money and effort is expended until the next war comes along. Then it's a question of who can most quickly recover from the shock of firmly held ideas being shattered on the battlefield.

By the end of World War I there were two types of tanks. Large, lumbering "infantry tanks" were intentionally slow so that the infantry could keep up, while the heavily armed tanks could use their cannons and machine guns to eliminate enemy resistance. Faster "exploitation" tanks were used to rush through the breach in the front line made by the infantry and their slower tanks. The exploitation tanks would plunge into the enemy rear area and shoot up artillery positions, logistical installations (trucks, horse-drawn wagons, railroad trains, and supply dumps) and any enemy infantry moving up to try and plug the hole in the front line. This latter exercise often did not work too well. Enemy artillery, at first in desperation, would fire directly at the light exploitation tanks and damage or destroy them with high-explosive shells. Soon solid metal shells were provided which did even more damage to tanks (often destroying them).

Had World War I gone into 1919, as military commanders thought it would until Germany surrendered in November of 1918, much more ambitious armored operations were planned. The Germans were ready with more vigorous antitank tactics. But the 1919 battles did not take place, and for the next twenty years there was a wild and much-varied period of experimentation. There were a lot of surprises when World War II opened with many tank battles. The tank officers of the 1920s and 1930s had their last practical experience with armored warfare in 1918, when most tank operations were against infantry in multiple trench lines. There wasn't much experience wandering about in the open, nor with encountering enemy tank forces.

While the tank officers accepted that they would probably still have to use armored vehicles to attack fortifications, they also realized that there would likely be more opportunity for mobile warfare. Indeed, World War I was seen as an aberration. There had never been trench warfare on that scale before. It was bloodier than any war Europe had ever experienced and something that no one wanted to repeat. But there were two schools of thought on future wars. One held that a future war would indeed see another round of large-scale trench warfare. But the tank officers saw things otherwise. They knew that it was tanks that had ultimately broken the trench lines and that it would eventually be tanks that would eliminate the need for all those trenches in a future war.

The tank officers had gotten it wrong. While tanks had played a part in breaking the three-year trench stalemate, it was actually new and more efficient infantry tactics that had first, and with the most decisive results, broken through the lines of fortifications. But the tank officers were right in believing that tanks would capitalize on any breakthrough. Where the tank officers went really wrong was to ignore how vital infantry would be to the efficient use of large units of tanks.

While the pessimists built more permanent fortifications all over Europe, the more optimistic armor crowd envisioned thousands of tanks stampeding across the countryside, crushing all before them. To satisfy the pessimists and their trench lines, there were larger and more heavily armed "infantry" tanks. But the tank gang's real love was with the lighter, more mobile "cruiser" tanks. The British accepted this specialization for tanks most enthusiastically. But everyone loved the idea of masses of tanks operating together. It was sexier, it was dashing, and it was easier to write optimistic articles about it in the popular and professional press. Slowly, through the 1930s, the "tank horde" school of thought gained more credibility.

The first two years of World War II seemed to vindicate the tank horde enthusiasts. But then reality set in. Even the Germans had ignored the fact that their superbly trained and led infantry were doing most of the real work in the battlefield. The tanks were prominent, but they would not have gotten far if the German infantry had not first cleared the way.

Theoretical Tanks Meet Real Warfare

EVEN BEFORE World War II, tank officers began to realize that tanks were no longer just a striking bit of new technology anymore. What made tanks decisive in World War II was more quantity and efficient engineering than breakthroughs in tank design. For example, the Germans had invaded France in 1940 fearing that they might lose. The French and British had more tanks and, on paper, superior tanks (more armor, bigger guns). But the Allied tanks were poorly designed. Yes, they looked more impressive on paper, and in person too. But the German tanks had been designed with a better concept of what tank combat would be. The German tanks had more powerful engines and internal layouts that allowed the crews to do more of what they had to do when the fighting got hot. The German tanks were also more reliable, because more attention had been paid when they were built.

Most importantly, the German tanks were used more intelligently. The French, of all the nations with a lot of tanks, were still wedded to the idea that tanks were more effective if they were spread out among the infantry. The Germans realized that if you gave the infantry antitank guns, they could defend themselves against tanks without needing tanks. Moreover, out in the open, the well-trained German infantry could move around and surround enemy troops that were inside fortifications. This even worked against trench systems, as it was the "storm trooper" tactics the Germans had developed in 1917 to breach trench lines that the Germans were still using in 1939. Even though the Allies had developed similar tactics, the Allied commanders preferred to depend less on nimble infantrymen and more on heavy "infantry" tanks. When all this was tested in combat, the Allies were wrong, the Germans were right.

The Germans were able to mass their tanks into a handful of tank divisions in 1939 and 1940. France and Britain didn't pay much attention to how the Germans smothered the Poles so quickly in 1939. They thought the Germans did it mainly with numbers. True, to an extent, but the German tank divisions made a big difference. How much of a difference did not become obvious until 1940, when the same techniques were used on France.

Russian Innovations

THE SOVIET UNION watched the early development of tanks with great interest and greater uncertainty about what to do about it. This did not stop the Russians from jumping right in and designing and building a large number of tanks. By 1939, the Soviet Union had the largest, and most modern, tank force in the world. What was extraordinary about this was that ten years earlier, Russia's armed forces were smaller than those of France in terms of tanks and artillery. In the late 1920s, France had 3,500, mostly World War I–era, tanks while Russia had 250 of modern design. Ten years later, the Russians had over 20,000 tanks. What had happened? Several things. In the 1920s, the Soviet Union was still recovering from World War I and its subsequent civil war. During the 1930s the new Soviet government began an ambitious program of industrialization. A lot of the new industrial capacity went into building tanks and combat aircraft. The Russians noted that the Germans were rearming during the 1930s, and this merely encouraged the Russians to do more of the same.

Russia was in the midst of "the Great Socialist Experiment." The feeling was that anything was possible, and anything could be changed. A lot of new tank technology was developed by the Soviets and during the 1920s they even shared it with the Germans (in return for technical assistance). During the 1930s, the Soviets licensed tank technology from American inventor Walter Christie that the U.S. Army had rejected as "too radical." Well, that wasn't unusual. But the Russians thought of themselves as at the forefront of social and technological change. So "too radical" suited them fine. The Red Army (as the Soviet armed forces were known) had a huge budget by 1930s standards, and they spent a lot of it on developing and building new models of tanks. Most of these Soviet tanks, like the BT series, were essentially light tanks. They were fast (over forty miles an hour) and maneuverable. By the late 1930s, the BTs were equipped with a large (for the time) 45mm gun. By the late 1930s, the Soviets had improved their quality control to the point where their tanks were pretty reliable. And the Soviets had a lot of tanks by 1941—over twelve thousand in European Russia alone. This was more tanks than the rest of Europe combined. Moreover, the Soviet government was very security conscious and pretty much kept this information to itself.

No one outside of Russia had any idea how large the Soviet tank inventory was. Nor did anyone realize how ambitious the new tank designs were, particularly the brand new T-34. This tank was introduced in 1940 and came as a big surprise to the Germans in 1941. By the end of the war, some forty thousand T-34s were produced. It was the best all-around tank of the war. But the T-34 was developed almost by accident, for the Russians never really figured out what they wanted to do with tanks and armored warfare until the Germans invaded in 1941.

First Lessons

THE RUSSIANS HAD plenty of warning of what was coming in tank warfare. First, there was the World War I experience, which was much written about. Then there was an avalanche of books after World War I. The Russians devoured all of these, but by the mid-1930s, no one was quite sure what would work. Then, in 1936, the Spanish civil war began, and the world now had a place to find out what the new tanks and new ideas could do. It wasn't a very inspiring exercise.

The Soviets sent hundreds of tanks to their fellow socialists of the Loyalist faction in Spain. These tanks were fast and well armed, but mechanically unreliable. Tanks did not do all that well in Spain, and all concerned were inclined to blame that on the nature of the fighting, much of it being in and around cities. No one drew any firm conclusions from the use of tanks in Spain. The successful use of airpower in Spain did impress all involved. Most nations (including the Germans and Russians) went and began forming more tank divisions rather than giving each infantry division a few tanks. By early 1939 the Spanish civil war was over, with no one drawing any particularly insightful or firmly held conclusions from the exercise.

In 1939, there was a lot of large-scale tank use. From May to August, the Russians fought a series of battles with the Japanese on the Manchurian border. The Japanese got the worst of it. The Russians used hundreds of tanks, as well as a lot of infantry and artillery. The largest of these battles, in the summer of 1939, had seventy thousand Russians defeating forty thousand Japanese. The Russians noted that the Japanese were generally inept even in those portions of the battles involving only infantry. While the Russian tank forces were successful, no conclusions were drawn regarding the capabilities of tank units in combat. The armored battalions did okay, so the Soviets kept building tanks and trying to figure out exactly what to do with them.

In September of 1939 there was a much larger use of tanks as the Germans invaded Poland. This was the first large-scale "blitzkrieg" and everyone, except perhaps the Germans, was shocked at how quickly (two weeks) the German mechanized forces smashed Polish resistance. By October 1, the war in Poland was all over. Again, the Russians attributed the success to the ineptness of the defenders. Keep in mind that, historically, the Russians have had a low opinion of the Poles and the Japanese. This despite the fact that the Japanese had defeated Russia in 1905 (the Soviets blamed that on the "decadent regime of the czar"), and the Poles had defeated the Red Army in 1920 ("They got lucky"). The Soviets did note that their forces had not done so well invading eastern Poland on September 17 (by prior arrangement with the Germans).

This Soviet invasion was led by two Russian armored divisions (or "tank corps") and resulted in chaos on the Russian side. Polish resistance was weak, with most Polish forces already off facing the Germans (and the Poles not expecting to be stabbed in the back by the Russians).

The Russians made much of the fact that the Germans had attacked thirty-eight Polish divisions with sixty-three of their own, and that only nine of the German divisions were tank divisions. The Germans used most of the tanks they owned in this attack, but these amounted to only 2,500 vehicles. The Russians had more than five times as many. Moreover, only 300 of the German tanks were heavy ones with large (for 1939) guns. The rest had either machine guns or 20mm cannons, and thin armor. Of course, that was all the Poles had, and most of the Polish tanks were distributed among their infantry divisions.

Based on what they had seen in Poland, the Russians decided to break up their tank divisions and distribute their tanks among the infantry divisions. This way, most of their infantry divisions would have enough tanks (50 to 100) to give a German tank division a hard time.

In November of 1939 the Russians finally discovered the real reason for the German victory in Poland: training. In that month the Russians invaded Finland. The better-trained Finns halted the much more numerous Soviet forces, and they did it without tanks. The Russians sent in hundreds of tanks with their infantry and it made no difference. The Finns invented the "Molotov cocktail" (a bottle of gasoline with a rag stuffed in the mouth to serve as a fuze) and used these crude devices to good effect against the very flammable Soviet tanks.

By the spring of 1940, the Russians agreed to make peace with the Finns. At the same time, the Soviets decided to institute a huge training program for their army. Part of the Russians' problem was that throughout the late 1930s, Soviet dictator Joseph Stalin had waged a vicious purge of the senior ranks of the Red Army. Many of the best officers were dead or in prison camps. It takes time for new officers to gain experience. The hastily conceived training program drawn up in early 1940 was a case of the blind leading the blind. No one dared criticize Stalin for the purge, but most officers were glad to see the increased emphasis on training.

But the spring of 1940 held some more shocks for the Russians, and the rest of the world. The Germans invaded western Europe. First Denmark and Norway, then France and the Low Countries. It was another successful blitzkrieg, but this time against well-equipped and -trained troops and not the Poles. The Soviets were stunned, and relieved that they had signed their non-aggression pact with the Germans in the summer of 1939.

The Germans were outnumbered when they attacked France. The Allies had 140 divisions, the Germans 122. The Allies had 4,000 tanks, the Germans

3,200. But, again, the Germans were better trained. Moreover, only 1,200 of the Allied tanks were of the same class (in combat capability) of those the Germans were using. The Germans had ten armored ("Panzer") divisions and several mechanized ("Panzergrenadier") divisions. The campaign in France was over in six weeks. The Russians held another conference during the winter of 1940–41 and decided that perhaps training *and* tank divisions had something to do with the German success. So the Russians began forming tank divisions again.

The Great World War II Tank Technology Competition

WHEN THE GERMANS invaded Russia in June 1941, they were again outnumbered. They had 34 mechanized divisions (19 of them tank divisions) and 138 infantry divisions (including 17 non-German allied divisions and a cavalry division). Facing them were 126 Russian infantry divisions, 47 tank divisions, and 24 motorized divisions. The Germans had 3,900 tanks, the Russians had over 12,000. West of Moscow the Russians had 3 million troops to face 3.5 million invaders. But the Russians also had over a million troops east of Moscow and a reserve system that could rapidly raise and equip over 10 million more troops. But the Germans already in combat were well trained and equipped and the Soviets were not. The first six months of that campaign were a continual romp for the Germans.

The enormous Russian tank superiority made little difference, other than to provide German tanks with a multitude of easy targets. Yet it was during 1941 that the great "tank technology race" began, a race that is still going on. Below are the main tank types built and used during World War II, and fifty years after that. You will see a pattern here, a pattern that repeats itself in all future military technology.

Table 1 / Tanks from World War II to the Present					
Nation	Model	Year of Use	Protection	Penetration	Production
USSR	BT-7	1939–42	20	57	12,000
USSR	T-28c	1939–42	55	50	4,000
USSR	T-34a	1940–42	60	57	10,000
Germany	Pz IIIh	1940–42	60	70	2,400
Germany	Pz IVe	1940–42	58	55	1,200
USA	M-4	1942–	108	95	48,000
USSR	T-34c	1942–44	82	90	10,000
Germany	Pz IVh	1942–45	65	125	7,100

Table 1 / Tanks from World War II to the Present (continued)

Nation	Model	Year of Use	Protection	Penetration	Production
USSR	T34/85	1944–45	95	110	20,000
Germany	Pz VIE	1942–45	110	140	1,355
Germany	Pz V	1943–45	120	121	5,500
Germany	Pz VIH	1944–45	150	205	485
USA	M-26	1945–	101	250	
2,428USSR	T-54	1948–	200	220	8,000
USA	M-48	1953–	122	220	9,000
USSR	T-55	1958–	200	265	30,000
USA	M-60	1959–	250	300	11,000
USSR	T-62	1961–	220	300	12,000
USSR	T-72B	1973–	250	450	11,000
USSR	T-72M	1987–	350	450	9,000
USSR	T-80	1984–	450	500	2,500
USA	M-1	1984–	400	435	3,100
USSR	T-90	1991–	600	550	400
USA	M-1A1	1989–	600	720	3,800
USA	M-1A2	1993–	800	720	500

Notes for the above table. Nation—The country that designed and built the tank. This nation is also the one that was the largest user of that tank. Model—How that particular tank was identified by the nation that built it. Year of Use—Years in which the tank was in use. If only one year is given, then that tank is still in use somewhere, and, the older the tank, the fewer the number currently operating. Protection—The maximum armor protection on the tank, in millimeters. This is usually the armor on the front of the tank, often the turret. The armor on the sides and rear is usually half or less of the greatest armor thickness. Penetration—Maximum armor that the tank's main gun can penetrate at normal combat range (five hundred meters in World War II, one thousand meters thereafter). Production—Number of that model produced. There was some variation among some of the models shown. The U.S. M-4 was equipped with a number of different engines and got somewhat more powerful guns as the war went on, and after the war (Israel installed 105mm guns in M-4s during the 1960s). There were several versions of the M-48 and M-60, the difference largely confined to engines and fire-control systems.

You can see several things in the chart, the main one being that each side continually leapfrogged the other in armor and penetration during World War II. The "tank race" went on at a more leisurely pace after World War II, but that was partially because there was no major war going on, and the tanks were getting much more expensive. Most World War II tanks cost one hundred thousand to two hundred thousand dollars or so (in current dollars) while the average cost is more like twenty to forty times that today. The first few tanks in the chart weighed ten to twenty tons. The heaviest today come in at some sixty tons. The armor quality has improved, as has fire control and weapons. But they are all still tanks.

What is given above is only some of the essential information about each tank. The key data are how well a tank can defend itself (protection) and how well it can destroy other tanks (penetration). While protection and penetration are the two most important items, they are not overwhelmingly critical. As has been proven during World War II and since, there are many other factors that go into making a tank a winner on the battlefield. Chief among these are:

• Mobility—A powerful engine, effective suspension, and wide tracks (those things the tank moves on) are key factors here. The first two items are things that a well-developed automotive industry can deliver. The Germans were leaders in automotive technology in this century and were able to come up with some novel ideas for their tanks. The width of the tracks was rather more specific to a particular nation. In Russia's case, the tank designers knew that theirs was a nation of few roads and much snow in the winter and mud in the spring. So a wider track was a natural addition to any tank design. The wider track reduced the ground pressure and made it easier for the tanks to keep going in soft ground, snow, and mud. The Germans learned about this the hard way when they invaded Russia. The entire world learned about the importance of ground pressure by watching the German and Russian experience. It wasn't until the 1980s that U.S. tanks achieved the kind of mobility that Russian tanks had long been known for.

• Communications—Tanks are like aircraft in that the crew, what with all the noise their own vehicle is making, need radios to communicate with higher headquarters and other tanks (and an intercom system to talk to each other). Before the war, it was understood by nearly everyone that radios and intercoms were a needed thing for all tanks. But once the war began, it was obvious that there would not be enough resources to provide every tank with a radio and an intercom system at all times. This was most widely seen in Russia, where, in most cases, only one tank in ten (that is, the company commander) had a radio. The company commander would communicate to his other tanks with hand and flag signals. Other nations also used this hand and flag signal system as a backup for when the still-primitive radio systems failed. There were also times, especially when a surprise attack was to be launched, when the radios were not used, lest the enemy overhear and the element of surprise be lost. The Russians equipped all their tanks with radios as soon as they could after the war. But during World War II, they used tanks in large groups and the lack was not a major impediment to their success. After World War II, more radio equipment was added to tanks.

• Internal layout—The layout of the inside of a tank turned out to be a lot more important than tank designers first realized. The Germans were quick to appreciate this and their tanks were, from the beginning, easier for their crews to operate. This sort of industrial engineering took into account what each member of the crew had to do and arranged things so that the crew member was able to do his job with a minimum of hassle and discomfort. This made a difference in combat, where fatigue or any additional hassles could have fatal consequences. French tanks in 1940 were particularly poorly laid out. Russian tanks were hit-or-miss. In order to keep their tanks small and low, the Russians stipulated that anyone serving in a tank be short (under sixty-five inches tall). There simply wasn't room for anyone taller. Beyond that, things were still cramped and more dangerous than in German tanks. The Russians lost some of their combat capability because of this, but they outproduced the Germans by such a large margin that they were able to overcome this shortcoming.

• Reliability—In combat, tanks don't last long. But while they are still undamaged by enemy fire, you don't want to lose many to mechanical breakdown. Alas, even in World War II, tanks were complex and touchy beasts. Breakdowns were frequent. The German tanks hastily designed once the war began (the Pz V and VI) were notoriously unreliable. Russian tanks were purposely simple and crude (to make it easier to mass-produce them), and once the crew had driven a new tank a hundred miles or so, they knew what its flaws were and could work around them. But American, British, and German tanks were more sophisticated and, except for the American vehicles, more likely to fail at a vital moment. This mechanical reliability is best illustrated when you consider that vehicles are most likely to be lost while moving toward a battle. A hundred Russian tanks might go the distance and lose twenty tanks, the Germans would lose nearly forty, and the Americans only ten. So reliability made a difference even before the shooting began. Since World War II, Russian tanks have remained relatively simple compared to Western vehicles. However, when the Russians went for the three-man crew and autoloader in the 1970s, they had a lot of trouble. These new tanks (the T-72) were more complex and had one less man in the crew to keep things going.

• Fire control—This is the gear that enables the gunner to find a target and aim the gun quickly and accurately to get a shot off. Russian tanks were at a disadvantage in this area during World War II. The sighting systems were crude and the turret could not be rotated as quickly as in German and American tanks. The Russians found ways around these deficiencies, the principle one being having a lot more tanks. Each tank would be given a narrow part of the front to aim at, and would fire at any enemy target that hove into view. The

Germans usually were much outnumbered and needed their superior optics and gun sights just to even things up a bit (but not enough). After World War II, Western tanks continued to have superior fire-control systems. The gap widened versus Russian equipment and the extent of that gap could be seen in the 1991 Gulf War. In particular, the heat sensors enabled Western tanks to see through night, smoke, and much else. The computer-controlled fire-control systems, and their third-generation laser range finders, allowed unprecedented accuracy and unprecedented range (first-shot hits at over two miles). Aiding the fire-control systems were stabilizers that allowed accurate firing while the tank was moving, and weather sensors that increased the accuracy of the long-range cannon.

• Shape—It wasn't until World War II that the shape of a tank was recognized as a crucial design element. Prior to that, tanks were put together in a rather haphazard fashion. It was the Russians who first began to make them low, wide, and with sloped armor. The low and wide angle made tanks harder to spot and allowed for the wider tracks that increased mobility over soft ground. The sloped armor made it more likely that enemy shells would either ricochet off or just have to travel through more armor in order to get inside a tank. By the end of World War II, everyone recognized the advantages of sloping the armor. Few other nations wanted to emulate the low and wide design of the Russians, because that meant cramped interiors and only short men being used for tank crews.

• Gun and shell construction—Gun quality varied somewhat, depending on how many good machinists and metalworkers you had. The Russians made up for their deficiencies in this area by using larger guns than the Germans. This required more manufacturing effort, and the tanks with these larger guns carried less ammunition, but it was a straight-ahead solution to the problem. The earliest antitank shells were "solid shot." In other words, just a hunk of metal, like a rifle bullet. Even before World War II, it was known that one could use different (harder) metals and shapes to get more penetration of enemy armor. Research on more effective shells showed results during and after World War II. The same model gun can fire different shell designs, some having more than twice the penetrating power of others. During World War II, the Germans had an edge in shell design, but because of German raw materials shortages, Russian and American designers were able to close the gap. After World War II, Russia still lagged in shell construction, and still tried to make up for the quality angle by producing larger guns. This has not been successful, as putting anything larger than a 125mm gun on the smaller Russian tank chassis is not practical.

• Countermeasures—This is largely a post–World War II development. During the war there was some use of smoke to hide tanks, but going into the

1980s, a lot more gadgets began to appear. These included radar-type sensors to detect incoming antitank missiles. Smoke-grenade dischargers also became more sophisticated, enabling a tank to quickly throw up a wall of smoke to hide behind.

It is well to note these items and keep in mind that the same pattern appears in other areas of weapons technology. It's a collection of superior aspects that makes the difference, not superiority in one or two. Thus the development of tank technology, more than any other aspect of ground combat, closely followed technology evolution in the air force and navy. The most modern tanks have more than a quarter of their cost devoted to the electronic components.

The Future of Digital Tanks

But tank technology highlights the fact that much of the high tech in this century has not been electronic. Tanks are, by weight, mostly metal, and vast improvements have been made in metallurgy technology. This has also been the case with aircraft, although even there, more attention is paid to the electronics improvements and less to the critical enhancements in metal tech. Even during World War II, new methods of making and fabricating metals made a big difference in improving armor, engines, guns, and ammunition. Progress in this area continued after World War II and only gained some attention during the 1991 Gulf War. There, the latest U.S. M-1A1 tank was noted as being practically invulnerable to enemy weapons. The M-1A1 was using a new composite armor. The British had invented composite armor (layers of different metal, plastic, and ceramic material) some twenty years earlier. American scientists had improved the idea to the point where the M-1A1 armor was almost impossible to penetrate by any current weapon. At the same time, some of the same technology (using very dense depleted uranium) was applied to the "penetrators" of U.S. tank shells. This produced a projectile that not only penetrated enemy tanks at long ranges, but often came out the other side and kept on going.

Engine technology also reached something of a peak in the M-1 tanks, giving U.S. vehicles a mobility advantage not seen since World War II, when Soviet T-34s often ran rings around less peppy German tanks. Finally, U.S. scientists had perfected the heat sensors and combined them with laser range finders and fire-control systems to produce the easiest to use and most effective tank weapons system ever.

What happened in 1991 was not the result of any sudden technological breakthroughs, but came after over half a century of minor improvements. The media like to play up "breakthroughs," but these rarely happen and then only sometimes in wartime. This can be seen from the chart above. There were dramatic changes in tank technology during World War II, a period of only six years. After that, progress was gradual for over forty years, culminating in the Kuwait battles of 1991.

The United States demonstrated a lead in tank design that was decisive, and that lead appears to be holding for a while. The M-1 tank was built to take advantage of upgrades, and American tanks are in the process of getting more, and better main guns, armor, computers and communications gear. It is this computerization and communications capability that makes the U.S. Army optimistic about creating a "digital battlefield" in which their M-1 tanks can play the same role as the air force's high-tech jets overhead. Indeed, the army wants to put its tanks into regular communication with the warplanes. This was a combination that was achieved during World War II, when the present U.S. Air Force was still a part of the U.S. Army. Such unity was lost after World War II and has taken nearly half a century to reestablish.

6

....

The Digital Aviator

THE AIRPLANE, A TRULY new technology in this century, has always had an affinity for new gadgets. Pilots can't get enough of this stuff, even if it often doesn't work or is counterproductive. During the 1995 Bosnian Scott O'Grady incident, we saw this in action. Captain Scott O'Grady was shot down by a Serb SAM (surface-to-air missile). Equipment was available to deal with these SAMs, but it's expensive to use the SAM warning stuff, so it isn't always carried by U.S. aircraft all the time. There was also high-tech gear monitoring the airspace, and the presence of hostile SAMs was noted just before O'Grady flew over, but this vital information didn't get delivered to the right people on time. O'Grady survived the crash of his F-16 fighter and was later rescued. People were shocked. American technology was supposed to prevent things like that. It can, it does, but technology has its limitations and the biggest limitation is the people that use the technology and, to an even larger extent, those who give the orders.

This was not the only instance of ill-trained or ill-informed people canceling out a high-tech advantage. When two U.S. helicopters were shot down by U.S. aircraft over Iraq in 1994, it was human errors, not lack of equipment, that caused the disaster. But the "zoomies" (a term pilots love) press on to ever greater degrees of digitization, even if it means less time to train the pilots and other folks to use it.

Aircraft that don't quite work the way you think they will are nothing new. During the 1930s, there was an avalanche of new developments in aircraft design, construction, and performance. There was also a plenitude of projects that got off on the wrong foot and generally got lost. World War II provided a reality check for many of these procurement disasters, and it is a good idea to review them once more.

The Great Decade of Aviation Progress

FROM 1935 TO 1945 there was an unbroken string of advances in aviation technology. The chart below shows the bare bones of this progress: the most widely used aircraft through the period, with some very basic statistics for each, plus the most notable combat aircraft developed from World War II to the present.

Table 2 / Combat Aircraft from World War II to the Present

Intro	Aircraft	Type	Nation	Speed	Range	Weight	Bombs
1936	Me-109E	Ftr	Ger	355	350	3.6	0.3
1936	A5M Claude	Ftr	IJN	273	746	1.7	0.0
1937	Hurricane I	Ftr	UK	316	460	3.8	0.5
1938	P-36	Ftr	USAAF	300	825	6.0	0.2
1938	Spitfire II	Ftr	UK	360	480	3.2	0.0
1940	B-17	Bmb	USAAF	280	2,000	29.7	8.0
1940	P-40	Ftr	USAAF	378	240	4.0	0.3
1940	A6M Zero	Ftr	IJN	354	976	2.7	0.0
1941	Halifax	Bmb	UK	280	1,200	30.0	6.0
1941	P-39	Ftr	USAAF	385	675	3.8	0.3
1941	P-38E	Ftr	USAAF	395	975	7.0	0.0
1941	Wildcat-4	Ftr	USN	274	770	3.6	0.1
1941	FW-190	Ftr	Ger	408	490	4.9	1.8
1942	F4U	Ftr	USN	470	1,100	6.4	1.0
1942	Lancaster	Bmb	UK	275	1,600	30.8	6.4
1942	P-47	Ftr	USAAF	428	590	8.8	1.0
1943	Spitfire IX	Ftr	UK	404	434	3.6	0.2
1943	Wildcat FM2	Ftr	USN	306	900	3.7	0.2
1943	F6F	Ftr	USN	370	945	6.5	0.9
1943	P-51B	Ftr	USAAF	437	1,300	4.4	0.9
1944	Me-262	Ftr	Ger	539	650	7.0	1.0
1944	P-38J	Ftr	USAAF	414	2,600	9.8	1.4
1944	P-51D	Ftr	USAAF	437	950	4.5	0.9
1948	MiG-15	Ftr	USSR	668	1,155	5.7	0.0
1949	F-86	Ftr	USAF	687	925	9.4	1.0
1956	MiG-21	Ftr	USSR	1,200	600	9.0	0.5

Table 2 / Combat Aircraft from World War II to the Present (continued)

Intro	Aircraft	Type	Nation	Speed	Range	Weight	Bombs
1958	F-104	Ftr	USAF	1,400	775	14.0	1.8
1961	F-4B	Ftr	USN	1,485	400	24.8	7.2
1967	F-4E	Ftr	USAF	1,430	595	27.9	7.2
1970	MiG-23	Ftr	USSR	1,400	600	14.0	1.0
1974	F-15A	Ftr	USAF	1,650	500	29.9	6.8
1979	F-16	Ftr	USAF	1,400	575	14.0	6.0
1984	MiG-29	Ftr	USSR	1,500	590	17.0	0.0
2001	F-22	Ftr	USAF	1,600	500	35.0	10.0

Notes for the above table. Intro—The year this aircraft was first put into service. Generally, the more recent the aircraft, the more capable it is. Aircraft—The name the aircraft was known by. Type—What the aircraft is primarily used for. Ftr is fighter (fighting other aircraft), Bmb is bomber, aircraft that primarily drop bombs on ground targets. Nation—Where the aircraft was designed. USAAF is U.S. Army Air Force, USN is U.S. Navy, UK is United Kingdom, IJN is Imperial Japanese Navy, Ger is Germany, USSR is Soviet Union, Fr is France. Speed—The top speed of the aircraft, in miles per hour, one of several measures of the aircraft's ability to defend itself. Range—How many miles from its base an aircraft can operate, another rough measure of an aircraft's performance, especially for bombers. Weight—In tons, fully loaded for combat. Gives you an idea of the size of the aircraft (bigger is heavier) and how much it cost (cost per pound for aircraft doesn't change that much in the same historical period). Bombs—In tons, the usual full load. Shows the relative destructive power of bombers, and the ability of fighters to do double duty as fighter-bombers.

Several things are obvious, and expected, in the chart. Aircraft got faster and heavier over time. In the first five years of World War II, from 1939 to 1944, the speed of fighters increased by over a hundred miles an hour and the average weight of the fighters nearly doubled. Heavy bombers pretty much disappeared, except in the American air force. But fighters and fighter-bombers were enormously popular. The Russian MiG-21 in particular became a prestige item for many poor nations, who were able to obtain these sleek-looking fighters cheap, or for free, from the Soviet Union. But in general, the U.S. warplanes were much smoother articles than their Russian counterparts. While aircraft like the MiG-15 looked impressive on paper, they were unstable and difficult to fly in combat. U.S. pilots chewed them up in large numbers. No other Russian fighters since have done much better, although the current generation (MiG-29) is well thought of.

There are more things that go into making one aircraft superior to another. Chief among these other elements are:

• Flight controls are systems of wires, flaps, and electrical systems that allow the pilot to make the aircraft maneuver in flight. Not a very sexy, or even obvious, part of the aircraft's design, but crucial in how well the aircraft performs. Aircraft that are otherwise equal on paper perform very unequally in combat if one has superior flight controls.

• Mechanical reliability is what it says, how well the components of the aircraft hold up in action. Many aircraft look great on paper, actually perform quite well in action, but tend to develop serious system failures after a few hours of use—things like engines locking up, wings falling off, or weapons failing to work. All of these things can be fatal for the crew and costly to the side so equipped. Russian aircraft suffered from these reliability problems throughout World War II and have suffered right to the present. Toward the end of World War II, Japanese aircraft were very well designed, but had serious reliability problems because of the U.S. bombing and blockade (which cut off access to vital alloys and raw materials).

• Crew quality is nothing more than how well trained the pilot or crew is to handle an aircraft. Actual combat experience can be useful, but not nearly as useful if the pilot has not had good initial training. Crew quality can change quickly in wartime as experienced pilots are killed, and if you don't have a system for training good replacements, the average quality of your pilots quickly tumbles. Japan was an excellent example of this in World War II. They entered the war in 1941 with the best-trained pilots in the world; but the Japanese had no plan for rapidly training replacements. As a result, heavy wartime pilot losses quickly sent the average quality of Japanese pilots plummeting. By 1943, after two years of fighting, American pilots were generally superior to their Japanese counterparts. American pilots have been the best trained in the world ever since.

• Navigation and flight aids, things that allow a crew to find its way around the sky safely and efficiently. At first, the only item used was a compass. Then came altimeters, airspeed indicators, and a growing list of electronic instruments, including radios. How many instruments an aircraft has, the instrument quality, and reliability all make a big difference in combat.

• Fire-control systems, which aim the aircraft's weapons, have grown from practically nothing to complex, computer-driven rigs that comprise over 20 percent of the aircraft's cost.

The amount of technical progress from 1935 to 1945 was amazing, and has never since been duplicated. This was because there was a major war going on, and wartime conditions mean things get done as quickly as possible. In 1935, biplanes (two sets of wings) were still in wide use and all-metal monoplanes (one set of wings) were just coming into use. Weapons and speeds were not much different than in 1918 (the end of World War I). Bomber aircraft were just coming into wide use, with the thought that they could operate by themselves. By 1945, all of that had changed. Jet fighters were being introduced, and long-range, four-engine bombers were available in the tens of thousands. But it was acknowledged that these bombers could not fend for themselves, and long-range fighters had been developed as escorts for the bombers.

Jets Take Over

FROM 1945 TO 1955, jets replaced propeller-driven warplanes. The jets became larger and faster. By 1965, it was noted that the American F-4 fighter (two engines, two crewmen) could carry more bombs than the workhorse World War II bomber the B-17 (four engines, eleven crewmen). The F-4 could also operate at longer ranges than the B-17, via the new air-to-air refueling. Technology was at the heart of all this. The B-17 had a pilot, copilot, navigator, bombardier, and radio operator, plus several gunners. The F-4 had only a pilot and a "guy in back" (or GIB) who handled most of the navigator, bombardier, and radio operator tasks. The F-4 pilot not only flew the plane all by himself, but also used the F-4 as a fighter, for this aircraft was correctly called a fighter-bomber.

Automation allowed two crew members to do the job of eleven. The rest of the B-17's crew consisted of machine gunners to fight off attacking fighters. The F-4, as a nimble fighter in its own right, did not need a lot of defense weapons. The new electronic equipment was more reliable, lighter, and more capable by 1965. It had to be. There was no opportunity for the operators to tinker with and fix radios, bombsights, and other gear in flight, as was the case with the relatively spacious B-17. The F-4 was built as a fighter, but increased engine power and equipment capability enabled it to operate as a bomber and a fighter with a two-man crew. The F-4 was also a much safer aircraft, with far fewer equipment failures than World War II planes. Indeed, in 1918, at the end of World War I, it was still common for more pilots to be lost from equipment failure than from enemy action. This changed during World War II, and the trend continues to this day. This improved safety record was necessary for another reason. In peacetime, pilots could expect a flying career of ten to twenty years. By World War II aircraft standards, a twenty-year flying career meant a better than 10 percent chance of death or injury from equipment failure. By the 1950s, this had dipped under 10 percent, and by the 1980s it was under 1 percent. This was great for pilot morale, as well as cheaper than constantly replacing pilots killed or crippled in accidents. Moreover, it ensured that the most experienced (and effective) pilots made it to the end of their flying careers in one piece.

Fighter-bombers could also operate with only the pilot, although it was found that the workload when bombing was a bit much for just one man. The GIB did make a difference. This problem has not yet been completely overcome, mainly because of the expense of automated bombing equipment. The F-117A "stealth fighter" (actually a light bomber) has only a pilot, and a lot of very expensive navigation, electronic warfare, radar, and fire-control equipment on board. To be affordable, most air forces consist primarily of cheaper aircraft. These either have one pilot, and limited bombing capability, or two crew members and less gear than the F-117A.

The High Price of High Performance

COST HAS BECOME the major factor in building modern aircraft. World War II fighter-bombers cost about a million dollars each (taking into account inflation and the smaller number of planes needed today). By the 1960s, the average fighter-bomber was costing some ten million (1996) dollars. By the 1990s, that average cost was closer to thirty million dollars. Unless this cost spiral can be brought under control, in the next century the same type of aircraft will cost over a hundred million dollars.

It's not that all this additional cost is wasted. The money buys many technical advantages. Saving weight is a major consideration. By using carbon-fiber composites and other new materials, such as synthetic fibers, aluminum-lithium alloys, and high-performance titanium, airframes have become much lighter. Some aircraft weigh less than half that of equivalent aircraft from the previous generation. This lighter weight means the aircraft can carry more fuel (for longer range and higher speed) and more weapons. The new aircraft also have more powerful engines, and lower fuel consumption. New design techniques, as well as new materials, have produced the new engines. This has made it practical to use supercruise (going faster than the speed of sound without using afterburners, and excessive amounts of fuel). In all military aircraft, more efficient and powerful engines provide for takeoff and landing on short or damaged runways, while fuel economies extend range.

A lot of money has gone into making new fighters easier to use. Instead of the old joystick and various foot pedals, many fighters now use center or side-stick HOTAS (hands on throttle and stick). This device is more efficient than the old joystick, and also uses a digital system in which data are received from sensors and sent via the interface and flight-control bus to the aircraft's flight-control computers. Some aircraft are also using direct voice input controls for noncritical functions like data entry, calling up different displays working the radio and other electronic devices. This, along with the HMS (helmet-mounted sight) that duplicates some of the functions in the traditional HUD (heads up display), eliminates a lot of the looking around and flipping of switches pilots have had to do in the past. Even when the pilot does have to look around for information, it is easier to find with the new cockpit display technologies. "Glass" cockpits provide electronic representations of traditional instruments on a few computer displays. Wide-angle heads up displays with computer-generated symbols allow pilots to see all the technical stuff they need to see without looking down.

It's increasingly common for new fighter aircraft to come with all-weather day-night capabilities as standard equipment. The electronics load in modern aircraft is enormous. Many warplanes now have several dozen different computers, fiber-optic links, and fly-by-wire or fly-by-light flight-control systems. These new flight-control systems allow the pilot to perform maneuvers that, without the computers furiously working the flaps and other control surfaces, would be impossible. Such computer-assisted flying makes the odd-looking stealth aircraft possible. This strangely shaped warplane is not controllable in the air with just a human flying it. The digital flight controls are also more resistant to combat damage because there is more redundancy. Unlike the older mechanical and hydraulic controls, you can have three or four sets of wires for the digital controls.

The radar and other electronic equipment is less than half the weight of the previous generation of gear. This also allows for a wider range of capabilities in the radars. There is usually one multimode radar that does air-to-air, air-to-ground, search-and-track, multitarget track-while-scan, and automatic fire control. There is also automatic terrain-following/terrain-avoidance/threat-avoidance with radar ranging and mapping. Some aircraft include Forward Looking Infra Red (FLIR) for night flying, plus day-night laser designator with thermal imaging. It's not surprising that nearly half the cost of new aircraft is in the electronics.

Self-defense is also a major consideration in modern aircraft. You have to include stealthiness in the design. This is most commonly done by using non-metallic composites and shaping of the airframe to make it harder for radar to pick up the aircraft. Active and passive electronic warfare (EW) measures include radar, infrared (heat sensors) search and track (IRST), laser, and missile-approach warning devices. With all that, you also need decoy systems like chaff dispensers and flares.

Counterstealth technology is becoming a major issue. Just because the United States has stealth technology doesn't mean U.S. forces won't be on the receiving end of weapons using stealth. U.S. air-defense radars and missiles have to be able to find and destroy stealthy enemy aircraft and missiles. The American Department of Defense has some highly secret programs to defeat stealth. This has to be highly secret, because it involves finding ways to defeat

America's own stealth systems. The major future threat is likely to be stealthy enemy missiles. It's very expensive, and technically difficult, to apply stealth the way American aircraft do. Missiles are a different matter, as it's much easier to retrofit missiles with stealth features and have a weapon that is much more difficult to detect and defeat.

All of this technology is expensive, even if most of it is currently used in many commercial applications. The trend has been to put more quality and quantity (of capabilities) into one aircraft. This results in fewer, and more expensive, aircraft. While most air forces continue to pursue this approach, there is another solution sneaking up on them.

The Future Is Robots That Fly

THE MOST LIKELY solution to the problems of being able to afford modern warplanes is robots. That is, aircraft without any humans on board. Air force commanders have resisted this for the obvious reason that it puts a lot of pilots out of work. Air forces are run by pilots, and being a pilot is considered the premier job in any air force and an essential experience for anyone seeking to achieve high rank.

But the trends in automation and aircraft capability have been pretty obvious for the past several decades. Pilotless aircraft have been used for decades to provide realistic targets for antiaircraft missiles. Cruise missiles, which are nothing more than pilotless bombers, have been in use for over twenty years and have proven themselves in combat. Pilotless reconnaissance aircraft have become increasingly popular.

A pilotless fighter can pull more G's and outmaneuver any fighter with a human on board. Humans tend to black out during high speed turns ("pulling G's") when the blood rushes from the head to the feet. Pilotless fighters have no such problems, and also have the advantage of being lighter as a result of not having a pilot and all the equipment a pilot needs. Without a cockpit and pilot, an aircraft can be a third or more lighter and nearly that much smaller. Many pilots have already noticed that the artificial intelligence in PC-based flight simulators has long been capable of smoking most human pilots (including the pros). And the flight-simulator aircraft are not even taking advantage of the "no human on board" angle.

In 1971 the U.S. Navy even went so far as to test an F-4 fighter (at that time, the best available) against one of its drone aircraft (normally used for target practice). The drone was equipped so that a pilot on the ground could control it. The drone won. Not only did it use its superior maneuverability to avoid two missiles fired from the F-4, but also turned the tables and scored several simulated hits on the F-4. But there never was much enthusiasm for pursuing this line of research, and nothing more came of this rather spectacular demonstration.

One factor always raised when discussing further work on fighter drones is the difficulty in getting the human "pilot" for the drone in position to fly the drone. One thing a pilotless aircraft lacks is a pilot's eyeballs and ability to rapidly size up a situation. But there are already sensors available that, if placed on different parts of an aircraft, will see even more than a piloted fighter. It's only a matter of time, probably by the end of the decade, before someone so equips a fighter and tests such an aircraft against piloted planes.

While turning pilotless warplanes loose scares a lot of people, we have already been doing it. Cruise missiles do it all the time, although their mission is a lot simpler than that of a fighter. But it is also possible to program a fighter to either self-destruct or disarm itself and return to base if there's a problem. Moreover, one can also fly these aircraft under ground control for all or part of a mission, which may be more preferable when using robot fighter-bombers against ground targets.

Many of the problems that have bedeviled the use of robotic fighters have long since been addressed. For example, telling friendly from enemy aircraft was a problem as early as 1941, when British aircraft began using IFF (identification, friend or foe) devices. An IFF is an electronic transmitter and receiver that sends and receives coded signals. The signals tell people on the ground or in the air if the airplane they are transmitting to is friendly. If the right signal does not come back, one can assume that the aircraft out there is either enemy, or a friendly with a broken IFF device. Despite this latter situation, IFF proved worth the occasional friendly-fire losses. For without the IFF, there would have been more friendly-fire losses as nervous pilots and gunners on the ground blasted aircraft they could not positively identify on sight, or raise on the radio.

In April 1994, everyone was reminded how valuable IFF is when two U.S. F-15 jets shot down two U.S. helicopters over Iraq because the helicopters' IFF gear was not functioning properly. You don't hear about the thousands of incidents where the trigger is not pulled because the IFF gives a timely and correct response, and all of this should remind you that things always get pretty murky in the heat of combat.

Pilotless fighters would still have to contend with IFF, and getting shot down by friendly aircraft if the IFF breaks down. But it obviously would not be as big a deal if a pilotless fighter were shot down under these, or any other, circumstances. You'd still be out a forty-million-dollar aircraft, but you wouldn't have to have the young life lost nor the grieving family. Politicians like to avoid that sort of thing. In the little wars of the next generation or so, the loss of a pilotless fighter also avoids the embarrassment of a pilot being captured and held for political ransom by the locals. This is another tremendous incentive politicians and voters will approve of. During the Vietnam War, some 90 percent of the American prisoners of war were from shot-down U.S. aircraft.

What will happen to pilots? They will be around for a while longer. There will be resistance to having pilotless passenger aircraft, and there will be a period of several decades during which piloted and pilotless aircraft will coexist. Sensor technology will hold back pilotless fighters for some time, perhaps a decade or more. Replacing the human eye is not easy, even though research on this has been going on for some decades. While there are already many electronic eyes in use, none yet developed has been as sharp as that used by human pilots.

Electronic eyes open doors and read bar codes. But a pilot's eye has to see far and in some detail. A human pilot learns to recognize a lot of different airborne objects. A bird at one mile may look like an enemy aircraft at many more miles. It hasn't been easy getting an electronic sensor (and its supporting computer) to operate as quickly as a human pilot. The pilotless aircraft will have the advantage of having several eyes looking in all directions at once. For some time there may be humans flying as section leaders, in charge of two or three pilotless fighters. Voice recognition is already in use for fighters, whereby a computer understands several dozen commands. These same commands could be just as easily transmitted to a pilotless aircraft. Just to close this loop, the pilotless aircraft could also respond with synthetic human speech. Each pilotless fighter could be given a different synthetic voice so the human flight leader could quickly tell them apart.

In other words, the digital aviator will, increasingly, be literally digital—a robot.

7

The Digital Sailor

B EFORE AIRCRAFT ARRIVED, ships were the summit of military technology. To a certain extent, they still are. While aircraft carry marvelous technology, ships can carry more weight, and thus more gadgets. And they do. But much of the money is still going to equipment for an opponent (the Soviet navy) that no longer exists. The U.S. Army and Marines need fast cargo ships to get to little wars in force before too much damage is done. But cargo ships, even though they float, are not something to warm an admiral's heart. On a more explosive level, the century-old disdain for naval mines in the U.S. Navy is still with us, with money for dealing with mines being painfully extracted from the navy budget as reluctantly as ever.

Even today, warships are the most complicated and high-tech weapons of war. As complex as aircraft have become, nothing beats a ship for sheer concentration of technology and complexity. With all that, ships have suffered less from technical problems than aircraft and ground forces. Maybe it's all that practice sailors get, or simply the effort it takes to keep anything functional in a corrosive, often stormy, saltwater environment.

Just as technology has been revolutionizing air and land warfare, it has also hit navies in several waves throughout this century. Big guns (twelve inches and up) and bigger ships (the first modern battleships) came just after the turn of the century. Radio, primitive sonar, and new types of engines all added new complexity to ships by World War I (1914–18). Keep in mind that, at the turn of the century, one-fifth of all shipping was still propelled by sails. Warships were almost all steam driven, but even this technology became much more complex in the first few decades of the twentieth century.

The shift from sail power to steam power in the late nineteenth century was supposed to reduce the size of ship crews. But as more technology was added to ships, the crew size stayed high. Historically, most of the men on sailing ships were needed to man all of those guns, and deal with the complex system of sails that propelled the ship. Steam power did reduce the number of sailors needed to keep the ships going, and larger guns meant fewer guns and fewer men, overall, to man them. But this economy didn't last long. More weapons were added, and more men were needed to make them work. By World War I, most warships had electricity and this brought with it radios and searchlights. The new guns now had complex optical and fire-control systems to make them more accurate. This meant still more sailors to man the fire-control gear. With all these new activities taking place over larger ships, there was a need for more communications. So more sailors were assigned to operate an increasingly complex communications system on the ship.

Bigger Ships, Smaller Crews

AT THE TURN OF THE century, the steam turbine was being introduced on a wide scale. This got a lot more power out of steam engines and allowed significantly higher speeds. In 1905, the first modern battleship (the British *Dreadnought*) was launched, and the race to have the biggest, heaviest-armed, and fastest ships began. Fast (over twenty knots), big (over twelve thousand tons) ships required much larger engines. Since these engines were coal powered, large numbers of guys shoveling coal and doing engine maintenance were needed. The first battleship had a crew of 770 (eighteen tons of ship per man). The tonnage per sailor was indicative of how crowded a ship was. Crews soon passed the 1,000 mark, something rarely seen before in a navy. The battleships were far larger than the old sail-driven, four-thousand-ton "ships of the line" with their 800-man crews (five tons of ship per sailor). But the sailing ships didn't have to carry a lot of mechanical equipment and fuel, nor were they nearly as fast.

During and after World War II, navies began shifting from coal to oil. This was very popular with the crews, as shoveling coal into the boiler was hard and dirty work. One of the earlier battleships so converted had a gold plated shovel mounted on a bulkhead in the engine room; below it was the inscription, "Lest we forget." The sailors were particularly grateful for relief from the periodic "coaling" exercise, in which tons of coal were manhandled into the ship's bunker spaces. Taking on oil was a lot easier, and cleaner. Oil allowed crews to be reduced, but more weapons and equipment were added and soon the savings were gone. This was particularly true in World War II, when radar was installed in battleships. But hundreds more sailors were needed to man the increasing number of 40mm antiaircraft guns. Not just the gun crews were needed, but also mechanics and more fire-control technicians.

Ship crews, and the ships, grew larger and larger throughout the twentieth century. This growth peaked in the current U.S. aircraft carriers, ships of ninety-five thousand tons with crews of over 6,000 sailors. This was about fifteen tons of ship for each member of the crew. During World War II, several classes, destroyer escorts and light carriers, had less than ten tons per crewman. Battleships were the roomiest, and the favorite ship for sailors to serve on. Adverse crew density was not unique to aircraft carriers; destroyers still often have only ten tons per man, while the larger ships had up to twenty-five tons per man.

As long as a lot of men were required to keep all the new technology going, the ships were going to be very expensive to run. You not only needed spare parts and fuel for the equipment, but food and supplies (and recruiting and training) for the sailors. The modern aircraft carrier costs over four billion dollars to build and about a tenth of that each year to run. For fifty years after World War II, navies struggled to automate their ships, lest the number of sailors grow too large for the ships to comfortably hold. By the 1980s, the U.S. was using eight-thousand-ton destroyers that had about twenty-five tons of ship per sailor. Not bad, but these ships had guns, missiles, helicopters, and massive amounts of electronic gear.

Yet it was the Russians that carried automation even further, to the point of being counterproductive. Wanting to put the maximum number of weapons and equipment on a ship, the Russians cut back even more. On a 9,700-ton ship, they had 30 tons per man and a lot more weapons and equipment. But the Russian ships were notoriously unreliable. They had far more breakdowns and accidents. The less heavily armed and more densely populated U.S. ships were generally more capable, and more of them were available to actually fight.

The way warships fight has changed since World War II. There is now a lot of complex electronic gear that requires constant maintenance. Moreover, much of this equipment is used all the time. There is a greater need for a larger crew just to man all the radars, sonars, and other sensors around the clock much of the time. Perhaps the biggest reason for maintaining large crews is the need to deal with "damage control." This is what the crew does when the ship is damaged, either in combat or otherwise. The latter condition is common enough on warships, as they carry a lot of explosives and accidents still happen.

While most navies have reduced their ship crews since World War II, the cost of these sailors has increased much more. Most of the World War II sailors were draftees, while most today are professionals, making up to five times as much (after taking inflation into account). More than half the cost of running modern warships is personnel, either their pay or portions of the ship devoted to their support.

Not only are sailors more expensive, but they are more reluctant to spend a lot of time at sea. More sailors are married and don't want to spend a lot of time away from their families. This is particularly a problem with the U.S.

Navy, which has to steam long distances to stand watch on out-of-the-way trouble spots. Most other navies don't have to travel that far and spend a lot more time in port or steaming nearby. With smaller crews, you would be able to depend on a larger proportion of those sailors who either enjoy, or do not mind so much, being at sea for so long. There are never enough of these old salts—there never have been. The U.S. Navy, with over four hundred thousand sailors in the early 1990s, found that several percent of the crew would leave the navy after a long (six-month or more) cruise because of the length of time spent at sea. Replacements have to be recruited and trained, a very expensive process.

Seagoing Robots

THE SOLUTION TO this problem is the same as with the other services: robots. No, not metal sailors scrambling over ships, but automation in many forms. Much of this automation has already appeared on civilian ships, where vessels larger than the biggest warships are run by a crew of less than fifty men. Most navies have held off on adopting much of this civilian-developed automation, but that changed in the 1990s as budgets got tight and the civilian automation continued to function efficiently.

The big problem was that there were many functions on a warship that had no counterpart on a civilian vessel, and thus there was no existing automated equipment on civilian ships. For example, damage control on warships and civilian vessels differs considerably. Civilian ships only have to deal with accidents (usually in the engine room) or acts of nature (storms or running aground). Warships have to worry about all that as well as getting hit by a wide variety of weapons. Moreover, warships are laid out much differently than civilian ships. Merchant ships, of whatever type (tanker, freighter, etc.) have a much simpler layout and do not carry nearly as much machinery and electronics as a warship. There's a lot more stuff on a warship that can break down in a violent way or get damaged. If a merchant ship breaks down, it can just sit there until help arrives. A warship has to fix itself as soon as possible because there's a battle going on, or because the damage tends to spread and destroy the ship.

Given that a warship needs numerous trained damage-control sailors, there are ways to reduce the number needed. Currently, most navies do not take advantage of automated communications equipment for damage-control crews. A large portion of damage-control crews are there to manage communications, and this could be taken care of by better equipment. More automation can be added to damage control by building in more extensive fire-extinguishing equipment and flotation devices ("air bags" and more automatic pumps). A major problem with all these swell damage-control automation ideas is that experienced naval officers are reluctant to try something new in this department. You see, it is not possible to thoroughly test new damage-control techniques. No one can afford to blow up existing ships for testing purposes, and you would need sailors on board to make the test realistic anyway. There's too much danger of losing people that way, and such losses in peacetime tend to attract unwanted political attention. Thus, installing new, damage-control gear on ships, whether it be automated or not, makes sailors nervous. Damage control is the most fearsome task any sailor faces, even more terrifying than combat itself or steaming through a major storm. No one wants to risk being the first crew to use a lot of new damage-control ideas. New damage-control gear is added all the time, but these are individual items that can be thoroughly tested, things like new fireproof gloves or suits, or new types of breathing apparatuses. Wholesale introduction of new damage-control systems is unlikely under these circumstances. What is more likely is the installation of new systems while keeping all the old gear, and crewmen trained in its use, until some combat or accident (a missile on board accidentally exploding) comes along to test the automated systems.

Perhaps the major opportunity to reduce crew size is in the area of equipment technicians. Modern warships have developed the capacity to repair themselves to a large degree. Even small ships have machine shops on board that can fabricate many spare parts needed. Sailors take it as a point of professional pride that they can fix just about anything on board and keep the ship going. In the last several decades it has become more common to use missiles instead of guns, and increasingly these missiles are loaded in sealed containers that, in theory anyway, require no maintenance. Instruments in the container, or via wires and test equipment, monitor the sealed missiles and report if they are ready for action. If not, they are simply not used, and are returned to a land base for repair. In the last twenty years, these sealed units have become more reliable. They are popular with sailors, as repairing things like torpedoes or missiles on board the confined spaces of a ship has never been popular and has often led to catastrophic accidents. By maximizing the number of "no maintenance" weapons and equipment, the crew shrinks. As the crew gets smaller, the space they require does also.

By cutting crew size, repair facilities, and spare parts carried, current ships could be one-third smaller, although not much cheaper. Well, not much cheaper to build, but a lot cheaper to use. The total cost of a ship over its customary twenty-year life consists mostly of operating expenses, and most of these have to do with recruiting, training, and paying the crew. Cut the crew size by at least half and the overall cost of a ship goes down by over 20 percent.

All of this is not a new idea. The radical aspect is taking the trends of the last thirty years (automation, sealed missile containers, etc.) to their logical conclusion. Many sailors are quick to point out that the logical conclusion is not the practical conclusion. It may not be practical to have too many highly automated ships, with few technicians on board, steaming long distances to a combat zone. It is for good reason that ships have long had the ability to repair themselves, or at least repair most of the things that can go wrong while at sea.

Ships, like tanks and aircraft, suffer wear and tear as they move about. Aircraft can't just stop when they have a breakdown and wait for a truck full of mechanics to show up and fix things. So aircraft must fly out, do something, and fly right back to a base. Tanks travel in large groups, accompanied by mechanics and trucks full of spare parts. The mechanics are kept busy repairing that percentage of tanks that are out of action at one time or another. While a ship can break down and just float around waiting for a repair ship to come along to set things right, this has not proven very efficient in practice. Ships usually operate in groups, but they also often proceed individually. Being able to perform minor repairs themselves, well-run ships are usually in good shape when they enter battle. A lot of battle damage is minor, and ships can repair this themselves, or at least fix themselves up so they can keep on fighting. More serious damage can be made less serious because of the onboard repair capability. And in many damage-control situations, the onboard repair facilities make the difference between saving and losing the ship.

Soviet Style

THE SOVIET UNION built a large fleet, the planet's second largest, using the "more weapons/less repair capability" approach. They never got to use their fleet in combat, and it is now wasting away in the wake of the Soviet Union's collapse in 1991. The Soviets did pioneer the use of antiship missiles, and scared the rest of the world into adopting this weapon on a wide scale. But we still don't know if the Soviet style of ship design would have worked. Basically, the Soviets sought to put as much firepower as possible into a first strike. If they succeeded, American carrier groups would be crippled. If they failed, the Soviet ships could retreat to their bases and the survivors would reload for another go at it. The Soviet bases were heavily defended by land-based aircraft, mines, and submarines, and hundreds of small, missile-carrying, fast attack boats (like the World War II era PT boats, but carrying antiship missiles instead of torpedoes). The Soviets also had the world's largest submarine fleet, with which to deny America and other Western nations access to the high seas.

The world did get to see this new style Soviet fleet operate for several decades. It was not a pretty picture. In addition to novel new designs, the Soviets had to gain experience and expertise in a form of naval warfare that Russians had never demonstrated an aptitude for. While working out the inevitable bugs in their new ship designs, the Soviets had a lot of problems one would expect from a large fleet short of experienced sailors and officers and lacking a long naval tradition. But the Soviets pressed on and they were making steady progress until the very end. At the end the nation could no longer afford the resources needed to maintain the ships, pay the sailors, and provide the fuel so the ships could stay at sea and continue their training.

What the Soviets did prove was that they could get a lot of their ships to sea and keep a lot of the systems (sensors and weapons) working. Cynics tend to concentrate on the frequent breakdowns of their ships and how one would regularly spot broken-down Soviet ships being towed back to port. American naval intelligence officers also were quite sure that a large percentage of the electronic systems on these ships was not working at any given time. But all this has to be put in the context of Soviet (and before that, Russian) military doctrine. The Soviets accepted that not every ship would be 100 percent ready. While 100 percent readiness is a laudable goal, and one American ships strive for, the Soviets had always been realistic about their ability to have everything good to go before a battle. During World War II, they won by piling on a lot of weapons and hitting the enemy hard with the ones that worked. Yes, we'll never know, at least in the foreseeable future, if this would have worked at sea, but the Soviets introduced some new concepts that could well work.

The U.S. Navy is already more automated than the American army or air force. The navy was the first service to use robot weapons (naval mines and torpedoes), so it's not such a strange concept for the U.S. fleet to build highly automated ships with much smaller crews. Repair and maintenance can also be automated, and the U.S. Navy has made extensive use of repair ships and floating dry docks for over half a century.

Throughout the 1990s, U.S. naval officers have suggested more automated ships, and heading toward the end of the decade, more and more senior admirals are getting these suggestions, previously only put forward by more junior officers.

Twenty-first-Century Ships

NAVAL PLANNERS HAVE noted the increased effectiveness of missiles, and the heightened vulnerability of manned aircraft. For the last twenty years, more and more people, inside and outside the navy, have been whispering about the coming demise of the aircraft carrier. The whispers have become louder in the 1990s.

In 1995, the USN proposed an "arsenal ship" as an apparently new form of capital ship, a supplement (for the moment) to the current carrier battle groups. The ship would be partially submergible, highly automated, and armed with some five hundred vertical launch system (VLS) missile cells. Crew size would be extremely sparse, the initial suggestion being under a hundred. This would call for nearly complete automation of damage control, an unprecedented step in the history of naval warfare. The models for this vessel are the numerous modern merchant ships, which use extensive automation to bring crew size for even the largest tankers to under thirty officers and sailors. In historical terms, this is an unarmored battleship. At forty thousand tons, it's as large as most of the battleships in use at the start of World War II. As far as being armored goes, a hundred years before World War II, most "battleships" were not armored and had rarely been so protected until the middle of the nineteenth century. Note that a World War II battleship, with nine large guns, carried some 80 shells for each gun, for a total of 720 "missiles." The arsenal ship missiles, at least the ones used for antiship work, have over ten times the range of World War II battleship guns. Missiles used against land targets have similar range.

Think of the arsenal ship as a modern freighter with double hull, lots of compartmentalization, larger engines, and the ability to fill ballast tanks and partially submerge (to make it harder to detect, and hit). In other words, part submarine and part freighter with no sharp edges (to make it harder for radar to detect). To further reduce its vulnerability to submarine and other attacks, the new ship would operate as part of a surface action group (SAG). Some of the arsenal ship's VLS cells would be devoted to SAMs of the same type currently used on U.S. Navy ships. These include the SM-2 and the Evolved Sea Sparrow (ESSM, a short-range missile). These different SAMs are effective at different ranges, giving the arsenal ship the ability to attack enemy aircraft or missiles far out or close in.

The arsenal ship design proposes to use the following features to help it survive enemy attacks:

• Active "torpedo defense." The navy is working on several systems to defend against torpedoes that are closing in on a ship. These include rocket-propelled missiles that hit the water close to where the approaching torpedo is and either try to lure the torpedo away, or destroy or damage it with an explosion. A sonar on the ship, or another ship in the task force, would detect and locate the incoming torpedo. The speed of a torpedo is not nearly as great as that of an incoming missile, perhaps fifteen meters a second, max. Given the speed of automated systems, this should give time to detect and stop the incoming torpedo. Of course, if it's a nuclear-armed torpedo, it's another story (these can detonate several hundred meters from a ship and still sink it).

• CEC (Cooperative Engagement Control), with the ship essentially providing an arsenal of weapons that can be fired and then handed off to off-board sensors or targeting systems on other ships or aircraft platforms. This turns something like the arsenal ship into, just that, an arsenal of weapons "used" by other ships and aircraft.

• Mine-resistant hull. This would include things like a double hull, many watertight compartments, with stiffeners and transverse frames. If the arsenal ship hit a mine, only a few of the hundred plus watertight compartments would be flooded. The stiffeners (extra metal supports) and transverse frames (watertight bulkheads going from one side of the ship to another) would prevent a mine explosion from doing fatal damage to the ship's structure. This is nothing new, but the building techniques for this kind of protection continue to get more effective.

• Missile countermeasures. The usual array of decoys, chaff dispensers, electronic gear, and the like.

• Tactical ballistic-missile defense, for local land and naval forces as well as the arsenal ship itself. This means whatever missile system the BMDO (Ballistic Missile Defense Office) program eventually comes up with.

• Stealth, in the form of ballasting, low top and side RCS (Radar Cross Signature), and radar absorbent materials. By having few structures above the deck, and being able to partially submerge ("ballast") so that only some five feet of the ship are above water, it would have a smaller RCS. That means that enemy missiles or aircraft would have a harder time spotting the arsenal ship with search or targeting radars. What an enemy cruise missile can't see, it can't hit. Even if an enemy missile manages to pick up the partially submerged arsenal ship, it will also have a hard time hitting it.

• Terminal missile defense. This would probably be ESSM and perhaps Phalanx or other new CIWS (close-in weapons system) guns for sea-skimming enemy cruise missiles coming in low, just above the water.

PROPOSED DIMENSIONS FOR the arsenal ship (as of 1995): length: 250 meters; beam: 32 meters; hull depth: 17 meters; transit (normal) freeboard (distance from water to highest point on ship): 6.8 meters; ballasted-down (partially submerged) freeboard: 1.5 meters; transit draft (distance from the waterline to the bottom of the ship): 10 meters; ballasted-down draft: 15.2 meters; transit displacement: 42,466 tons (metric); ballasted-down displacement: 75,034 tons; reserve buoyancy (how much water the arsenal ship can take on before sinking) when ballasted: about 10,500 tons. Compare this to the last active battleship class, the Iowas (to which the famous *Missouri* belonged). These weighed 57,000 tons, were 270 meters long, 33 wide, and 11.6 deep. The arsenal ship will not carry the thousands of tons of armor and sixteen-inch guns that the Iowas had, thus accounting for most of the difference in weight. The arsenal ship will also be slower than the thirty-knot Iowas, but fast enough to keep up with a carrier task force (twenty to twenty-five knots).

Estimated cost is about $740 million. The way things work in this area, expect the final price to be at least a billion dollars. That's still less than a quarter of what it costs to build a carrier, and less than what cruisers and B-2 bombers cost. The initial proposal had the first ship converting from prototype to fleet use in 2001. Feasibility studies and system development are scheduled for 1996, with construction to begin in 1997.

In a comparison with the B-2 bomber force and a navy carrier task force, using the Rand think tank study data, a single arsenal ship was able to destroy 4,000 mobile targets (armored vehicles and trucks) out of a future 15,000-target Persian Gulf War scenario. This compares to 420 targets destroyed by B-2's in the same four days. The navy's argument is that since, by its own calculations, a carrier task force can destroy 1,080 mobile targets in the same period (something the Rand study did not say), and its arsenal ship can nail 4,000, the navy can destroy the magic 30 percent of the enemy force, and thus stop the (Iraqi or Iranian) offensive. The air force generals (and the navy's own carrier admirals) will no doubt question the theoretical effectiveness of the arsenal ship. But the cruise missiles have been in action four times between 1991 and 1995 (three times against Iraq, once against Bosnian Serbs) and performed well each time. After years of uncertainty, the air force and navy pilots have fully accepted missiles in the past decade. So it's hard to make a case against the missiles.

The arsenal ship is not the only design the USN is considering for the twenty-first century. The United States Navy is also looking at a follow-on class for the DDG-51 Burke class destroyer, to come into service in 2005. This program, the Surface Combatant–21 (SC-21), received approval from the Pentagon's Defense Acquisition Board in 1995.

The new cruiser is being called a "battlespace dominance ship." Battlespace is a new concept that defines an area of some six hundred kilometers in all directions as a zone to be made free of any enemy forces. The SC-21 class thus has design features that are an interesting cross between current ship design and the arsenal ship.

The proposed specifications for SC-21 include: Crew: as small as possible, with heavy use of automation, perhaps one hundred to two hundred; displacement: 11,900 tons (cruiser class); weapons: 256 VLS missile cells capable of handling Tomahawk land/sea attack cruise missiles, Harpoon antiship missiles, Standard antiaircraft missiles, as well as future anti-theater ballistic and anti–cruise missile point defense missiles; two automated 155mm (six-inch) guns, with 2,400 "smart" shells (each shell having its own guidance system);

two lightweight torpedo launchers (mainly for use against submarines); an antitorpedo point defense launched via either VLS missile or torpedo tubes.

Electronic combat equipment—An improvement over the current system found in the Aegis class cruisers. The new system would have more capable "cooperative engagement capability" so that the cruiser could cooperate with any friendly ship or aircraft from sea level to earth orbit. The Aegis is the current cruiser-type ship with an elaborate radar system that can spot aircraft hundreds of kilometers away. Also planned are "telepresence" remote operating capabilities—that is, the ability to use both onboard sensor information with similar information from other ships, aircraft, and ground units. This makes it possible for the JTF (Joint Task Force) commander to efficiently direct all forces under his control by employing all the sensors these forces are using. It's not so much a matter that the JTF commander can order around every individual air, ground, or naval unit in his area, but that he can see what they see and sort out what is going on. Then the JTF commander can issue orders to subordinate commanders that allow everyone to work together and not at cross-purposes. These orders and this coordination are particularly important now that there are so many electronic weapons. These include electronic-warfare transmitters as well as dozens of different types of radars. The battlespace concept requires that one commander get the army, navy, and air force to work together. This JTF commander cannot do that unless he can see what all the army, navy, and air force sensors can see. The SC-21 also contains electronic equipment that is more difficult for an enemy to detect and jam. In effect, this is "stealthy" electronics. Items like passive sonar (it just listens) and IR (infrared, heat-sensing) "radars" are becoming more popular because enemy missiles cannot home in on them as they can on normal radars and sonars, that emit signals.

Aircraft carried—two helicopters, SH-60 (navy version of the army Blackhawk, or its successor). One unmanned aerial vehicle (UAV) for reconnaissance. Two unmanned remote mine-hunter helicopters. Plus two unmanned underwater vehicles (for clearing mines, and whatever new uses can be found).

The navy has established several criteria for whatever final shape the SC-21 takes.

First, the ship must have a very large VLS missile capacity. It is expected that any far-off emergency (Persian Gulf, Far East) will require a quick response with a lot of firepower. This is especially true if the foe is a relatively small force and can be intimidated by a massive show of force. A hundred or more cruise missiles delivered from one ship can do that. If the foe is larger, the SC-21 (and other ships) must be able to slow down the enemy until reinforcing American units can arrive.

Second, to back up the missiles, it is considered necessary to have two heavy guns on the SC-21. The choice of the moment is a new 155mm (six-inch) gun and a supply of 2,400 guided shells. This combination of gun and shell would enable the SC-21 to fire over 100 kilometers (over 80 kilometers inland) and help destroy or damage enemy ground units and bases. The shells would mainly be high-explosive shells, while the antitank munitions would be carried on the Tomahawk cruise missiles. This combination of guns and missiles would also provide adequate support for friendly ground units that are landed.

Third, another type of missile carried by the SC-21 would be for theater missile defense, for shooting down Scuds and others of their ilk. This is increasingly important as more nations obtain ballistic missiles. In regional conflicts, there will be a need to defend friendly ports, ships, and airfields from weapons of mass destruction, while waiting for reinforcing units to arrive. This will require sea operations within a thousand miles of the battle area, as friendly transports move forward with air and ground units. The SC-21 is expected to be one of the first ships on the scene and will have to keep the area safe until the reinforcing units are ashore.

Finally, the unmanned vehicles on board the SC-21 will be needed for clearing mines and performing reconnaissance so that the ship's guns and missiles will know what targets to hit during the early stages of the operation (when no other friendly aircraft are available).

Getting the Job Done with Fewer Sailors

ONE OF THE MAJOR issues with both these new ships will be the crew size. The SC-21 and the arsenal ship are naval ships and must operate like them, not like commercial ships. Navy ships do a lot more maneuvering and station taking. Warships perform a variety of distinct missions. For the new ships this will include task-force defense, support of land operations, underway replenishment (taking on supplies while at sea), and station keeping (maintaining a fixed position in a formation). All of this takes a lot of changes to a ship's speed and course. Warships don't go in straight lines for hundreds or thousands of miles while steaming from one port to another, which is about all commercial ships do, except for loading and unloading at either end. Warships do constant drilling on damage control and engineering casualties, which puts a lot of stress and strain on equipment and people. Warships must train constantly so the crew can react on instinct when something happens. The real revolution will come in actually cutting down on the amount of repair and maintenance that is performed while these new ships are at sea. Eliminate most of this and you can get away with a good half of the crew. Warships also have traditionally had a fully manned bridge, engineering spaces (engine room and power plant), and combat information center while at sea. Commercial ships are quite different in that they can get away with one man on the bridge, or none now and then by using Iron Mike (autosteering with cruise control). Leaving the bridge empty is technically a no-no on commercial ships, but that's just another of the corners that warships cannot afford to cut (except perhaps when traveling alone.) If the navy converts over to commercial requirements then we could really reduce manning.

That said, the navy already has an example of ships with hundred-man crews, and this is in the form of nuclear submarines. The larger (16,000-ton) ballistic missile boats have 160-man crews while the smaller (7,500-ton) attack boats have 140-man crews. Nuclear subs are very complex ships, not least because of their nuclear power plants. Yet the U.S. Navy knows that one can go ever further with automation on nuclear subs. Russian nuclear attack subs have gone to sea with crews as small as 50 men. The Russians were not as successful in automating their nuclear subs as they would have liked, but that can be said for a lot of Russian engineering. In many technical areas where the Russians have tried and failed, American engineers have succeeded.

The Ships of the Future, Yesterday and Tomorrow

NUCLEAR SHIPS ARE also the one type of modern ship that is essentially untried in combat. A British nuclear sub sank an Argentine cruiser in 1982, but that's the only time a "nuke" has been in combat against ships. Peacetime exercises consistently demonstrate that the nukes can get close enough to use their torpedoes on surface ships under nearly any circumstances. These exercises also show that nukes are nearly as lethal against other nukes. These nuclear submarines, which did not become common until the 1970s, are the highest-tech warships ever put to sea. Even without combat experience, they are much valued, and feared. While the nukes are the most dangerous warships at sea, their prey is largely limited to surface ships and other subs. While some nukes are equipped with cruise missiles that can attack land targets, not many of these missiles can be carried. A dozen missiles can be carried on the older, and much more numerous, U.S. Los Angeles class attack subs, while the two or three new Seawolf class boats that will be built may carry two or three dozen land-attack missiles. More of the Tomahawk missiles can be carried by any nuke, but at the expense of torpedoes for attacking other ships.

The biggest problems nuclear subs have are communicating and finding targets in the air or on land. Both of these problems arise from the fact that submarines are submerged under the water most of the time. This is what makes them hard to find and attack. But this works both ways, and subs require enormously expensive sensor systems (costing over a hundred million dollars, if you want the best) to find anything at all. So, while nuclear subs can provide a model of what a high-tech, highly automated ship can be, you have to transfer a lot of that technology to surface ships in order to obtain warships that are worthwhile in an era where navies have to participate in operations ashore.

In the U.S. Navy, the "automation gang" has put down a large bet that they can translate nuclear-sub technology and experience to surface ships. The current navy leadership seems inclined to take that bet and accept the consequences if it doesn't work. It probably will work, eventually. And with the cold war over, this appears to be a favorable time to try something like this. In wartime, or a time of superpower confrontation, the debugging of such a radical new system would cause a lot of casualties. During a time of relative peace, one has the leisure to work things out more deliberately.

PART III

High Tech and the Future of Modern Warfare

What kind of future wars will the U.S. be called on to fight?

What kind of technology will be most effective in these wars?

What kind of tools will the troops have available and how well will
their gear work?

What has history taught us about situations like this?

8

Modern Battles

IN THE LAST TWO centuries, armies have moved away from the set-piece battle (everyone crowded into one place before fighting) toward the "spread-out battle" (groups of troops wandering all over a vast battle area). Communication and navigation have become major problems and technology has provided a lot of overhyped solutions.

Battlefield communications has always been a problem. Until the invention of the telegraph (1844), the telephone (1876), and the radio (1898), military communications consisted of messengers, flag signals, and musical instruments. These ancient forms of communication were, in the hands of well-trained troops, quite effective—but only when the commander could see all, or most, of the battlefield. As armies began to spread out in the 1800s, things became rather more complicated and unpredictable. Navies had fewer problems, for they did not have to worry about spread-out battles until the aircraft carrier came along, and by then radios were in widespread use and the communications problems were largely solved.

But on the ground, even radios were not enough help for the sprawling armies of the twentieth century. First telegraph, then telephone, and finally radio were all hailed as revolutionary battlefield communications devices. They were useful tools, but not decisive ones, as some had hoped. Everyone soon got these gadgets and, as always, victory went to those who trained longest with them and put the largest number of them to work on the battlefield.

But as the twentieth century comes to an end, many really useful gadgets have arrived that actually work consistently and well in the communications and navigation area. The most startling example is the GPS (Global Positioning System), which allowed troops to wander around the Kuwaiti desert without getting lost in 1991. Getting lost on the modern battlefield has been a very common occurrence, and deserts are the easiest places to get lost in. GPS changed all of that in a very dramatic way during the 1991 Gulf War.

Satellite communications, essentially the same gear that civilians have been snapping up, has also proven useful in combat. This is all because, even in peacetime, these aspects of warfare get a good workout. The downside, as always, is that the bad guys will also have most of these gadgets in future wars. The United States had an advantage in the Gulf War with GPS only because it was very new, and American troops were just getting the GPS receivers. Today, Iraqi troops have the GPS gear too.

Everyone has radios of one sort or another, from sophisticated military communications equipment to cheap CB equipment from discount electronics stores.

But effective military communications is more than just having a working radio handy. You also have to be able to move around easily. This has always been, for the soldier, the other meaning of the word *communications*.

Getting There

IN THIS CENTURY, technology has put most troops on wheels. This has been horrendously expensive, and it wasn't until the 1950s that the last of the major armies, the Soviet Red Army, got rid of the last of its horse-drawn transport. Actually, the Chinese army still has a lot of horse-drawn transport, even though they have been working hard for the past twenty years to motorize everyone. This rush to motorization, a technological advance without parallel, has created as many problems as it has solved.

Okay, everyone is riding on a truck or tracked vehicle. Yet these armies are not able to move any faster than a medieval cavalry army (in particular, the Mongols, but others were as swift). The reason for this inability to pick up much speed has been "the tail." While horses can stop and start munching grass, motor vehicles need refined fuel (gasoline, diesel, and lubricating oil). Trucks also need spare parts, from tires to spark plugs to—well, just about every part of a vehicle wears out eventually. At least you can (and often do) eat a dead horse, whereas the wreckage of vehicles just gets in the way (or, at best, provides a source of spare parts). Motorization, like many new technologies, has been a mixed blessing.

The immediate appeal of motor vehicles was that they could, until they broke down or ran out of fuel, move faster than horses. This they could do, but not for long periods. Throughout this century, vehicles have been designed and built to be more robust and sturdy. But rarely have they been robust enough to overcome all those limitations these machines are prone to.

By the 1990s, the number of vehicles in a combat division was more than double the number found in World War II divisions. Modern divisions have 3,000 to 4,000 vehicles (over two-thirds are trucks). Each day, this division needs 1,000 tons of supplies (if just sitting there) to 4,000 tons (if in heavy combat) to do its job. While the same types of weapons are being used now that were available fifty years ago during World War II, the sheer number of weapons has increased. A good example is the growth of the Russian tank division from 1946 to 1996. The 1996 version was based on their experience in World War II and was pretty much a spiffed-up version of their World War II "tank corps" (same size, different name). The 1946 unit had 11,541 troops, 336 tanks and 84 assault guns (essentially tanks without turrets), 24 towed artillery guns, and 1,500 trucks of various sizes. The 1996 tank division had 11,470 troops, 328 tanks, 250 infantry fighting vehicles and armored personnel carriers (the former are like the latter, except with a turret and more weapons). There are 90 self-propelled artillery and 90 towed (including mortars and rocket launchers). There are 4 ballistic missiles, 6 helicopters, and 2,500 trucks. A lot more stuff, and it all needs lots of fuel and spare parts to keep going.

For every vehicle in the combat divisions, there are two or more behind them, moving forward supplies, fresh troops, and support units. Think of a modern army as a few combat divisions being "pushed" forward by a mass of trucks. Of course, if you advance too far, the trucks cannot get back to ports or working railroads fast enough to bring forward fresh supplies before the tanks run out of fuel and spare parts. This limitation of motor transport was first discovered during World War I, and the lesson was hammered home again and again during World War II. As recently as the 1991 Gulf War, the victorious Coalition tank army was limited more by supplies than by anything else. Lack of fuel, not Iraqi troops, would have dictated how long it would have taken Coalition troops to get to Baghdad. As it was, the dash across the deserts of Kuwait and southern Iraq exhausted the fuel of many motorized units, leaving them motionless inside Iraq for up to a day until more fuel could be rushed forward over the roadless desert.

The technical solution to this problem has been manifold. Larger trucks, which can move more supplies cross-country while burning less fuel in the process, have helped somewhat. But in the meantime, more, and larger, armored vehicles have been put into service. These vehicles burn a lot more fuel, which is the main reason divisions need twice as much supply tonnage today as they did fifty years ago. Other solutions have taken the form of easily laid (over ten miles a day) fuel pipelines. Large rubber fuel bladders that can be carried forward by helicopter are available for emergencies, when a battalion or two need to be refueled quickly. These solutions haven't really worked. As more and more technology has been added to armies, more troops and trucks have had to be added to support the new gear. The tail has gotten larger. The only saving grace in all this is that the troops behind the divisions don't need nearly as much supply, mainly because the support soldiers aren't shooting off a lot of ammunition or burning as much fuel in heavy armored vehicles. Nevertheless, a hundred thousand ground troops (including two combat divisions) require about one hundred pounds of supplies per day per soldier. That's five thousand tons of material each day, every day. That's only an average. During heavy combat, this can double. During periods of inactivity, it can fall by half. Logistical problems, as much as wanting to avoid a lot of casualties, is why generals prefer to hammer the enemy from the air before sending in the ground troops.

Feeding the Sortie Rate

BUT THE AIR FORCES have their own problems. A modern air force is concerned with getting as many combat aircraft into the fight as possible. This is known in the trade as "sortie generation." A sortie is one trip out and back by an aircraft, particularly a combat aircraft. Modern combat aircraft, in addition to being very expensive, are also very sturdy. With sufficient supply and support, they can fly several sorties a day. Thus aircraft are prodigious consumers of fuel, bombs, and spare parts. While each member of an army needs about a hundred pounds of supplies a day, each member of an air force unit requires over half a ton. Modern aircraft gobble up many tons of supplies each time they fly a sortie. The chart below shows the average tonnage of supplies needed for different types of aircraft each time they fly off to fight (a "sortie").

Table 3 / Modern Warplanes and Supplies Needed for Combat

Aircraft	Function	Tons Carried Fuel	Tons Carried Weapons	Average Sorties	Total Tons per Day
Russian Type					
MiG-21	Fighter	2.1	1.5	1	3
F-6	Fighter	1.8	0.5	1	2
MiG-23	Fighter	4.7	1.5	1	6
MiG-27	Fighter-bomber	4.7	4.5	1	9
MiG-25	Recon	15.1	2.0	0.5	17
MiG-29	Fighter-bomber	4.0	4.5	2	16
Su-17	Bomber	3.3	4.5	1	7
Su-24	Bomber	24.0	4.5	1	28
SU-25	Ground-attack	3.5	6.5	2	20

Table 3 / Modern Warplanes and Supplies Needed for Combat (continued)

Tons Carried

Aircraft	Function	Fuel	Weapons	Average Sorties	Total Tons per Day
Su-27	Fighter	5.0	2.0	2	14
Tu-22M	Bomber	13.4	8.0	1	21
Mi-24	Gunship	1.5	1.7	4	12
Western Type					
F-4	Fighter-bomber	5.7	7.2	2	24
F-16	Fighter-bomber	3.2	6.9	3	26
F-15	Fighter-bomber	6.1	7.2	3	36
A-10	Ground-attack	6.1	7.2	5	65
Harrier	Fighter-bomber	3.5	3.6	5	32
Tornado	Fighter-bomber	5.2	7.2	2	24
F-111	Bomber	15.4	10.0	1	24
AH-64	Gunship	7.0	1.7	4	30
US Carrier					
F-14	Fighter	7.5	6.5	2	20
A-6	Bomber	7.2	8.1	3	44
F-18	Fighter-bomber	5.1	7.7	3	35

Notes for the above table. *Aircraft* is the official name of the aircraft. *Function* is what the aircraft does most of the time. Fighter-bombers can operate either as fighters (attacking other aircraft) or bombers (dropping stuff on ground targets). Gunships are helicopters that are designed and used as combat aircraft. *Fuel* is the tons of fuel usually carried for a sortie. *Weapons* is the tonnage of missiles, bombs, and cannon ammunition carried. *Average Sorties per Day* is the average number of times the aircraft can fly each day on a combat mission. For a day or two they can fly up to twice this rate (and even more, depending on the supply situation and how good the ground crews are). *Total Tons per Day* is the tons of supplies used each day to support the average number of missions flown. This tonnage includes ammunition, missiles, and fuel an aircraft will not use on a mission, but also includes an allowance for spare parts. Russian aircraft, for example, require new engines more frequently than Western aircraft. All the missions are bombing missions for fighter-bombers. For fighter-bombers acting as fighters, just deduct two-thirds of their weapons tonnage (all fighters would use is some of their air-to-air missiles). The F-6 is a Chinese (they have thousands of them) copy of the Russian MiG-19; they also make the F-7, a copy of the MiG-21. The Tornado is a European design and the Harrier is a British design. All the other Western aircraft are American.

At the start of an air offensive, 500 Western-type aircraft could fly some 3,000 sorties in the first two days. This would require some 100,000 tons of supplies just for the aircraft. If the air offensive continued for another 18 days, that would mean another 25,000 sorties and another 750,000 tons of supplies. Normally, in a Western air force, each pilot will fly some 200 hours (50 to 100 sorties) per year. There are usually two pilots for each combat aircraft, so in a normal year these 500 aircraft would only fly some 75,000 sorties and in a 20-day period, only some 4,000 sorties. Thus wartime demands have combat aircraft flying six times as many sorties for a major offensive. This makes a big difference in terms of supplies.

Thus the three-week air offensive would gobble up 850,000 tons of fuel, munitions, and spare parts. On average, each aircraft has about 50 support troops working on the ground. The 500-aircraft force would thus equal 25,000 troops. But we cannot leave out the other half of the air strength involved. For every combat aircraft, there will be one noncombat aircraft. This gives us a total force of 1,000 aircraft, with a total troop strength of 50,000. Using our half-ton-per-man-per-day yardstick, we have this force using 25,000 tons a day, or 500,000 tons over this 20-day period. This tonnage includes bringing in all the equipment needed to maintain these combat-zone airfields and support the aircraft flying off them. While the normal tonnage is 500,000 for 20 days, at times of peak activity, we can see how it can increase to nearly a million tons for the same 20 days. Normally, the aircraft are not operating at peak capacity, thus the difference in the two numbers. When there is not a major offensive, the noncombat aircraft will carry troops and supplies in and out, and some of the combat aircraft will fly reconnaissance and training missions.

The 1991 Gulf War air offensive used 2,700 aircraft of all types, flying 112,000 sorties over a six-week period. Over five million tons of supplies were brought into Saudi Arabia to support this air offensive.

Air forces have watched this growing need for tonnage and come up with many innovations to control it. Of course, the cruise missile and robotic aircraft are one solution, and may be the ultimate solution. But even these pilotless planes require logistical support. Ever since mass use of airpower was first employed during World War II, efforts got under way to cut down the logistical load such air operations entailed.

The World War II Experience

But during World War II, the mass use of airpower was seen as a novel application of technology in warfare and, for the United States, the best way American industrial might could be applied quickly. When America entered World War II in December 1941, it had a miniscule army, not much of an air force, and a navy that was in the midst of building a lot of new ships. What could America do in the meantime? It would be 1943 before America combat divisions and warships would be available in any numbers. American war planners quickly realized that the United States did have enormous capacity to produce light metals like aluminum and complex machinery like aircraft engines, and had the skilled manpower needed to assemble aircraft. A new warplane could be built in a few days, and one factory could turn out hundreds a month. Pilots took a few months to train and the resulting air force units could be flown across the ocean, or knocked down and shipped in crates, quickly. Moreover, the Germans and Japanese had already demonstrated how devastating airpower could be when used in conjunction with ground and naval forces. Americans decided to play their strong hand and built a lot of aircraft quickly. During World War II, the United States produced 283,000 aircraft. That was 44 percent of all the aircraft produced during the war. Getting these new aircraft and pilots into action was another matter, but American airpower hit the Germans and Japanese a lot more quickly than U.S. infantry and warships did. Below is the number of American combat aircraft in action overseas on the dates indicated.

Table 4 / U.S. Combat Aircraft in World War II

Date	USA Aircraft Overseas	Annual Production	% of World Production
December 1941	957	19,163	28%
June 1942	1,902		
December 1942	4,695	44,479	40%
June 1943	6,586		
December 1943	11,917	81,028	49%
June 1944	19,342		
December 1944	19,892	91,456	47%

These aircraft operated first from bases throughout the Pacific, then in Britain and North Africa, and moved to Italy in late 1943 and to France in mid-1944. By the end of the war, there were an even greater number operated by Allies, shipped as part of the Lend-Lease program, as well as thousands operating in the United States itself. In December 1941, America had 17,000 aircraft, at the end of the war, 107,000. Some 40,000 aircraft were lost, with 23,000 being combat losses. These operational and training accident losses were greater than combat losses, largely because of bad flying conditions, inability to provide first-rate maintenance in primitive overseas air bases, and the rush to train pilots. In order to maintain the growing frontline strength of aircraft units, it was necessary to ship an ever growing number of new planes overseas. Most aircraft flew overseas, being a form of supply that could transport itself to the battlefield. Thus America was able to use the quantity of aircraft technology, as well as improving technology itself, to gain an upper hand on distant battlefields.

The World War II experience convinced America that airpower was the key to any future military success, and this attitude, firmly held for over half a century, continues to drive U.S. military thinking.

Doing More with Less during World War II

BUT THE LOGISTICAL requirements of such a huge air fleet were enormous. Ever since World War II, air forces the world over have tried to do the same work with fewer, more reliable, aircraft. To a certain extent, this approach has succeeded. A single-engine, single-seat fighter-bomber can now deliver more bombs, over the same distance, as a four-engine, eleven-man World War II–era bomber. While aircraft have gotten much more efficient over the last fifty years, they have also gotten a lot more expensive. Even adjusting for inflation, your average modern fighter costs about three times as much as the most expensive World War II–era bomber (the B-29). It's human nature that once you have more resources, you come to expect you will be able to do more. While it took the United States over six months to mount its first offensive in World War II (August 1942, at Guadalcanal), we now expect to be able to do it in a few weeks, if not quicker.

There are sound reasons for moving faster, as it gives the bad guys less time to do evil things and ultimately makes it easier to defeat the enemy. The 1990 Iraqi invasion of Kuwait is the best current example. Had the Iraqis decided to keep advancing through Kuwait and two hundred miles into Saudi Arabia, they would have controlled a third of the world's oil reserves and over half the current production. The first thing that America did was fly in several hundred combat aircraft and their ground crews. At that point, had the Iraqis kept coming, it would have been a matter of how much aircraft munitions and spare parts could have been flown in to generate sorties against the advancing Iraqi tanks. No American commander wanted to test the air force assurances that fighter-bombers could do the job. Yet without those fighter-bombers, the Iraqis stood a good chance of pulling it off.

Comparing the weight of bombs, fuel, and spare parts needed to what can be delivered quickly by air, you discover that this puts a severe limitation on combat operations. U.S. transport aircraft were only able to deliver fifteen thousand to twenty thousand tons of matériel per month. While Saudi Arabia had supplies of jet fuel on hand, you still needed about ten tons of matériel per sortie. And you had to use the transport aircraft to fly in the ground crews and their equipment in the first place. At best, the transports could support some two hundred fighter-bomber sorties per day. U.S. carriers were coming into the area in a few days, but these ships are designed mainly to protect themselves at sea. This doctrine has changed since the dissolution of the Soviet Union in 1991 and the subsequent decline of the Soviet fleet. But even with this change in mission, the average carrier has enough bombs and aircraft fuel on board for only two hundred to three hundred ground-attack sorties. A somewhat greater number of air-defense sorties can be flown, and this is what the carriers did in the Persian Gulf, to defend themselves as well as nearby Coalition land bases. Carriers can only take on new supplies of bombs, fuel, and spare parts from supply ships, and these can take awhile to arrive. So, while carriers can arrive rather quickly, they are not a long-term solution to a distant crisis involving more than a few divisions of enemy troops.

Attacking ground targets has become more effective in the last half century, but it is still rather inaccurate. Your average fighter-bomber still doesn't have the whiz-bang fire-control systems that got so much attention during the Gulf War. These systems are very expensive, and less than 20 percent of Western aircraft have them. So each sortie is doing well if it can destroy two or three enemy tanks or armored vehicles, and the average is often just one ground vehicle per sortie. A lot depends on the terrain and what kind of air force the enemy has. In deserts, you can do a lot more damage from the air. If there are mountains and forests, not to mention bad weather, you do a lot less. If the foe is coming cross-country with an armored division (over five hundred armored vehicles and two thousand trucks), it will take a thousand sorties to stop that one division (or at least bang it up so much it halts or retreats).

Technology has its limitations.

Putting Troops on the Ground

WHILE AIRCRAFT CAN get there first, ground troops have to get there eventually to settle most overseas crises. As much as people might wish otherwise, there are few diplomatic crises that can be taken care of using only firepower. Even the early 1990s crisis in Bosnia required some friendly ground troops in the danger zone. While the nations contributing these troops were reluctant to see them get involved in heavy combat, it was realized that this particular peacekeeping mission could not call in bombers unless it had people on the ground to decide who was good and who was bad (and eligible for a bombing).

In most cases, such as a crisis in the Persian Gulf, Korea, Taiwan, or wherever, ground troops will quickly, or eventually, be needed to settle the matter once and for all. Getting the troops there fast enough and in sufficient numbers is a technological problem that has still not found a complete solution.

As early as World War II, it was proved that you could send some troops by air, often a barely adequate number, into a situation and come out a winner. But just sending in ground troops by air has a lot of drawbacks. The major shortcoming is that the airborne troops are rather more lightly armed and supplied than their opponents. Coming in by air meant that you often must accept that the opposition will confront you with greater numbers and more heavily armed. The incoming troops must have some degree of surprise and a substantial superiority in training, leadership, and morale to prevail. German paratroopers did it this way when they invaded Belgian fortifications in early 1940 and the island of Crete a year later. But the latter battle was such a costly and close-run thing that the Germans backed off from further major airborne operations.

Not so the Allies. American and British paratroopers participated in a number of successful landings in 1943 and 1944. Even the failure in the battle for Arnhem ("the Bridge Too Far," September 1944) did not dim Western enthusiasm for dropping lightly armed troops out of airplanes onto more numerous and more heavily armed opponents. After World War II, there were several successful operations in Africa, the Middle East, and Asia. But there were also several failures and some questionable successes. French airborne operations in Indochina were often failures. America finally realized that paratroopers are too lightly armed and too scattered on landing to be successful most of the time. So U.S. troops began to come in by helicopter. While this method brought the infantry into an area with more precision and more heavily armed, it also greatly reduced the distance the airborne troops could cover before they hit their targets. Helicopters had a range of two hundred miles at best, while paratroopers could fly over two thousand miles before jumping out onto their targets. To deal with this conundrum, America maintained nearly two divisions' worth of paratroopers plus several divisions of troops who could travel by helicopter.

The Soviet Union, and many smaller nations, followed the American example. But in practice, these nations maintained these elite air-transportable troops so they would have some very capable and mobile troops for all manner of emergencies. The airborne (landing via parachute) and air-landing (via helicopter) troops most often came into the combat zone via truck or commercial airliner.

Pre-positioning

ONE SOLUTION TO getting a lot of fire-power to a distant trouble spot in a hurry is to store the equipment in the area. That way, all you have to do is fly in the troops; they use the pre-positioned equipment, and there you are.

Getting heavy weapons (armored vehicles, artillery, and lots of ammunition) to a battle zone takes a lot longer than flying in paratroopers. The additional time is a big problem, because whatever crisis created the need for troops to go in will only get worse the longer it takes for the troops to get there. The classic example is the 1990 Iraqi invasion of Kuwait. Within a few days, American paratroopers were brought in (via an airport, not parachutes) and had only their light weapons with them. Because Iraq chose not to continue its advance into Saudi Arabia, there was time (about a month) to bring in U.S. Marines (with their heavier equipment). After several months, it was possible to ship in U.S. Army tank units from Europe and North America.

For decades, pre-positioning had been used in Europe, where several divisions' worth of equipment had been stockpiled. Each year, the system was tested as the personnel for several brigades were flown over to take the equipment out for field exercises. Before the 1991 Gulf War, heavy equipment for a marine division was stockpiled on an Indian Ocean island (Diego Garcia, 2,500 miles to the south), and this was brought north to Saudi Arabia after the 1990 Iraqi invasion. Based on that experience, arrangements were made to stockpile heavy equipment in the Persian Gulf.

The problem with the pre-positioning of equipment is that it's expensive. Two sets of equipment have to be maintained for the unit in question: one that is used wherever they are normally based, and the other set (maintained by civilian technicians) at the potential trouble spot. Moreover, you need sets of equipment at each trouble spot and, to make sure all this works, you have to regularly fly some (or all) of the troops over to take the pre-positioned equipment out to make sure everything is in order.

A variation on the pre-positioning concept is to keep additional sets of equipment on ships. These commercial vessels can be moved to wherever a trouble spot develops, or simply kept anchored nearby an area for as long as needed. This is more expensive than storing equipment in a land base. Not just any ship will do. You will need relatively speedy ships that have their own unloading equipment. This type of ship is more expensive. For an armored division you'll need several of these ships, say half a billion dollars' worth. The ships need crews on them at all times and the ships have to be maintained even when at anchor somewhere.

There are new types of high-speed ships being built that can move at twice the speed of earlier high-speed ships (about forty knots, versus twenty knots). These ships are nearly twice as expensive, but allow pre-positioned equipment to arrive at most trouble spots in a week or so rather than a month or more.

Technology has been of limited use in solving the problems of getting troops to where they are most needed in a hurry. This has become more of a problem now that the cold war is over and attention has turned to dealing with a large number of local crises. In the past, these local wars and massacres would have been talked about, but there would not have been, as there is now, a public outcry over "doing something." Even the things that can be done, like buying more heavy transport aircraft or high-speed transport ships, are not popular with the military or the taxpayers. This is a bit of a paradox. But the troops would rather have better weapons and equipment for battlefield use. Freighter aircraft and fast transport ships are a hard sell when trying to get a military budget passed. Although the American Congress forced the navy to buy some fast transports in the 1980s, this was not normal. It's much more common for new weapons to be bought. They are an easier sell to the public and have enough expensive components built in enough congressional districts to get the votes needed.

Moving Around

JUST GETTING TO the battlefield in a timely manner is a major chore. But once you are there you encounter many more problems that can be solved, somewhat, by technology. The key to battlefield mobility is machines that move. There are those machines that fight (tanks and other armored vehicles) and those that carry the enormous quantity of supplies needed to keep all the machines going.

The number of trucks in armies has increased at a faster rate than the fighting vehicles, and there are now thousands of "flying trucks" in the form of helicopters. Throughout the twentieth century, the logistical "tail" has grown far more rapidly than the fighting "tooth." World War II was won by two armies with quite different attitudes toward the "tooth-to-tail" ratio. The Russian army put most of its troops up front in the fighting units. Its tooth-to-tail ratio was nearly one to one. The Western armies, in particular the United States, had a lot larger tail, the tail outnumbering the tooth by more than three to one. Both of these army types were victorious. The fact that both used different tooth-to-tail ratios led to an ongoing debate over how large a tail was necessary.

On one side of the debate, there were proponents of the lean tail the Russians used. But the other side pointed out that the Russians were fighting in their own country while the United States had to send troops thousands of miles, and supply them over the same distance. Also, when it became known how meagerly the Russian troops were supplied with medical care, food, shelter, and so on, attitudes changed. The final argument against the lean tail was the huge noncombat losses the Russians took. It was also pointed out that the Japanese had an even leaner tooth-to-tail ratio than the Russians, and suffered even heavier privation losses.

As the lessons of World War II were fully absorbed, the size of the logistical tail in all armies increased. Even the Russians realized that they would get more out of their troops if they supplied them more generously. But the Russians were caught up, as was everyone else, in the rush to add more weapons and equipment to their combat units. There was a lot more electronics gear, both for communications and electronic warfare. This stuff needed a lot of maintenance, and that meant technicians and spare parts. There were a lot more weapons and more complex weapons.

Thus modern, "Western-style" armies are represented by swarms of trucks and people in uniform who do not fight. (Or at least that is not their principal job, and if forced to fight they would not do a very good job of it.) The most common opponents of these armies are locals who are not organized into a formal army, or at least not an army as we know it. Bosnia, Somalia, Rwanda, Chechnya and a dozen other post–cold war battlefields have all shown this pattern. The local "irregulars" live off the land and the humanitarian aid that usually accompanies the foreign troops. The irregulars are part-time troops, turning out with their weapons when they feel like it, and then turning into civilians again.

When, as was the case with Iraq in 1991, there is a more formally organized army to fight, Western armies must deploy huge numbers of trucks (over one hundred thousand in this case) and tons (seven million) of supplies before a proper battle can be fought. The commanders of these troops know that their people can fight with a lot less, and are prepared to do so. But this would result in many more friendly casualties and this would be politically unacceptable. It would also be the end of the military career and reputation of any general that was in charge of such a low-budget battle. So it is accepted by political leaders and military commanders that you don't send in the tooth unless you also put in all the tail.

The sheer mass of supplies needed to sustain a modern army has made use of new technology. Fifty years ago the standard military truck carried two to three tons of cargo. Today, it's more common to see trucks that carry five, ten, or more tons. Forklifts and other devices for quickly loading and unloading trucks are common. Portable fuel and water pipelines are common, and these can be laid down and taken up again at the rate of many miles a day. Helicopters are used widely, as are freighter aircraft that can land on dirt fields or highways.

The volume of supplies going to a modern army, as well as the sheer number of different items, has made the use of computers and inventory tracking systems mandatory. Bar-code readers and microchips attached to cargo containers are more common. Military transportation and logistics has become big business, if only because it is what most of the troops are doing these days. There are more soldiers engaged in moving supplies than in fighting the foe.

Throughout history, the most successful generals have been those who mastered the movement of supplies, and this has become even more important today. It doesn't sound, or look, very exciting, but that's the way it is. For every tank and its crew of three or four men advancing to the fight, there are twenty or more men, and often women, behind that tank (often only a few kilometers behind) bringing up the fuel, ammunition, and other supplies the tank needs to keep going. Along with all the supplies comes a swarm of technicians and other administrative type "soldiers" to keep the entire organization running.

High-Speed Warfare

MODERN ARMIES ARE not just more heavily armed, and more lavishly supported, versions of their World War II ancestors. Modern armies are much faster. While they may not move forward much faster than they did in the 1940s, they move about at a higher speed. This is all the result of technology. But, as you have seen, it is a good news/bad news situation. While that much larger logistical tail slows down forward movement of the entire army, helicopters and all those lively modern tanks allow the troops to dash back and forth while under fire at a much higher speed. This is not just for show, for when fighting, "speed is life." Russian T-34 tanks were so successful during World War II largely because they had more get-up-and-go when moving about on the battlefield. Many decades went by before equally frisky Western tanks were built.

Oddly enough, and this is an important point to remember, Americans didn't discover this until North Korean T-34s were captured intact in 1950 and tested. The speed and agility of these tanks came as quite a shock. While American forces had access to information about Russian equipment during World War II, either from captured German records or from Russian military attachés, the knowledge did not become common. It did during the Korean War, and began to influence the design of future American tanks.

By the 1980s, most tanks were not only twice as heavy as their World War II counterparts, but also nearly twice as fast and mobile. Infantry now kept up with the tanks in equally fast armored vehicles. Most artillery was self-propelled. All that kept these speedy behemoths from breaking battlefield distance records was their enormous fuel consumption and the difficulty their fuel trucks had in keeping up.

Adding more speed, and fuel requirements, to the modern battlefield was the widespread introduction of helicopters during the 1960s. Military helicopters were introduced at the end of World War II by the U.S. Army Air Force. Choppers were restricted to transportation, reconnaissance, and medical evacuation until the 1960s, when the UH-1 (the "Huey") was introduced. This was a much more efficient design, and made possible large-scale use of helicopters on the battlefield. Late in the 1960s, the UH-1 design was modified to produce the first helicopter gunship, the AH-1. This was a purely combat aircraft, but unlike any conventional warplane. Heavily armed with machine guns and rockets, the AH-1 could hover like a helicopter (which it was) and blast away like a warplane (which it also was, at least as far as firepower went). The military got one benefit from Vietnam: practical knowledge on how to use helicopters on the battlefield.

In the 1960s, helicopters were the first really radical new weapon for ground warfare since tanks first appeared some fifty years earlier. Tanks provided mobility, and some protection, to their users. Helicopters provided a lot more mobility, but were more vulnerable. During the Vietnam War, helicopters flew 36 million sorties. But as vulnerable as they appeared, flying slowly over a hostile battlefield, only 4,642 were lost. That's one loss for every 7,786 sorties. Only 3,500 crew members were lost for those 4,642 choppers lost, and only 1,755 passengers. Helicopters were a lot safer than they looked, even though about half the losses were for noncombat reasons. These often occurred when pilots took their birds out in nasty weather to pick up wounded troops, or simply to accomplish the mission. While their aircraft were more reliable, Vietnam-era helicopter pilots thought of themselves more like the fearless young men in their primitive fabric-and-wire biplanes of World War I. The UH-1 flew slowly and close to the ground. The highly maneuverable birds gave pilots the feeling they could do anything, and often they did. The chopper pilots felt a real closeness, psychological and physical, to the ground troops they supported.

The main problem with the UH-1 (and helicopters in general) was range. The low cruising speed of about a hundred miles an hour was not a real problem, but the fact that these birds could only stay in the air for about a hundred minutes was. Making allowances for a fuel reserve (for emergencies), the range from a helicopter's base was only sixty to seventy miles. And helicopters did need their bases. Several man-hours of maintenance (at a minimum) was needed for each hour in the air and, more importantly, some six hundred pounds of fuel were consumed for each flying hour. Helicopter bases were gas stations and repair shops, with several ground-support troops for each chopper supported. Fuel was the major problem, and was usually trucked in. With a useful load of about two tons, the UH-1s could (and sometimes did) fly in their own fuel to bases deep in the bush. But, basically, helicopters were tied to their bases. For example, a combat aviation battalion would have some five hundred troops, 34 helicopters (24 UH-1s, 6 AH-1s and 4 small observation birds), and nearly 60 trucks. It was as if the helicopters were attached to their base by a rubber band. The choppers could go out, but they were yanked back once they had used up nearly half the fuel on board.

Even with their range limitations and seeming vulnerability, helicopters changed battlefield tactics. While aircraft had, for over fifty years, allowed radio-equipped observers to call in artillery or bomber strikes, the helicopters could now bring in infantry to finish the job. As always, victory is not final until your infantry have defeated the enemy's. In Vietnam, the North Vietnamese and Viet Cong feared the helicopter-borne American infantry. Not only were the U.S. groundpounders dangerous in themselves, but they were also able to clearly identify enemy infantry positions and bring in artillery fire and air strikes. Indeed, it was this last capability that the enemy feared most, for there was no defense against a sudden artillery or bomber strike. You could at least shoot it out with the American infantry. There was no escaping the shells and bombs.

Capitalizing on their artillery superiority, U.S. commanders developed tactics whereby helicopters would airlift guns, ammunition, and crews to hilltop firing positions, thus extending the reach of the artillery. Infantry would also be flown in and the entire hill fortified and the North Vietnamese challenged to try and take it. Should the enemy assault these forward fire bases, bombers, gunships, and nearby artillery would take a heavy toll. If things got too hot, helicopters could evacuate the hilltop garrison.

Even in Vietnam, where air-landed infantry could fight on equal terms with the North Vietnamese light infantry, most helicopter sorties were combat support. While getting people moved around the battlefield quickly was useful, getting things moved quickly was equally beneficial. What the troops appreciated most in the combat zone was the quick evacuation of casualties, both to the aid stations to the rear and from there to hospitals farther back. Helicopters proved to be a logistical lifesaver too, moving food, ammunition, spare parts, and equipment quickly to where it was needed.

The extensive use of helicopters to move people and things around denied the enemy many opportunities to ambush trucks carrying the same things cross-country. When truck convoys did move into hostile territory, they often did so with helicopters hovering above to spot ambushes, and sometimes a gunship or two came along to deal with any enemy troops encountered. This forced the enemy to make more attacks on U.S. bases, situations in which the American troops had a big advantage.

Helicopters added a new dimension to warfare in many ways that no one anticipated. While conventional aircraft were still much in evidence, the helicopters were down there with the troops. The soldiers on the ground regarded the choppers as *their* air force. And indeed it was, as any ground unit could quickly get helicopter support via a call on the radio. Getting air force bombers to help out required a lot of planning, as well as special radios to communicate with them. Helicopters were always there, right on the ground some of the time, and crewed by people wearing the same uniform.

Most, but not all, of the helicopters used in Vietnam were the UH-1 and its AH-1 gunship variant. There were a lot of smaller observation choppers and larger transport birds. This is still the case today, when the U.S. Army has some seven thousand helicopters. About 20 percent are gunships, 30 percent the older UH-1, 20 percent the newer UH-60 (gradually replacing the UH-1), and the rest smaller scout choppers or larger cargo birds.

With this, the largest helicopter fleet in the world, the U.S. Army intends to change the tempo and style of warfare in any future campaign. The world already got a preview of this new style of fighting during the 1991 Gulf War. American ground forces broke speed records with their lightning advance. Several other things happened during that hundred-hour battle that many observers may have missed. An airmobile division (the 101st) not only advanced by air 120 kilometers into the Iraqi desert, but landed and set up a base so that hundreds of gunships and transport helicopters could advance another hundred kilometers into the Euphrates River valley and cut southern Iraq in half. This was the biggest helicopter assault since Vietnam and far more ambitious. The capacity and reliability of the equipment had improved since the 1970s, and many logistical problems had been solved.

The Benefits of Moving Just a Little Faster

A STUDY OF history shows that those armies that could simply move and react a little faster on the battlefield had a significant advantage. This was noted during the 1967 and 1973 Arab-Israeli wars. The 1973 war was a particular shocker, as the Arab armies, previously thought inept, managed to make progress against the Israelis. More worrisome was the Arab use of Soviet equipment and, to a large extent, Soviet training and tactics. The Israelis recovered from their early defeats and, using superior speed and American equipment, won the war. But at great cost. The Russians, based on their World War II experience, had long been preaching speed in executing battlefield plans. American military leaders realized they would have to be even speedier, and helicopters were one way to achieve that speed.

Although the Vietnam War showed that helicopters were useful in combat, an experience shared by Russian troops in Afghanistan during the 1980s, it wasn't until 1991 that anyone got to see helicopters used on a battlefield against armored forces on a large scale.

Other nations with large helicopter fleets (such as Russia) or those that wanted to use helicopters in a big way, or find ways to deal with nations that did, found the helicopter assault into Iraq rather shocking. Here was the type of airmobile operation that had long been theorized about and talked about, actually happening under combat conditions. The U.S. troops were constantly moving, seemingly around the clock. The relentless nature of the advance, and the ability of the Americans to instantly put devastating firepower on any Iraqi unit accidentally, or deliberately, getting in the way, caused most Iraqi troops to just surrender at the first opportunity. The Americans were doing it, performing a truly new and overwhelming form of mobile warfare. And they were doing it quickly, efficiently, and apparently without any problems.

But there were problems, and the Americans were aware of them. High-speed warfare involves more than fast-moving tanks and aircraft. The high-speed operations greatly increased the risk of either blundering into the enemy or shooting at your own troops. While much was made of the number of friendly-fire casualties during the Gulf War, it could have been a great deal worse had not a lot of precautions already been taken.

Direction from Above

THE MAJOR PROBLEMS of high-speed warfare are control and coordination, and they have been known for a long, long time. The potential for disaster was first noted during World War II, when operations involving over a thousand aircraft in the air at once demonstrated how out of hand things could get. Forming up all these airplanes, each traveling at 150 to 250 miles an hour, and sending them toward distant enemy targets in some semblance of order was much more difficult than it first appeared. Although more capable aircraft appeared after World War II, these were also faster aircraft (more than twice as fast as their World War II predecessors). As the cold war proceeded, thousands of combat aircraft formed up on both sides of the Iron Curtain in central Europe. By the 1970s, it was obvious that any future air war would be a mess unless some way were found to control all those aircraft efficiently.

This problem had been noted even in World War II, but no technical solution was available. That is, you could not mount a very powerful radar in an aircraft. The U.S. Navy did plan to use radar-equipped TBF Avengers to control the fighter screen protecting the fleet from Japanese suicide bombing attacks during the planned 1945 invasion of Japan. But the invasion never came off and the navy pursued the radar-equipped control aircraft at a more leisurely pace. The E-1 airborne early-warning aircraft first flew in 1956 and entered service in 1960. While mainly used to extend the radar coverage of a naval task force, this type of aircraft also had a vital role in controlling large numbers of friendly warplanes in air battles.

The new U.S. Air Force also kept working on the idea of airborne control aircraft, and waited for technology to catch up with its needs. By 1953, the air force was able to send propeller-driven transports (EC-121 Lockheed Constellations), equipped with powerful radar and radio equipment, off the coasts of North America to watch for Russian bombers. Beginning in 1965, the first of thirty EC-121s were sent to Vietnam, where they controlled combat operations in the northern part of the country. As useful as these aircraft were, it was obvious that, with a little more technology, one could *really* control air-combat operations. New computer and radar technology made this possible by the late 1960s.

The solution came in the form of a four-engine jet transport converted to a flying radar station and control tower. This was the E-3 AWACS (airborne warning and control system), whose development began in the late 1960s. The first prototype was flying in the late 1970s, and it went into regular use in 1982.

Flying far enough inside friendly territory to avoid enemy antiaircraft missiles, the AWACS has a radar range of between two hundred kilometers (for small aircraft or cruise missiles flying close to the ground) and six hundred kilometers (for large aircraft flying at high altitude). The AWACS tracks several hundred friendly and enemy aircraft at once. The AWACS acts as an airborne command center for aircraft. Friendly planes are kept out of each other's way. (There was not a single friendly air-to-air collision during the 1991 Gulf War.) Enemy aircraft are spotted and identified, and friendly interceptors are assigned to take care of the hostile planes.

One or more AWACS are used to control an air operation, and each can stay up eleven hours at a time, or up to twenty-two hours with refueling and extra crew on hand to man the equipment. The AWACS functions as a combination radar platform and command center. Once in action during the Gulf War, other uses were found. The AWACS could spot a ballistic missile (like a Scud) as the missile was taking off, and nearby combat aircraft were directed to the launch site to destroy the launch vehicles or, if they were lucky, missiles that had not launched yet. If the AWACS was close enough, enemy aircraft could be spotted taking off from their airfields. Naturally, friendly fighters were promptly sent to shoot down these enemy planes before they could even gain much altitude.

During its first wartime workout, during the 1991 Gulf War, the AWACS proved its worth, often in more ways than anticipated. The use of over a hundred tankers to refuel combat aircraft would not have been possible without the AWACS being there to efficiently link tankers and aircraft needing fuel. Forming up the Wild Weasels, and coordinating their use with the bombers they escorted, was much easier using an AWACS. Just keeping track of who was who and going where would not have been possible without the AWACS.

The communications equipment on board an AWACS allows information gathered by one AWACS to be quickly shared with other AWACS in the vicinity, other combat aircraft in the area, and units at sea or on the ground. This function, which was eventually made to work, gave generals and admirals the goal of trying to link together all the sensors and communications of every ship, aircraft, and ground unit in the area. But first, an AWACS for ground operations was needed.

Even before the AWACS was finished developing, the army commanders realized that they could use a similar aircraft to control their units on the ground. So in the 1970s they began working with the air force to develop the E-8 JOINT STARS (or J-STARS). Like the AWACS, this aircraft had a radar, but on the bottom of the aircraft, rather than a saucer-shaped device on the top. The primary task of J-STARS is tracking ground activity, and this aircraft was designed to better integrate air and ground operations by quickly locating targets for our aircraft and coordinating those attacks with friendly ground operations. The radar has two modes: wide area (showing a 25-by-20-kilometer area) and detailed (4,000 by 5,000 meters). Each E-8 has ten radar displays on board plus a dozen or more on the ground with army headquarters units. All the radar displays could communicate with each other. The radar simultaneously supported both modes and covers several different chunks of terrain being watched. While an operator might have to wait a minute or two for an update on his screen, this was not a problem because of the relatively slow pace of ground operations. The radar could see out to several hundred kilometers, and each screenful of information could be saved and brought back later to compare to another view. In this manner, operators could track movement of ground units. Operators could also use the detail mode to pick out specific details of ground units (fortifications, buildings, vehicle deployments, etc.).

For the first time in history, commanders were able to see and control mechanized forces over a wide area in real time. J-STARS was able to perform its primary function, getting bombers to ground targets with a minimum of fuss. As fast as the ground forces were, they could be slowed down by enemy armored units. With J-STARS, the enemy armored units could be spotted before friendly tanks came into range. Bombers and gunships could then work over the enemy armor so that when the friendly tanks reached the scene there was less resistance to slow down the advance. Keep in mind that, even with this prompt air support, most of the enemy armored vehicles destroyed in the Gulf War were done in by Coalition tanks and IFVs (Bradley infantry fighting vehicles). Darkness, dust, and sandstorms, even if they didn't always prevent any air attacks at all, always reduced the effect of these attacks. Not so with the U.S. M-1 tanks. It still takes ground forces to stomp ground forces.

Without this "eye in the sky," aircraft and tanks could not be so well coordinated. So meticulous was the coordination that friendly ground units were seen as they approached an area where bombers were pounding the enemy, and were ordered to halt until the bombing was finished. This was frustrating for many of the tank commanders, but were it not for the J-STARS, friendly armored vehicles would have entered the battle area and gotten hit by their own aircraft and helicopters. J-STARS also prevented different friendly units from running into each other with cannons blazing. This was a common occurrence in previous wars. It happened a lot less in the Gulf War.

During the Persian Gulf War, J-STARS performed its designed mission well and speeded up the development process (and guaranteed the spending of billions of dollars on additional J-STARS aircraft). The two E-8s flew forty-nine missions during Desert Shield and (mostly) Desert Storm, each lasting about eleven hours. The success of the J-STARS energized the movement to electronically "network" all of the army's sensors and communications so that commanders could get an accurate picture of what was going on, and information could be quickly shared.

The success of J-STARS and AWACS also gave a boost to other "big airplane" projects. The one that benefited the most was the airborne laser. The airborne laser (ABL) is designed to detect and destroy enemy ballistic missiles as they are slowly rising into the air after launch. The ABL uses a multimegawatt laser on a modified Boeing 747 to zap the missile, causing enough damage to either make it explode or ruin its aim. While it's preferable to destroy missiles before they can be launched, the next best alternative is to destroy them while their booster rockets are still firing. This has the advantage of attacking the missile when it's easiest to spot and destroy, and it means that debris falls back on enemy territory. The initial plan for the ABL was to zap enemy aircraft, and that's still a possibility. But there are still a lot of technical problems to be overcome before the ABL is a practical weapon.

Synchronization and Digitization

THE GULF WAR provided an opportunity to test two new buzzwords in the military, synchronization and digitization.

Synchronization meant more precise coordination of combat and support units, in order to allow even faster operations on the battlefield. In the past, tanks and support units (lots of men and equipment in trucks) could move a lot faster than commanders could keep track of things. This meant that units had to either halt until the boss could figure out who was on first and what to do next, or keep going and allow for a free-for-all. The Germans solved this problem somewhat by having the unit commander up front with the troops, while his chief of staff was back at headquarters taking care of the more mundane coordination problems and radioing the commander with updates. Meanwhile, the commander would be up front, able to see what was happening and to make decisions on the spot. The major drawback with this approach was that the commander could only be in one place at a time. The "commander up front" approach works for a battalion (500 to 800 men) or a regiment (2,000 to 4,000), but it breaks down a lot when the unit is a division (10,000 to 20,000) or an army (100,000 and up). Still, it often helped a lot, and was often decisive, for an army commander to be up where the action was. During World War II, many generals (Rommel, Patton, etc.) used the technique with great success.

Synchronization is a deliberate attempt to find out what aspects of running a combat unit slow down the flow of information and order. Find the bottlenecks and come up with better ways to do it. Often something as simple as changing the way radio messages are handled, or the format in which orders are given, can make a big difference. But all the work in this area led to the conclusion that communications had to be improved with new hardware. In effect, the goal is to enable the commander to run his unit (battalion, brigade, division, etc.) with a laptop computer and satellite hookup.

Synchronization also demands that you can make decisions more quickly than the enemy. To do this you never put any of your troops, or especially your leaders, in a situation in which they have to call any higher-ups to get permission to act in any situation they could have reasonably been expected to encounter. Your troops have to be able to think for themselves, not consult higher authority for every little thing. The net result is that, while the enemy is still figuring out what to do, or getting permission to do it, you are all over him. This works wonders on the battlefield.

Digitization comprises the nuts-and-bolts solution for synchronizing the vast amount of communications and sensor equipment armed forces now have. It's nothing radically new; warriors have sought ways to coordinate the exchange of information on the battlefield for thousands of years. But the appearance of vast numbers of radios and increasingly powerful sensors takes the coordination problem to a whole new level of difficulty. A crude example of this communications and sensor problem comes from the early days of World War II. Many warships had radar by the early 1940s, but at first often only one or two ships in a group would be so equipped. This ship, often a cruiser or battleship that was also the flagship, would spot the enemy first. Rather, the radar operator would spot the enemy, then notify the commander, who would then decide when to fire, and signal the other ships to aim for where the flagship's shells were exploding. Or perhaps the commander would first order star shells (illuminating shells, which give off a lot of light when they detonate) fired to reveal the enemy ships to all. You can see the communications problem. Digitization would have the other ships in the task force equipped with radar sets that could instantly see whatever the flagship's radar could see. Taking the digitization scheme one step further, all the ships' radars would be tied into the fire-control systems, so that the guns would automatically fire at the target once the task-force commander gave the word (electronically). Of course, all of that kind of technology was not available during World War II, but it is now. All the armies, navies, and air forces have to do is get everyone's electronic systems talking the same language and talking to each other. This is no small order.

Talking to Your Friends

FOR THE LAST fifty years, the proliferation of electronic devices in the military has, as is fairly normal, been done without much coordination. Air force, army, and navy radios cannot, with a few exceptions, talk to each other. There are often technical reasons for this, but when the same cacophony shows up in the aircraft radios of all three services, you have a problem. As long as these incompatibilities have existed, people in each service have tried to achieve some degree of standardization. Until recently, there was no strong push from the very top to do this. But now there is. And the prize is not simply interservice cooperation, but the benefits of instantly sharing information.

An example of the proposed digitization of the battlefield would be when, say, an air force fighter-bomber flying at night picked up an enemy tank formation on its FLIR (infrared, or heat-sensing, "radar.") The bomber can see the bad guys in the distance, but he hasn't got the ammunition on board to do anything about it. He hits a switch and passes the data over to army units below (if this isn't already being done automatically) so that the army troops can take advantage of the fighter-bomber's broader view of the battlefield. The army infantry battalion below passes the images and target location back to its supporting artillery battalion. Soon shells are landing on the enemy unit, and the friendly infantry battalion is headed for the target zone some kilometers distant in order to finish the job.

Right now, some U.S. Air Force fighter-bombers have FLIR. But if they spot something, they either have to attack it themselves, or radio the information back to their headquarters. The air force headquarters then radios the local army headquarters and, eventually, the army units in the area are notified. But that might be hours later, and the enemy unit might have moved on. The information, while valuable when fresh, becomes virtually useless after a few hours. Digitization, and the synchronization it makes possible, changes all of that.

Alas, digitization is not easily implemented. For one thing, it requires that new types of radios be used, preferably digital types. The first radios, and most of those still in use, are analog. That is, the transmissions depend on gradual differences in the electrical signal. Digital transmissions, which are becoming more common, send out a stream of zeros and ones (or "dits" and "dots."). Digital transmission allows for more information to be sent and with greater accuracy. Digital transmission depends on microprocessors (as used on personal computers, cellular phones, and all manner of other gadgets) to work, and these microprocessors are, every year, becoming cheaper and more powerful.

The most important hurdle, recognizing the need for digitization and synchronization, has already been taken care of. But it will take years to get the new radios in the hands of the troops. It will take more years to get the synchronization techniques worked out and perfected. But as long as the military leadership recognizes this as the way to go, work will continue on it. As U.S. troops get involved in combat over this period of transition, they will do so with greater degrees of digitization and synchronization. What works will be noted, as will what doesn't. The combat experiences will speed up things and, depending on how much combat exposure digitization and synchronization get, the new methods will arrive sooner (with more combat) or later (with less combat experience).

Moving and Feeding the Ships

WE COVER NAVAL logistics last, and separately from army and air force operations, because the navy is usually a force unto itself. Out at sea, the sailors are pretty much all by themselves.

Warships are by far the most agile combat units available. As fast and long-ranged as aircraft are, they are still tied to land bases. Aircraft are better thought of as "ships" that can fly out for a few hours, hammer something in the air or on the ground, and then return. Warships *are* bases that carry every-thing they need with them and can stay out at sea for months at a time. Orga-nized into task forces, usually around an aircraft carrier, plus up to a dozen cruisers, destroyers, and nuclear subs, warships prowl all over the globe. All this is not without its cost. Warships still have to be refueled and resupplied.

The current naval logistics situation is both the same as, and different than, that faced by land units. Because of automation, and the demise of the large Soviet fleet, there are now fewer sailors out there on fewer ships. The U.S. Navy now possesses the bulk of the world's large warships and thus dominates the high seas. But the more warships you send out, the more supply ships you must dispatch to maintain your fleet at sea.

Nuclear power has reduced the need for bunker oil (for ship propulsion). But many of the nuclear-propelled ships are aircraft carriers that need prodi-gious amounts of aircraft fuel and other supplies for the five thousand to six thousand sailors that man these huge vessels. The aircraft are used constantly, and each time one of these jets leaves a carrier deck, another five or more tons of fuel, munitions, and spare parts are consumed. Thus the nuclear carriers have to take on fresh supplies up to twice a week. This frequent resupply of aircraft carriers is a custom founded in the World War II experience of aircraft-carrier operations. Those many task forces contained over a hundred carriers and thousands of other ships. Some of these World War II task forces stayed at sea for over six months at a time. The logistical problems of modern fleets are nothing new. The problems, and solutions, have been known for over half a century.

Nuclear submarines are a different matter, and the only new element to ap-pear since World War II. Because of their small crew size (80 to 160 sailors), they can ship out with ninety days' worth of supplies on board and not surface until three months later. This is now seen as the wave of the future. If the crews can be made smaller and missiles substituted for most of the aircraft, you can "sortie" ships like you do aircraft. While the most an aircraft can stay out is twelve hours or so, ships, at least nuclear-propelled ones, can be sent out for months without resupply. This is actually a return to the days of sail-propelled warships, when resupply at sea was rarely done and ships would stay at sea for months, until wear and tear forced them to land for repairs.

Nuclear power is very expensive, doubling the cost of most warships; thus oil propulsion will remain the standard for the foreseeable future. The princi-pal resupply item at sea will remain, as it has been for over fifty years, fuel. Depending on the tempo of operations (how much high-speed steaming is be-ing done), surface ships with small crews could refuel as little as once every few weeks. A carrier task force can easily consume over five thousand tons of supplies (mainly fuel) a day. Depending on how far the task force is operating from friendly ports, three or more groups of resupply ships will be shuttling back and forth from these ports to the task force with fresh supplies.

Naval logistics is more expensive than the land-unit equivalent, as the fleet has to use specially built ships to move the supplies forward. Sometimes these ships of the "fleet train" have to be guarded from hostile ships and aircraft, making their use even more expensive, especially if some get sunk or damaged in enemy waters.

9

Gold-Plated Bombs

U SING TECHNOLOGY TO make bombs, bullets, and other flying objects go where you want them to is a twentieth-century innovation. Late in the nineteenth century, metal and instrument manufacturing became accurate enough to produce artillery that could fire a shell ten miles or more and hit a target it was meant to hit. Before that, you had to fire a lot of shells at a not-very-distant target in order to guarantee a hit. These first twentieth-century artillery shells were the first guided missiles, even though they were only guided by the precise amount of propellant used, the exact alignment of the gun barrel, and the accurate work of surveyors and mapmakers. This was, at the time, a true triumph of technology. These techniques were given an extensive work-out during World War I, when the technology was perfected.

Right after World War I came more technological advances that produced bomber aircraft. These planes were designed specifically to carry, and drop accurately, large quantities of bombs. By the mid-1930s, there were twin-engine bombers like the German Ju-88 that could carry three tons of bombs, and the single-engine Ju-87 that could carry a ton of bombs. Even before World War II began, the Ju-87 and Ju-88 (and similar aircraft) found that bombs dropped from aircraft were missiles of much less accuracy than artillery shells. This was a major problem for bombers until guided bombs were developed. The Germans developed radio-guided bombs during World War II, and sank some warships with them. But these guided missiles were crude and not much use except at sea, where the target (a large ship) stood out at a distance and gave the bomb controller in the launching aircraft sufficient time to guide the bomb onto the target.

As is often the case, bomber pilots improvised in order to obtain results. One- and two-engine bombers would "dive-bomb." That is, they would dive on the target and release their bombs when they were so close they were assured of getting a hit. The downside of this was the amount of fire from the ground these dive-bombers were exposed to. If there were enough enemy antiaircraft guns around the target, it might be virtually impossible for a dive-bomber to get through. Not only would many of the dive-bombers be shot down, but even those that were not would find their aim spoiled by all the enemy fire. Early in the war, it was not understood how lethal (read "accurate") dive-bombing could be and how effective strong antiaircraft defenses were against dive-bombing. By 1942, it was becoming increasingly dangerous to engage in dive-bombing.

A safer approach was "level bombing." With this method, the bomber flew straight and level while the bombardier sighted the target below and released the bombs at the point calculated to give them the best chance of hitting the target. With level bombing, the quality of the bombardier and his special bombing sight made a big difference. If you did the level bombing at a few thousand feet up, you had a good chance of hitting something. But at that altitude, you were still exposed to a lot of antiaircraft fire. Flying higher reduced the amount of fire from the 20mm and 40mm heavy machine guns, but degraded bombing accuracy considerably.

When the Allies introduced heavy (four-engine) bombers like the Lancaster and the B-17, in 1941, it was necessary to drop the bombs at altitudes over ten thousand feet, in order to avoid the numerous small-caliber, under 75mm, antiaircraft guns. The United States developed what it thought was the ultimate bombsight: the Norden bombsight. But even with this marvelous bit of engineering, accuracy was poor. On average, a B-17 with a Norden bombsight could expect half its bombs to fall within a thousand meters of the intended target. This was also known as the Circular Error Probable (or CEP). Thus the B-17 bombs had a CEP of one thousand meters. This accuracy problem was overcome by using large numbers of bombers, often a thousand at a time, to hit a target.

Since the target was often a large factory complex, the fact that 9,070 bombs (each leaving a six- to seven-meter-wide crater) would be needed to hit one eighteen-by-thirty-meter building was less meaningful. There would be dozens of buildings spread over several acres in such a complex. The B-17s were able to destroy a lot of their intended targets by simply depending on some accuracy and large numbers of bombs dropped all at once on the same target. Of course, even to obtain this accuracy it was necessary to attack in daylight, when enemy fighters and antiaircraft guns had a better view of *their* targets.

The British, who flew about as many bombing missions over Europe as American bombers, had another solution: saturation bombing of cities at night. While there were some industrial facilities and many administrative organizations in the cities, the most common target was the German people. This did serve a military purpose, as the Germans had to divert military resources to defend the cities (without much success) and to deal with all the damage. Millions of Germans were thus unavailable to support the war effort.

The British method, after much trial and error, was to send in a few aircraft as pathfinders. These planes carried electronic navigation equipment, expert bombardiers, and a few incendiary bombs. When the target was found, even if the sky was overcast (the electronic navigation was used), the incendiary bombs were dropped, starting fires in the target area. Behind the pathfinder were up to a thousand bombers, who would drop their bombs on the fires below. Crude, but effective. American bombers used this in daylight when it was overcast; otherwise the target could not be found.

Over three million tons of bombs were dropped during World War II. To say that this was a futile effort is nonsense. The bombing did not always do what it was supposed to do, but it did do a lot of damage and, in many cases, won battles that would otherwise have been lost. But when the war ended, there was a vigorous debate over what kind of bombing was the most effective, and what future technologies might bring to this new weapon.

Precision Bombing That Works

AS JET AIRCRAFT were introduced after World War II, bombing became even more difficult. The slowest speed of the jets was about twice the minimum speed of the older prop-driven aircraft. Higher speed led to less bombing accuracy. This was somewhat counteracted with more accurate bombing sights, incorporating computers and better optics. During World War II, advances had been made on the primitive sights used for bombing. Pilots were trained to calculate the effect of their altitude, speed, and angle relative to the ground before releasing their bomb. There was also enormous opportunity to practice with real bombs. After all, there was a war going on. It was clear, however, that in peacetime an air force could not allow its pilots to practice that much in order to perfect their bombing skills. Technology would have to make up for the lost practice opportunities.

By 1945, pilots and aircraft designers could see that in the future there would be even more capable aiming equipment, resulting in ever more accurate bombing by these swift jet aircraft. The speed of the jet bombers also allowed these aircraft to get in and out of the target area more quickly, giving the defending antiaircraft gunners less opportunity to hit the jets.

During the Korean and Vietnam Wars, jet fighter-bombers achieved a CEP of some 120 to 130 meters. This, however, meant that, on average, only 1 in 176 bombs would hit the same 18-by-30-meter target the World War II B-17s were going after. This was as accurate as electromechanical bombing sights could make it. One innovation that overcame some of the CEP problem was the introduction of cluster bombs during the 1960s. This involved filling a bomb with dozens or hundreds of smaller bombs. When dropped, the container would open and spread the bomblets (or "submunitions") over a wide area. The bomblets could be of any type, from hand-grenade types that attacked people, to incendiaries for burning things down, to high explosives for destroying things in general. A more recent type of bomblet is a small antitank weapon (a shaped charge) that detonates when it hits something hard (like the top armor of a tank). The antitank bomblet has enough penetrating power to get through the thinner top armor of a tank and kill or damage the tank in the process.

Computers were needed to make bombing still more accurate.

Fighter-bomber fire-control systems got their computers during the 1980s and by the 1991 Gulf War, a CEP of sixty to seventy meters was achieved. At this point, thirty bombs were required to hit that eighteen-by-thirty-meter target. These results were achieved by using the new computers as well as by taking advantage of another new device: the HUD (heads up display, which was a transparent glass panel in front of the pilot). On this HUD panel was displayed crucial information for navigation and bombing. In the HUD systems, the bombing data were coming from a bombing computer system that constantly calculated where the bomb would go if it was released at that instant. This made it much easier for the pilot to line up the ground target with the moving crosshairs (or diamond, or whatever) on the HUD. Then, when the HUD gave a signal that it was close enough to release the bomb, the pilot could do so with a good chance that the target would get hit.

To improve accuracy still more, the bomb would have to be guided.

As early as World War II, it was obvious that guided bombs were another solution for increasing bombing accuracy. The Germans had done it during the war, although only in a few cases. The guided bomb was nothing more than a bomb with small wings attached, which allowed the bomb to glide downward toward the ground instead of just dropping. Electrically controlled motors allowed a human controller to transmit radio commands to the bomb and guide it to the target. German research on this weapon began in the late 1930s, and by 1942 it had been perfected. The 1.5-ton Fritz-X was meant for use against ships, and the Germans expended 500 of these to damage or sink 79 ships (40 of them warships). Although 48 launch aircraft were lost in the process, this was still a notable achievement considering Allied air superiority and the considerable antiaircraft defenses found on, or around, most Allied ships. This latter characteristic made it increasingly impractical to use dive-bombers against Allied ships, something the Germans learned the hard way in the first years of the war.

The Fritz-X was a standard armor-piercing bomb containing four small wings and radio-controlled fins for guidance, plus flares to assist the operator in keeping the eleven-foot bomb in sight. Normally, it was dropped from an altitude of twenty thousand feet, while still some five kilometers from the target. This resulted in about forty seconds of flight time. The launching aircraft would throttle back to minimum speed (to avoid getting any closer to the ship's antiaircraft guns) while the operator guided the bomb in. The aircraft still had to release the bomb on a fairly accurate trajectory, as the operator could only adjust the distance traveled by about 500 meters and direction by about 350 meters. Still, achieving 14 percent hits was a lot better than what could be achieved by any other bombing method.

Allied researchers managed to duplicate the German technology during the war. Some three thousand U.S. AZON glide bombs were used in Europe. The AZON could only adjust the fall of the bomb laterally, and in Europe the bomber generals did not think that they were worth the trouble, as the bomber had to hang around for a few minutes until the bomb-guidance operator was finished. In the Pacific, it was a different story. There were no huge fleets of bombers available, and there were lots of difficult Japanese targets in places like Southeast Asia. Some five hundred AZONS were used to knock out twenty-seven bridges, several of which had resisted repeated attacks with conventional bombs.

As World War II was ending, two improved models (RAZON and TARZON) were completed. But with the end of the war, development was halted and the existing weapons were put into storage. When the Korean War came along in 1950, the stored bombs were taken out and used. Half of them were defective due to their years in storage. Even so, the RAZONs proved twice as effective as conventional bombing. The heavier, and more reliable, TARZON was used with spectacular success. Six targets were destroyed using only twenty-eight bombs. This was ten times as effective as conventional bombs.

The Navy had its own "smart bomb" development program which produced two even more remarkable weapons. First came BAT, a radar-guided thousand-pound bomb with more elaborate flight controls than the Army AZON series. In the last few months of the war, BAT proved quite successful in the Pacific attacking ships and bridges (both large metal targets the radar could spot and home in on.) With a range of sixteen to thirty-two kilometers (depending on altitude dropped from), this glide bomb looked like a miniature aircraft. A similar, and simpler, weapon was Felix. This was a kit that was attached to standard half-ton bombs. On the nose was attached a heat-seeking device. On the rear was placed a set of fins to guide the bomb as it glided to earth. With less than half the range of BAT, Felix worked well in tests but was put into production too late to be used in the Pacific war. Both BAT and Felix were potentially susceptible to countermeasures, but the Japanese had none for these weapons. But, again, when the Korean War was over, the guided bombs were withdrawn from service. Why? Mainly because the emphasis was on nuclear weapons. The air force did not want to divert funds to develop and build "exotic" conventional bombs.

This reluctance to energetically pursue "smart bomb" technology would prove a costly oversight in the 1960s, when the Vietnam War would again provide a nonnuclear war with heavily defended targets conventional bombers could not get at.

But work on guided bombs was not completely abandoned in the 1950s. The U.S. Navy went ahead and developed the Bullpup (AGM-12 in the USAF) for use against enemy ships. Work began in 1954 and the first model was put in service by 1959. It was a missile, rather than a guided bomb. Pre-1964 models weighed 571 to 1,800 pounds, had a 250- to 1,000-pound warhead, and had a range of 11 to 30 kilometers. Its rocket motor gave it a peak speed of over 1,700 kilometers an hour. This meant that the pilot, using his gunsight and a joystick, had fifteen to forty seconds to guide the missile to the target. It was a very popular weapon, with over thirty-five thousand being built. But the warhead was not large enough for many key land targets, like large bridges and bunkers. Moreover, while the Bullpup was accurate, it was not capable of really precise hits. It was guided by radio commands automatically sent via joystick movements and what the aircraft's gunsight could see. A good combination, but not a great one.

In 1962 the U.S. Navy used television technology to develop the Walleye. This was a glide bomb. The first version had a thousand-pound warhead and a range of twenty kilometers. Some 4,500 were built when production stopped in 1970. Later upgrades doubled the warhead size and range, as well as increasing the accuracy. But the first version was quite accurate. The TV camera was in the nose of the bomb and the operator in the launching aircraft, using a joystick, only had to put his crosshairs on the target as it appeared on his TV screen. The bomb then used that TV image, its own TV camera, and guidance fins on the bomb to home in on the target. This was called an EOGB (Electro-optical Glide Bomb). But like the Bullpup, the warhead wasn't always large enough and the guidance systems often didn't work reliably. The technology was almost there, but not quite. Moreover, both the Bullpup and the Walleye were much more expensive than bombs alone. The guided version of a bomb costs four to ten times as much as the unguided ("dumb") version. (Depending on the size of the bomb, the guidance equipment costs about the same no matter what size the bomb.) The laser-guided bombs cost a third to a quarter of what the more complex EOGB ("drop and forget") systems cost. For this reason, the laser-guided bombs are more popular.

The Vietnam War, especially the bombing campaign against North Vietnam, had presented some really difficult targets. The classic example was the Thanh Hoa Bridge in North Vietnam. By 1972, 871 sorties had been flown against the bridge, without success. Even the Walleye had been unable to bring down the bridge, because its half-ton warhead was too small. Eleven aircraft had been lost in the effort, all when going in with plain old "dumb" bombs. But during the late 1960s the guided-bomb research had made some real breakthroughs in the use of lasers. The new generation of bombs, the PAVEWAY series, was first used in 1972 against the Thanh Hoa Bridge. Four USAF F-4s attacked the bridge with these laser-guided bombs and brought it down. None of the F-4s was hit.

Targets like bridges were particularly difficult because they were relatively small, and stoutly built. To bring down a bridge, you had to put a bomb onto a few key areas. Even B-52s using hundreds of bombs dropped in the area of the bridge would not do it. You had to get one bomb in just the right spot. Laser-guided bombs could do it, and they did.

These Vietnam-era laser-guided bombs were a great advance in bombing, as the bomber could now drop the bomb a distance away from the target and easily guide it in. The optics and laser designator were carried on one aircraft, while another could go in and actually drop the bomb. Thus both aircraft could stay out of harm's way and still get the job done. That distance protected the bomber from all the enemy antiaircraft guns that usually defended such key targets. By the 1980s, these laser-guided bombs achieved a CEP of under ten meters, and they could be dropped from low altitude in bad weather, making the weapon accurate for most small targets and combat conditions. These bombs have changed air warfare more than any other technology.

The World War II–era guided bombs had to be flown into the target by a human controller, usually in the plane that launched the bomb. This worked well enough as long as you had a skilled operator at the controls and the enemy wasn't jamming the radio signals. But a lack of skilled operators and the presence of enemy jamming were likely in wartime. This limited the appeal of radio-controlled bombs. The EOGBs and laser-guided bombs were more acceptable, as they could not easily be jammed and were cheaper than radio-controlled bombs.

The appearance of the laser in the early 1960s made guided bombs much more easy to use, reliable, and, overall, more practical. The laser is a thin beam of light that can be projected over many kilometers. When the laser light hits something, it reflects light of a particular frequency that can be picked up and identified by special optical instruments. This could be used for range finding, as well as providing reflected light for a glide bomb to home in on. Unlike the World War II glide bombs, the laser-guided ones only required the operator to keep the laser on the target. The bomb had computer-operated fins and a seeker in the nose of the bomb that looked for the reflected laser light and used the movable fins to keep the bomb headed for that light. It was a simple system, and has undergone constant improvement since it first appeared in the early 1970s. While some four thousand guided bombs were dropped in nine months of use in Vietnam, four times as many were used in six weeks of operations in the 1991 Gulf War. The guided bomb had come of age, and bombing would never be the same again.

The importance of guided bombs was lost in the more familiar jungle mayhem of Vietnam. In a guerrilla war there are few specific targets for highly accurate bombs. More effective, and more widely known, was carpet bombing by the B-52s. This made much more of an impression on the enemy and friendly troops. Flying in groups of three at thirty thousand feet, the B-52s would drop over two hundred five-hundred-pound bombs in an area one kilometer wide and three long. Inside that box there would be devastation. But this was simply World War II brought up-to-date. The future was the guided bombs, used mainly in North Vietnam, where there were few friendly witnesses.

Through the Mist, in the Dark of Night . . .

BUT EVEN BEFORE laser-guided bombs came into use, air forces were addressing an even more pressing problem: how to bomb at night and in bad weather. The goal here was to create "all-weather" bombers. This required special radars and navigation equipment that allowed aircraft to fly safely at night or in weather in which they couldn't see much. In most parts of the world, clear flying weather occurs only for a third of the day. The rest of the time it's either night or cloudy, misty, or foggy. Even if you control the air, your opponent will make the most of those parts of the day when your aircraft cannot fly. Even before the laser bombs were perfected, all-weather fighter-bombers were put into service. These cost about twice as much as clear-weather aircraft, so only a small percentage of the warplanes available were of this type. Since these aircraft were the most capable bombers, they also tended to be the ones that got the laser bombing equipment.

The big problem with all-weather aircraft using the guided bombs was the expense of the electronic equipment needed (several million dollars per aircraft) and the cost of training the aircrew (two-seat fighter-bombers were preferred for this sort of thing) to use these weapons (another few million dollars per crew). As the weapons, and the electronic equipment, become cheaper, more aircraft are equipped with them. The 1991 Gulf War gave some telling demonstrations of the value of the more efficient, and much more expensive, fire-control equipment. The F-117A stealth aircraft flew only 1.2 percent of the sorties during the Gulf War, dropped about 3 percent of the bomb tonnage, and did about 10 percent of the damage. The F-117A was the latest, and most effective, of the high-tech bombing aircraft. There were others (F-15E, A-6, F-111F, and LANTIRN-equipped fighters), but all of these, including the F-117A, flew but 20 percent of the bombing missions, dropped only 8 percent of the bombs, yet did about 30 percent of the damage. Only about three hundred bombers had advanced (laser guidance) bombing equipment. These included existing all-weather aircraft like navy A-6s, air force F-117As, F-111Fs and twenty sets of LANTIRN laser-targeting pods that could be mounted on F-15s (usually) or F-16s (sometimes). These aircraft dropped an average of some two hundred laser-guided bombs every twenty-four hours during the forty-two-day war. These bombs had an 80 to 90 percent hit rate. This was in spite of the need to change tactics during the war, to avoid the high volume of anti-aircraft fire from machine guns and light cannons. Bombers had to stay at altitudes over three thousand meters to avoid this fire, and this put even heavier demands on the fire-control equipment.

These aircraft were, and still are, expensive (F-117As and F-15Es go for about fifty million dollars each), but they get the job done with fewer bombs, fewer sorties, and fewer losses. The lower loss rate has become increasingly important since World War II. In the last five decades aircraft have become much more expensive, and much fewer in number. Each lost aircraft counts for a lot more. And it's not gotten much more difficult to bring aircraft down. Even during World War II, many troops learned that just firing up in the air when under air attack would do damage to the low-flying fighter-bombers. During the Korean War, the Chinese and North Korean troops adopted the practice of immediately firing into the air when under attack by low-flying jets. More than their prop-driven predecessors, jets were vulnerable to stray bullets. Now we have a large number of shoulder-fired antiaircraft missiles and even more automatic weapons on the ground. Moreover, it does wonders for pilot morale and confidence if they see that aircraft losses are very low. Such was the case during the Gulf War, and this has become the model for all future operations.

The Pod Pilots

THE LANTIRN pods, which allow most clear-weather fighter-bombers to be turned into all-weather laser bombers, appear to be the future. The LANTIRN system is two electronic containers (called "pods") that look like bombs and are slung under an F-16 or F-15 just like a pair of bombs. The LANTIRN (Low-Altitude Navigation and Targeting Infrared for Night) system was originally developed as a cheaper way to obtain more high-performance bombers without building all that expensive electronics into fighter aircraft that would spend some of their time operating as fighters and some as bombers. Cheaper clear-weather warplanes can still be built, and converted to all-weather bombers by strapping on the LANTIRN equipment as needed. The pods can already be mounted on a variety of fighters, giving them similar capabilities to the F-117A, A-6, and F-111F.

The U.S. A-6, F-111F, and F-117A already had LANTIRN capabilities built in. Putting all this capability into two pods proved a difficult task and took most of the 1980s to accomplish. LANTIRN had not yet officially been placed into service by late 1990. A dozen LANTIRN sets were undergoing final testing, and eventually twenty sets were shipped to the Gulf, where they went into service and performed admirably. One of the LANTIRN pods uses terrain-viewing radar that allows the aircraft to fly low and fast at night or in bad weather. This enables the aircraft to avoid most enemy radar and antiaircraft weapons, although the terrain-viewing radar can be detected. This was not a problem in the Gulf, where most Iraqi air defenses were destroyed after the first week, but would be in many other times and parts of the world.

The second pod, the targeting one, did most of the work. It enables the pilot to see his target five thousand to fifteen thousand meters (twenty to sixty seconds' flying time) away. The target can be magnified six to fifteen times and accurately "painted" with the weapon system's laser. Maverick missiles or laser-guided bombs can then "see" the laser-painted target, memorize its location, be released, and go after the target while the aircraft flies away or picks out another target. Videotapes of some of these missions were shown and the media were suitably impressed.

The downside of LANTIRN goes beyond its expense. A set of two pods costs nearly five million dollars. Moreover, they tend to break down, on average, every fifty to one hundred hours of use. If the failure occurs during a bombing run, the target usually doesn't get hit. Another limitation of LANTIRN (and similar systems used on other aircraft) is that it only provides a limited view of what is in front of the aircraft. This severely limits what the pilot can see and puts a heavier workload on the pilot. While LANTIRN works, it's not quite "turning night into day." But LANTIRN and similar systems get improved over time. The United States and other Western air forces have them now, and most potential adversaries do not. This makes a big difference once the shooting starts.

Although a set of LANTIRN pods is very expensive, the experience of the Gulf War convinced many generals and legislators that this expense was not as great as it appeared. The cost of flying many more bombing missions, and dropping the ordnance the old-fashioned way, turned out to be greater than the cost of more LANTIRN systems. By the time NATO aircraft were unleashed on the Bosnian Serbs during the summer of 1995, nearly all bombing missions were done with the high-tech bombers. The results were devastating for the targets and the aircraft losses were very small. The point has been made. All-weather, laser-bomb-equipped bombers are the future and, for many air forces, the present.

The Navy Way

SUCH TECHNOLOGICAL advances are not inevitable, however. Despite the experience with guided bombs in World War II and Vietnam, going into the 1980s, the U.S. Navy did not equip itself with guided bombs and instead went for more expensive (and more accurate) guided missiles. The U.S. Air Force stuck with guided bombs, particularly the laser-guided ones, and this difference in direction showed up during the 1991 Gulf War. In that conflict, only 3 percent of the bombs dropped by navy warplanes were guided. The U.S. Air Force figure was 17 percent. Moreover, as was the case in Vietnam, the navy guided bombs were lighter than the air force ones. The navy was concentrating on longer-range cruise missiles with smaller (under five-hundred-pound) warheads. At these longer ranges (over twenty kilometers), lasers were impractical anyway. So the navy used radar (to home in automatically) or data links that allowed a distant operator to use a TV camera in the nose of the missile to guide in the final approach to the target.

The navy was not being stupid. They knew what they wanted, and that was longer-range and more accurate missiles to better destroy enemy ships at sea. These ships are high-value targets, and often great precision is needed. This is particularly true if one is shooting at surfaced (usually nonnuclear) submarines or one of the hundreds of small missile boats the Communist navies were fond of. The air force was more intent on going after sturdier land-based targets. Concrete command centers and aircraft shelters required larger, and cheaper, guided bombs because there were so many more of them. These targets could not move, so the air force could afford to shut down antiaircraft defenses before taking out the concrete structures. Thus the air force bombers didn't need the long standoff range that navy bombers required against ships armed with antiaircraft missiles.

The navy developed the Harpoon, and an even more accurate variant, the SLAM. The latter weapon had a infrared camera in the nose, the better to put the missile's five-hundred-pound warhead through a specific porthole on a ship, or window in a building, as was demonstrated during the Gulf War. The navy policy was not necessarily wrong, for until 1989, the major foe of the navy was the Soviet Union's navy, and those of its Communist allies. When the navy was called to help in the air war against the Iraqis, it was largely bombing concrete structures, not enemy ships.

Where Are All the Smart Bombs?

THE 1991 Gulf War was the most extensive use of smart bombs to date. But it pretty much emptied the U.S. inventory of smart bombs. The chart below shows what was used during that war.

Table 5 / Type, Cost, and Quantity of Bombs and Missiles Used during the 1991 Gulf War

Bomb or Missile	Number Used	$ Cost Each	$ Total Cost
Unguided Iron Bombs			
Mk-82 500lb High Explosive	69,701	498	34,711,098
Mk-83 1000lb High Explosive	19,018	1,000	19,018,000
M-117 750lb Demolition	43,435	253	10,989,055
CBU-52/58/71 Fragmentation	17,831	2,159	38,497,129
CBU-87 Combined Effects	10,035	13,941	139,897,935
Mk-20 Rockeye II	27,987	3,449	96,527,163
CBU-78 Gator Antitank	209	39,963	8,352,267
Total Unguided Bombs	**210,004**		**$431,960,550**
(includes some not listed above)			
Guided Bombs			
GBU-10 Laser 2000lb	2,637	22,000	58,014,000
GBU-12 Laser 500lb	4,493	9,000	40,437,000
GBU-15 EO-IR 2000lb	71	227,600	16,159,600
GBU-16 Laser 1000lb	219	150,000	32,850,000
GBU-24 Laser 2000lb	284	65,000	18,460,000
GBU-24 Laser/BLU-109 2000lb	897	85,000	76,245,000
GBU-27 Laser/BLU-109 2000lb	739	75,539	55,823,321
GBU-28 Laser 4000lb	2	100,000	200,000
Total Guided Bombs	**9,342**		**298,188,921**
(includes some not listed above)			

Table 5 / Type, Cost, and Quantity of Bombs and Missiles Used
during the 1991 Gulf War (continued)

Bomb or Missile	Number Used	$ Cost Each	$ Total Cost
GUIDED MISSILES			
Anti-Radar Missiles (ARMs)			
AGM-45 Shrike	78	89,000	6,942,000
AGM-88 HARM	1,961	257,000	503,977,000
Air-to-Surface Guided Missiles			
AGM-132A Skipper II	12	31,240	374,880
AGM-62B Walleye II	133	70,000	9,310,000
AGM-65B Maverick (EO)	1,673	64,100	107,239,300
AGM-65C Maverick	5	110,000	550,000
AGM-65D Maverick (IR)	3,405	111,000	377,955,000
AGM-65E Maverick (Laser)	36	101,000	3,636,000
AGM-65G Maverick (IR)	177	269,000	47,613,000
AGM-84E SLAM	7	346,000	2,422,000
Air-to-Air Missiles			
AIM-7M	88	225,700	19,861,600
AIM-9M	86	70,600	6,071,600

There were also 333 cruise missiles used, costing a total of $330 million. Army helicopters fired 482 Hellfire and TOW antitank missiles costing $11.1 million. The total cost of all bombs and missiles used was $2.2 billion. Some 90 percent of the items dropped were unguided bombs, and these accounted for only about 20 percent of the cost of all items dropped. The average cost of an unguided bomb was $2,057, while the average cost of a guided bomb was $31,918, or about fifteen times more expensive.

Despite the success of guided bombs and all-weather fighter-bombers, there is still a reluctance to buy a lot of them for a future war. Although it takes twelve to twenty times as many old-fashioned "dumb" bombs to hit a target as it does when using guided ("smart") bombs, some 95 percent of the U.S. bomb inventory still consists of dumb bombs. Current plans call for only having 30 percent of fighter-bombers capable of using smart bombs. The explanation given is that there is not enough money to do everything and that, rather than increase the number of smart bombs in the inventory, it is more prudent to spend the money on developing even smarter, and cheaper, bombs.

There is also a lot of money being spent on the new generation of fighters (F-22) and more heavy bombers (B-2). Given that no one else is likely to have anything that will come close to matching the F-22, and that the mission of the B-2, dubious to begin with, disappeared with the end of the cold war, there are obviously other things at play. The U.S. Air Force is run by bomber and fighter pilots, who have a hard time conceiving of an air force without better and better (if fewer and fewer) bombers and fighters. Moreover, the cost of these new aircraft, one hundred million dollars for each F-22 and two billion dollars for each B-2, means votes to many in Congress. The result is fewer smart bombs, the weapons that win wars and save American lives.

Big Bombers Forever

DURING THE 1930s, the United States embarked on a program to design and build strategic bombers. No one else had done this before, although a few nations had built some large and not very successful bombers. America took the lead in this area and, for over sixty years, has not relinquished it.

The first truly effective strategic bomber was the B-17, the "Flying Fortress." This thirty-two-ton aircraft first flew in 1935 and entered service in 1939. By 1945, 12,731 were built. It could carry up to 8.5 tons of bombs and had a maximum range of 2,000 miles. A more usual mission was about 1,000 miles with some four tons of bombs. The B-17 could cruise at 250 miles an hour and was heavily armed with ten or more fifty-caliber machine guns. The four-engine aircraft was quite rugged, and often came back literally shot to pieces with large chunks of the airframe missing.

Even as the B-17 was going into production, a second four-engine bomber was in development: the B-24. This thirty-two-ton aircraft first flew in 1939. It was a more advanced design than the B-17, and eighteen thousand were built by 1945. Entering service in 1942, the B-24 "Liberator" was just a little better than the B-17 in most respects. While the B-17, because it entered service first, grabbed most of the headlines, the B-24's overall superiority led to its being produced in greater numbers than the older airplane.

When World War II ended, the United States had built 33,000 four-engine heavy bombers and still had thousands of them left. Nearly all were scrapped, but many of the B-29s (of which 3,965 were built) were kept, as this was the one bomber type that could carry a nuclear weapon. The B-29 weighed sixty-four tons, and carried nine tons of bombs. It had a maximum range of four thousand miles. In 1945, the air force had 3,873 B-29s. Unlike the B-17 and

B-24, many of these were kept in service until new generations of heavy bombers could be put into service. This was an expensive proposition. B-29s cost nine millions dollars each (in 1996 dollars), but that was only because so many were built. Later heavy bombers became progressively more expensive, because they were more complex and fewer of each model were built. This culminated in the current B-2, costing some two billion dollars each. These aircraft would still cost over a hundred million dollars each if 4,000 were built. But that's the cost of high technology.

Table 6 / The American Heavy Bomber Fleet: 1945–2000

Year	B-29s in Service	Total Heavy Bombers
1945	3,873	3,988
1946	3,352	3,400
1947	2,830	2,830
1948	2,309	2,580
1949	2,048	2,449
1950	1,787	2,410
1951	1,467	2,568
1952	1,147	2,186
1953	504	2,816
1955		2,635
1960		1,951
1965		1,022
1970		600
1975		500
1980		411
1995		200
2000		181

Once B-29s went out of service in 1954, the American heavy bomber fleet always consisted of a number of different types, in steadily shrinking numbers.

Table 7 / New Heavy/Strategic Bomber Types, Year of Introduction

Name	In Service	Max Weight (tons)	
B-17	1939	32	
B-24	1942	32	
B-29	1944	64	
B-32	1945	50	
B-50	1947	85	
B-45	1948	55	
B-36	1948	200	
B-49	1952	100	"Flying Wing" canceled in 1952
B-47	1952	91	
B-52	1955	240	
B-58	1960	74	
FB-111	1969	47	
B-70	1970	260	Project canceled in early 1962
B-1	1985	236	
B-2	1992	181	

Notes for the above table. Development time for bombers varied from a few years for the earlier models to over ten years for the more recent ones. Weight (maximum takeoff weight) for each is given as a best indicator of each aircraft's size. After 1945, in-flight refueling gave all of these bombers sufficient range to reach any target on the planet.

Ever since the end of World War II, the U.S. Air Force has built new bombers. Between 1939 and 1955, ten strategic bomber–development programs were undertaken. Nine of them resulted in bombers that entered service. That's ten projects in seventeen years, but a lot of this can be attributed to the needs of World War II. In the forty years since the mid-1950s, only five new bomber projects have been undertaken. While the tempo of new bomber projects declined after the 1950s, the amount of money spent on strategic bomber development did not. Indeed, during the 1980s, more was spent on long-range bombers than on ICBMs, even though the latter were a more certain weapon if it came to nuclear war. The list of post–World War II bomber projects is impressive, even if few of the aircraft ever saw combat.

During World War II, the B-29 was not the only "superheavy" bomber built. As a form of insurance, another was designed and built: the B-32. It was not nearly as capable as the B-29, weighing only fifty tons and carrying ten tons of bombs for only 2,400 miles. Only 115 were built and these were taken out of service in 1947.

In 1947, an improved B-29, called the B-50, was introduced. The main difference between the B-50 and B-29 was the larger engines, with the B-50 engines generating about 55 percent more horsepower. The B-50 also had a new wing, tail, and landing gear, and some 75 percent of the B-50 was new. Still, it looked very similar to the B-29, although it was significantly heavier at eighty-five tons. But the B-50 was a dead end—only 370 were built. It never saw combat, even during the 1950–53 Korean War. It was phased out of bomber service in the late 1950s and a few were converted to recon use. In this role, some continued in service as late as 1965. The B-50s got lost in the shuffle because the air force had already flown a B-29 replacement in August 1945, the B-36.

The B-36 was a huge aircraft by any standard, with a maximum weight of two hundred tons. It first flew in 1946 and was meant to be the first truly intercontinental bomber. The B-36 began entering service in 1948, the B-50 being something of a backup in case the monster B-36 took any longer to get all the bugs out. The maximum bomb load of the B-36 was about the same as the later B-52 (thirty-eight tons) and it had a range of 6,800 miles. But the B-36 was propeller driven, with later models having four jet engines added. This meant ten engines had to be taken care of, an enormous maintenance burden. Only 385 were built and it was withdrawn from service in 1959.

High-Tech Bombers Forever

THE INTRODUCTION OF jet-powered aircraft during World War II meant that new designs for all types of aircraft were now possible. In effect, jet engines made all the propeller-driven aircraft of World War II obsolete. Nations were reluctant to junk all their brand-new nonjet aircraft right after the tremendous expense of World War II, so it took awhile before new jet designs were introduced. This was just as well, for the first jet engines were cranky beasts and it took another decade or so before a lot of the bugs were worked out. But the United States was not deterred. Once the jet engines were added to the B-36, bombers propelled solely by jets were already in the works.

The fifty-five ton B-45 first flew in 1947. It was originally designed to fly with propellers, but was converted to use four jet engines before its first flight. Thus it was the first U.S. all-jet bomber. It entered service in 1948 and no more than 106 were ever in service, out of 143 built. It was withdrawn from service in 1956 as more of the superior B-47s came into use. The B-45 could carry ten tons of bombs and had a range of 1,900 miles. It was the first jet bomber to be refueled in the air (by a B-29 modified for that purpose). In effect, the B-45 provided a testing program for future jet bomber designs.

The ninety-one-ton B-47 first flew in 1950 and entered service in 1952. Powered by six jet engines, 2,040 were built. It carried nine tons of bombs and had a range of four thousand miles. It had a maximum speed of 630 miles an hour but, more importantly, could cruise at nearly 500 miles an hour. It was phased out of service by 1965, although some continued to fly as recon aircraft for a few more years. The B-47 was basically a warm-up for the more capable B-52. The B-47 was also built in large quantities before it was realized how effective ICBMs would be taking nuclear weapons deep into heavily defended enemy territory.

The 240-ton B-52 first flew in 1952 and entered service in 1955. It could carry nearly 40 tons of bombs and had a maximum range of ten thousand miles. Only 744 B-52s were built, at a cost of some thirty-five billion dollars in current dollars. This was about fifty million dollars each, more than five times the cost of the B-29, the new bomber only twelve years earlier. The B-52s were overhauled and maintained so well that forty years later, over a hundred were still flying. The B-52 is the only post–World War II strategic bomber to see extensive combat. Over Vietnam and Kuwait, the B-52 was used repeatedly because of its long range and enormous bomb-carrying capacity.

The seventy-four-ton B-58 first flew in 1956, and entered service in 1960. It was withdrawn from service in 1970. The B-58 was in development for a long time, for it was a very advanced design. Thirty B-58 aircraft were built during its test phase. Eventually 10 of those were converted to production configuration. Another 8 of the original batch of 30 were converted to make the TB-58 trainer version. Production ended in 1962 after 86 production models were built, making 116 total. In all, 26 were destroyed in accidents; 10 or so of those were due to loss of control for one reason or another, the majority of those occurring from 1959 to 1962. In addition, 3 were lost due to landing gear or tire failures, 3 due to hard landings, and 3 due to flying too low (undershooting an approach, low-level bomb run, and showing off at an air show). B-58s first became operational in 1960. They were not placed on alert until 1962. B-58s were expensive to build and, more importantly, to operate, costing about three times as much as a B-52. In 1969 it was announced that the B-58s would be withdrawn because of improved bombers and ICBMs (i.e., FB-111, Minuteman, and Polaris). This was also at the height of the Vietnam War and B-52s were cheaper and dropped lots of conventional bombs, whereas the B-58 could drop only one nuclear weapon. They were all retired by 1970. Nonetheless, the B-58 did very well in bombing competitions, coming out in first place in its first effort six weeks after becoming operational. It did have much more sophisticated navigation and bombing systems than the

B-52. It was very fast, being the first supersonic strategic bomber. But the B-58 was also a portent of things to come, for jet bombers were pushing the limits of what available technology could do. The B-58 established a pattern of high-tech, high-cost, and low-reliability new bomber designs. This is a pattern that, after forty years, is still with us.

The 260-ton B-70 was a dead end. Originally conceived as a replacement for the B-52, work was begun in 1957, but the project was halted in 1962, after spending some seven billion (in 1996 terms) dollars. The B-70 was basically an advanced military version of the commercial Concorde supersonic airliner. The B-70 was meant to fly high and fast, and it was quickly realized that such an aircraft would be defenseless against antiaircraft missiles and interceptors. Even in the early 1960s, it was apparent that strategic bombers would often have to come in on the deck to avoid enemy defenses. The B-70 wasn't built for this. Also, as with the American attempts to build a Concorde-like aircraft, it was soon discovered that this technology would be too expensive to be worth the effort and expense. ICBMs were coming into use, and they were a much cheaper way to deliver nuclear weapons against heavy defenses. Work was continued anyway, purely to explore the technology. The B-70 was first flown in 1964. Development was halted in 1966 when one of them crashed. Only two B-70s were built, both prototypes for testing. However, neither ever carried any weapons system, aside from having a bomb bay, and they only carried a crew of two. A third B-70 was under construction and was to have the weapons systems installed and a crew of four. It was not completed and was scrapped.

This was the second major bomber project to be canceled. The first was the B-49 "Flying Wing." This aircraft used the same shape as the later B-2, but the late-1940s technology was not up to making it work soon enough for the air force, and it was canceled after only fifteen were produced.

The forty-five-ton FB-111 first flew in 1964 and entered service in 1967 as a fighter-bomber. While 501 F-111s were built, 76 were converted to the slightly heavier FB-111 strategic bomber. This aircraft could carry ten tons of bombs and had a range of 3,800 miles. The FB-111 was meant as an interim measure while a replacement for the failed B-70 project could be completed. The F-111 was designed to fly low and fast, just the approach that would be most successful in penetrating modern enemy air defenses. Ironically, the FB-111 has seen action in more different conflicts (Vietnam, Libya, Kuwait) than the B-52. Criticized for being too ambitious, the FB-111 turned out to be the most versatile bomber of the post–World War II era. It could fly very low, at high speed, and drop its bombs with great accuracy. With air refueling, the FB-111 could go just about anywhere.

The 236-ton B-1 first flew in 1974. It was planned during the 1960s as a replacement for the B-70, but the fiscal demands of the Vietnam War on the air force budget slowed progress to a crawl. Work was begun in earnest during 1970. The B-1 was to take advantage of the latest stealth and engine technology to produce an aircraft that could fly fast either low or high. Its shape and onboard electronics would make it difficult for enemy radars to detect. In other words, it would be stealthy. But the project was canceled in 1979, again because of the cost of the aircraft and uncertainty of achieving all its technological breakthroughs. The project was revived in 1982, and by 1988 a hundred B-1Bs had been built at a cost of some four hundred million dollars each. Unlike the original B-1, the B-1B became mainly subsonic when the engine air inlets were redesigned for low-altitude, high-speed flight, and to make the aircraft a lot cheaper to produce. Few airplanes fly supersonic for very long anyway, so this was an economy that would not cost anything in combat. The B-1B is actually able to outrun the fighters on the deck because few fighters can fly at very low altitude at very high speeds before running out of gas. The B-1B has the fuel, and shape, to keep going at high speed at low altitudes. It also carries twenty tons of weapons over four thousand miles. But as impressive as the B-1B performance is, its technology did advance rather further than was prudent. The reliability of the aircraft is low, as was the earlier high-tech B-58. The extensive, and expensive, electronics are also of questionable reliability. The B-1B has, as of 1995, not been tested in combat.

The 181-ton B-2 was in development throughout the 1980s and went into service in 1992. It is a combination of radically new and untried technology that is very advanced, very difficult to perfect, and very, very expensive. Over twenty-five billion dollars was spent before the B-2 even flew, and projected costs were over seventy billion dollars for 132 aircraft. Only twenty were built as of 1996, pushing the cost per plane over two billion dollars each. This means that three B-2s cost more than a nuclear aircraft carrier, and one B-2 cost more than half a dozen of the latest Peacekeeper ("MX") ICBMs and their hardened shelters. The B-2 can carry twenty tons of bombs for over five thousand miles.

Both the B-1 and B-2 are capable long-range bombers. With aerial refueling, they can be sent to bomb any place on earth within twenty-four hours. Their stealthy shape and onboard electronics hide them from all but the most robust antiaircraft defenses. But the expense of maintaining four (B-52, FB-111, B-1B, B-2) different types of strategic bombers is a bit much. This is especially true since the total number of strategic bombers is about three hundred. There are plans afoot to retire the FB-111. Although thirty years old, the FB-111 is a proven airplane. Its replacement, the B-1B, is of dubious reliability and has not been tested in combat. The former problem can be solved by the application of lots of maintenance and modification, the latter by many realistic exercises. Both of these solutions require lots of money, something the air force won't have a lot of in the next decade or so. The B-2 is also there to replace the FB-111, but at two billion dollars each, it makes air force generals nervous to use such a golden bird in combat. The B-52 soldiers on because it is reliable, has long legs, and carries lots of bombs.

Smart Missiles Begin to Replace Bombers

EVEN AS THE U.S. Air Force built more and more new types of bombers, they realized this was not enough. As good as a new bomber design was, enemy defenses were such that it was not always practical to expect a bomber to survive long enough to fly over its target and drop a nuclear weapon. So missiles were developed that could be carried by bombers. When close enough to the target, the missile would be launched and then make its suicide run to the target. The first of these missiles was the five-ton AGM-28 Hound Dog. A B-52 could carry two of them and each missile in turn carried a one-megaton nuclear warhead. With a range of 1,100 kilometers, the AGM-28 depended on its own inertial guidance system to find its target. The missile was in use from 1960 to 1976. In 1972, the lighter (one-ton) and shorter-range (55- to 220-kilometer) AGM-69 SRAM (Short-Range Attack Missile) entered service. It carried a smaller nuclear weapon (two hundred kilotons) and was to be used for attacking enemy antiaircraft defenses (radars and missile sites) as well as the usual strategic targets (factories, military bases, and cities). A total of 1,500 AGM-69s were built and it continued to be used into the 1980s, when it was replaced by the cruise missile. The AGM-86 ALCM (Air-Launched Cruise Missile) entered service in 1981. It weighed 1.5 tons, had a range of 2,500 kilometers, and carried a two-hundred-kiloton nuclear bomb. Some 1,700 were built and a B-52 could carry 20 of them. The ALCM used a terrain-following guidance system, based on an electronic map of the terrain the missile was flying over. Traveling a hundred feet off the ground, the ALCM could fly a complex course to its target.

Weapons like the ALCM showed that missiles were becoming smarter and more like robots. Bit by bit, missiles were taking over jobs once done by aircraft with pilots. The air force missed the irony of putting robot bombers (cruise missiles) on their increasingly expensive manned bombers, but their critics did not. The zoomies thought they were being made fun of when it was suggested that cheaper Boeing 747s be bought and loaded up with cruise missiles. The critics were serious, but the bomber mafia was clueless. The army and navy are pushing the use of cruise missiles and recon droids to replace a lot of aircraft. Well, they are pushing this approach more vigorously than the air force. This makes sense—the army and navy have other things to do besides baby-sit a lot of expensive airplanes. But no air force general wants to command a bunch of robots. Machines don't look good in a uniform and they can't salute.

The B-2 may be the last new strategic bomber we see from the air force, or anyone else, for some time.

The Hidden Advantage of Air-to-Air Refueling

BOTH THE RANGE and bomb-load capacity of the long-range jet bombers were the result of another technical innovation: the KC-135 air-to-air refueling tanker. This aircraft was a development of the cargo version of the B-29, the C-97. The manufacturer (Boeing) put swept wings and jet engines on the C-97 and produced 820 C-135 transports (as well as a commercial craft, the B-707). The first prototype flew in 1954 and 732 eventually entered service as the KC-135 tanker.

A British firm had perfected an air-to-air refueling system before World War II and versions of the B-29 were converted to tankers (KC-97) right after World War II to provide extremely long range for nuclear bombers. Aerial refueling was not used during World War II because the ranges were not that great and it was the later jet bombers that had truly huge fuel consumption. The KC-97 refueled B-50s in the late 1940s during around-the-world flights. The object of this exercise was to show what aerial refueling could do, and show the Soviet Union that American strategic bombers could go anywhere.

A jet tanker was needed for the B-52; otherwise the cruising-speed differences between a jet and a prop-driven aircraft made refueling difficult and inefficient. Thus the need for the all-jet KC-135. Not only did the refueling increase the range of the B-52 (and other jets), but it increased the load carried by the refueled aircraft. A bomber or transport can fly at a heavier weight than it can take off with. It takes more engine power to get off the ground than it does to stay in the air. Thus an aircraft can take off with more cargo and less fuel, and then take on more fuel once in the air. For a bomber, more fuel can be taken on after returning from its mission, while it still has a ways to go before reaching its base. KC-135s transfer twenty to twenty-five tons of fuel per sortie. This sounds like a lot, but a B-52 normally carries over a hundred tons of fuel. Thus it takes two or more KC-135s to replenish a B-52's fuel supply.

Aerial tankers revolutionized air warfare. Jets could now fly farther and with more weapons without devoting a lot of onboard weight and space to fuel. America's fleet of six hundred KC-135s (and over a hundred other, mostly smaller, tankers) gave U.S. aircraft an advantage no other nation had. This is a technology that doesn't get much attention, sort of like the local gas station. But take away two-thirds of the local gas stations, and all of a sudden everyone would pay a lot more attention to the fuel supply.

The technology of aerial refueling is not very complicated, but the manner in which you assemble a significantly large force of tankers and trained crews is. America has over forty years' experience with aerial refueling. The United States also has lots of combat experience with it. While only 50 refueling sorties were flown during the Korean War (1950–53), during the Vietnam War (1964–72) tankers flew 195,000 sorties, delivering over 4.5 million tons of fuel. When there wasn't a war going on, the tankers got a constant workout refueling combat aircraft flying training missions. This paid off during the 1991 Gulf War, where tankers refueled 49,950 aircraft with over 350,000 tons of fuel. There were no accidents, or at least none that resulted in the loss of an aircraft.

The dark side of aerial refueling is that it makes air operations a lot more expensive. During the 1991 Gulf War 20 percent of the total number of sorties were tanker sorties. Those four-engine KC-135 tankers are expensive to operate, costing several thousand dollars per hour in the air. And tankers spend a *lot* of hours in the air. The refueling routines used for the Gulf War were developed many years earlier for potential air operations against Soviet forces in Europe. Tankers circled for hours, creating flying gas stations. Thirsty aircraft, usually fighters and light bombers, came by, picked up a few tons of fuel, and went on their way. The tankers, when empty, returned to base, took on another load of jet fuel, and went out to circle again, and again.

Because the KC-135s are old aircraft, most built over thirty years ago, they require a lot of maintenance and periodic overhauls. All have gone through several sets of engines and upgrades in their electronics and refueling equipment. Many of the crew members are younger than the tankers they serve on.

Without the tankers, the USAF would have much shorter legs. Without tankers, American combat, control (AWACS and J-STARS), and freighter aircraft would need two or three times as many days to arrive at the scene of a future conflict. Moreover, this dependence on tankers makes it mandatory that American aircraft always have air superiority. Too many enemy fighters in the air would severely restrict aerial refueling. Tankers are basically defenseless and make great targets.

Technology continues to play a role in aerial refueling. Better navigation equipment, particularly GPS units and passive sensors, makes refueling more efficient. The GPS, using satellites to precisely guide tankers and thirsty aircraft, eases the task of quickly setting up rendezvous points in the air. Passive sensors, which don't broadcast signals, enable tankers to refuel in bad weather while not giving the enemy a signal to home in on.

But tankers also have much to fear from new technology. Robotic cruise missiles, turned loose to search the sky with passive sensors while themselves being hard to spot, may become the bane of tankers. Traveling slowly, and often in circles, tankers make the perfect target for such soon-to-be-deployed weapons. Tankers can be equipped with some countermeasures, but this makes them still more expensive to operate and reduces their fuel capacity.

There is also a trend toward fewer, and larger, tankers. The U.S. Air Force is already using a jumbo tanker, the KC-10 (based on the commercial DC-10). These tankers, weighing 267 tons, can carry 160 tons of fuel. The first KC-135s weighed 136 tons (with 86 tons of fuel) and the latest upgraded version weighs 146 tons (92 tons of fuel). As a practical matter, the KC-10 can deliver about three times as much fuel as the older KC-135. The KC-10 is also a lot cheaper to operate. In this age of shrinking defense budgets, newer, larger, and cheaper-to-operate tankers are the future. Moreover, within the next twenty-five years, the older KC-135s will reach the end of their useful life. You can only maintain and overhaul an aircraft for so long before it costs more than it's worth.

The combination of high-tech bombers and hundreds of aerial tankers has produced a situation where America can put bombers over any point on the earth within twenty-four hours. The bomber force and the tankers cost billions of dollars a year to develop and maintain. The bombers are used infrequently, and when they are, not that many bombs are dropped. So when all the costs are added up, the bombs dropped might just as well be made of gold. Smart bombs themselves cost over $300,000 a ton, and this cost is easily tripled or quadrupled when you add in the life cycle cost of the bomber dropping it. Okay, gold currently goes for some twelve million dollars a ton. But at over a million dollars a bomb, you could easily gold-plate them.

10

Missiles That Miss

WAYWARD MISSILES are a phenomenon that began during World War II (and even earlier). The accuracy of many weapons systems has been grossly exaggerated. The precision-guided bombs of the Gulf War were first used successfully in 1943. But it took nearly half a century before such weapons had enough kinks worked out of them so that they could be used on a wide scale.

Air-to-air missiles also took nearly twenty years of widespread use before pilots were able to make them their main air-combat weapon. The common experience is for these missiles, and their capabilities, to be oversold and produced in large quantities before they have achieved any degree of usefulness. Blame it on Hollywood, where the missiles always work, and on politicians, who rarely meet a high-tech weapons program they don't like. The claims and the performance have started to come closer together, but even slight degrees of error have catastrophic consequences in today's battlefields.

Yet guided missiles are not all that recent a development. The use of guided missiles in warfare goes back over fifty years. German V-1 cruise missiles were first launched against southeast England in June of 1944. Development work on the V-1 cruise missile began in June 1942, and the first successful flight took place in December of that year. The Germans eventually fired some 9,200 V-1s at Britain. This still comprises the bulk of the cruise missiles used in combat. About 5,000 made it to their target, usually the largest target available, the city of London. This also comprises the largest number of cruise missiles that have hit military or civilian targets. Most of the V-1s that didn't make it were shot down by flak or fighters.

The V-1 was pretty crude by current standards, but really high-tech for 1944. It was basically a jet aircraft with a rudimentary guidance system. The missile had to be launched directly at the target, as the V-1 flew in a straight line, at a constant speed (about three hundred to four hundred miles an hour) and altitude (three thousand to four thousand feet). It used a simple pulse jet engine and plunged to the ground after it had gone a programmed distance. Only slightly faster than contemporary fighters, the V-1s could be shot down by antiaircraft guns or intercepted by fighters. The V-1 was relatively small, and radar did not always spot it. In effect, it was "stealthy." The technology of the period did not allow for a very accurate guidance system. The V-1 basically attacked area targets, like cities, that were large enough that wherever the V-1 landed it would do some damage. In that respect, it was not really efficient. It was, indeed, a vengeance weapon, attempting to lower the morale of the British civilian population. This it did, but that had no effect on the war effort (other than the diversion of some antiaircraft guns and fighters to deal with it).

Table 8 / World War II and Modern Missile Characteristics

	Weight (lbs)	Range (km)	Warhead (lbs)	CEP Accuracy (meters)	Year in Service
FZG-76 (V-1)	4,850	200	1,874	12,000	1944
A-4 (V-2)	28,380	320	2,200	6,000	1944
Scud	13,500	300	2,000	2,000	1957
Styx	6,600	42	800	Homing	1957
Regulus II	22,000	1,600	Nuclear	1,600	1958
Minuteman I	76,000	11,000	Nuclear	2,000	1962
Exocet MM-38	1,653	42	364	Homing	1972
Gabriel	882	21	397	Homing	1972
Harpoon	3,200	110	500	Homing	1977
AGM-104	3,000	2,500	1,000	50	1984
Peacekeeper	195,000	10,000	Nuclear	100	1986

Notes for the above table. *Weight* (in pounds) of the missile when launched. *Range* (in kilometers) of the missile. *Warhead* (in pounds), which is largely explosive. Those warheads that were nuclear are so noted. In that case, the weight of the warhead doesn't matter. Missiles have an advantage over bombs or artillery shells in that the weight and mass of the missile structure add to the destruction when the missile hits something. The metal of the missile body turns into fast-moving, and often lethal, flying objects in the aftermath of the missile's impact, while any remaining fuel continues to burn. *Accuracy* (in kilometers) is represented by the CEP (Circular Error Probable). What this means is that the missile has a 50 percent chance of landing within a circle whose diameter is the CEP. Thus the V-1 had a 50 percent chance of landing within six kilometers of where it was aimed at. Where missiles homed in on their target (usually with radar), the CEP is replaced with "Homing." The later ballistic missiles (ICBMs) also used multiple warheads, up to a dozen or more on one missile.

V-1 and V-2 were not the official designations of these weapons. The V stood for *Vergeltungswaffe* (vengeance weapon). The official designations were FZG-76 (the V-1) and A-4 (the V-2A). Comparison with their modern descendants is instructive. Scud and Styx are NATO names for two early Russian missiles. Regulus is the last of the first-generation U.S. cruise missiles. Most of the early U.S. V-1 clones were built to provide target practice for antiaircraft weapons or fighters. Exocet is the widely used French antiship missile (shown is the ship-launched version), and Gabriel is the Israeli missile built in response to their loss of a destroyer to the Styx missile in 1967. Harpoon and the AGM-104 (Tomahawk) are U.S. cruise missiles launched from ships. Most of the improvements in post–World War II ballistic (V-2) and cruise (V-1) missiles were to make them lighter and able to fly farther and more accurately. If you look at the missiles developed in the 1950s and later you can see the connection to the German World War II missiles.

During the 1991 Gulf War, America fired over two hundred Tomahawk cruise missiles at Baghdad. At the time, this was proclaimed as the first wartime use of cruise missiles, apparently by people who had forgotten about the V-1 "buzz bomb" attacks on Britain in 1944. The U.S. cruise missile was a much more capable weapon; it could accurately hit small targets most of the time and cost a lot less than a contemporary aircraft. But as a concept, the cruise missile took some forty years to go from the first combat use of such a weapon to the development of one that was really useful on the battlefield. Through the 1990s, American continued to use cruise missiles against land targets, usually ones that were heavily defended and likely to result in lost pilots if manned bombers were used instead.

The V-1 cruise missile was a simpler weapon than the V-2 ballistic missile, but the German example inspired both the Soviets and Americans to develop postwar versions of both cruise and ballistic missiles. The United States dropped cruise-missile work in the 1960s in favor of ballistic missiles while the Russians continued development, especially on ones that could be used against ships. One of the last American cruise missiles developed was the Regulus II, intended for delivering a nuclear weapon deep inside enemy territory.

The Revolution at Sea

IN THE 1950s the Russians had developed cruise missiles for use on ships against other ships. The first of these were basically copies of the original German V-1. That is, they were jet aircraft (a version of the obsolete MiG-15) without a pilot. Unlike the V-1, the Russian Styx models had a homing radar, and in 1967, Russian-made Egyptian missile boats fired three Styx missiles at an Israeli destroyer and sank it. When the Americans realized how lethal cruise missiles could be on (and against) ships, they began working on these weapons again. The first U.S. antiship missile subsequently put into service was the Harpoon, a weapon that remains in service to this day. Israel and France got antiship missiles into service even sooner, as they did not have all those aircraft carriers, like the Americans did. But the Russians had demonstrated that every ship, when equipped with cruise missiles, could be turned into an aircraft carrier capable of launching kamikaze-type bombers.

The earlier Russian cruise missiles could be seen as obvious knockoffs of the V-1, but the post-1960s U.S. weapons took full advantage of modern propulsion and guidance technology. The Harpoon and Tomahawk look quite modern. The Russian versions, although similar in appearance to the German V-1, used more sophisticated guidance, including radar and other sensors, to seek out enemy ships. The modern U.S. cruise missile (the Tomahawk) uses sensors and a powerful microcomputer to scan the terrain below it and literally "follow the map" to its target. This allows for very high accuracy. Accuracy aside, all the cruise missiles since 1944 have had the same mission: to hit enemy targets. Since the V-1 was aimed at urban areas (London) it usually hit something and did, indeed, cause considerable damage and loss of life. The V-1 attacks didn't stop until Allied troops overran the Channel coast sites from which the short-range V-1s were launched. Most of the descendants of the V-1 have become the principal weapon for ships at sea.

Throughout this transition from big guns to cruise missiles, there was little opportunity for antiship missiles to show what they could do. But as a result of one of their destroyers going down from a cruise missile hit in 1967, the Israelis spent a lot of time and effort on figuring out how to defeat these Russian-made missiles, while also building missiles of their own. During the next Arab-Israeli war, in 1973, the Israelis had their own antiship missile, the Gabriel. This weapon was ready to go in 1972. It had a shorter range than the Styx (twenty kilometers versus forty-two), but had a much better guidance system. During the 1973 war, the Israelis were also able to jam the guidance systems on all the Styx missiles fired at them while most of their Gabriels hit their targets. This came as a big disappointment to the Arabs, as the Styx had been used in the 1971 India-Pakistan war, where eleven of twelve missiles hit their targets.

This reminded everyone that slow-moving cruise missiles could be stopped and were, indeed, more vulnerable to interception than the "primitive" V-1s of 1944. The earlier German missile had what amounted to an autonomous guidance system: the mechanism in the V-1 that caused it to dive to the ground once it had gone a set distance could not be jammed. The later

Russian cruise missiles used an "active" guidance system. That is, the Russians put a small radar set in their cruise missiles so that when a missile got close to a target the radar would pick up the target and the missile would then home in on it. But radars can be jammed, and that's what the Israelis did in 1973. This jamming problem is still with us, and shows no signs of going away, despite large amounts of money and effort thrown at it. Your missile has to be able to find its target, and, if the target is moving, that requires some kind of sensor. A sensor is always subject to jamming.

Several solutions have been tried to overcome the jamming problem. Depending on how well equipped the defender is with jamming, and other defensive, gear, these techniques may work.

• Multiple sensors. Radar was the first sensor, because it was a proven and reliable technology. But by the 1960s, heat-seeking (infrared) technology had matured to the point where it could also be used. Ships give off a lot of heat. About the same time, it became possible to install a TV camera in the front of the missile so that a distant operator can manually guide the missile to its target. One could also use a laser designator, from a friendly aircraft or ship, for the missile to home in with. More sensors in the missile took up more room and weight. But if two or more sensors guaranteed a hit, it was worth the smaller warhead size.

• Frequency hopping. Radars operate at a set frequency, just like a radio station. But improvements in electronic technology have made it possible to have a radar that could rapidly switch between a number of frequencies. Any frequency can be jammed, but it takes jammers specially built for the task to jam a lot of frequencies. Moreover, you have to be careful that you don't jam your own radars in the process. Frequency hopping isn't a cure-all to jamming, it just makes it more difficult for the target ship to shut down your cruise-missile radar.

• Radar homing. The target ship has radar and, if it is being used when the missile is inbound, then those radar signals can be used like an electronic beacon that the cruise missile can head for (if equipped for radar homing).

• Launcher guidance. For shorter-range missiles, the launching ship can use laser designators, radio control, and the like to guide the missile to its target. This is a modern version of firing a large battleship gun at a distant target. With a missile, as long as you can see the target and your radio commands are not jammed, you can guide the missile right to the target. Laser designators eliminate the need for radio commands, although the laser beam can be jammed with chaff (small strips of metal that dissipate or break up the laser beam and degrade the "painting," thus depriving the missile of the reflected laser light it is homing on).

• Third-party targeting. Missile attacks usually involve a ship or aircraft that launches the missile in the general direction of the target. After that, it's up to the sensors on the missile to find and hit the target. Shorter-range (forty kilometers and under) missiles use radar on the launching ship to spot distant targets. Because of the curvature of the earth, a ship at sea can't spot anything with radar (or optics) much farther than forty kilometers away. If an aircraft, or another ship closer to the target, is available, this "third party" can assist in guiding the missile to the target. This is a popular method with the Russians. It's more complicated, as your "third party" can be blown out of the sky or water, and leave your missiles blind.

• Sea skimming and terrain tracking. With the right kind of navigation and flight-control system, a cruise missile can be made to approach its target while traveling only five to ten feet above the waves. This makes it more difficult for the target ship's radar to spot the incoming missile. Unless the missile is being assisted by friendly aircraft, the missile still has to "pop up" (increase altitude to a thousand feet or more) to confirm there is a target nearby, before going back down on the deck to make its final run in. But an attack from just above the water continues to make the missile a difficult target, even if the "pop-up" revealed its presence to the target ship. Most modern antiship missiles are sea skimmers.

• High speed. It's always been advantageous in warfare to be fast. The Russians concluded that, since they could not keep up with Western electronics technology, they could gain some advantage by increasing the speed of their cruise missiles. This they did with new models introduced in the 1980s. Traveling at 1,500 to 2,000 miles an hour, these missiles gave the defender less time to get its defenses going, and a more difficult target to hit. On their final approach to the target, most missiles turn off their sensors and just keep going straight. This solves the jamming problem, if the missile can get a few kilometers from the target. A high-speed missile can make this final run from farther away because the ship will not have enough time to move away. High-speed missiles have to be larger, to carry more fuel. But this is also an advantage, as the high-speed missile will weigh five or more tons when it hits and do a lot more damage than slower, and lighter, missiles. Only the Russians went with this approach. Western missile designers preferred to rely more on electronics to get the missile on the target, and not pay the weight and size penalty a larger, heavier, and faster missile would impose on the ships and aircraft used to launch it.

• Size. Smaller missiles are harder to spot and hit with antiaircraft fire. You can also carry more smaller missiles. Western nations have preferred to make their missiles smaller.

• Multiple attacks. Sending more than one missile against the same target will tend to overload the ship's defenses. This is an ancient technique, and in the age of missiles it can easily be done in the deadliest of ways, with attacks from many different directions. It is fairly common to launch two or more missiles at one target, if only to cover yourself in case one of the missiles doesn't make it because some onboard mechanical or electronic system failed.

• Coordinated attacks. There are multiple attacks, often with missiles coming from several different ships and aircraft, where you plan it so that all the missiles will arrive at the target within the space of a few minutes. This is a coordinated attack that is even more likely to overwhelm the best defenses. The Russians had long planned to use such attacks against the heavily defended U.S. carrier groups. Indeed, anything less would have had little chance of success.

NAVIES ARE KEENLY aware that all of their countermeasures may fail. With that in mind, for the past two decades, more ships have been equipped with an automatic radar-guided cannon. This weapon is a twenty- to thirty-millimeter, high-rate-of-fire machine gun that can quickly spot an incoming missile and put dozens of explosive shells on it. These weapons (the American one is called Phalanx), once turned on, act completely automatically, without any human intervention (except to turn them off). This enables the weapon to act quickly when missiles evade jamming and are only a few kilometers from impact. Since cruise missiles are unlikely to carry a jammer to disable the machine gun's radar, these "last chance" weapons do give an added, and final, measure of protection.

Despite all the countermeasures, antiship cruise missiles have proven effective in many cases. This is particularly the case with Western models. U.S. Harpoon missiles easily sank two Libyan ships in 1986, and proved themselves again later in the Persian Gulf. French Exocet missiles were effective against British forces during the 1982 Falklands War and throughout the 1980s against ships in the Persian Gulf. The older antiship missiles, like the Russian Styx, are still abundant among Third World nations and still effective, as these countries don't have much in the way of jammers or other defenses against any kind of cruise missiles.

But using high-tech missiles against ill-prepared Third World navies is an optimal situation. The history of cruise missiles is laden with instances of system failure. Many of the first Exocets used in combat turned out to be duds (the warheads did not explode). As the missiles become more sophisticated, so do the chances of something going wrong. Moreover, opponents have often come up with simple, but effective, countermeasures. There is no perfect weapon.

Ballistic Missiles Get Big, Really Big

WHILE CRUISE MISSILES proved quite good for use against ships, they were not seen as all that effective against land targets. For this a faster and longer-range weapon was needed. That weapon was the ballistic missile. But before these were developed to their present state, there was a detour into attempts at making cruise missiles strategic weapons.

After World War II, the United States developed a number of submarine- and surface-launched cruise missiles, culminating in the late 1950s Regulus II. But the Soviet Union put a satellite in orbit in 1957 and demonstrated what large ballistic missiles could do. If such a missile could put an object in orbit, it could also be used to drop a nuclear warhead anywhere on earth. Thus was born the ICBM (intercontinental ballistic missile). Things would never be the same after that.

Again, right after World War II, the smaller ballistic missiles the Germans had built quickly mutated into bigger, and longer-range, models. The Soviet Union took the lead in this, but they were quickly overtaken by the United States when it was realized that the Soviet Union had nuclear weapons (as of 1948) and that the Soviet Union was ahead of the United States in big missile development.

It turned out that the Russians were not as far ahead as first thought. Most Russian efforts had gone into launching satellites. This was a lead the Russians never lost, if only because they were never able to develop satellites as sophisticated and efficient as the American ones. Thus they had to constantly put more satellites into orbit than the United States. But two years after the first Soviet satellite launch, America also had satellites in orbit. More importantly, in 1959 the first true ICBM, the U.S. Atlas, went into service. It had a CEP of 3,300 meters. This wasn't much better accuracy than the original German V-2. But the Atlas had a nuclear warhead and a range of 11,500 miles. It weighed 125 tons. By 1960, there were seventy-two in service. At the same time, Russia had only four operational ICBMs.

The Russians made a few false starts with their ICBM development, but got some SS-6s into service during 1960. The SS-6 had a CEP of 3,600 meters. Thus began the greatest, and most expensive, arms race in history. During the next thirty years, the two superpowers would spend over a trillion dollars developing and building new ICBMs. It was a race that nobody won, but no one really lost either, as none of these missiles were ever used in combat. There was a cost no one anticipated, however. The Soviet Union collapsed in 1991, with the cost of its ICBM program being a major factor. The United States was not unscathed, as a large chunk of the nation's multitrillion-dollar national debt can be traced to the expense piled up during three decades of ICBM work.

In 1961, the first full-scale test of the U.S. Minuteman ICBM was successful. This was the next generation of ICBMs, using solid fuel, rather than liquid. The solid fuel was much easier to use in a missile designed to sit in a concrete hole in the ground for years. In 1962 the U.S. Minuteman I (CEP 2,000 meters) and Titan (liquid fuel, but only 1,200 meters CEP) came into service. By 1963, the U.S. had 424 ICBMs, 105 shorter-range MRBMs, 224 SLBMs, and 786 long-range bombers aimed at the Soviet Union. Together, all of these systems carried over 5,000 nuclear warheads. The Russians had only 100 ICBMs, 48 sea-based cruise missiles, and 190 long-range bombers. In all, about 500 nuclear weapons pointed in our direction. The Russians noted this disparity, so after 1963, things really began to heat up on the Russian side of the Iron Curtain. Although the Russians were still building only liquid-fueled ICBMs, these rockets were better suited for launching satellites. The solid-fuel rockets could only launch much smaller loads, but the United States had figured out how to make small warheads, a technology the Russians would require another decade to master.

In 1966 the United States fielded the Minuteman II (500 meters CEP) and in 1970 the Minuteman III (400 meters CEP). This raised the stakes again, as better accuracy made it more expensive for the other side to build silos capable of withstanding closer hits by nuclear warheads. Russia was slower in the accuracy race. Some SS-7s (2,700 meters CEP) appeared in 1962 and the mass-produced SS-8 (1,800 meters CEP) in 1964. The SS-9 (900 meters CEP) appeared in small numbers in 1966. In that same year the SS-11-1 (1,400 meters CEP) showed up. The SS-13-1 (1,800 meters CEP) entered the picture in 1969.

By 1970 each side had nearly a thousand ICBMs capable of blasting each other's cities into oblivion. But the Russians noticed that U.S. missiles had continued to become more accurate, more accurate than required just to hit large urban areas. It was apparent that the Americans were out to develop the ability to destroy Russian missile silos, a job that required a very small CEP. Attacking Russian silos would only be useful if Russian missiles were still in those silos and this would be the case only if the United States attacked first. This scared the Russians, as they were historically nervous about being hit with surprise attacks. Although American engineers were increasing accuracy mainly because they were working to perfect all aspects of their ICBM technology, there was never anything said that could convince the Soviets that the United States was *not* trying to build a first-strike force.

So through the 1970s the Russians strove to catch up, often simply replacing guidance systems in existing missiles. In 1973 the SS-11-2 (1,100 meters CEP) showed up, as did the SS-13-2 (1,200 meters CEP). In 1974 the SS-18-1 (500 meters CEP) came along. In 1975 there were the SS-17-1 (500 meters CEP) and the SS-19-1 (500 meters CEP). In 1977 they finally brought out a model that matched the Americans', the SS-18-2 (400 meters CEP), but only in small quantities. There were also a number of multiple-warhead versions of their missiles introduced, another area where the United States had a large lead.

Through the 1970s, most Russian ICBMs were only accurate enough for city busting. In 1979 there were a few SS-18-3s with a CEP of 300 meters. But that same year the United States introduced the Minuteman III with a CEP of 220 meters. The MX Peacekeeper, with a CEP of 100 meters, had already been designed, but production was delayed until 1986 because of budgetary and political problems. In the late 1980s Russia brought out the SS-24 and SS-25, but neither achieved CEPs of better than 300 to 400 meters. The Russian approach with these last two missiles was to make them mobile, thus rendering U.S. CEPs less critical.

Russia has had even less success with CEPs in their SLBMs. Both sides had SLBMs through the early 1960s with CEPs of 3,600 meters. Then the United States brought out the Polaris A3 in 1964 with a 900-meter CEP.

In 1971 there came the Poseidon with a 500-meter CEP. The Trident C4 of 1983 had a CEP of 220 meters and the Trident D5 of 1989 a 100-meter CEP. Russia never got their SLBM CEP lower than 800 to 900 meters. Moreover, U.S. SLBMs carried more warheads per missile and traveled in quieter subs.

American was unable to deploy mobile ICBMs for political reasons. Few people wanted trains carrying ICBMs wandering around the countryside. Other approaches were tried. A Minuteman III (sixty feet long and thirty-six tons) was successfully dropped (and fired in midair) from a C-5 aircraft. Again, this would not fly politically, particularly since one of these ICBM-carrying aircraft could crash on takeoff or landing. Moreover, building and maintaining the aircraft would be very expensive, another political minus.

The "race" for greater ICBM accuracy, and thus the theoretical ability to launch a "first strike" at enemy missile silos, was rather absurd when you think about it. The engineers on both sides of the Iron Curtain were simply trying to make their missiles more effective. If they didn't do this, they would be out of a job. Missile building was good work, and there was more work if you came out with new and improved models every year or so. Both sides knew that the other was improving its missiles. As is usually the case with arms races, it took a while (the late 1980s) before both camps could muster the courage to say "Stop!"

Table 9 / Nuclear Warheads Deliverable at Intercontinental Ranges

Year	U.S. Warheads	Russian Warheads
1950	450	0
1955	4,750	20
1960	5,437	327
1965	4,862	716
1970	5,522	1,914
1975	9,744	2,830
1980	10,394	5,909
1990	12,100	10,300

The United States had an early lead, and no one in the West knew how much the Russians were at a disadvantage through the 1960s. Once the Soviet Union had over a thousand warheads, they had reached the point where they were likely to destroy America if there were a nuclear war. After that, the Russians just kept on building.

During the 1980s, Russia began to catch up to the United States in the number of warheads, and by the late 1980s both nations found that they each had over ten thousand warheads aimed at each other. Both countries saw this coming in the early 1970s, when negotiations began to try and limit the growth of nuclear warheads sitting on top of ballistic missiles. Even as the negotiators talked, the engineers and scientists worked on. The major problem was the increasing use of ICBMs that could deliver more than one warhead. First three, then up to a dozen or more warheads were mounted on each missile. The Strategic Arms Limitation Talks (SALT) tried to restrict this item, as well as the overall increase in the number of nuclear warheads aimed at either nation. What was particularly worrisome was an accidental launch of one or more ICBMs. This could trigger a launch by the other side, thinking that it was about to be the victim of a first strike. One SALT treaty was signed in 1972 (SALT I) and another in 1979 (SALT II). But all either of these treaties did was stabilize, on paper, each side's warhead inventory at over ten thousand warheads each.

Finally, beginning in 1986, a series of disarmament treaties were signed that drastically reduced the number of warheads aimed at each other. This has not stopped work on even more advanced warheads, it has only slowed it down.

Ballistic Missiles in Action

ALL CURRENT BALLISTIC missiles are direct descendants of the earlier World War II German weapons. The Soviet Scud and American Corporal (the U.S. "Scud") were both developed using the World War II German V-2 ballistic missile as a model. Indeed, German scientists and technicians who worked on the V-2 also worked on the later Soviet and American versions.

Work began on the V-2 in 1938 and the first successful launch was in October 1942. Unlike the V-1, which had to be launched from catapult-equipped concrete ramps, the V-2 was mobile. The trailer the missile was towed around on contained hydraulic jacks that put the missile into a vertical position. Its liquid fuel was then loaded, the inertial guidance system was adjusted, and the missile was launched. Between September 6, 1944, and March 27, 1945, the Germans launched 4,300 V-2s. Most (2,500) were fired at targets on the Continent; the rest were aimed at England. This is still the largest wartime use of ballistic missiles. The only other major use of ballistic missiles since was the firing of over 600 missiles by Iran and Iraq at each other during the 1980s. In 1991, Iraq fired 81 Scuds at Saudi Arabia and Israel. Thus Germany still holds the record for the largest number of ballistic missiles fired in anger.

By early 1944, the Germans were producing three hundred V-2s a month in an underground missile factory in the Harz Mountains. The V-2 was originally designed to hit military targets beyond artillery range, and this was largely how it was used. Hundreds were fired at logistics facilities in Antwerp, and had some success in hurting Allied supply efforts. Against London, however, the V-2 was used as a terror weapon, and it had some success there. Because it was a ballistic missile, you couldn't hear it coming. There was no warning and no defense. All of a sudden there was an explosion. As Londoners soon learned, if you heard the explosion, you were safe.

Thus far, the city of London has the distinction of having suffered the most from ballistic-missile attacks. Starting in October 1944, about a thousand V-2s were sent against southeast England. Some 2,700 people were killed by the V-2 attacks, another 6,500 were wounded. Damage to real estate was greater, with 123,000 buildings receiving some damage, and many destroyed.

The next widespread use of ballistic missiles occurred during the 1980–89 Iran-Iraq War. The weapon used was very similar to the World War II V-2. During the 1950s, the Soviet Union developed the Scud, an improved German V-2. By the 1980s, the Soviets were selling Scuds to just about anyone with the money to pay for them. The Scud is thirty-seven feet long, thirty-five inches in diameter, and weighs six tons. It carries 3.7 tons of highly toxic liquid fuel and a 1-ton high-explosive warhead. It can land within a thousand meters of its target (a CEP of one kilometer) at its maximum range of three hundred kilometers. Between 1982 and 1985 the Iraqis fired 143 Scuds into Iran. At first, Iran could not return the favor, mainly because the Soviets could not get away with supplying both sides in that war, and the Iraqis were old customers who paid in dollars. But in 1985 the Iranians were able to obtain some Scuds from Libya, and later Syria, North Korea, and China. The Iranians fired their Scuds into the Iraqi capital, Baghdad.

Tehran, the Iranian capital, was five hundred kilometers from Iraq, so the Iraqis could not hit the Iranian capital. Between 1985 and 1987 the Iranians fired 40 Scuds. The Iraqis were unsuccessful in obtaining longer-range missiles but finally bought 300 more Scuds from Russia and used East German technicians to boost the Scud's range to six hundred kilometers. This was done first by reducing the warhead weight from 2,200 pounds to 300 pounds. Thus modified, 25 Iraqi Scuds were launched at Tehran in 1987 and a further 193 in 1988. Some of the 1988 attacks were made with a new Scud modification. This one cannibalized fuel tanks from another Scud missile to allow a one-ton warhead to hit Tehran. In that same year, the Iranians fired 231 Scuds back. A total of 632 Scuds were fired between 1982 and 1988, two-thirds of them in 1988. The modified Iraq Scuds had a CEP of two to three kilometers. But when aimed at a city as large as Tehran, they would hit something. It was the same situation the Germans had faced over four decades earlier when attacking London. Moreover, during World War II, the Germans also had their own longer-range designs on the drawing boards when the war ended, using essentially the same modifications the Iraqis came up with. An added irony was that (East) German technicians were hired to modify the Iraqi Scuds and oversee the launching of the missiles.

Because of all this ballistic-missile warfare in the 1980s, it was a seller's market for Scuds. Iran and Iraq each paid about a million dollars for each missile. In addition, about 340 shorter-range (under one hundred kilometers) rockets were fired. All told, about a billion dollars was spent on this "rocket war." Over fifty thousand casualties were inflicted.

Using missiles was considered preferable to aircraft because neither nation could afford to lose what few long-range bomber aircraft they had, nor their irreplaceable pilots. Ballistic missiles, a high-tech weapon, were preferable for a low-tech nation, because they were easier to use than high-performance aircraft. Ballistic missiles will become easier to use in the future. Like many smaller missiles currently available (portable antiaircraft missiles) they will come "ready to fire," in sealed containers that need little maintenance and minimal training for the operators.

In 1991, the Scuds were fired again, this time at Saudi Arabia and Israel. Casualties per Scud fired were fewer than ten per missile. Militarily, the Scud was a bust in 1991. Allied countermeasures against the Scud were impressive.

The Coalition air attacks against Scud launchers sharply reduced the Iraqi capability to launch the missiles. When the Coalition air campaign began against Iraq in January 1991, the Iraqis promptly began firing back Scuds.

Table 10 / Iraqi Scuds Fired during Each Week of the Coalition Air Campaign

Week	Scuds Fired
1	35
2	18
3	4
4	5
5	6
6	4
Total	**72**

Iraq apparently launched at least eighty-one Scuds (forty-three Scuds were fired at Saudi Arabia and thirty-eight at Israel) before the war ended. About half the Scuds were so off target that they fell harmlessly in the desert or water. About 50 percent of the Scuds fired at Israel and 90 percent of those fired at Saudi Arabia were fired at by U.S. Patriot missiles. The Patriot was an anti-aircraft missile that could, under the right conditions, intercept missiles like the Scud. Unfortunately, the modified Scuds used by the Iraqis broke up as they plunged to earth, providing several targets for the Patriot. Since only one of these missile fragments was the high-explosive warhead, the Patriot usually intercepted a larger fragment (usually the Scud fuel tank, which showed more prominently on the Patriot's radar) rather than the smaller warhead.

While all of the ballistic missiles used in combat so far, from 1944 to 1991, have been as terror attacks, ballistic missiles do have the potential to be effective weapons that can accomplish something useful in wartime. Chemical or biological warheads can be fitted to these missiles, although the technology of such warheads is as complex, if not more so, than that of the missiles themselves. Nuclear warheads are also a possibility. But, once more, it's not enough just to have a nuclear weapon. Getting such a weapon to work in a ballistic-missile warhead, a warhead that makes its final plunge to earth at speeds faster than a rifle bullet, is a difficult feat of engineering. Eventually, some aggressive nation will get the missiles, and warheads, and do more with ballistic missiles than terrorize civilians.

Who Has What Ballistic Missiles

WHILE ONLY A handful of nations have ICBMs (United States, Russia, Britain, France, and China), many more have shorter-range missiles, and some of those countries have nuclear weapons to put on their ballistic missiles.

There are roughly five categories of ballistic missiles, and these categories are not equal at all. Many nations have low-level missiles. What is worrisome is the increasing availability of the more capable types of ballistic missiles.

Missile Types

BATTLEFIELD BALLISTIC missiles. Have a range of 10 to 100 kilometers; examples: U.S.-made Lance, Russian FROG-7 (Free Rocket over Ground-7). These are widely available, and have been used to bombard cities and military targets in several wars over the past few decades.

Tactical ballistic missiles. Have a range of 100 to 300 kilometers; example: Russian Scud A, the most exported ballistic missile. The Scud has been the most widely used ballistic missile to date. Interestingly, the Scud is an improved copy of the original World War II V-2. There are thousands of Scuds available these days, and many nations have them, or could easily buy them. Obsolete technology does not mean useless technology.

Short-range theater ballistic missiles. Have a range of 250 to 800 kilometers; examples: improved Scuds and many of the new models several nations are developing. Many nations are building these missiles, often from new designs, and selling them on the world market.

Intermediate-range ballistic missiles or theater ballistic missiles. Have a range of 800 to 5,000 kilometers; example: Chinese-made CSS-2, another popular research project in many nations. For many nations at odds with their neighbors, these missiles are as good as an ICBM. Indeed, in that respect, they are more useful than ICBMs because these shorter-range missiles are cheaper and more available for purchase.

Intercontinental ballistic missiles. Longest-range missiles, currently have a range of 3,500 to 15,000 kilometers; examples: U.S. Minuteman II, Russian SS-18, and new Chinese models. None of these have appeared on the arms market yet, but it's only a matter of time.

BELOW IS a list of the nations currently owning various types of ballistic missiles, or in the process of designing and building their own.

Table 11 / Ballistic Missiles in Use by Anyone Who Can Afford Them

Nation	Missile System	Range	Status	Warhead(s)
Afghanistan	Scud types	250–400	In Use	
Argentina	Condor-II	1,000	R&D	
Brazil	MB-EE 600	500	R&D	
China	CSS-X-4	10,000	In Use	N
	CSS-1	1,000	In Use	N
	CSS-2	2,000	In Use	N
	CSS-N-3	2,000?	In Use	N
	DF-25	1,700	R&D	
	M-18	1,000	R&D	N
	Scud types	250–400	In Use	C,N
	Improved Scud	500	In Use	C,N
	Frog-7 type	65	In Use	
Egypt	Scud A/B	250–400	In Use	
	Frog-7	65	In Use	
India	Prithvi	200	In Use	
	Agni	600–750	In Use?	N
Iran	Scud types	250–400	In Use	C
	Improved Scud	300–550	In Use	C
	Frog-7	65	In Use	C
	Iran-700	700	R&D	C
	Al-Fatah	950	R&D	
Iraq	Scud types	250–400	In Use	C
	Al Hussein	300–550	In Use	C
Israel	Jericho I	450–600	In Use?	N
	Jericho II	1,500	In Use?	N
	Lance	130	In Use	
Japan	Type-30	40	In Use	
Kazakhstan	SS-18+	10,000	In Use	N
Korea, North	NK Scud-C	300–600	In Use	C,N
	Frog-7	65	In Use	C
	Nodong 1	1,000	R&D	C
	Nodong 2	1,500	R&D	C
	Taepo-Dong 1	2,000	R&D	C
	Taepo-Dong 2	3,500	R&D	C

Table 11 / Ballistic Missiles in Use by Anyone Who Can Afford Them (continued)

Nation	Missile System	Range	Status	Warhead(s)
Korea, South	"Korea SSM"	400	In Use	N
Libya	Scud A/B	250–400	In Use	C
Pakistan	Hatf 3	600	R&D	N
Saudi Arabia	CSS-2	950	In Use	
Spain	Capricornio	1,300	R&D	
Syria	Scud B	300–400	In Use	C
	Frog-7	65	In Use	
	SS-21	800	In Use	C
Taiwan	Ching Feng	90	In Use	
	Tien Ma	950	R&D	
Ukraine	SS-18	11,000	In Use	N
	Frog-7	65	In Use	C
Vietnam	Scud types	250–400	In Use	C
Yemen	Scud types	250–400	In Use	

Notes for the above table. *Nation*—Who owns it. *Missile System*—The name of the missile. *Range*—Range of missile in kilometers. *Status*—In Use is a missile that is available for use, R&D means the system is still undergoing research and development, ? means the missile may be in service, or its capability is unknown. *Warhead(s)*—All missiles, except those over 1,000 kilometers range, have high-explosive warheads. All may have C for chemical warhead or N for nuclear warhead, only those known to have them are so listed.

In addition to the systems listed above, Japan and India have satellite launchers that could easily be converted to ICBMs, or at least to ballistic missiles with a range of about four thousand kilometers.

Most of these missiles are quite inaccurate; many are lucky to be as precise as a World War II B-29 bomber operating under optimal conditions. But, unlike B-29s, or any other aircraft, ballistic missiles are difficult to stop. If a nation absolutely, positively has to put a warhead into a neighbor's capital city, a ballistic missile will do the job. Iran and Iraq demonstrated this during the 1980s. Iraq did it again in 1991 against Saudi Arabia and Israel. Add a chemical, biological, or nuclear warhead and you have a real showstopper.

Eyes in the Sky

MANY MISSILES ARE highly dependent on an extensive network of space satellites. In 1957, the Soviet Union launched the first space satellite. Over a trillion dollars and nearly 3,500 satellites later, we have quite a formidable system of military satellites up there. While nearly all ICBMs are built and never used, similar missiles for launching satellites are all used to put satellites in orbit (or at least try to—about 10 percent of launches fail). With the end of the cold war, many ICBMs are being converted to satellite-launcher duty.

While civilian communications, weather, and broadcast satellites do most of the work, the majority of the birds put in orbit have been for the military. While many of the "defense" satellites are up there simply to expedite communications, most are for more warlike purposes. The most common combat-support job of satellites is to make missiles more accurate. This function covers a lot of territory.

• Finding targets. Taking photographs from space was an early objective of satellites, and the military was keen on finding out exactly where the best targets were. In this manner, bombers and ICBMs knew what to hit and exactly where it was.

• Launcher positioning. A ballistic missile–carrying submarine (SSBN) can only launch its missiles accurately if the sub knows exactly where it is when the launch takes place. The guidance system of a ballistic missile works by using precision instruments to guide it to a designated point so many miles, and in a precise direction, from where it was launched. Thus if you miscalculate the launch point by ten miles, it will arrive ten miles from the target. To overcome this problem, the U.S. Navy began launching navigation satellites for its SSBNs in 1960. The first ones sent a signal to submerged subs that allowed them to pin down their exact location to about one mile. Subsequent navigation birds improved this. These satellites were the beginning of the GPS system now in service (which provides location to within fifty to sixty feet). For land-based systems, it is easier, cheaper, and more accurate to use conventional surveying methods.

• Target designation. Finding targets by satellite is a slow process, for the photos have to be transmitted to earth and analyzed. This takes days or, at best, hours. Some satellites, using radar, have the capability to spot targets quickly enough to enable an immediate attack. This was first applied using radar satellites that scanned the oceans for hostile ships. Once the enemy ships were spotted, ships, missiles, or aircraft could be sent after them.

• Missile guidance. The introduction of lightweight GPS receivers in the late 1980s made it possible to use satellites to allow missiles to more accurately find their targets. The downside of this is that any satellite signal can be jammed. So at the moment there is a constant struggle between the satellite builders trying to make their signals more jamproof, and potential target nations working on better jammers. Note that every nation is a potential target, for anyone can buy cheap (a few hundred dollars) GPS receivers for their missiles.

• Countermeasures support. From the very beginning of electronic warfare, the first step in creating a countermeasure was to find out what kind of signal the system to be jammed was broadcasting. Special low-orbit satellites have been employed for several decades to collect this information. Since all electronic equipment has to be extensively tested, and then used even more by the troops who are to learn how to operate it, there are ample opportunities for these low-orbit "ferret" satellites to pick up the transmissions and make possible countermeasures. However, this is not a perfect solution. The Russians tried, and apparently succeeded in some cases, to make the ferret satellites part of a deception. Knowing when the ferret birds would be overhead, the Russians would have their "new" electronics transmit a false signal. The U.S. electronics experts would then be fooled into developing a countermeasure that would not work on the real signal of the new Russian electronic equipment. This only worked for a short time once a war began, but that was enough time to do a lot of damage before a workable countermeasure could be developed.

• BDA (battle damage assessment). "Did we hit it the first time and do we have to try again?" Satellites are often better at checking out targets after they have been hit to see if another attack is necessary. Various deceptions are often used to make the initial attack miss, and the true extent of the damage cannot be determined until the smoke, so to speak, has cleared. The defender may have used deceptions (false targets, camouflage, etc.) to fool the first attack. Countermeasures may have thrown off the aim of aircraft or missiles. If the target was heavily guarded and/or deep in enemy territory, the only practical way to get a look at the damage is with a satellite.

For all of the above reasons, nations are nervous about any threat to their satellites. Moreover, those few nations that possess military satellites have a considerable advantage over those that don't.

But even with a lot of satellites, there are shortcomings in the use of these expensive devices. The two nations with the most military satellites, America and Russia, have both built enormous bureaucracies to safeguard and analyze all the data gathered from their expensive birds. Until this information was first needed for an actual war, no one knew there was a problem. But during the 1991 Gulf War, people from the commanding general of the Coalition down to a lot of lower-ranking people roundly condemned the bureaucrats and their sloth and stringency in passing on all this valuable information. There was much talk, and a little shouting, over this. But it remains to be seen if the satellite barons have loosened their grip on their expensive data. The lesson in all this is that it's not enough to possess spectacular technology. You have to be willing, and able, to use it effectively. Pretending you are does not cut it.

Air-to-Air Missiles and the Elusive Target

WHEN AIRCRAFT FIRST went after each other in a hostile fashion, machine guns were the preferred weapon. At first, these were the same weapons used on the ground. By World War II, heavier machine guns (20mm and 30mm cannons with explosive shells) were used to increase the chances of taking down larger and more robust aircraft. The major shortcoming of machine guns has always been the need to get in close and to be a good shot while firing at a fast, violently maneuvering aircraft from an equally agile warplane. For this reason, many sorties were flown for each enemy aircraft brought down. Indeed, during the formative days of air-to-air combat (World War I, 1914–18) more aircraft were destroyed by accidents and equipment failures than by enemy action.

The shortcomings of machine guns and the need for something better were recognized early on. The basic problem was that there were only a few pilots who had the knack for getting off an accurate shot with machine guns. It was, and is, a very tricky business. It was, and is, thought that automation would solve this problem. Missiles and radar, perhaps. Even during World War II, attempts were made to use missiles to do the job. The appeal of missiles was that they carried a larger warhead, the better to destroy the target with one hit, and had a longer range. Using radar to spot the enemy first, you could guide in a missile from afar. The farther you are from your target, the better your chances of avoiding enemy return fire.

Table 12 / Range of Aircraft Machine Guns by Caliber

Caliber (mm)	Effective Range (meters)
7.5–8 (infantry weapon)	200
12–13 (".50 caliber")	400
20	500
30	700

For going after enemy fighters, 20mm weapons were good enough, as you still had to get in pretty close to insure a hit on these agile aircraft. But two- and four-engine bombers were another matter, and this is where 30mm cannons and rockets came in. The Allies had the bombers and the Germans were doing the shooting. The Germans came up with two air-to-air missiles for use against bombers. The first was an unguided missile, the R4M. The R4Ms were carried in packs of twelve and fired like a shotgun, the idea being that one or more of the eight-pound, 55mm missiles would connect with an eighteen-ounce warhead. German fighters, coming in at 150 to 200 meters a second, would let go with up to forty-eight R4Ms when about 1,000 meters away and then fly until within range for their 20mm or 30mm cannons and open up with these also. When within range of the bombers' (B-17s' and B-24s') many .50 caliber weapons, the fighter would turn away and, if it had any ammunition left, make another pass.

This combination of rockets and cannons was particularly lethal when the Germans were flying their Me-262 jet fighter. Allied fighter escorts had a hard time catching up with the Me-262s before they had made their pass on the bomber formation. The Me-262s would then scoot away to land, rearm, and refuel, and come up for another go at it. The Allies found that the best way to deal with the Me-262s was to go after their airfields.

The second German air-to-air missile, the X-4, was more modern, but because the factory building them was bombed, it never got into action. The X-4 was a wire-guided air-to-air missile. It weighed 132 pounds and a fighter could carry four of them. It had a range of about 5,000 meters. The missile-control flaps were linked to the fighter's gunsight via the wire. The pilot maneuvered the missile via a joystick next to the gunsight. The X-4 rocket motor burned for about seventeen seconds and the pilot had control of the missile for about twelve to fifteen seconds (before it ran out of wire). The forty-four-pound warhead had a proximity fuze that detonated when it came within seven meters of the two-hundred-hertz frequency emitted by U.S. bomber engines. Thus the pilot only had to get the X-4 close to the bomber to score a hit. Given the size of the warhead, a hit would have been fatal most of the time.

After World War II, work on air-to-air missiles continued, although it was another ten years before something workable was put into service. Development of air-to-air missiles began in 1947, when the design of the U.S. AIM-4 Falcon missile got under way. This was to be a thoroughly modern weapon, using radar guidance. It entered service in 1954, as a weapon for use against large, slow-moving Russian bombers carrying nuclear weapons to the United States. The AIM-4A weighed 120 pounds and had a range of nine kilometers. The missile was fast, moving along at a top speed of some 900 meters a second; meaning that at maximum range, it would hit its target in less than fifteen seconds. The problem was that it could easily be jammed, as the missile followed the radar signals, reflecting off the target, from the radar in the aircraft that launched the missile. Also, at lower altitudes, where the radar signal would be bouncing off the ground too, the missile seeker could get confused. This was a common problem with radar-guided missiles.

Table 13 / American Air-to-Air Missiles, 1954–Present

Missile	In Service	Weight	Range	Effectiveness
AIM-4A	1954	120	9	1
AIM-4F	1960	200	15	2
AIM-7A	1955	440	40	3
AIM-7M	1982	500	40	9
AIM-9B	1956	155	3.5	4
AIM-54A	1972	985	140	8
AIM-9M	1983	190	16	7
AIM-54C	1986	1008	150	9
AIM-120A	1989	335	40	10

Notes for the above table. *Missile* is the official name of the missile. *In service* is the year that model entered service. *Weight* is the weight of the missile, in pounds. Most of these missiles are ten to twelve feet long; the Falcon is seven feet long. Diameter ranges from five to eight inches (plus fins and such). *Range* is the normal effective range, in kilometers. *Effectiveness* is a ranking of the missile's ability to hit and destroy a target, with 10 being the best and 1 the worst. All of these missiles have made air-to-air kills in combat.

In 1956, the AIM-4C version came out, using a heat-seeking (infrared) warhead. This was more difficult to jam, but the primitive heat-seeker technology of the time made the AIM-4C good only for shots directly at the target aircraft's heat source; that is, the target's engine exhaust. You had to be pretty much directly behind the target to get a good shot. In 1958, improved radar-homing and heat-seeking models came out, followed by even more improved models in 1960. Several more versions of the Falcon were produced over the next twenty years and eventually some sixty thousand of all versions were built. The missile was withdrawn from U.S. service in 1988. A few are still in use with foreign air forces. The Falcon shot down very few aircraft in combat. In fact, it was a turkey.

Note that despite its shaky prospects, the Falcon enjoyed a long service life and went through many upgrades and improvements. Peacetime testing showed that under just the right conditions, the Falcon would do its job. There was even a longer-range (sixteen kilometers) version (AIM-26A) that carried a nuclear warhead. Some 1,900 of these were built, for use against bomber formations. Some 10,000 of the AIR-2A unguided rockets, also armed with nuclear warheads, were also built. The AIR-2A was cheaper than the AIM-26A and did the same job: delivered a nuclear warhead into a formation of Russian bombers.

The Falcon was developed to deal with a real threat, Russian bombers carrying nuclear weapons to the United States, that never appeared. The heat-seeking version proved less capable than the AIM-9 Sidewinder.

Other 1950s-era air-to-air missiles were designed to deal with fighter-versus-fighter combat, and they eventually succeeded. During the 1991 Gulf War, there were thirty-nine air-to-air kills (of enemy aircraft). AIM-9 Sidewinders accounted for eleven of them, and AIM-7 Sparrows twenty-five. But this success was a long time in coming. It wasn't until thirty years after these missiles first appeared that they finally replaced cannons as the air-to-air weapon of choice. The experience with these missiles taught pilots that missiles often do miss, no matter what the boss, or the manufacturer, says. But it was something of a hollow vindication of air-to-air missiles. For eighty-eight AIM-7 Sparrows were fired, with only 28 percent scoring a hit. The AIM-9 did even worse, with ninety-seven fired and only 12.6 percent making contact. That said, most of these hits could not have been obtained with cannons, especially when the AIM-7 was used against a target that was likely fleeing. Moreover, U.S. pilots knew they could fire at least two missiles at each target, there being few Iraqi warplanes in the air to fight. Two missiles made "long shots" more likely to bring something down.

The AIM-7 Sparrow was basically a longer-range AIM-4. It entered service in 1955, weighing 440 pounds, with a 66-pound warhead and a top speed of about a kilometer a second and a maximum range of forty kilometers. This maximum range is only for attacks from the front or the side of a target. If chasing a fast jet, the effective range is only about eight kilometers. The first version did not perform so well, for it used a form of guidance (beam-riding) that required too much effort from an overworked pilot. The beam rider literally flew within a radar beam broadcast from the radar in the nose of the launching aircraft. The pilot had to keep this beam on the target, for the missile guidance system automatically changed course to stay within the beam. If the target aircraft moved around too much, the launching aircraft would not be able to keep the beam on it.

In 1958 a workable version of the Sparrow appeared, using semiactive radar homing (SARH), and this version has been constantly upgraded to this day. But because of its size and type of guidance, the AIM-7 was not suitable for fighters going after other fighters. The heat-seeking Falcon was supposed to arm the fighters for their air-superiority work, but the AIM-4 was never really good at it. Eventually, the AIM-7 would get better, and the AIM-4 would be replaced.

Relief came in the form of a secret, and unauthorized, development project begun in 1953 that produced the AIM-9 Sidewinder. This was done by a bunch of curious and resourceful navy weapons engineers who decided to turn a World War II–era air-to-ground unguided rocket into a guided missile by simply making a few unauthorized modifications. This proved to be the most successful air-to-air missile in history. The Sidewinder was designed to be simple (it had twenty-four moving parts), cheap (the first version cost twenty thousand dollars in 1996 dollars), and effective. Initially weighing 155 pounds and with a range of 3,500 meters, some seventy thousand of this version, the AIM-9B, were produced between its introduction in 1956 and 1962. The Sidewinder was effective. It was meant to be nothing but a heat-seeking missile for fighters. It was simple to use. All the pilot had to do was:
• Turn his aircraft toward an enemy aircraft;
• Turn on the Sidewinder's heat (infrared) sensor;
• Wait for the "growling" noise to come through his earphones (indicating the missile's heat detector had spotted the target—the louder the growl, the better a fix the heat sensor had on the target and the more likely the missile was to hit the target);
• Then press another button to fire the missile, and press it again to fire another. Two or more were often fired to insure a hit.

At that point the missile was on its own and the pilot could go about other business. Most importantly, a Sidewinder was used to shoot down an aircraft in 1958. The Sidewinder now had the ultimate stamp of approval, "proven in combat."

By 1960, U.S. air commanders thought the future had arrived. Air-to-air missiles would replace machine guns as the principal air-to-air weapon. When U.S. fighters went to Vietnam a few years later, many went with just missiles. No machine guns were needed. Combat experience with the North Vietnamese air force provided a sharp reality check. The American air-to-air missiles were not a wonder weapon against North Vietnamese pilots. A modern jet fighter had too many moves for the current generation of missiles. The heat seekers had to be directly behind the enemy jet, and even then a bit of violent maneuvering could fake out the Falcon or Sidewinder. The heat seekers were also fooled if they were too close to the ground, or if fired toward the sun. The radar-homing missiles were even easier to evade. The pilots demanded their 20mm cannons back, and then went off with missiles and guns.

While the original Sidewinder worked, but only under just the right conditions, this was largely a result of the heat seeker, which had limited ability to detect heat. Heat-seeker technology was available before, and during, World War II, but it was not sensitive enough to really be useful. By the early 1950s, a fairly sensitive heat seeker was available for the early AIM-4 Falcon and AIM-9 Sidewinder missiles. But these could only detect heat straight ahead, or a few degrees to either side. It was like picking up a target by looking through a straw. The aircraft carrying the heat-seeker missile had to get almost directly behind the target aircraft before the heat seeker in the missile would detect the target. Then, when launched, the missile could easily lose the trail if the target aircraft turned sharply and could no longer be detected by the heat seeker. Over the next four decades, more sensitive seekers were developed. The AIM-9M (used in the 1991 Gulf War) could "see" a target twenty-seven degrees to either side. This made it easier to pick up a target, and keep on the target's tail.

By 1967, a new model of the Sidewinder, with a more sensitive heat seeker and better controls, was in service. The Sparrow had already proved itself capable for longer-range missions in the air battles over North Vietnam. The first two enemy aircraft downed by U.S. warplanes, in 1965, were due to Sparrows. For close-in work, there were the new Sidewinders, with more sensitive heat seekers and more maneuverability. By the end of the Vietnam War, during the last air campaign over North Vietnam in 1972, the Sidewinder was hitting enemy aircraft over 80 percent of the time it was used. The following year, when Israel was at war with the Arabs and needed fresh supplies of air-to-air missiles, late-model Sidewinders were sent over and achieved a 92 percent hit rate.

Israel repeated the success with Sidewinders, and Sparrows, in its lopsided aerial victory over Syria in 1982. In that same year, Britain used the latest Sidewinders with equal success in the Falklands.

The AIM-9L came out in 1976, with a more powerful rocket motor as well as improved tracking and maneuvering ability. An improved fuze increased the warhead's effectiveness and resistance to electronic countermeasures (like a signal to detonate prematurely). The AIM-9L had better tracking ability and was the first Sidewinder with the ability to attack from all angles, including head-on.

The current version, the AIM-9M, introduced in 1983, has the all-aspect capability of the L model, but provides all-around higher performance. This includes improved defense against infrared countermeasures, better ability to pick out a target close to the ground, and a reduced-smoke rocket motor. These modifications increase ability to locate and lock on a target and decrease the missile's chances of being seen. Many of the earlier Sidewinders had "smoky" rocket motors that made it pretty obvious where the firing aircraft was, so new propellant was used. Several new, and rather minor, modifications to the AIM-9M were made in response to experience in the 1991 Persian Gulf War.

Missiles That Don't Miss as Much

BUT NO ONE in the air force wanted to rest on their laurels. A new generation of air-to-air missiles was under development by the 1980s. The new missiles shared two characteristics: they would do what we have done and do it better, and they would do new stuff with the latest technology.

For longer-range missiles, this meant a missile that had its own radar and countermeasures, so that, once fired, the pilot can go off and do something else, like escape or take on another target. Once launched, the missile would be on its own. This was actually done in the 1960s, at great cost, to create the U.S. Navy's AIM-54 Phoenix missile. This weapon, costing over a million dollars each (then, a lot more now), was to be the ultimate weapon for fleet defense. Its range was 150 kilometers and it weighed 985 pounds. After fourteen years of development and extensive live tests, it was in service by 1974, and it worked. What made the Phoenix so expensive, and so effective, was its ability to fly most of the distance using radar homing and then, for the rest of its flight, to use its own built-in radar, plus a heat seeker and proximity fuze. Later versions also had countermeasures built in and the missile's software was modified to deal with high-speed cruise missiles.

The main point of the Phoenix, which could only be used on the F-14 fighter, was to nail enemy bombers or cruise missiles as far away as possible from friendly ships (especially aircraft carriers). Because of the long range of the missile, and even though it could move at better than one kilometers a second, the F-14's radar and fire-control computer could send up to six AIM-54s at six different targets simultaneously. This capability was there because the navy knew that anyone attacking a ten-billion-dollar carrier task force would do so with multiple aircraft and missiles. Over two thousand AIM-54s were built, and older versions were upgraded. If you include the cost of the F-14, the Phoenix program was on the same scale as the World War II Manhattan Project to produce the atomic bomb (taking into account inflation). One of the additional benefits of the AIM-54 program was that it proved that such a missile could be built successfully and used without a lot of embarrassing failures.

Out of this came the AMRAAM (Advanced Medium-Range Air-to-Air Missile) project. Begun in 1978, it got into service in 1989 and managed to shoot down something over Iraq in 1993. The AIM-120 AMRAAM was the lighter and more capable successor of the AIM-7 Sparrow. The AIM-120 weighs 340 pounds, has a range of fifty kilometers, and, like the AIM-54, is launched by a fighter, after the fighter's radar has spotted a target. When the AIM-120 gets to within a few kilometers of its target, the missile's radar takes over and leaves the launching aircraft to do something else. The AIM-120 is more resistant to countermeasures and, in general, more effective than the AIM-7. At over half a million dollars, it's also four times more expensive. But that's the price of progress. Moreover, the AIM-7 will remain in service. It seems that, as complex and effective as the AIM-120 is, when the counter-measures get really exotic, the older, and less elaborate, AIM-7 still has an edge—sort of like an aircraft using its cannons when the enemy has jammed the air-to-air missiles. No one ever figured out a way to jam cannon shells.

But this takes nothing away from the AIM-120. Being a newer missile, it is more amenable to upgrades. One proposal is to add another rocket motor to it so that it can shoot down ballistic missiles during the first fifty to sixty seconds of flight (when they are moving relatively slowly and can be spotted by an AWACS). While zapping ballistic missiles like the Scud may be appealing, getting the money to upgrade a missile that already costs over half a million dollars each will be difficult in these post–cold war times. Actually, just get-ting the sophisticated and expensive AMRAAM into service was difficult, and that was before the cold war came to an abrupt end.

The companion to the AIM-120, the AIM-132 ASRAAM (Advanced Short-Range Air-to-Air Missile) is having a more difficult time getting into service. The AIM-9 Sidewinder has, since it was first introduced, proved such a capable weapon that there was not a tremendous incentive to completely re-place it. Over the last forty years, the Sidewinder has been continually im-proved. Usually, a new component was developed and older versions of the Sidewinder were simply equipped with the new item (warhead, guidance sys-tem, rocket motor, controls). Some Sidewinders were in service several decades, and had most of their components changed, before they were used in combat, or training. At the moment, the AIM-132 project is being carried on largely by Europeans. Meanwhile, more improvements to the AIM-9 are ex-pected to take it into the next century. One of the more ambitious is to make the AIM-9X faster and use it to attack larger, slower, and longer-ranged radar-homing missiles. This will bring the air-to-air missile to an ultimate battle, with missile fighting missile.

Several lessons can be learned from this history of air-to-air missiles:

• New high-technology weapons may not work at all that well when first released. But if you keep improving them, they will eventually become quite capable in combat. A decade or two of use will usually turn any new weapon into something useful on the battlefield.

Targets will try to defend themselves. Pilots quickly found that they could perform sharp maneuvers that would throw off the missile's aim. This is less likely today, with much more maneuverable missiles, so other countermeasures, like flares (for heat seekers) and jammers (for radar-guided missiles) continue to come into use. New versions of missiles are needed just to deal with the latest wrinkles in countermeasures technology. For example, flares and aircraft are not, obviously, the same thing. Seekers on missiles can be made "intelligent" enough to tell the difference. This can, in turn, be countered by designing flares that look (to a heat seeker) more like an aircraft. It goes on and on. Therefore,

• Technology marches on, and while new technology often creates proposals for new weapons, more often it solves technical problems with existing ones and makes them more reliable and effective.

• Air-to-air missiles are not a perfect weapon, as many of their early promoters exclaimed. But eventually, new tactics were developed to make use of the missiles and eventually the cannon and machine gun became obsolete for air-to-air combat.

• All of the basic types of air-to-air missiles were developed by the United States. The Soviet Union made copies first, then began developing its own variations. As far as anyone knows, from combat experience, Russian air-to-air missiles were never able to catch up to, or surpass, the capabilities of the latest American weapons. This is not to say that claims to the contrary have not been made, nor that the Russians could not build a better mousetrap. All we know so far is that no one has demonstrated Russian superiority in air-to-air missiles, yet.

But this may be changing, ironically and providentially, since the cold war has ended. During the 1980s, British and Russian scientists developed heat seekers that could see sixty degrees on any side. The British are trying to build this new seeker technology into the AIM-132 ASRAAM, while the Russians have, since 1985, already installed the new seekers in their AA-11 missile. The Russians' problem, it was always thought, was that they could produce small quantities of very effective technology, but were unable to produce it in large quantities. The Russians always did excellent laboratory work, but rarely managed to transfer that excellence to the production line.

But throughout the 1980s, the Russians appeared to have solved many of their problems with the mass production of high-tech items. This could be seen in the new generation of Soviet warplanes, particularly the MiG-29 and Su-27. But the most compelling example was the AA-11 heat-seeking missile. What the Russians had done was take two existing technologies and combine them in a weapon that leapfrogged every other short-range air-to-air missile. The AA-11 had a seeker that could detect heat sources up to ninety degrees on either side. The pilot of a Russian aircraft wore a helmet with a built-in sight that allowed him to identify the target he wanted a missile to go after. Pressing a button sent the missile on its way, even if the AA-11 had to promptly turn around and go after an aircraft that was going the other way and was now behind the launching aircraft.

After the Communist government in East Germany collapsed, and the two Germanys were united in 1990, the German Luftwaffe (air force) inherited a squadron of Russian MiG-29s and their AA-11 missiles. Also inherited were the East German pilots trained, by the Russians, to use these aircraft and missiles. This was unprecedented, and rather sobering. It turned out that the AA-11s were quite good, even though none had, as yet, actually been used in combat.

The key to making the AA-11 work was the targeting helmet. This was a device widely used in the West, but not in fighters, or at least not in American fighters, where the emphasis was on long-range missiles. America had an excellent short-range missile, the Sidewinder, and no one in the United States saw any need to change anything.

The AA-11 had entered service in 1984 and was widely known about by 1985. Israel promptly did something about it. The Israeli solution was similar to the Russian system: a helmet-mounted tracking system and a short-range missile (the Python 4, based on the Sidewinder) that entered service in 1993.

Meanwhile, back in the United States, the attitude was one of "so what?". The United States had developed a helmet sight in the early 1970s, and used it in jet warplanes from 1973 to 1979. But the missiles of that time were not really up to making the most of the helmet sight. Most importantly, the missiles did not have seekers that would allow the missile to look "sideways" before it was fired. The U.S. helmet sight (the VTAS) was abandoned except for versions used by attack helicopter pilots.

More importantly, the U.S. attitude was that close-in air-to-air fighting was to be avoided, for the very simple reason that the weapons were becoming so effective that everyone involved was likely to get hit. Since American doctrine went for quality over quantity, the idea of taking equal losses was a losing proposition. The Russians, on the other hand, did believe in quantity. Getting equal exchanges in air-to-air combat was fine with them, especially when they were exchanging their aircraft for American warplanes that cost more than twice as much. The American doctrine was to go for the long-range shot with missiles like the AIM-7 Sparrow or the AIM-120 AMRAAM. American air commanders are not surprised that the Israelis would develop their own version of the Russian AA-11. It makes sense, because Israel is relatively small and air battles have always been at relatively short ranges because it doesn't take long for enemy aircraft to get into Israeli airspace.

This is not the first time there have been two quite different attitudes toward air-to-air combat, and not the first time that American doctrine played down close-in air combat. During World War II, the Japanese had fighters that were superb at close-in air-to-air combat. The Zero was the best example, but American aircraft managed to get the upper hand anyway. Built for speed and durability, U.S. fighters simply did not get in close with Japanese fighters. Instead, they would use their speed to make high-speed diving passes at Japanese aircraft, or simply to get away to fight another day. Even against roughly equivalent German aircraft over Europe, American pilots used the same type of tactics. American pilots have never been big fans of "dogfighting." After World War II, when the first air-to-air missiles were developed, the intention was to get kills at longer ranges.

Well, it didn't work out that way.

As attractive as the long-range shot was, and is, pilots are understandably nervous about firing a missile at a distant aircraft that might be friendly. While there have only been a few incidents of these long-range missile shots taking out friendly aircraft, it happened enough times to make the fighter pilots reluctant to use those long-range missiles. Moreover, until the last decade or so, long-range missiles were not capable enough to consistently take down their intended victims. But over the years the long-range missile shot has become more attractive to pilots. The equipment is better able to tell friend from foe, and the missiles are more lethal. One of the great confidence builders has been the use of AWACS air-control aircraft. Fighter pilots know that the AWACS can see everyone in the air and is in a position to guarantee, as much as this sort of thing can be guaranteed, that the "hostile" aircraft on your radar scope is indeed a bad guy and not one of your buddies who got lost.

This is not to say that U.S. pilots won't get new helmet-mounted sights. They will, and the new helmets will have a lot of new features. The basic technology is still the head-tracking system. This monitors the pilot's head position and permits weapons sensors and seekers to be pointed in the same direction as the pilot's eyes. The new technology is more reliable and less likely to suffer interference from other equipment on the aircraft. The new helmets take care of more than targeting; they handle navigation, air-to-ground and air-to-air combat, and fire-control calculations.

Using the MiG-29s and AA-11s of the German air force, American pilots have found that they would lose most of the time if they got into a dogfight. But they would also win most of the time if they used their long-range missiles and avoided a close-in fight. U.S. warplanes have yet to encounter AA-11–equipped jets in combat. The Russians are exporting the missile and the head-mounted sight that works with it. But it is felt that U.S. fighters are unlikely to get into trouble with any AA-11–equipped adversaries. For one thing, in the hands of inept pilots, the AA-11 won't do the enemy much good. Of course, if a number of U.S. fighters got whacked by AA-11s in air-to-air combat, that attitude could change in a hurry. But for the moment, the U.S. Air Force and U.S. Naval aviation prefer to follow their long used, and generally successful, tactics of avoiding the close-in battle. Only time will tell if this is a wise move.

The Ultimate Countermeasure

WHILE JAMMING AN enemy radar is effective, at least for a while, blowing the radar up is permanent. This was recognized during World War II, but the radar operators were also aware of their vulnerability. Radar stations were fortified and well protected with antiaircraft guns. Moreover, radar equipment was difficult to destroy and relatively easy to repair. The antennae were easy to spot, but they were more frequently separated from the more valuable electronics equipment. The latter was increasingly put in a hidden underground bunker. It wasn't until the end of World War II that the Allies were able to put enough airpower over Germany to enable them to smash the enemy radar system, or at least knock it down and keep coming back to keep it down.

After World War II, more thought was given to the problem. It was soon realized that, with the advances in missile technology made by the 1950s, it was possible to take a long-range air-to-air missile and fit it with a seeker that went after radar signals. Presto, there was an accurate antiradar missile that went directly at the source of the radar transmission. The AIM-7 was used as the model for the AGM-45 Shrike antiradar missile. Development began in 1961, to provide a weapon that could knock out the growing number of Soviet radar systems. Thirteen different seeker modules (for the wide array of different Russian radar frequencies) were developed for the 390-pound weapon. It had a range of up to forty kilometers and a 145-pound warhead. The AGM-45 entered service in 1964.

There were problems. These were first encountered when the Shrike was used to shut down the Russian-supplied radar systems used in Vietnam. The Soviet "advisers" operating North Vietnamese radar stations quickly adapted to the new antiradiation missiles. The simplest countermeasure to this countermeasure was to simply turn off the radar when it was thought that aircraft carrying Shrikes were in the neighborhood. Actually, there were several variations to the "turn it on, turn it off" routine that would confuse the Shrikes and cause them to miss. The AGM-45 also had reliability problems that led to further failures, and a series of upgrades that kept it in production until 1986 and in service into the 1990s, at least with the U.S. Navy.

As a result of the Vietnam-era problems with the AGM-45, the AGM-78 was developed and entered service in 1968. It wasn't much of an improvement over the AGM-45, was produced in smaller numbers (three thousand, versus over twelve thousand for the Shrike), and was withdrawn from service in the 1980s. Until the 1980s, the AGM-45, with constant upgrades and modifications, remained the primary antiradiation missile in Western arsenals.

Table 14 / U.S. Antiradar Missiles

Missile	In Service	Weight (pounds)	Range (km)	Length (feet)
AGM-45	1964	400	19	11
AGM-78	1968	1,356	30	15
AGM-88	1983	805	70	14
AGM-122	1986	195	17	9
AGM-136	199?	430	200	8

Notes for the above table. *Missile* is the official name of the missile. *In Service* is the year that model entered service, or was being tested if an experimental missile that was never in service. *Weight* is the weight of the missile, in pounds. Most of these missiles are ten to twelve feet long; the Falcon is seven feet long. Diameter ranges from five to ten inches (plus fins and such). *Range* is the normal effective range, in kilometers.

Although Israel used the AGM-45 successfully against Soviet radars during its 1973 war, it was obvious that a new antiradiation missile was needed. There were too many ways to defeat the Shrike and there was only so much that upgrades and modifications could do to overcome this. After over a decade of work, the AGM-88 HARM (High-speed Antiradiation Missile) entered service in the early 1980s. This was a much more capable weapon. For one thing, it was faster and used more sensitive electronics to detect enemy electronics on the ground. In addition to going after radar transmitters that were turned on, the HARM could also detect many transmitters that were turned off. This feat was possible because, even when turned off, radar equipment gives off some signals, and these can often be detected. In addition, the HARM was very good at "memorizing" the location of a radar site so that, even if the radar was turned off, the missile remembered where it was and went after it. With this last mode, the missile can be fired in the general direction of suspected transmitters. If it detects some of these low-level transmissions, it goes after the enemy equipment; if not, the missile self-destructs (so the enemy does not get its hands on an intact missile, and its secrets).

As the name HARM indicates, speed was an important feature of the AGM-88. At some five hundred meters per second, the HARM was nearly twice as fast as earlier antiradar missiles. But speed alone was not the key to nailing enemy radars. From the earliest use of the Shrike during the Vietnam War, it was obvious that the same rules applied against radars as against enemy warplanes. Namely, you had to ambush them, and then outsmart them. Enemy ground radars would use deception and countermeasures to hobble attempts to blind the enemy defenses.

The aircraft that used antiradiation missiles received more sensitive radar receivers as time went on, and more powerful computers to sort out all the signals and identify, and locate, the ones that posed the greatest dangers. Keep in mind that enemy defenses would use several different types of radars. Some of these would be for spotting incoming aircraft; others would guide antiaircraft missiles to their targets. Each different type of missile system—and you might encounter three or more different ones at once—would use different radar frequencies. Some of the more modern radars can switch frequencies. Thus while the speed and homing capabilities of the antiradiation missile were important, it was often more important that the aircraft carrying the missile have the equipment on board to sniff out enemy radars before turning the missile loose. This also explains why antiradar missiles can vary considerably in their capabilities, depending on what aircraft they are carried on. For this reason, the AGM-88 HARM had, in addition to speed, a lot of built-in electronic capabilities. But there's only so much you can build into a missile. Most of the electronics sniffing for radars, and then sorting them out by type and capabilities, is still best done by using the more extensive electronics carried on the Wild Weasel (electronic warfare) aircraft. The Weasels can not only pinpoint the best target for a HARM, but can also jam or deceive radars. There are often more radars than HARMs carried on Weasels. So you jam what you can and blast the rest with HARMs. Deciding which radars to use missiles on is easy. If you can't jam it, and it's going to guide surface-to-air missiles at you, then it's worth an antiradiation missile. Range is often a factor, which was one of the major reasons for developing the larger AGM-78.

Antiradar missiles have proven to be rather tricky to develop. It's something of a dark art, and several systems have died from a bad case of budget overruns. Each U.S. antiradiation missile developed to date has suffered from the "low capability–high cost" problem. The first missile, the AGM-45, was a modified air-to-air missile (an AIM-7 Sparrow). As the first of its type, it wasn't all that expensive to develop. But then the enemy began to come up with ways to fool the missile, and the development of new seekers and electronics to overcome that became a cost spiral that never ended. The range of the surface-to-air missiles also became a factor. If the defender could get off some longer-range (than your antiradiation missile) shots, you were in trouble. His missiles would hit you before your missiles shut down the antiaircraft radar system. Oh, you might be able to jam him. But then, you might not. So a little extra range on the antiradiation missile was seen as a good thing. The AGM-88 HARM had a much longer range than its predecessors. But this was not seen as enough. The AGM-136, which eventually got into trouble because of cost overruns, had more range, and it had endurance. The AGM-136 could slowly cruise about the battlefield for several hours, listening for any enemy radar. If said radar came on-line, and it was one of the radars the AGM-136 was programmed to attack, the radar would be attacked by the missile. The problem was cost, putting all those expensive electronics into a missile that would eventually make a suicide run on a radar.

Another missile that never got into widespread use was the AGM-122 Sidearm. This was a "HARM lite" for helicopters and low-flying jets. It was a Sidewinder with a radar seeker. It was small, it was cheap, and it was too limited in its capabilities to be useful. Making antiradiation missiles like the AGM-122 can be too little, or, as with the AGM-136, too much. However, the AGM-136 is expected to be replaced with a drone aircraft that can be reused. It will wander over enemy territory, using its sensors to capture information about enemy radars. Friendly jets can then come in and use that information to bomb the radar sites.

Antiradiation missiles will be around for a while. In fact, new types are under development. It has not gone unnoticed that more and more aircraft, and missiles themselves, are using radar. Any aircraft or missile that broadcasts is making itself a target for an antiradiation missile that knows its frequency. At one point, the United States experimented with equipping AIM-7 missiles with seekers that went after the radar of enemy fighters. But it didn't work out, and much money is still being spent to make this work. Many fighters are using their radar more sparingly anyway, if only to avoid giving away their position. Meanwhile, a very popular target for antiradiation missiles are aircraft like the AWACS, which can control hundreds of warplanes and tankers in aerial battle. Take down the AWACS and you cripple the coordination of the aircraft the AWACS was directing. An AWACS is moving at over seven hundred kilometers an hour (two hundred meters a second) and will detect an incoming antiradiation missile several hundred kilometers away. Well, the missile could use its own countermeasures and be very fast.

One proposal for attacking an AWACS is a missile with a jet engine, plus a rocket booster for the final approach to the AWACS. Such a stealthy missile could approach the AWACS at extremely low altitude using passive radar (homing in on the AWACS radar signal). Once under the AWACS, it would ignite its rocket and home in on the AWACS using radar or infrared. This would be difficult for the AWACS to avoid, as it might only be twenty or thirty seconds before such a fast-moving missile from below connected.

You could also use a ballistic missile with a radar seeker in the warhead. You would have to move fast, as the AWACS is moving fast and a ballistic missile is aimed at a specific area when launched. However, you wouldn't have to hit the AWACS directly; you'd only have to damage it and put it out of action. Its radar dome is very vulnerable to any kind of damage.

So you can see why the antiradiation missile, while not a perfect countermeasure, is certainly the ultimate one if it does connect.

Such a Great Idea: Surface-to-Air Missiles (SAMs)

IN 1945, AMERICAN scientists began working on a guided missile that would destroy aircraft. Actually, such a device had already been developed and put to use three years earlier. That was the radar fuze for antiaircraft artillery shells. This device was a miniature radar set in the nose of a shell. If the shell came close to an aircraft, the radar detected this and caused the shell to explode. This made antiaircraft guns several times more lethal. But it was obvious that aircraft could fly higher than the largest antiaircraft gun could fire, and something else was needed to bring these high-altitude bombers down. This became particularly urgent with the appearance of nuclear bombs. These could, indeed must, be dropped from high altitude and don't require the accuracy of conventional bombing.

The solution was obvious: a guided missile. By 1951, the first American SAM, the Nike-Ajax, was tested. Two years later, Nike-Ajax batteries began to show up on the outskirts of American cities. Over ten thousand of these missiles were built before the Nike-Hercules replaced the Nike-Ajax in 1958.

The Nike-Ajax missile weighed 2,500 pounds and was 35 feet long. It had a range of 40 kilometers and could reach aircraft as high as 19 kilometers (62,000 feet). The Nike-Hercules was a larger missile, 42 feet long and weighing 4,700 pounds. But it had a range of 130 kilometers and could reach targets 100,000 feet high. Both missiles were essentially radio-controlled. Radar was used to track aircraft and missile, sending commands to the missile so that it would collide with the aircraft. It worked during tests. More importantly, it worked in 1960 when the Russian version of the Nike-Ajax, the SA-2, shot down a high-flying American U-2 reconnaissance aircraft.

The Russians had noted U.S. work on SAMs and had used captured German technicians and documents to start their own program. In 1956, the SA-1 entered service. This was similar in size to the Nike-Ajax, but was inferior in performance. In fact, it was quite unreliable. Two years later, the much more effective SA-2 came out. This was a two-ton, 35-foot-long missile with a range of 50 kilometers and a maximum altitude of 60,000 feet. While the U-2 could fly higher than this, there were times when the U-2 dipped to lower altitudes. And during one of those times a U-2 got nailed by SA-2s. This gave the missile a good reputation inside, and outside, Russia.

Even before the U-2 incident, American air force commanders were worrying about how to get past whatever SAMs the Russians would eventually develop. The problem did not seem overly formidable. SAMs were radar-directed, and radar had been jammed or deceived during World War II. At first, the World War II model was followed, with special aircraft equipped with radar detectors and jammers operating just outside the combat zone. These electronic-warfare aircraft were not warplanes, but simply flying platforms for all the electronic gear and the operators. But it wasn't enough to detect the SAM radars, or to try and jam them. Some of the SAM launchers and radars would have to be destroyed, one way or the other. The Russians were using powerful radars that were not easily jammed from a distance. The only way you could be sure that the SAMs could not get through was to destroy them.

Thus began, in the early 1960s, the Wild Weasel concept. The Wild Weasel aircraft was the answer, a fighter-bomber loaded down with radar detectors, jammers, and antiradiation missiles. The two-man crew consisted of a pilot, to keep the aircraft out of the way of enemy fire, and the GIB (Guy in Back), who operated all the electronics. Originally, these were second-line fighter-bombers that used their electronic sensors and jammers, plus antiradiation missiles as needed, to clear the way for friendly bombers. The sensors were crude, and at first the Weasels had to depend mainly on larger electronic-warfare aircraft to the rear to feed them information on enemy radars. But the Weasels would bore in, strafing and bombing radar, SAM, and antiaircraft gun positions. The new AGM-45 Shrike antiradiation missile had teething problems initially, but by 1965 was in regular use. The results were pretty spectacular. Between the Weasels and new electronic countermeasures (ECM), North Vietnamese antiaircraft defenses were made much less lethal by 1968. For example, the percentage of SA-2 missiles that hit a U.S. aircraft from 1965–1968 shows this.

Table 15 / SAM Effectiveness in Vietnam

Year	Percentage of SA-2 SAMs Hitting a Target
1965	5.7%
1966	3.0%
1967	1.8%
1968	0.9%

Some nine thousand SA-2s were fired by the North Vietnamese, bringing down 150 U.S. aircraft. That's one warplane shot down for every sixty missiles fired. When first used, it took fewer than twenty SA-2s to hit something. Four years later, more than a hundred SA-2s were needed to achieve the same result. It wasn't just the Wild Weasels that turned the tide, but numerous new electronic devices that canceled the effectiveness of the SAMs. One of the more important items was the RHAW (Radar Homing and Warning, pronounced "raw") device. Nearly all combat aircraft were equipped with RHAW, a gadget that warned that they were being "painted" by a SAM radar and, if a missile was launched, told which direction it was coming from. The SA-2s were fast (up to a thousand meters a second), but not maneuverable. With RHAW warning, a fighter could quickly turn away from an oncoming SAM. The old World War II standby, chaff, was also widely used, as were jamming pods.

All of these countermeasures were so effective that the North Vietnamese often had to launch the SA-2s as unguided missiles. With the defeat of the SA-2s, the Vietnamese fell back on the old World War II weapon, massed antiaircraft cannons. But even these were rendered much less effective by jamming of their radar. This left only the most primitive weapon of all, small-caliber (57mm and under) guns that were aimed visually. These were lethal at low altitudes and, by the early 1970s, were the cause of most U.S. air losses. But the U.S. defenses were so superior that when B-52s were sent over North Vietnam in the early 1970s, jamming and Wild Weasels rendered the high-altitude bombers relatively immune to SAM attacks. The B-52s were too high for cannons to reach them. These attacks were demoralizing for the Vietnamese, and especially for the Russian technicians manning the Soviet SAMs and radars.

The Vietnam War also saw the development of the modern "strike package," in which a dozen bombers would be escorted by a dozen or more specialist aircraft to defeat enemy SAMs and interceptors. There would be Wild Weasels to detect and jam radars, as well as to launch antiradiation missiles (ARMs). Other fighter-bombers would be sent down to finish the job after ARMs had destroyed the radars. Thus the missiles and antiaircraft guns would be destroyed so that they could not fire at all. High-flying fighters would guard against enemy interceptors and other aircraft would drop chaff to block the use of other SAM sites. To the rear, larger and slower aircraft equipped with radar and radar detectors would oversee the entire operation. These larger electronic aircraft were the predecessors of the present AWACS.

The United States knew that there were several thousand Russian technical advisers in North Vietnam helping to maintain and operate the SA-2s, and these were the same troops and weapons NATO aircraft would face in Europe.

The battle against the SAMs was seen as a practice session for a war with the Russians themselves, a battle that the Soviets seemed destined to lose. But not everyone got the message.

The Soviets also took their Vietnam experience to heart and worked vigorously to come up with weapons and technology that would defeat the American techniques for suppressing air defenses. The Russian reaction was to develop a number of responses.

• They produced still more missile systems. This complicated the job of Wild Weasels and enemy aircraft. Countermeasures often worked only against one type of missile system. By 1990, the Soviets had over two dozen different SAM systems in use.

• They added more variety in the frequencies used by each radar, complicating the job of enemies trying to jam or detect these radars.

• They continued their use of old-fashioned deception. This was most commonly seen in how they established several fortified positions for each actual missile battery. Some of these unused positions were not empty, but contained dummies and/or electronic equipment that tried to make it seem like there was a radar there.

• They did not export all of their missile systems, so that the ones kept at home were harder for American experts to figure out, and devise countermeasures for, ahead of time. The systems they did export were often what they called "monkey models," with key features deleted.

• They attempted to hide the true characteristics of their radars and electronics. This was an old Soviet technique. Some equipment would not even be distributed to the troops in peacetime, but would be brought out if there was a war.

• They developed an elaborate plan for air defense, with over a dozen different types of SAMs providing overlapping defended zones. In addition, there were several different types of radar-guided antiaircraft guns. On top of all this, there were special electronic-warfare units to analyze enemy electronic devices and, if possible, jam or deceive them.

The first victims of the new Soviet techniques were the Israelis. During the 1973 Arab-Israeli war, the Arabs were equipped with the latest Russian SAMs and techniques. The Israelis had ignored the American experience in Vietnam and refused to spend a lot of money on the expensive U.S. equipment developed to defeat Soviet-style air defenses. The Israeli air force paid the price in the opening days of the war. Their warplanes suffered unprecedented losses. U.S. equipment was quickly rushed in, and the Israeli air force was able to recover. After that, everyone took to heart the new face of air defense.

Thus, by the early 1970s, the future of air warfare was already laid out in detail. The "strike package" and the ongoing battle between electronic gadgets is still with us and will be for some time to come.

Or will it?

Ever since Vietnam, there's been an ongoing effort to make Wild Weasels more effective against SAMs and enemy electronic devices. Wild Weasels are expensive, especially if these aircraft and their crews do nothing else but Wild Weasel work. Instead of having Wild Weasels, air forces are now trying to develop internal countermeasures gear, and pods that allow any aircraft to be an electronic countermeasures aircraft. Electronic warfare has become so complex that, rather than depend on highly trained aircrews to handle it, it's easier to program the skills and strategies into computers that can be carried on any aircraft. This is nothing new. For decades, combat aircraft have had more "black boxes" added that automatically perform complex tasks previously taken care of by skilled pilots or other aircrew members. Fifty years ago, a bomber would have a navigator to keep track of where the aircraft was, a radio operator to deal with communications, a flight mechanic to look after electrical and mechanical systems, and a bombardier to do the intricate actions needed to get the bombs on target. There were also several men manning defensive machine guns, and on some aircraft one or two specialists to operate electronic-warfare equipment. Today, a bomber carrying a heavier weight of bombs over a greater distance than its World War II predecessor does all of that with one or, at most, two people. Everything else is automated.

So why not automate electronic warfare? This automation has been creeping in as individual aircraft are given more and more of their own countermeasures—things like warning radars for attacking missiles, and flare dispensers and jammers to shake those incoming missiles. So why not go all the way? Why not get rid of the Wild Weasels and only equip a few of the aircraft on a strike with the equivalent of the Wild Weasels' equipment? This gear would be in the form of a pod or two and some HARM missiles. The "designated Wild Weasels" would carry fewer bombs, or perhaps none at all. You would no longer have to maintain a fleet of Wild Weasel aircraft, and there would be one less type of specialist to be trained (to operate the Wild Weasels).

There are those who insist that electronic warfare is an arcane dark art that requires flying human specialists. This crew appears to have lost their argument, and the Wild Weasels are going the way of the flight mechanic and tail gunner. What really sealed the fate of the Wild Weasel was the end of the cold war and the growth of the electronics industry.

The tremendous effort that went into the Wild Weasels was driven by the "Soviet Threat." The Russians had spend hundreds of billions of dollars on air defenses. The Soviets were quite fearful of Western aircraft shooting up their troops before battle could be joined. So the Soviets constructed a massive and intricate air-defense system using surface-to-air missiles, antiaircraft guns, interceptor aircraft, and dozens of different radar types. But Western, notably U.S., air forces knew they had to get through these Russian defenses in order to bomb Soviet ground forces. Without this bombing support, Western troops would be outnumbered and, everyone feared, defeated. To get through the Soviet air defenses, special measures would be needed.

The search for special measures began in the 1950s, and these measures were put into practice during the 1964–73 Vietnam War. But with the end of the cold war, the massive Soviet air defenses are no more, and the likelihood of fighting what is left is remote. What is left as potential opponents are nations that bought Soviet equipment, like Iraq and North Korea. What is more dangerous are smaller nations with more sophisticated Western weapons, sometimes even American SAMs and electronics.

The explosion of electronics equipment, popularized by the personal computer industry, has made the equipment carried by Wild Weasels, and other aircraft, far more capable. In the 1960s, you needed a separate piece of complex equipment for each enemy radar to be detected and jammed. With modern electronics, you build a smaller device that can detect thousands of different radars and other electronic devices. Jammers have become smart, or "brilliant" according to their developers' press releases. Using microprocessors like the ones that power your PC, jammers analyze any signal they come across, identify what it is or is likely to be, and then jam it. Radars have become almost as smart, scrutinizing what is out there and trying to defeat stealthiness and jammers to identify a target and send a missile on its way. The West always had a lead in the development of these electronic devices, and this has put Soviet equipment ever further behind American gear. At least in theory. The reality is that electronic warfare has become more and more of a chess game on an ever growing board.

Countermeasures designers must be ready for things they did not anticipate. This is why most ECM gear today is reprogrammable. Not only is the software itself designed for rapid modification, but many changes can be made by the users. This is done much the same way one would change the ever growing array of options in modern word processing or spreadsheet programs.

Missiles Versus Tanks

THE IDEA OF using missiles against tanks came up over fifty years ago. The first antitank guided missile (ATGM) was developed by the Germans during World War II. This was the X-7. Originally planned as an antiaircraft weapon (to follow the X-4), the X-7 project was taken over by the German army and was about to enter production in early 1945, but some key factories were bombed and the X-7 never made it to the battlefield. The X-7 was a solid-fuel rocket that was guided by commands sent over a wire the missile played out behind it. The missile operator used a joystick to direct the missile to the enemy tank, where a shaped-charge warhead detonated on contact and destroyed (usually) the tank.

Table 16 / Typical Antitank Guided Missiles (ATGMs)

Intro.	Name	Armor Pen (mm)	Effective Range (meters)		Speed (mps)	Made By	Missile/ Launch System Weight (lbs)	
			Min	Max			(lbs)	(lbs)
1945	X-7	200	200	1,000	100	Germany	22	35
1956	SS.10	420	300	1,600	80	France	33	25
1960	AT-1 Snapper	350	500	2,300	90	Russia	49	45
1965	AT-3 Sagger	400	500	3,000	120	Russia	25	40
1971	DRAGON	500	65	1,000	100	US	30	32
1971	TOW	750	65	3,000	360	US	40	184
1989	TOW2	1,200	65	3,750	360	US	47	191
1986	Hellfire	900	500	8,000	300	US	95	

Notes for the above table. *Intro.*—The year the weapon was introduced. All systems went into service, except the German X-7. *Name*—The name of the system. The Russian systems use the code names assigned by NATO (which are more familiar to most people reading this). *Armor Pen* (*mm*)—The amount of armor the warhead could penetrate. All of these weapons used a shaped-charge warhead, which sent a jet of very hot gas through the armor. If the hot jet got inside the tank, it would make things burn and explode. *Effective Range* (*meters*) *Min Max*—The minimum range that the warhead would be armed and the operator could take control of the missile, while the maximum range that the operator could control the missile (limited by the length of control wire used). *Speed* (*mps*)—The speed of the missile in meters per second. Slower missiles could be more easily guided, although this also made it easier for the enemy to see it coming and get out of the way. *Made By*—The nation that originally designed and built the system. *Missile /Launch System Weight* (*lbs*)— the weight (in pounds) of the missile itself and of the launching system (the mechanism to send the commands to the missile, as well as the joystick and power supply).

Although the Germans successfully tested their X-7 during World War II, the first operational ATGMs didn't show up until 1956. It was France, which began working on ATGMs in 1945, that first fielded the SS.10 in 1956. Another French firm came out with a similar weapon, and a few years later, so did a German company. By 1960, the Russians had gotten into the act. At first, America did not appreciate the enthusiasm other countries felt for this new weapon. After all, no one had given it much of a workout in combat yet. France had used a few in the 1950s, but the first real workout they got was during the 1973 Arab-Israeli war. The results were quite revealing.

Egypt diligently trained hundreds of Sagger (AT-3) operators. This was the third ATGM the Russians had built, and it was about as good a weapon as you could get using a joystick to guide the missile. The Egyptian operators spent hundreds of hours practicing on crude simulators. The Egyptians quickly discovered that, despite Russian pronouncements that the Sagger was "easy to use," accuracy depended a great deal on the proficiency of the operators. The French had admitted as much when they first produced these joystick ATGMs in the 1950s. Although an 80 percent hit rate was claimed, and shown in demonstrations, in the hands of your average user, hit rates of 65 percent or less could be expected. The Egyptians did better than that, at first. But the Israelis were quick to adapt to this new (to them) weapon. The Israelis noted that you could see the Sagger coming, as its flight time varied from ten to thirty seconds, depending on range. The Israelis knew there was someone out there guiding the missile via a joystick. If you could distract the operator, the missile would miss. So the Israelis quickly adopted the tactic of having troops designated to look out for Sagger launches. When a Sagger took off, it left a noticeable amount of smoke and dust behind it. While the Sagger could be launched fifty or so meters from the operator, the joystick guy had to be able to see the missile and the tank he was aiming it for. The Israelis soon became quite good at firing all their machine guns at likely places the operator would be. You didn't have to hit the operator, just put a few bullets close enough to make him flinch. Also, the tanks under fire could promptly start maneuvering, behind some cover if it was available, to further complicate the Sagger operator's job. Between the "Sagger Watch" and various countermeasures, the Sagger was soon a lot less effective.

The Israelis themselves got to use the new U.S. TOW ATGM in 1973. This was a second-generation system that was three times as fast as the Sagger and did not require as much effort from the operator. Put into service in 1972, the TOW only required that the operator keep the sight's crosshairs on the target. The fire-control system took care of the calculations and sent commands to the missile via the wire. The TOW was a great success and became the most widely used ATGM in the world, with over half a million missiles built so far. Several other ATGMs have been built in large numbers (over one hundred thousand), including several of the earliest, first-generation, models.

While a few Hellfires were used in the 1990 Panama operation, these third-generation ATGMs literally began the Coalition attack during the 1991 Gulf

War. Some three thousand Hellfires were fired after the first few opened the battle by destroying an Iraqi radar installation. The Hellfire used a laser to designate the target, and the missile homed in on the reflected laser light. This did away with the wire and allowed for longer-range attacks (up to eight thousand meters).

By the 1980s, ATGMs were all over the place. APCs had them, and some tanks fired them out of their smooth-bore cannon barrel or from racks on the turret. From the beginning, ATGMs were seen as in the tradition of motorized antitank weapons used in support of infantry units. The earliest ATGMs were often mounted on light trucks. The truck was parked behind the slope of the hill or some other cover, while the operator crouched with his joystick, and a view of approaching enemy vehicles. But the ATGMs could also be carried forward by the troops and placed near the operator. One operator could have several missiles nearby, all hooked up to his joystick. As one missile was seen to hit its target, another could be fired.

While tanks are often touted as the ultimate antitank weapon, World War II experience showed that tanks were more effective if they were using their speed to reach the enemy rear area. There, tanks could tear up artillery, headquarters, and supply units. It was better, if possible, to fight enemy tanks with cheaper antitank weapons. In World War II these were either towed or self-propelled antitank guns (usually the same guns tanks carried, but without all the expensive stuff that makes up a tank). As a last-ditch defense, troops could use bazookas (shoulder-fired antitank rockets). The ATGM was warmly embraced by everyone because it had a longer range than antitank guns, was relatively light, and packed more punch than most antitank gun shells or bazooka rockets. Also, the ATGMs were high-tech, which was good for morale.

Because there were few opportunities to test the first generation "joystick" ATGMs, over half a million were produced before it became obvious that the joystick approach had some serious disadvantages. These were made clear to all in the 1973 war. But even in the 1960s, these problems were recognized and the second-generation models (like the TOW) were in development. But just as the second-generation ATGMs began to appear in large numbers, tanks acquired more defenses.

The most effective countermeasures were advances in tank armor. There were two approaches to better protection against ATGMs. First, there was the "Chobham" (after the British organization that developed it) or "composite" armor. This armor is a combination of layers of armor, plastic, and ceramics. It absorbs and breaks up shot-type shells before they can penetrate. It is also effective against HEAT (High-Explosive Anti-Tank) shells used on ATGMs. Spaced armor has come back into vogue to defeat ATGM HEAT warheads. This is nothing more than thin armor sheets mounted a few inches from the main armor. Basically, it causes the HEAT shell to detonate prematurely and form its penetrating plasma jet inefficiently. Spaced armor can in turn be defeated with a special fuze. And so it goes. The latest wrinkle is reactive armor, which is composed of explosive material. When struck, it explodes and makes HEAT shells' penetration much less efficient. Most nations can, or do, use spaced armor. The U.S. M-1 is the best example of a tank using composite armor, while Russian tanks prefer the reactive armor. Some tanks have composite and reactive armor, plus spaced armor. All of this increases the weight of the vehicle somewhat, but does make it less likely that an ATGM will do fatal damage to a tank.

The other countermeasures were the ones the Israelis developed on the spot in 1973. In other words, go after the guy operating the ATGM. Each ATGM gunner has several missiles to fire. Even if the first ATGM fired connects, you can still get him before he can do the job with any of his remaining missiles. Machine guns and artillery were both seen as excellent ways to spoil an ATGM gunner's aim.

In the 1980s, the ATGM crowd upped the ante once more. Three new items made ATGMs more lethal. First came better warheads. To defeat, or at least minimize the effects of, new forms of armor (composite, reactive, and spaced), ATGMs were equipped with two warheads, detonating one after another. This reduced the ability of reactive or spaced armor to protect a tank from the penetrating power of the HEAT shaped charge. The Swedes also developed an ATGM warhead that sidestepped the whole issue of better armor by detonating its warhead while the missile was passing over the tank. The smaller warhead thus penetrated the much thinner armor on the top of the tank. Tanks would be prohibitively heavy if they had thicker armor on top. However, tanks did soon begin putting reactive armor on top. No one yet knows how effective that will be because no one has seen large-scale use of either "top attack" ATGMs or reactive armor (no matter where it is on the tank).

The third ATGM innovation may turn out to be the deadliest for tanks. The United States introduced its Hellfire ATGM in the late 1980s. This was a longer-range ATGM, somewhat like the TOW in most respects except that it was "third generation." The Hellfire was a "fire and forget" missile. Well, not completely fire and forget, but a helicopter could fire a Hellfire in the general direction of enemy targets, and allow another helicopter or someone on the ground to "paint" the target with a laser. The Hellfire homed in on the reflected laser light. In the 1990s, improved versions of the Hellfire were developed that could resist countermeasures and use different homing methods. Plans were also made to use the Hellfire from ground launchers. At a hundred pounds, seven inches in diameter, and nearly five and a half feet long, the Hellfire was more at home on a helicopter.

The Hellfire was the first of the third-generation ATGMs to get into use before the cold war ended. With the end of the cold war came the end of the need for new ATGMs. The Soviet Union had been the chief source of "enemy" tanks, and the disarmament treaties that accompanied the end of the cold war saw most of those tanks destroyed or put into storage. But as the cold war was ending, there were several even more powerful ATGMs in development. Some were ready to go into production.

One would think that weapons like the Hellfire would be a hard act to follow. Such was not the case. The "next generation" consisted of smaller, smarter, and much more independent missiles. Actually, most of these new missiles were submunitions, with several of them being carried in a bomb, artillery shell, or rocket to wherever the enemy was thought to have armored vehicles present. Only one of the new systems looks familiar. The new kids on the block are:

• SADARM (Sense and Destroy ARMor). This is a twenty-five- to thirty-pound "smart bomb" that contains a small radar and heat sensor. As the bomblet slowly descends, it spins and scans a hundred-meter-wide circle with its sensors. If it spots a vehicle, the shaped-charge warhead explodes when it is pointing at the target. This shaped charge is rather different than the usual one, as it does not form a hot jet of gas, but uses the special metal in front of the explosive to form a jet of molten metal. This "molten bolt" is effective for over a hundred meters, and the ones in SADARM can penetrate over one hundred millimeters of armor. Since the SADARM attacks the top of a tank, this penetration is more than adequate to damage or destroy most armored vehicles it hits. The U.S. Army fires 155mm artillery shells that each carry two SADARM or MLRS rockets that carry six SADARMs each. Each weapon uses a time on target–type fuze on the shell that ejects the SADARMs once the shells are over the area where enemy armored vehicles are reported. Troops on the ground or observers in aircraft or helicopters report the position of the enemy armor to the artillery, who then do the calculations (with a computer) to get the shells or rockets in the right place at the right time. SADARM has been in development since the early 1980s. It's been tested a lot and was scheduled to go into production in the early 1990s. With the end of the cold war, this schedule has been slowed down, but not stopped.

• WAM (Wide-Area Mine). This is a ground-based weapon using SADARM warheads. A forty-pound contraption, looking like a flat, squat robot, is placed on the ground. The WAM contains sound and ground sensors and a computer that knows what different types of vehicles sound like. When the sound and ground rumblings of a vehicle are detected, the computer calculates if the vehicle is within range. If so, one of the two SADARM-type warheads is rotated into position and a small explosive charge sends the warhead several hundred meters into the air. As the SADARM comes down, it does what a SADARM normally does and attacks any vehicles it can find. A WAM often comes with built-in booby traps, plus some antipersonnel mines scattered around. All of these mines have timers and will self-destruct after a set time. The WAM has been in test and development for about as long as SADARM, and is still scheduled for production sometime in the 1990s. The big selling point for the WAM is that it will replace troops in exposed positions. Whenever there is a ground battle, there are always some troops at the front who, because of the geography of the battlefield, will be hit first and hardest. These guys are usually wiped out. If they can be replaced by robots (WAMs), then the robots will take the heat instead of humans.

• Antihelicopter mines. These are a variation on WAMs, with the sensors set to detect helicopters and the SADARM modified to attack aircraft instead of ground vehicles. These mines have been successfully tested and are expected to go into production in the 1990s.

• BAT (Brilliant Antiarmor Submunition). This is the "next-generation SADARM." A forty-four-pound missile is released from a higher altitude than SADARM and uses three-foot foldout wings to glide and more powerful sensors to scan a wider area (over a square kilometer) for a variety of targets. A more capable onboard computer enables BAT to look for a number of different targets. In the wake of the 1991 Persian Gulf War, this now includes stationary tanks, antiaircraft missile equipment, and trucks. The masses of tanks these weapons were originally conceived for are gone now that the massive Warsaw Pact armored force has been junked. So it's difficult to justify the billions needed to get weapons like BAT into production. But there are hostile nations out there that can threaten U.S. interests. Iraq proved that in 1990, and nearby Iran continues to arm and to threaten American allies. So the BAT sensors were tweaked so they could pick up the other types of targets that nations like Iraq presented. In addition to tanks, there are trucks, aircraft hidden in villages, numerous antiaircraft guns, radars, missile launchers, and so on. BAT can use several different sensors, including acoustic, infrared (heat), and radar. More powerful microcomputers and memory storage can stockpile the "profiles" of many different types of equipment and attack only what the BAT programmers tell it to.

• Other successors to SADARM and BAT. The basic technology for SADARM and BAT is relatively cheap and the arms makers are keen to mass-produce new and "smarter" weapons. One example is LOCAAS (Low-Cost Antiarmor Submunition). Low cost in this case is fifteen thousand to twenty thousand dollars. There are two versions. The unpowered forty-to-fifty-pound army version is two feet long, one foot wide, and nine inches tall, with three-foot foldout wings, in shape a lifting body that slowly floats to earth, using a laser radar to find targets. The variation in weight depends on the power of sensors and warhead carried. The air force version weighs ninety-five to one hundred pounds and includes a miniature (four-inch diameter) turbojet with a thirty-minute fuel supply. This allows the LOCAAS to travel about 180 kilometers, scanning an area 750 meters wide for targets. If none are found, the LOCAAS destroys itself. The self-propelled LOCAAS carries a GPS so that it can fly a precise pattern and watch a specific area. Both versions, like SADARM, use a self-forging warhead. But the LOCAAS radar can tell the difference between different types of vehicles, and use the warhead in different ways depending on the type of targets detected. So in the most elaborate version of the warhead, tanks get hit with one large rod of molten metal. For smaller armored vehicles, the warhead explodes differently, sending out several smaller rods. This does more damage to the less well armored vehicles. For trucks and other unarmored targets (like radars), the warhead sends out a spray of fragments. LOCAAS can be carried in bomblike containers. (A B-1 or B-2 could carry about two hundred of them; an A-10 or F-16 could carry forty.) You can also put a half dozen or so in an ATACMS or similar type missile.

• FOG-M (Fiber-Optic Guided Missile). A surface-to-surface, hundred-pound missile, somewhat like the Maverick, with a TV or infrared sensor in the nose that transmits the signal back to the launcher by an optical fiber (which cannot be jammed). It has a range of some eight kilometers. The fiber-optic data link carries information from the sensors in the warhead to the operator's TV-like screen. The sensors penetrate smoke, fog, and darkness. The operator sits in front of TV screens with a trackball, guiding the missiles to target. A truck or armored vehicle carries one TV-equipped gunner and a magazine of six to eight FOG-Ms. These are expected to cost $125,000 per missile initially, some ten times what a TOW costs. The comparable Hellfire (used on helicopters) costs about $50,000, and a Maverick (used on jets) costs some $80,000. FOG-M has several advantages over TOW. The operator and launcher are less vulnerable to attack by the enemy, since FOG-M is fired straight up, then levels off and heads for its target. The guidance system is more accurate and, because of its larger size, carries a more powerful warhead. Lastly, the FOG-M attacks its target from the top, hitting an area where armored vehicles have less protection. FOG-M does not completely replace the lighter TOW and other ATGMs, but it does a lot of the antitank work. Targets are picked up by troops at the front, helicopters, and other sources. FOG-M is in another part of the digital battlefield, sitting in a safe place, waiting for orders to launch and go after targets in a specific area. The target's location is passed to the FOG-M's guidance system, to get the missile close enough so the sensors can give the operator something to get in his crosshairs. This is an ambitious system, and has run into money problems with the end of the cold war. But all of the FOG-M technologies are basically off-the-shelf. Putting them together in a reliable weapon is expensive and will get done if anyone sees a need to have that kind of weapon.

• Fire and forget warheads. Missiles are kept in service by upgrades, usually to their guidance systems (and less frequently to their warheads). The most popular guidance system in the 1990s is the "fire and forget" feature. This is a computer-based feature in a guidance system that enables the missile, once it has identified the target, to keep going after it until the target is hit. This feature requires a lot of onboard computing power, and the rapid advances in microcomputer technology during the last few decades have made this kind of power available for missile-guidance systems.

• High-velocity missiles. Advances in rocket motor technology have made it possible to produce relatively small missiles that can go very fast, very quickly, and punch a hole in any known armor. One proposal has 170-pound missiles, mounted on any vehicle that can currently carry a TOW, with a range of five or six kilometers against ground targets and up to ten kilometers against aircraft. The 22mm-by-91mm penetrator is moving at 1,800 meters a second by the time the missile is 200 meters from its launcher. A guidance system enables the missile to make precise adjustments so it hits the distant target. But at that speed (about twice as fast as a bullet), you basically point and shoot. Another variant on this has a "shotgun"-type warhead that disperses a 20- to 30-meter diameter cloud of eighty to one hundred smaller penetrators. Each projectile can go through about an inch of armor. In other words, such a missile would shred incoming aircraft or missiles.

Countermeasures against Antitank Weapons

ALL OF THE NEW antitank technologies have not gone unnoticed by tank users and designers. As each new antitank weapon came out, the tank designers came up with a countermeasure. This has not resulted in all, or even most, new antitank technologies being defeated. The problem is that, because there are so many new antitank weapons appearing in the past few decades, it is not possible for any but the wealthiest nation to produce countermeasures for all of them. The way it works is that the rich countries, like the United States, can buy the countermeasures for the more exotic antitank weapons that potential (less wealthy) adversaries cannot afford. Put another way, America has to worry about any of several foes somehow getting their hands on some new antitank weapon that the United States could, at great expense, equip its tanks with, such as devices to defeat something like SADARM. Less wealthy armed forces can buy some countermeasures, but this only provides partial defense against most of the new antitank weapons.

The original antitank weapon was a gun that could fire a powerful enough shell to penetrate the tank's armor. This is still the principal antitank weapon, and the only thing that will defeat it, most of the time, is heavy and expensive composite armor. The U.S. M-1 tanks have the latest Chobham (composite) armor. The U.S. M-1 tanks have this special armor built in three layers. On the outside there is 50 to 75 millimeters of armor, then several inches of composite armor, then another 100 to 150 millimeters of regular armor. The tank is first built with the two layers of steel armor; then the composite armor is fitted into the space between the two layers of steel, and the openings that allowed the composite armor panels to be inserted are welded shut. A shell hitting the tank would first, in the case of a tank shell, go through the outside layer of armor. But when it hit the composite armor, it would hit several layers of quite different material. What this composite stuff does is force the high-speed (about a mile a second) "penetrator" to twist and break up before reaching the inside (next to the crew) layer of steel armor.

But the first Chobham armor designs were "brittle." When the Russians discovered this, they developed a blunt, high-speed penetrator that would literally shatter the composite armor. The first such round might not make it all the way through, but a large chunk of the tank's composite armor would now be worthless and another shot in the same general area would destroy the tank. In response to this, the U.S. Army developed the depleted uranium (the densest material known) mesh to reinforce the composite armor panels on the M-1A1 and defeat any "blunt penetrator" attack. This worked in the 1991 Gulf War. No U.S. tanks were destroyed by Iraqi tank fire. And the Iraqis did score a lot of hits, but at best their shells went through the first layer of steel armor and were stopped by the composite armor. Shaped-charge warheads are also stopped by composite armor.

Any time an M-1 takes a hit that penetrates to the composite armor, the composite material is damaged and must eventually be replaced. Several hits in the same spot, without such repairs, will eventually lead to a shot getting through. The U.S. Army has an armor-cutting machine that opens up the armor and replaces the damaged composite armor panel in about half an hour per tank.

Like all other tanks, the M-1 armor is thickest in the front. An M-1 can still be destroyed if you can get a shot at the front or rear. For this reason, tank crews always try to find out where the enemy is and, if they can't turn the tank in that direction, they turn the turret, and its thick frontal armor. The M-1 has "skirts" over the running gear that use a different kind of composite armor that protects this vulnerable part of the tank from small shaped-charge shells found in portable rocket launchers, or from tank shells hitting at an extreme angle.

Only a few nations can afford tanks like the M-1, and none are quite as impregnable as the M-1. The antidote to the composite armor has been to attack from a different direction, namely from above or below. The weapons from above are the new items like SADARM, which only America has. However, Russia has also been building a weapon similar in operation to SADARM and will probably sell it to anyone who has the cash. Delivered by artillery shell or rocket, the "SADARMSKY" would likely do in a number of M-1 tanks. Of course, even before SADARM, there was another submunition for bombs that contained a shaped-charge warhead powerful enough to get through the top armor of a tank. But this had to be delivered by aircraft to be effective, and no one has been able to take control of the air away from U.S. forces since 1944.

The most common antitank weapons to be encountered on the modern battlefield are the ATGM and the bazooka. The latter, because it has to remain portable, has become increasingly less effective against increasingly better protected tanks. So ATGMs are the big threat. A number of countermeasures are out there as a means of dealing with these missiles. Oh yes, there are also the mines. No major progress against them. Pesky little critters, just won't go away. But there are some countermeasures.

Favorite countermeasures against antitank weapons are:

• Reactive armor. This is widely used by Russian tanks and is the cheapest and most reliable protection against ATGMs. Blocks of explosive material that detonate when hit hard. Not much help against metal penetrators or self-forging weapons. But against the shaped-charged warhead of most ATGMs, reactive armor is quite effective. Problem is, it can only be used once. When it does go off, it is dangerous to any troops (friendly or otherwise) that are within a few meters (or more, depending on the angle). Reactive armor can also do some minor damage to the tank using it.

• Missile sensors. The same basic technology used on aircraft. A form of radar that alerts you when an object over a certain size is moving toward you at greater than a certain speed. In other words, you get a warning that an ATGM is headed for you. This warning device is linked to other countermeasures that actually try to keep the missile from hitting you. A Russian technology.

• Smoke dischargers. A longtime countermeasure. The most primitive approach to this was to pour oil on the hot parts of the tank engine. Crude, but it gave you a place to hide. In the last few decades, tanks have come to have several grenade "throwers" (small shotgun-type devices) mounted on the front of the turret. The crew can then throw one, two, or up to six or more smoke bombs over a hundred meters in front of the turret. This quickly puts smoke between yourself and those pesky ATGM operators. Special types of smoke are available which make infrared (heat) sensors less effective.

• Antilaser lasers. Since so many weapons use lasers for guidance, a favorite device is one that detects laser light (on themselves) and then searches the vicinity to find the source (not too difficult) and zaps the source with its own laser beam in order to destroy the offending laser's optics (and often the eyesight of the operator). Devices like this are becoming popular on the battlefield, mainly because so many weapons are laser guided, not just antitank weapons.

• Jammers. Not many weapons use radio guidance, mainly because it is so easy to jam. But it is possible to broadcast signals that will directly affect the electronics in guidance systems. Such a weapon would best be kept secret during peacetime, as many jamming vulnerabilities can be overcome by redesigning the guidance system in question.

• Soft layer. The Soviets came up with this when they saw the United States coming out with cluster bombs carrying hundreds of dartlike shaped-charge bomblets that would burn through the thin top armor of tanks. The "soft layer" was a layer of softer metal on the top of the tank that was soft enough to prevent the detonators on bomblets from working. Kind of dumb, actually, as the detonators can be redesigned. Not many tanks were converted to soft layer, and not many of these shaped-charge bomblets are in service anywhere anyway.

• Decoys. Just like aircraft, tanks can now use everything from flares (to draw away heat-seeking missiles) to chaff (to confuse radar-equipped missiles). As the ATGMs become more complex, the decoys will become more common.

• Offsets. An additional layer of armor mounted on the tank, with an empty space between the new armor and the original stuff. This one goes back to World War II, when portable antitank rocket launchers first arrived on the scene. The offset made the rocket's shaped-charge warhead much less effective. Since most ATGMs still use shaped-charge warheads, this offset technique still works and is still used.

• Plows, rollers, and explosives. For mines delivered by missile, or otherwise, a special plow fitted to the front of a tank will literally plow up (and push aside) any mines in the way. Heavy rollers can also be attached to explode mines, if the ground is too hard for plowing. Missiles deliver small mines that lie on the ground and blow the tracks off tanks. This does not destroy tanks, but does render them immobile for as many hours as it takes for the crew to make repairs. Various special forms of explosives are also used to clear an areas of these small mines (as well as larger antitank mines that will, indeed, destroy a tank).

• Tactics. As the Israelis demonstrated in 1973, one can quickly counteract the effects of ATGMs by changing your tactics. Keeping an eye out for the missiles and firing at likely places where the missile operator is, works wonders. Other tactical changes are to have helicopters on hand to hammer the missile operators and unlaunched missiles. One can also make creative use of smoke when you have to pass an area that might expose the tanks to ATGM fire. Carefully studying the terrain the tanks have to pass through, long a useful practice, becomes even more crucial when faced with a lot of ATGMs. One also has to keep in mind that Russia makes and sells ATGMs that can be fired from the 115mm and 125mm tubes of Russian-made tanks. The most recent versions of these ATGMs are "top attack." That is, they use a smaller, downward-firing warhead that detonates as the missile passes over the target tank.

Where Missiles Don't Miss

THE U.S. DEPARTMENT of Defense spending on military aircraft declined from $25.7 billion in 1991 to $17 billion in fiscal 1995. But spending on missiles increased. Systems like the AIM-120 Advanced Medium-Range Air-to-Air Missile, the AGM-154 Joint Standoff Weapon, the Brilliant Antiarmor Submunition, and the Sensor Fuzed Weapons are getting billions more each year. Missiles, for all their faults, are increasingly a better investment than manned aircraft. Missiles are smarter, more reliable, and more lethal. As expensive as missiles are, increasingly they are cheaper than any of the alternatives.

11

Electrons at War

F OR FIFTY YEARS, ever since the air war over Germany during World War II, aircraft have fought each other with electronic devices. It comes as a big surprise to many people that all the electronic give-and-take that characterized the 1991 Gulf War was also taking place fifty years earlier over Europe.

Slaughter Above

THE AIR WAR OVER Europe was the longest, most intense, and bloodiest air campaign ever waged. It went on around the clock, 365 days a year, from early 1940 to early 1945. That's five years of the Germans and the Allies (mainly the United States and Britain) locked in aerial combat. Overall, this campaign saw 1.5 million Allied troops and 69,000 aircraft battling 2.2 million German troops (plus two million civilians repairing the damage) and 61,000 Nazi aircraft. The air war over Germany and Britain began in 1939, but didn't really get going in a big way until 1943, when the "Strategic Bombing Offensive" against Germany was begun. The four-engine strategic bombers dropped 1.5 million tons of bombs on German cities and industry, but all other combat aircraft (single- and two-engine) dropped another 1.1 million tons, mostly on German combat units.

There were actually two bombing campaigns going on against German factories, cities, transportation, and armed forces. The British effort had a peak strength of 718,628 pilots and ground crew who dropped 1.2 million tons of bombs, mostly at night. The Americans had a peak strength of 619,020 troops supporting the dropping of 1.5 million tons of bombs, mostly in daylight. To put this American effort into perspective, the bombs dropped in Europe comprised about 75 percent of total bomb tonage dropped by the USAAF worldwide in the entire war.

Losses over Europe were heavy, as 159,000 airmen became casualties (about evenly split between British Commonwealth and American). Aircraft losses were enormous, with 21,914 bombers lost (11,965 British) and 18,465 fighters (10,045 British) destroyed. The bombers flew 1.5 million sorties and had a loss rate of 15 aircraft destroyed per thousand sorties. The fighters flew 2.7 million sorties, for a loss rate of seven destroyed per thousand sorties. It was actually worse than it appears for the bombers, as many aircraft that survived their missions would be shot up with dead and wounded crew on board. The heavy four-engine bombers had crews of ten or more men. The German losses were higher in terms of aircraft (over 60,000) and lower in terms of aircrew (about 100,000), because most of the German aircraft were single-seat fighters. Moreover, many of the German aircraft were destroyed on the ground, especially after the middle of 1944. But some 600,000 German civilians were killed by the bombs, as well as over 100,000 military personnel. Over 250,000 homes and apartments were destroyed as well as thousands of industrial, military, and transportation installations.

In the first half of 1944, Allied aircrews flying over Europe were suffering horrendous casualties. The chart below shows those killed or missing in action (usually meaning dead, but some were taken prisoner). It was worse in late 1943, and got a lot better after the summer of 1944. Overall, about 45 percent of the U.S. and British men serving in bomber crews were killed over Germany.

Table 17 / World War II Aircrew Killed or Missing over Europe
(January–June 1944)

Heavy Bombers	71%
Medium Bombers	48%
Fighters	24%

Most of these missions were flown out of Britain. Half the bomb tonnage was dropped on Germany, with another 22 percent landing on France. Aircraft based in Italy accounted for most of the bombs delivered to Italy (14 percent), Austria, Hungry, and the Balkans (7 percent) and sundry other locations (the remaining 7 percent). The air war was largely British and American aircraft versus Germans, for the Germans occupied most of Europe during this period.

The Dawn of Electronic Warfare

WHILE THE BOMBING itself got off to a slow start (see the chart below), the electronic warfare did not. The massive use of bombers hit rather suddenly in 1944. But for three years before that the electronic warfare went on with rather high intensity.

Table 18 / Percentage of All Bombs Dropped over Europe Each Year

Year	Bombs Dropped (as a percentage of the total of those dropped)
1940	0.8%
1941	2.0%
1942	3.0%
1943	12.8%
1944	57.9%
1945	23.5%

Going into World War II, aircraft had little electronic equipment on board except a radio, and many nations didn't even equip all their warplanes with radios. But there was a lot of new electronic gadgetry being developed in the laboratories and universities during the 1930s. The needs of wartime quickly brought a lot of that speculative and experimental gear into use.

One of the first of the modern electronic devices to be introduced over Europe was the German Knickebein in February of 1940. This was an airborne navigation system using signals from ground transmitters. This allowed bombers flying at night to find targets and accurately bomb them. This was a classic, and oft repeated, case of an unexpected military situation (bombing at night) bringing forth a technical solution to a seemingly intractable problem (finding targets at night).

While the Germans pioneered the bombing of cities in the 1930s, particularly in Spain during the civil war (1936–39), they always assumed that they would first clear the air of enemy fighters and then bomb accurately by day. When the Luftwaffe (German air force) ran into the RAF (British Royal Air Force) in 1940, it was quickly obvious that British fighters could make bombing in daylight a very expensive proposition. Bombing at night avoided the fighters, but created seemingly insurmountable navigation problems. Flying above the clouds, one could navigate well enough by the stars to find and bomb cities, but not smaller and more critical targets like aircraft factories and air bases.

But the Germans (and other nations) had already been working on the use of radio beacons to guide aircraft. These were actually quite simple in theory, and practice. Radio beams were pointed in a certain direction, and the navigators on aircraft listened to the radio signals, instructing the pilot when to make a slight turn this way or that to stay on course. The beam was about four hundred meters wide. The navigator noted the distance traveled, and listened for the second beam that crossed the first beam at the target, so that he could alert the bombardier when the aircraft was near the target. If there was nothing but clouds or fog below, when the aircraft hit the point where they heard both radio signals, it was time to drop the bombs.

You could still use visual identification of the target being bombed. But if you could get the aircraft close, and clouds or fog did not interfere, a river or shape of a coastline would let you know when the target was found. Once a few bombs were dropped, the rest of the bombers would have the fires below to light up their target.

It took awhile for the British to figure out how the Germans were doing it, for the Knickebein device was hidden on the bombers and the crew members who knew about it were instructed to keep quiet on the subject if captured. But eventually the British did find out about the Knickebein, and in September 1940 they introduced their countermeasure: Asperin. This was nothing more than an electronic jammer that sent out a lot of noise on the same frequencies as Knickebein, rendering it useless.

The Knickebein was something that aircraft engineers were interested in before the war, for purely commercial reasons. Such a system could just as easily move commercial aircraft from city to city. Even before the war, such a system was used to allow aircraft to land when the weather was so bad that they could not see the airfield below. Systems for long-range navigation (LORAN) were constructed after World War II and are still in use.

During the Battle of Britain (summer of 1940), the outnumbered British came up with a number of innovative, and not always high-tech, ways to better deal with the German bombers. Although the principal German bombing attacks during 1940 were in daylight, there were also night attacks against cities. The British were the first to develop airborne radar for their night fighters. The first system was the AI (airborne interception radar), with a minimum range of 240 meters and a maximum one of 3,200 meters. Given the crude tracking ability of the ground radars, this was often not enough to get the night fighter close enough to the German bombers to get a contact.

So the British came up with another simple device, a transponder (radio transmitter) called Pip Squeak that gave out a signal periodically that was picked up by ground stations and, using triangulation, gave a precise position of the British aircraft. There was also a series of radar beacons that allowed the night fighters to quickly find out what their own current position was. Most important was a nontechnical innovation, centralized control of air defense. This was nothing more than reporting all sightings of enemy aircraft (by radar, human spotters, or pilots) to one location. This control center would then allocate interceptors and alert antiaircraft units. While seemingly obvious, this technique was not immediately adopted by every nation. The British were the first, and it was a key element in their winning the Battle of Britain against the German Luftwaffe.

In September 1940 the British introduced a better night fighter (the eleven-ton Beaufighter, with four 20mm cannons), equipped with an improved airborne radar (AI Mk IV) that had a minimum range of 120 meters and a maximum range of 4,800 meters. The Beaufighters began shooting down German night bombers in late November 1940, and the night skies became increasingly unfriendly for German bombers. By March 1941, for the first time, British night fighters shot down more German bombers (22) than did British antiaircraft guns (21). In April the score went up to 48 bombers for the night fighters, versus 39 for the guns. In May, the larger number of radar-equipped Beaufighters took down 96 German bombers. At that point, most of the Luftwaffe aircraft were shifted to Eastern Europe, for the German invasion of Russia in June of 1941. This was just as well, for the total German bomber strength was 1,300, and losing nearly a hundred a month to British night fighters was more than the Luftwaffe bomber force could take. The aircraft were easy enough to replace, even if losses were two hundred a month. But experienced crews were another matter. The British had won the aerial battle over the night skies.

When the night bombing began in 1940, it was going both ways. Britain began sending night bombers against Germany in May 1940. Until the Luftwaffe was sent off to Russia in the spring of 1941, the British and Germans continued to battle for control of the air and send night bombers against each other's cities. The British noted a problem with telling the difference between their own returning night bombers and German bombers headed for British cities. Friendly and enemy would both be shot at by the antiaircraft guns or attacked by the few primitive night fighters available. The solution was a device that is still in use: IFF (identification, friend or foe). The IFF was a special radio device that sent out a specific signal on a specific frequency. A friendly radar would recognize the signal and then would know if the aircraft was sending back the right signal. If it was, that aircraft was friendly; if not, it was presumed to be a foe and was attacked. Early IFF devices were only used by radar stations, so that antiaircraft units could be told to open or hold fire. Oddly enough, the Germans did not pick up on this device until near the end of the war. They knew of it, but did not fully appreciate its usefulness. Eventually they did.

IFF became a standard piece of equipment after World War II, as most nations had radar and antiaircraft artillery guarding their borders, or at least key targets. By the 1960s, as long-range air-to-air missiles became more popular, IFF became even more important. With guns, fighters had to get close enough to be sure that the target was not a friendly before they opened fire. Missiles were often fired at a blip on the aircraft's radar. Without IFF, the chance of friendly fire was too great. Even with IFF, it was a decade or more before pilots became somewhat comfortable with the idea of firing on an unseen plane just because a machine (the IFF) said it was okay.

IFF is still somewhat suspect to many pilots and commanders of antiaircraft units. If an enemy finds out what the IFF codes are, it provides free passage into protected territory, there to shoot up antiaircraft positions and unsuspecting aircraft passing nearby.

But during World War II, IFF was widely used by the British, and later the Germans. Enemy aircraft with purloined IFF codes never became a problem. It was more likely for a friendly aircraft to fly into range of friendly antiaircraft guns and get shot up because the IFF was broken that day.

As the war went on, the Germans had more important electronic problems to solve, namely how to improve their radar system to deal with the increasing number of British (and later U.S.) bombers headed east. The original German radar in use in 1939 was quite advanced, probably the best in the world. But in 1940 British scientists discovered how to make microwave radar. This greatly increased the power of radar, as well as its accuracy, while making the equipment smaller. This latter advantage made it possible to put long-range radar sets in aircraft. This British advance in radar transmitters was combined with the U.S. lead in radar receivers. Together, British and American radar manufacturers saw to it that the Allies maintained a lead in radar technology throughout the war.

The Germans kept using the older technology until they discovered the microwave angle in 1943, via a shot-down Allied aircraft and its radar. The Germans didn't get their own microwave radars into use until late 1944, too late to have any major effect on the outcome of the war. Oddly enough, the Japanese had also discovered how to use microwave radar in 1941, but had not shared this with their German allies. This shows how valuable military secrets can be. Had the Germans gotten the secret of microwave radar in 1941 or 1942, their antiaircraft defenses would have been more formidable when the Allied bombing campaign went into high gear during 1944. There would have been a lot more Allied losses. It wouldn't have changed the outcome of the war, but it would have killed a lot more British and American airmen.

The 1940 British radars had a range of 150 kilometers, and went up from there as wartime improvements were made. In the middle of 1940, the Germans were just introducing their Wurzburg, an "improved" radar with a 40-kilometer range. Since it could plot altitude, it was used to control flak (antiaircraft) guns as well as night fighters. What the Germans needed the most was a longer-range radar that could, like the British radar, spot the enemy coming at a longer distance. In September 1940 the German Freya radar went into service. This was a very powerful radar with a 120-kilometer range. Although it could not detect altitude, it did give the early warning of bombers approaching. The Freya, with periodic improvements, remained Germany's main early-warning radar for most of the war.

The increasing number of British air raids on Germany was very embarrassing to the Nazi government. Although it was impossible to stop the raids, measures could be taken to reduce their impact. For example, if the night had enough moonlight, and there was enough warning, German fighters could be directed to the oncoming British bombers and could get some hits in. Moreover, the longer the warning, the sooner more civilians in the target area could get into the air-raid shelters.

With typical wartime vigor, the improvements in German radar kept on coming. In October 1940 the Wurzburg II went into service. This was a case more of cleverness than of some kind of scientific or engineering breakthrough. A pair of Wurzburg radars was used in this system, one to track bombers and another to track German interceptors. This was deadly when used at night, which was the reason for developing it in the first place. The German night fighter pilots could not see far at night, but their radar operators on the ground could see everything in the sky about them. This dual radar system guided the interceptors to a position behind and below the British bomber stream. This was the ideal position for the night fighters to spot the bombers and attack them. Unlike the British, however, the Germans had not yet centralized their air-defense control. It wasn't until 1943 that the Germans had a centralized air-defense system similar to what the British had in 1940.

In September 1941 the Germans introduced the Wurzburg Reise, an improved Wurzburg with a 65-kilometer range. In the previous twelve months, the new 1940 systems were manufactured and installed. Because of the short range of the German radars, more of them were needed to cover the large area of airspace the British bombers operated in.

The new technology also had to be organized in a way that could do maximum damage. This is one side of new technology that is often overlooked.

New gadgets by themselves are not of much use. Moreover, not everyone will organize new technologies the same way. The air war over Europe in World War II provides many examples. One was the use of night fighters. Before they equipped theirs with radar, the British preferred to use ground radar to guide the night fighters to an interception with the bombers, and then let the fighters use whatever light was available to find and attack the bombers. This did not allow attacks quite as lethal as in daytime, mainly because the bombers could be spotted only at relatively short range (a few hundred meters, out to a few kilometers, depending on position and available light from the moon) and because the fighters could not operate in groups, lest they collide with each other in the heat of combat. Often it took several passes at an "intercept point" before a fighter found a group of bombers. So individual night fighters were kept under tight control by their ground controllers, and kept apart as the attacks were made.

The Germans came up with another approach. They used a line of radar-guided searchlights not only to spot, and spotlight, bombers, but also to guide in and control the night fighters. The searchlights made the bombers much easier to find, and this technique increased the losses among the British bombers. Fortunately, politics intervened, and the searchlights were ordered back to "defend the cities" in May of 1942 (that is, to make a show for the civilians that "something was being done to defend them"). Even in a dictatorship, the Nazis had to pay attention to public opinion.

But in February 1942 the Germans introduced Lichtenstein, their airborne radar for night fighters. Since it was not a microwave radar, its range was short, varying from a minimum of 200 to a maximum of 3,500 meters. But this radar enabled night fighters, once directed by ground radar to the general area behind where the bombs were spotted, to eventually find them. Then would follow a pursuit, as the night fighter crept up behind a bomber, got it in sight, and opened up with 20mm or 30mm cannons. Coming in, the bombers were full of fuel and bombs, and the attack often resulted in a violent explosion and one less bomber. A single night fighter could often get two or more bombers on one sortie. The attacks were made from below, to minimize the effects of the bombers' own machine guns. The first radar-equipped German night-fighter kill was in early August 1942.

In response to the more lethal German night-fighter attacks, the British did what electronic warriors have been doing to this day: they tried to find out more about the new German airborne radar so that they could deal with it. While ground-based radars were too powerful to jam with 1940s technology, airborne radars were another matter. These smaller radars put out a much weaker signal and could be jammed, if you knew what kind of signal they emitted. To find out this information, the British sent out bombers equipped, not with bombs, but with special monitoring equipment and operators who could use it to quickly sort out the German radar's characteristics and radio this information back to Britain. The information had to be quickly radioed back because it was likely that the bomber would not survive its encounter with the night fighter, and the crew would be killed or captured in the process. This was not a job for the faint of heart.

What the British learned in World War II about collecting information on enemy electronic equipment is still valid today. Such information is not cheap to get, and is even more expensive if you don't get it. Today ships, submarines, aircraft, and satellites are used to get this information on other nations' radars and electronic gadgets. Even during peacetime there are losses, for often the gathering involves getting close to foreign territory, and sometimes nations get violent about such actions. Hundreds of Americans have died in the past half century while collecting these electronic signatures in peacetime. In wartime it is an even more costly process. But without this information, wars begin with enemy electronics operating at peak capacity, rather than crippled by jamming and other countermeasures. The need for this electronic information was appreciated early in World War II, thus beginning a process that will continue as long as weapons use electronic transmitters.

Going into 1942, Germany began introducing new generations of radar equipment. In March, they began using two new, complimentary, radars. First there was Mammut, a more powerful early-warning radar with a range of 330 kilometers. However, this device could not plot altitude, only detect that something was out there. Introduced at the same time was the Wassermann, an early-warning radar with a range of only 240 kilometers, but one that could plot altitude. Thus by using both radars, enemy aircraft could be spotted 330 kilometers out and interceptors ordered aloft. It took the approaching bombers less than half an hour to get from 330 kilometers out to 240 kilometers out, at which point the Wassermann radars could detect their altitude and the interceptors could be sent in at the right location and altitude.

In early 1942 the Allies also tried out their own version of the earlier German Knickebein. The Gee airborne navigation system used signals from ground transmitters, but differently than the earlier German system. Gee was also usable over longer ranges. At 600 kilometers from the transmitters, aircraft knew their location to within 10 kilometers. In June of 1942, the Allies introduced the Shaker system. This was Gee-equipped "pathfinder" aircraft that dropped bombs on the target (as best they could), to provide aiming points for other night bombers following behind. The use of pathfinder aircraft was an extremely useful innovation for night bombers, and required no technical innovations. This sort of thing is quite common in warfare. Technology is not always the answer. Anyway, in August 1942 the Germans introduced Heinrich, a jamming system the made Gee unusable by the end of 1942.

During the summer of 1942 the Allies raised the stakes in the electronic war. They began using Moonshine, a device carried on aircraft that detected German long-range radar signals and increased the strength of the signal bounced back, making it look like a larger bomber formation. This caused the Germans to send interceptors after the wrong groups of bombers, at least until the incoming bombers were picked up by the shorter-range fighter control radars. By the end of 1942, the Allies began using Mandrel, an electronic jammer carried in the lead aircraft of a formation to jam the German early-warning radar.

The new radar jamming was not a wonder weapon, for the Germans had several different types of radars, operating on several different frequencies. Each radar frequency had to be jammed separately, a problem that current jammers still have to contend with. What these first jammers did was make the German air-defense system less effective. The Allies knew what they were doing, and following up on the radar jamming they introduced Tinsel, an electronic jammer that disrupted ground-to-air communications. This made the German night fighters less effective, as the night-fighter pilots would find themselves without a working radio just as they were getting final instructions on how to close with British bombers that were being traced by radio.

The Allies also realized that the Germans depended on more primitive devices to track bombers crossing Germany at night. So a device was fitted to some bombers that amplified the bombers' engine noise so as to confuse ground observers who tracked bomber formations by their engine noise. This was not a big success, but it shows you how eager people are to try just about anything in wartime in order to gain an advantage.

At the very end of 1942, the Allies introduced Oboe. This was a 430-kilometer range ground radar device that calculated a friendly bomber's precise location and sent a signal to the bomber about when bombs should be dropped. This was used during the day as well, when overcast prevented bombers from seeing their targets. This was limited by the range of the Oboe radar, and was of no use for the many targets deep inside Germany. It was also, for all practical purposes, impossible to jam.

The year 1943 saw the introduction of many new devices that, fifty years later, would still be considered high technology. The first of these "modern" electronic devices was introduced by the Allies. H2S was a ground-mapping airborne radar that could distinguish between water, cities, and rural areas. For 1943, this was really high tech and all the bugs were not worked out until the end of 1943. The advantages of ground-mapping radars were enormous. Since

Europe was crowded with rivers and urban areas, navigators with the proper maps could always figure out where they were, day or night, no matter how much overcast there was. For large targets, like cities, ports, or large industrial complexes, "bombing by radar" became a possibility, and an accurate one at that (at least by World War II standards). In September the Germans responded to H2S, after a fashion, when they began using Naxburg. These were receivers that could detect the allied H2S ground-mapping radars over 300 kilometers away. In January of 1944, the Germans came out with yet another H2S detector, Naxos. When the Allies discovered the use of these detectors, they ordered aircraft crews to be sparing in their use of H2S. Of course the Allies knew that H2S signals could, in theory, be detected, but the warnings to H2S operators meant more when they could be backed up with evidence that the Germans were able to home in on H2S.

In March of 1943 another high-tech electronic gadget came into use. This was the Allied Monica, a tail-warning radar for night bombers. The device would alert the crew when another aircraft was within a thousand meters of the bomber. This was particularly useful for the rear gunner in a bomber. With sufficient warning he could spot the night fighter and put some firepower on it.

By 1943, the principal British night bomber was the thirty-ton Lancaster (the current F-15E fighter-bomber, with a crew of two, weighs thirty-two tons). Its crew of seven men included a rear gunner who had quadruple 7.7mm machine guns. Although the German night fighters carried heavier, and longer-ranged, 20mm and 30mm cannons, the night fighter had to get so close to its target to take aim in the darkness that the British 7.7mm machine guns were within range. The real purpose of using heavier 20mm and 30mm cannons was to knock out the bomber before its 7.7mm machine guns could be brought into play.

The Lancaster was a relatively new aircraft design, only going into production at the end of 1941. Compared to the earlier, mainly two-engine, night bombers, the Lancaster was larger, far more robust, and able to carry the new electronic gadgets developed for its protection. The principal German night fighter was the Me-110, a ten-ton, twin-engine fighter-bomber with a three-man crew that found itself better suited to attacking bombers at night. The Me-110 had a fifty- to eighty-mile-per-hour speed advantage over British bombers, and it was this additional speed that enabled the night fighters, operating independently of each other, to catch up with the night bombers. In 1942, most of the 1,400 British aircraft lost over Europe were shot down by the 200 to 300 night fighters the Germans had in service at any given time that year.

During 1942, Britain had shifted over to night bombing of cities, recognizing that there were no other targets that could be accurately hit at night. Because of the danger of flying at night in formation, the British bombers proceeded spread out in a "stream." Faster two-engine pathfinder aircraft would use highly skilled pilots and bombardiers to drop a few bombs on the target to start fires and provide an aiming point for the other bombers (from several hundred to a thousand or more) following behind. Night fighters were encountered approaching and leaving the target, while over the target itself there were searchlights and antiaircraft fire. The bombs were usually released at an altitude of twenty thousand feet.

In addition to the Monica tail-warning radar, early 1943 also saw the Allies' first use of Boozer, a "radar warning receiver" (RWR) that alerted a crew when they were being detected by the German radars that controlled night fighters, as well as by the night fighters' own radar. The Allies also began using night fighters against the German night fighters. Later, during the summer of 1943, the Allied night fighters received a much improved radar (AI Mk IX, or, in American parlance, the SCR 720). At the same time, Serrate was introduced for Allied night fighters. This device detected the German Liechtenstein airborne radar. This enabled Allied night-fighter pilots to determine where a German fighter was and engage it. Since all this usually took place above the clouds, there was enough star- and moonlight to allow engagements if you knew where to look. This made for some very active combat in the night sky, as the German night fighters stalked British bombers and the Germans were in turn hunted down by Allied night fighters.

In the summer of 1943, the electronic countermeasures war really heated up. The Allies introduced Window (chaff) to jam German radar. Window was tinfoil strips, cut to the right length to cause German radar to see a "wall" of, well, tinfoil strips. Bundles of it were tossed out of Allied aircraft and this, in effect, created an electronic smoke screen behind which anything could be happening. The Allies began using separate groups of aircraft equipped with jammers and chaff to create deceptions and lure the German night fighters to them and away from the real bomber screen.

To further befuddle German night fighters, the Allies brought on-line Special Tinsel, an updated transmitter that jammed the new German aircraft radios modified to operate in spite of the original Tinsel jammers. Noting that the weak link for German night fighters was their radio communication with their ground controllers, more attention was paid to jamming this vital link between fighter and ground radar. Thus in October 1943, the Allies deployed ABC, airborne transmitters that would jam the new series of "jamproof" radios in German night fighters. At the same time, the Allies also began using Corona, which were Special Tinsel jammers that, instead of jamming, sent out false instructions to German fighters.

The Germans were now having the tables turned on them, with their electronic detection and communication devices being attacked electronically by skilled airborne Allied electronic countermeasures (ECM) experts. Thus was born a job category that has increased enormously in the past fifty years. The World War II ECM specialists would, just like their 1990s descendants, fly ahead of the bomber stream and use all manner of tactics and electronic equipment to confuse and neutralize enemy ground radars, radar-equipped interceptors, and radio communications between the two. Eventually, the Allied ECM became so effective that some bombing raids suffered no losses to German night fighters.

But the Germans fought back. In late 1943 they deployed the SN-2, an improved night-fighter radar that was immune to Window and had a range of four hundred to six thousand meters. The use of chaff was a major blow to the German use of radar and they quickly responded. In November 1943 they began using Wurzlaus. This was a modified Wurzburg radar that could sometimes differentiate between stationary tinfoil clouds and nearby aircraft that were, of course, moving.

The Germans also modified their Wurzburg radar (the "Nürnberg" version) so that it gave an electronic sound to the operator, as well as the blip on the radar screen. After some training, an operator could use his ears to tell the difference between the radar signal coming back from a chaff cloud and one coming back from moving aircraft. Chaff, like so many other measures, was only a temporary advantage and soon was compromised by countermeasures.

Perhaps the major flaw of electronic devices was that, if they sent out a signal, that signal could be traced. Thus by the end of 1943 the German night fighters were using Flensburg, an airborne receiver that could detect the allied Monica tail radar for up to a hundred kilometers. This enabled the night-fighter pilot to carefully stalk the bomber and get in his attack without as much danger from the bomber's tail guns. But Flensburg, and the Naxburg device for detecting the H2S ground-mapping radar, also made an earlier (summer of 1943) innovation even more useful. This little item was not a piece of high-tech gear, but a simple modification of a German night fighter and was called Schrage Musik ("Jazz"). Despite this flurry of electronic measures and countermeasures, it was still the case that simple, nontechnical ideas had a major impact on the night battles in the air. Thus the Germans managed to increase the lethality of their night fighters, while reducing their vulnerability, by the simple expedient of mounting a pair of upward-firing 20mm cannons behind the pilot. Whether alerted by Flensburg or not, the night fighter came up under the bomber and Jazzed it with the 20mm cannons. The pilot had to be careful to get out of the way as the bomber began to go down, but at least the fighter did not have to worry about those four machine guns mounted in the tail of the bomber.

There was a flurry of new devices introduced in early 1944. First there was the Allied Dartboard, which jammed German radio stations that were used to send coded messages to fighter pilots (whose normal radios were now frequently being jammed). Then came the Allied Oboe 2, a new version of the navigation with a new and improved type of radar signal. This made Allied bombing missions 300 or so kilometers inside Germany more accurate.

But the Germans also came up with Jagdschloss, a ground radar with a range of 150 kilometers that could switch between four different frequencies and thus be more resistant to jamming. They also began using Egon, a 200-kilometer-range fighter control radio that was more resistant to jamming and enabled ground controllers and radars to continually guide fighters.

From the end of 1943 through the spring of 1944 it appeared that the Germans were winning the battle for the night skies. Despite all the Allied efforts at jamming German radios and radars, the Germans were more successful at using radar and jammer detectors. And the use of Schrage Musik greatly reduced their night-fighter losses. Between November 1943 and March 1944, the British sent out 35 major attacks against German cities. The night fighters destroyed 1,047 bombers and damaged 1,682 others. In one major raid, the British sent out 999 bombers, of which 97 were shot down. Night fighters launched 247 sorties and accounted for 79 of the British bombers lost. The difference in men lost was even more striking: 11 Germans versus 545 British.

The German success was misleading, however, in that most of the British bombers were still getting through. Moreover, the British night bombing was a stopgap until such time as daylight bombing could be done. This was what the American bombers began doing in late 1942. By late 1943, escorted by long-range fighters, the American B-17s and B-24s were ranging all over Germany making accurate raids on German industrial targets. The British bombers were still dropping more bombs. Even in 1944, at the peak of the American effort, the British night bombers dropped 525,000 tons of bombs versus 389,000 tons for the American daylight bombers. The British bombing, although now considered "terror" raids against cities and their civilian population, did have a serious impact on the German war effort. Millions of workers were diverted to dealing with the damage and the refugees. Over half a million German troops were assigned to antiaircraft defenses around the cities. And the night-fighter force kept increasing, from 611 fighters at the end of 1943 to 1,256 in January 1945. The night raids made the cities unlivable and helped cripple the German transportation network.

The Germans did make their point, in early 1944 and throughout the war, that night fighters were a formidable weapon. Of the 11,965 British night bombers lost during the war, night fighters accounted for half (5,730) of them. But the Allies did not give up because of the night fighters' ascendancy in early 1944. June of 1944 brought the Allied invasion of France and many of the night bombers were diverted to bombing missions in France, and adjacent areas, to support the invasion.

During the summer of 1944, more Allied technology was applied to the night bombing effort. In August, Jostle was introduced. This was an airborne "barrage" jammer that jammed a large range of frequencies simultaneously. This could shut down many of the German electronic devices at the same time and prevent coordination of their effort. This is a method that is still quite useful today, for there is really no easy countermeasure for it.

In September, Window 2 came into use. Chaff cut to different lengths would jam the new German SN-2 airborne radar. Window had to be cut to the right length to jam a specific radar frequency, and this became a regular practice. The right chaff for the right radar, and sometimes different lengths of chaff went out the aircraft at the same time to jam all the German radars being used.

In October the Allies introduced Serrate 4, a new radar detector that could detect and locate the new German SN-2 airborne radar. At the same time, the Allies began using Perfectos to turn German IFF against them. The Germans were now using electronic ID (IFF, identification, friend or foe) and Perfectos could trigger the IFF and use the subsequent ID signal to locate German fighters. It was this experience that has, ever since, made pilots a bit wary of IFF. At the end of 1944 the Allies introduced Micro-H, an alternative to the Gee navigation system, which would again be useful until the Germans figured out a countermeasure.

In addition to more powerful electronic weapons, in 1945 the Allies had sufficient control of the air over Germany to attack the German radar and control network. With its radar and control centers gone, the effectiveness of the German air-defense system nosedived.

By early 1945, Germany lay in ruins, in good measure because of the 955,000 tons of bombs dropped by the British night bombers and the 623,000 tons dropped by the U.S. daylight bombers. The American air force officers that planned and flew all those missions over Germany came away with ideas and expectations that have resonated for fifty years and that form the core attitudes of air force technology and tactics to this day.

Setting Course in 1945

THE CARNAGE OF THE European air war was also a crucial influence on how air forces were manned, equipped, and organized after World War II. No one was willing to fight such a bloody air campaign again. Several of the weapons and technologies developed during the war were seen as the means to avoiding any more aerial slaughter in the future. Chief among the World War II items that transformed air warfare during the next few decades were:

• Nuclear weapons. This was what the air force leaders saw as their principal weapon. Until the late 1940s, America had a monopoly on nukes, and built larger and faster long-range bombers to carry them. No more thousand-bomber raids would be needed, no more massive casualties among bomber crews. One bomber, one atomic bomb, one target destroyed for sure. The downside of the one-bomber, one-target tactic was enemy resistance. But there were other technologies to deal with this. Countermeasures were to become the one crucial system essential to getting the nuclear weapons through to the target.

• Jet engines were powering combat aircraft by 1944. Jets meant speed and speed was life, and victory, in air combat. The Germans were the first to get a jet fighter into action (the Me-262), but the Western Allies were only a few months behind. By 1946, America was on its way toward an all-jet air force. This would not happen for another two decades. But year by year, the proportion of jet-powered combat aircraft increased. Jet bombers could not outrun jet fighters, but they could get to their targets quicker, and maneuver more rapidly to avoid approaching jet interceptors. Jet engines, and the speed they provided, made many countermeasures more useful. Enemy radars are usually prepared to deal with many countermeasures, but the speed of jet aircraft will often put the bombers over the target before the enemy can overcome the jets' countermeasures and locate the oncoming enemy again. In that sense, one might even consider speed a countermeasure.

• Electronic warfare, even more than nuclear targets, defined aerial combat after 1945. Electronics were new, only coming into their own twenty years before World War II began. It was all new, it was all different, and most of it was invented during World War II. But electronic measures begat countermeasures, and this aspect tended to get played down a bit. The emphasis was on things like keeping nuclear-armed jet bombers safe from enemy fighters. Individual bombers, coming from many directions with their nuclear weapons, would have to be spotted and tracked by enemy radar before fighters could find and attack them. Flying low and fast was seen as a safer course than trusting electronic countermeasures. If electronic countermeasures could defeat enemy sensors, then the nuclear-armed bombers could reach targets anywhere in the world and bring any foe (particularly the Soviet Union) to its knees. Unknown or untried electronic weapons, however, always lurked in the background, waiting to screw up a lot of carefully laid peacetime plans, and often succeeding.

• Command and control was something few nations appreciated at the beginning of World War II, but that all recognized as the crucial glue that holds everything together by the end of the war. The "headquarters," where the supreme leader and his assistants hung out, was an ancient notion, but the "command center," where the war leader communicated electronically with his many troops, was a late nineteenth-century invention. The "command and control center" concept was most successful in directing air-defense forces, both on land and at sea. It was obvious that, as radars and communications became more powerful, it was only a matter of time before the attacking air forces, as well as the ground forces, could also be controllable by these new systems. The crude British control centers of 1940, the ones that won the Battle of Britain, had become vastly more elaborate, effective, and vulnerable by 1945. The future was clear: whoever lost their command and control centers first in a future war would lose the war. The command centers, so dependent on electronic communications, were more vulnerable to countermeasures than to bombs. The latter would merely destroy one command center, and another could then take over. But countermeasures deceived, and made the command center carry on ineffectively. When antiaircraft missiles came into use during the 1950s, command centers became even more worth spoofing electronically. Aircraft sent off in the wrong direction by an electronically befuddled command center had pilots who would eventually sort out the problem. Missiles, once sent in the wrong direction, could not recover. Command and control centers were one of the biggest advances in warfare to come out of World War II. But because of that other child of that conflict, electronic countermeasures, command and control centers arrived in the post–World War II world with some fatal flaws and vulnerabilities.

How We Got Where We Are

IT'S OBVIOUS NOW where all of the modern electronic systems came from. Even missiles, in the form of guided bombs, were present in World War II. But missiles were the one post–World War II system that did not appear in its modern form until after World War II. Missiles were not seen for what they were, or would become, in the 1940s, although many recognized their future potential. No one was sure exactly what missiles would eventually do, but from the beginning it was recognized that missiles, by definition pilotless aircraft, would have electronic pilots. And electronic pilots would be far more susceptible to countermeasures than human ones.

Slowly, decade by decade, more electronics appeared in aircraft, ships, and vehicles. What these electronic gadgets could do often caused the development of countermeasures. As the electronic systems became more complex, so did the countermeasures. Thirty years after World War II it reached the point where "electronic surprise" was seen as a major tactic in future wars. By keeping the inner workings of electronic systems and countermeasures top secret, one hoped to pull off a fatal deception on the enemy when the shooting began. The only problem with this approach was the difficulty in keeping the secrets secret. Security was a sometime thing as the cold war approached its conclusion. So many secrets were for sale that most electronic confidences were breached and countermeasures were compromised. But that was only between the superpowers. For the smaller nations, like Iraq or Libya, that bought electronic gear from the big boys, well, you never sold little people your best stuff.

Until the 1980s, combat electronics and countermeasures were generally unknown to the public or, at most, considered some kind of dark art. Then came video games and the proliferation of personal computers. All of a sudden many of the new recruits had experience, from playing video games, with electronic weapons and countermeasures. Not only did the weapons and electronics-systems operators now take more quickly to their gadget-laden equipment, but the public came to appreciate, perhaps too much, what these new wonder weapons could do. The public has a short memory. Few realized that the whiz-bang electronic weapons had been around for half a century. There was also a split-personality attitude toward combat electronics. On a good day, people felt that these were the silver bullets that would guarantee bloodless victories. On the days that the press noted the price of electronic systems, and the frequency with which these systems failed, popular opinion was rather less enthusiastic. This sudden celebrity status for electronic weapons was generally a good thing, for the more attention they got, the more realistic people were about what these gadgets could do.

One thing that many people now appreciate is that in frontline situations (like the Gulf War), they are quite effective. But in guerrilla theaters (as the Vietnam War proved), electronic weapons and their countermeasures are much less capable.

We are now in a situation where we have so many electronic weapons, and possible countermeasures, that we have an enormous amount of uncertainty. Countermeasures have become so expensive, in their continued attempts to counter every potential threat, that they have become unaffordable, and unwieldy to the point of uselessness. Users, and the governments expected to pay for all this, are learning to live with less and make do with what they can get their hands on.

The impossibly large number of systems that countermeasures must deal with developed because so many weapons, over the last five decades, have had electronics built in. One likely solution to the problem is programmable and, generally, more flexible countermeasures systems. For example, your air force realizes that it may be flying against more different radar systems than it can afford to buy countermeasures for. The only viable solution, aside from the suicidal one of doing without countermeasures, is to create more flexible countermeasures. The key to this is software, or programmable countermeasures. The most advanced of these new countermeasures systems think for themselves, after a fashion. When a new electronic system is encountered, and this is quite likely to happen in the opening moments of any future war, the countermeasures system analyzes its electronic foe and selects the most likely signal to jam or otherwise defeat the foe. Given the speed of electronic warfare, this new approach, as risky as it might be, is the only practical one. Time for technicians to confer and think about it is no longer available. If the new electronic threat is not figured out and countered in seconds, you're toast.

As risky as this new approach is, it does not mean a lot of friendly troops are going to be killed. Increasingly, robots, in the form of things like cruise missiles and recon drones, are going in first and taking the hits if the new countermeasures don't work the first time around.

12

The Nonlethal Battlefield

ELEVISION HAS BROUGHT the reality of wartime carnage to everyone's home. Often in real time. It is not a pretty sight and people do not like what they see on this kind of "reality TV." Thus, there has developed a movement pressing for the development of "nonlethal weapons." These weapons are high tech extraordinaire and have already advanced more than a few military and political careers. The only problem is, they don't work.

Not to put too fine a point on it, when your troops are firing rubber bullets and other nonlethal weapons (NLWs) while the other folks are shooting back with the more conventional stuff, you will lose. The proponents of NLWs counter with the argument that one can incorporate NLWs and lethal weapons, using the former to save lives when possible, and the latter otherwise. But this approach gives the opposition an opening they are sure to exploit.

Looking at the past situations where NLWs could have been used, we see that the stronger users already worked under a number of restraints. These restrictions have largely been self-imposed. Any nation thinking of using NLWs is already in possession of armed forces that avoid generous applications of lethal force. Like the British in Northern Ireland, Israel in Palestinian areas, and many similar situations, the side with the big army tended to use NLWs for riot control. But whenever the "little guys" tried to duke it out with anything stronger than rocks and homemade firebombs, the regulars unlimbered the heavy weapons and went to war. Russia did this, most of the time, in Chechnya, because the Chechens preferred to use their own rifles most of the time.

Nonlethal weapons have always been around. The oldest one was simply a large stick or a whip. "Beating the crowd back" is an ancient phrase and classic nonlethal combat. Nonlethal weapons have been used for thousands of years to control angry people you were not exactly at war with. These weapons were for imposing restraint on an angry people. There were also weapons for annihilating an angry mob, and these were used on people you felt you could do without.

Television Wars

BUT SINCE THE 1960s, there has been another element to encourage restraint: television news cameras. These do have an effect on the troops, even when they are in situations where they might easily be killed themselves if they hesitate to use lethal force. This happened in the early 1990s in places like Somalia and Bosnia.

Another factor that has always been and will always be present is uncertainty. Many of the peacekeeping-type missions currently fashionable involve walking into the middle of a civil war. Such a conflict is always murky to the participants, and much more so to the outsiders. Human beings in general and soldiers in particular get very edgy when in an unpredictable situation. While it's easy to advise the troops to use NLWs when confronted by a mob of rock-throwing civilians, how do you know that there are not people in that mob with automatic weapons? Just such a strategy was used several times in Somalia, where throngs of women and children crowded around UN peacekeepers, allowing armed Somalis to get close enough to wipe out the UN troops with automatic weapons. While a risky tactic, the Somalis knew it had a good chance of success. If the opponents are bloody-minded enough, they will always exploit the humanitarian attitudes of their adversaries. Another recent example is how the Bosnians and Serbs attacked their own people and UN peacekeepers in order to create "atrocities" they could blame on their opponents. Several times the perpetrators were found out. Moreover, both sides had speakers going on in public about how good their side was at deception and subterfuge.

Humane Weapons

THE CONCEPT OF "humane" weapons is an old one, but usually in terms of some weapons being "too horrible," not ones that will do the job without hurting anyone. In medieval times, the Catholic Church came out several times against weapons deemed "too horrible" for use against Christians. There was often the caveat that such implements of war could be used against non-Christians. Attempts to make war more humane are not new and won't go away. In a way, it's just the other side of the same coin. Excessive violence (war) gives rise to bizarre attempts to tone it down.

Some of these attempts to impose restraint have worked, but more for practical reasons than for idealistic ones. The most common practical reason is to reduce those aspects of warfare that cause your own troop morale to decline or that increase the resistance of enemy troops. All this has more to do with psychology than technology. For example, the Geneva Conventions, a series of international agreements dating from 1864, have provided mutually agreed upon guidelines regarding how "civilized" nations are to conduct war. In much the same spirit as the declarations of the medieval popes, the Geneva Conventions forbade really nasty behavior. For example, prisoners were not to be killed outright and were to receive humane treatment. Most soldiers liked that one, because without it, troops who saw they had no way of escaping or winning would not surrender. Instead, they would fight to the death and take a number of their opponents with them. As war became more violent in the twentieth century, this protocol was seen as a way to keep up troop morale as they marched off to what appeared to be hell on earth. Experienced officers know that if the troops are too intimidated by what may happen to them out there, they won't be very useful on the battlefield, and many will endeavor to desert before they get to the combat zone.

Certain types of weapons were also outlawed, like shotguns and hollow head bullets (that caused more horrible wounds than the normal kind). Again, this played to the soldiers' fear of mutilation. Getting chopped up was seen by most soldiers as worse than just getting killed. If you were dead, that was it; if you had several key body parts shot off, you have to live with the results for years.

After World War I, chemical weapons were outlawed. Although such weapons were used extensively from 1915 to 1918, the generals could not help but notice how the presence of chemical weapons slowed everything down and drained the troops of any enthusiasm for being anywhere near the front. Chemical weapons were too successful. Not only that, they were actually more humane than the earlier weapons (machine guns and artillery). Chemical weapons killed fewer troops and wounded more. Most important, the nature of chemical weapons (silent, affecting the lungs, eyes, and skin) more easily panicked soldiers. It was this last reason that turned military leaders against chemical weapons. These were terror weapons, and terrified troops tend not to follow orders.

This did not stop some nations from using chemical weapons against opponents who could not return the favor. Thus French used chemical weapons against the Algerians in the late 1920s, Italians used them against the Ethiopians in the 1920s, the Japanese used them against the Chinese before and during World War II, the Egyptians used them against the Yemenis in the 1970s, and Iran and Iraq used them against each other in the 1980s. This last case was rather disturbing, but explainable. At first. Iraq used chemical weapons because the Iraqis thought they were going to lose their war with Iran and thought that Iran would not be able to manufacture chemical weapons soon enough to make a difference. The Iraqis were largely correct in this assessment, although Iran was able to get its hands on and use some chemical weapons before the war ended. This points out the real possibility of a nation using chemicals even when there is a risk that they will be used in return. When a nation sees the situation as desperate, anything is possible.

Nuclear weapons had a similar impact on commanders as did chemical weapons, even though nukes have only been used twice, and then against cities and not combat troops in the field. For several decades after that first use in 1945, commanders seriously planned for the use of nuclear weapons. But as the effects of nuclear weapons were studied and the psychological impact became more clear, it was seen that, in addition to the enormous damage, there would be crippling demoralization. By the 1980s, Russia and the United States were becoming more reluctant to even plan for the quick use of nuclear weapons in any future war. Aside from the mutual devastation if two opponents both used nukes on each other, there was the growing realization that the armed forces involved might just fall apart as discipline and the will to fight disappeared.

Biological weapons are, in a way, ancient. It has long been noted that disease is more likely to occur under some circumstances. Even without understanding the scientific reasons for this, from antiquity, some generals have noted this relationship and sought to take advantage of it. The most obvious example of this is the poisoning of water supplies by putting poisonous plants or dead animals into wells or other water sources. Some generals would leave poisoned food for their foes to find, or sling diseased animals into a besieged city. The twentieth century has brought forth more sophisticated biological weapons that no one has dared use yet. The major problem with modern biological weapons is that you have to immunize your own troops, and be prepared to deal with enemy retaliation in kind. But, as with Iraq and its desperate situation in the 1980s, some nation may eventually feel compelled to use biological weapons. This may cause more civilian than military deaths, but it is unlikely to spread very far. The most likely biological weapons are not exotic "plagues," but rather nasty diseases that are robust enough to be delivered by artillery shells and missile warheads, and are quick acting. Given prompt and adequate treatment (not always possible on battlefields and in Third World countries), these diseases can be treated. In theory, biological weapons can be a lot worse, launching diseases that are difficult to treat and spread quickly. But that's the future. For the present and the near future, biological weapons are not much more effective than chemical weapons and have about the same effect.

The New Nonlethal Weapons

IN THIS CENTURY, especially since World War II, a number of nonlethal weapons have been developed. The most common are tear gas (at first also called "riot gas"), rubber bullets, and water cannons. This last item is actually a variation on the use of fire department equipment, especially their high-power water hoses. Other old standbys are attack dogs, cattle prods, and blinding searchlights. But in the 1990s the notion caught on that modern technology could provide even more, and more effective, nonlethal weapons. The result has been an interesting list of new "weapons."

• Airborne antiengine sprays. These would be dropped as bombs or sprayed from an aircraft. The chemical would disable or destroy engines by causing components to corrode and fail. The trick with this stuff is making it nonlethal to humans and most other critters.

• Blinding Lasers. Lasers used against human eyes and optical/electronic cameras, fire-control optics, and similar equipment. This is as powerful as lasers can get at the moment. Effective range is more than adequate for riot control and dealing with opponents within a few kilometers. In the next ten years or so, we'll see lasers powerful enough to damage or destroy lightly built things like aircraft and trucks. But that won't be nonlethal warfare.

• Antimaterial chemicals and biological material. One of the better examples of this is a bioengineered Central American fungus that causes the plastic used for computer circuit boards to turn into a green goo. Basically, these are chemicals or living things like fungus that will damage materials used to build roads, bridges, railroads, and even the hulls of ships. Some of these items will, for example, cause rubber to crumble. This will stop cars and trucks, not to mention aircraft (which take off and land on rubber tires). Other materials in this category can be used to contaminate fuel and turn high explosives into low or no explosives. Of course, these items also make swell terrorist weapons, so there are mixed feelings about putting this stuff into wide use.

• Entanglement munitions. Long, thin, and strong fibers that would disable propellers, jet engines (which have propellers in them), helicopter rotors, axles on trucks and trains, and, in general, anything that spins around. Some versions of this are proposed for use on people, to entangle them in sticky fibers so they cannot move, or move very effectively.

• High–power microwaves (HPMs). These generators are light enough to be carried on a soldier's back, or installed in an unmanned (and expendable) aircraft. These generators direct a beam of microwaves that do many of the same things as an electromagnetic pulse (EMP) generator. In addition, HPMs can detonate ammunition fuzes, shut down engines, and damage military electronics by broadcasting very powerful microwaves. If a person gets in the way of these beams, the effects can often be fatal, if not immediately, then eventually.

• Infrasound. Very low frequency (ultra bass) sound that sickens and disorients. This could be used to keep people away from places you don't want them near. Infrasound can also be used instead of land mines to protect fortified positions.

• Nonnuclear electromagnetic pulse (NN-EMP). EMP generators and EMP bombs (explosives create the pulse) used to destroy commander communications, electrical power systems, and electronic devices, usually civilian, that are not shielded against EMP. These items are still in development, but tests have shown that they will work and can be built.

• Radio frequency (RF) systems. These are radio transmitters that jam and short-circuit the human nervous system. This temporarily disables the people the radio beams are aimed at. Think "Phasers on stun" and you'll get the idea. A tricky bit of business, this, for it can also cause long-term effects. It works on animals; no one is admitting to human experiments.

• Short-circuit fibers. These are long strings of material that conduct electricity. When dropped over electrical equipment or electricity transmission lines, everything is shorted out. These were used in the opening hours of the 1991 Gulf War to shut down the Iraqi electrical system. This method was quicker than bombing the power plants, and was more humane in that much less equipment had to be repaired or replaced to get the electricity flowing once more. A dust form is now available.

• Sticky/slippery foams. Liquids that are either supersticky or very slippery. In either case, application of these materials would immobilize vehicles, or make them uncontrollable. It has a similar effect on people, but use of the stuff in places like Somalia has shown that people quickly figure out ways to overcome these "weapons." These materials can also have a negative effect on machinery, especially vehicles and their moving parts.

Many of these nonlethal weapons are nonlethal only to a degree. Those items that disable engines or vehicles can, if the vehicle is moving when incapacitated, cause a fatal accident. All of the NLWs can, because few have been widely used, have some nasty side effects. For example, those items that use chemicals and bioengineered organisms might have effects beyond what tests have shown. The fungus that eats PC electronics might not disappear after its first meal, but might mutate and trash most of the world's electronics before an antidote can be found.

When the U.S. Congress found that the U.S. Army wanted money for more laser "dazzlers" (to destroy enemy optics and lasers), questions were asked about the effect the dazzler would have on the human eye. Why, of course the dazzler could blind an enemy soldier. Just like the medieval popes, Congress passed a law outlawing such an inhumane weapon. Well, outlawing it for American troops. No telling what enemy soldiers will do with it, but you can make a good guess.

Sorting Out the Impact of New Weapons

WHAT IS INTERESTING about this is how long it takes to comprehend what impact the new technology will have on the battlefield. It sometimes takes several years even when there's a war going on, and usually decades when there isn't.

Nuclear weapons were at first seen as merely another form of artillery. Chemical weapons were also first seen primarily as a more powerful artillery weapon. What is ironic about this is that modern artillery (rapid firing, large supplies of ammunition, fired from a distance at targets the gunners could not see) got its first real combat test in World War I. No one was quite sure what impact this new form of artillery would have until about the same time chemical weapons were first used. Although the first chemical attacks were made by waiting for the wind to blow in the right direction and then releasing the gas from canisters, within a year it became obvious that it was much more effective, and safer for the user, if shells containing the chemicals were fired instead. It wasn't until after three years of heavy use that effective artillery tactics were figured out. These new tactics (short, intense bombardments and mobile guns for the advancing infantry) got the war mobile again, but chemical weapons were also slowing it down. So everyone agreed to refrain from using chemical weapons after World War I. For those who were keen on "humane" warfare, the outlawing of chemical weapons seemed like the humane thing to do. Those generals who wanted to avoid seeing battles turned into a mass of demoralized troops in gas masks went along.

The use of nuclear weapons on the battlefield was a problem that had to be sorted out in peacetime; this took over thirty years. At first, military leaders were a little fuzzy about exactly how radiation fit into all this. The other effects of nuclear explosions, blast and heat wounds, they had seen plenty of while touring the wards in field hospitals. It wasn't until the 1960s that radiation began to loom as a major obstacle to the battlefield use of nukes. Even then, what changed things most was the decades of attention (none of it favorable) nuclear weapons and their radioactive fallout got in the media. Books, magazine articles, TV, and movies gave the new generation something to think about, and their military commanders something to worry about. Going into the 1980s, few soldiers on either side of the Iron Curtain saw nukes as "just another form of artillery." Nuclear weapons had been demonized, and troop morale could be expected to collapse if the nukes were used.

Nuclear weapons were unique in the history of weapons, and NLWs, not just because of their highly technical nature, but because of how they became quite potent just as psychological weapons. When nuclear weapons were first used, each one was able to do the work of about a thousand B-29 bomber sorties. The advantages for the attacker were that fewer aircrews were at risk. Each atomic bomb used saved from a few dozen to over a hundred American lives, mainly because so few B-29 crews would be in action. Even if twenty or so nukes were used during World War II, it still would have been cheaper, in money terms, to use lots more B-29s and conventional bombs instead. If twenty nuclear weapons had been used, each would have cost, in 1996 money, nearly a hundred million dollars. What was unique about the nuclear weapons was that they were radically new technology; one bomb from one bomber did as much destruction as thousands of conventional bombs from a thousand bombers. The implication was clear, and intentional: if the conventional bombs could (and already had) devastated most of Japan's cities, then those same bombers carrying atomic bombs could incinerate all of Japan. The chief benefit of radically new military technology is not what it is doing, but what the enemy can be made to think it can do. In that sense, nuclear weapons began their battlefield career as terror weapons, and have continued in that vein up to the present. As time went on, atomic bombs became more and more terrifying, even though they were never again used after August 1945. Nukes became the ultimate nonlethal weapon. So frightened had everyone become of nuclear weapons, that confrontations were avoided between nuclear-armed nations lest there be a diplomatic accident and nuclear weapons be used once more.

The Downside of Nonlethal Weapons

YOU CAN ALSO SEE how new protocols calling for the use of NLWs would encourage more people to confront armed troops, secure in the knowledge that they would not be shot down on the spot. Use of existing NLWs has clearly established that demonstrators are as often encouraged as discouraged from their violence by the use of NLWs. But, then, the new theory of NLWs is that if they are used on a massive scale, the enemy will be overwhelmed. Perhaps, at least in some cases. But it is also true that if the opposition is using lethal weapons, they will go right on using them.

Currently we have a movement to ban the use of land mines. Now mines are very nasty weapons, especially as they have been used massively during the last sixty years, and increasingly used haphazardly. But if some nations renounce their use, that will not eliminate the use of mines. No weapon has ever been successfully banned. The United States has also put restrictions on the use of laser devices by American troops. While lasers can blind people, they can also detect fire-control equipment and quickly disable it. Giving your own troops nonlethal weapons while the enemy loads up on the more deadly stuff will present some ugly situations once the shooting starts. You can disarm your troops a bit in peacetime and not notice it, but the consequences will be unavoidable if these soldiers are sent into combat.

Nonlethal Weapons in Perspective

THAT SAID, nonlethal weapons are not without their uses. First, we must realize that there have always been nonlethal weapons and they have proven useful on the battlefield. Smoke has been a widely used weapon in this century, and was often found on ancient battlefields as a deliberate combat tool. Smoke blinded the enemy to your whereabouts and, if you planned your operations the right way, allowed you to throw the opposing army into a panic, thus achieving a relatively bloodless victory.

Barbed wire is another NLW that became prominent in this century. It's nasty, but basically nonlethal and no more dangerous than a lot of the new NLWs being proposed. Barbed wire served the same purpose as mines, in that it kept the enemy out of areas you didn't want him in or at least slowed him down if he was determined to come through. Against civilians, barbed wire was also useful as a nonlethal way to keep people out of places. If you look around, you'll note that it is a favorite NLW off the battlefield.

Electronic warfare is another nonlethal weapon unique to the twentieth century, and many of the proposed new NLWs are merely new variants of long-used electronic-warfare techniques. But electronic warfare is more of a hassle for the high-tech soldiers than for the less well equipped opponents they encounter in places like Somalia and Bosnia.

Nonlethal weapons are a hot item among the politicians, but are less welcome among the troops who are being ordered (not asked) to use them. This is nothing new, especially in the United States. But the troops are not stupid and can see ways to make the most of the NLWs forced on them. Many of the NLWs that attack equipment are simply joining similar equipment already long in use. During the 1991 Gulf War, NLWs in the form of electrically conductive strips of material were used to take out the Iraqi electrical system. Antilaser equipment was used, as was a wide range of electronic-warfare gear. The new items that damage vehicles and enemy equipment of all kinds could be used, in large quantities, to attack enemy vehicles far from the front lines. It has to be this way because most of this stuff can't tell the difference between enemy and friendly equipment.

Many of the crowd-control devices, such as "stun rays" and slippery or sticky stuff, will only work if you can see your opponent. If you are fighting your way through an urban area, all you're likely to see of the enemy troop is their bombs, bullets, and booby traps. But these realities will only become clear to the civilian proponents of NLWs after the truth has been revealed in combat. It won't be pretty. The truth rarely is.

PART IV

Dollars, Media, and an Uncertain Future

Digital soldiering involves more than high-tech weapons and the troops that use them. There are also the people that design and build the gadgets, the government officials that decide what gets built, and the media that write about the builders and bureaucrats. All of these groups are very much a part of the action, and the media play a crucial role in keeping the games going.

Finally, here are some thoughts on where it is all going.

13

Paper Bullets and Iron Contractors

O NE OF THE PRIME movers behind the development of digital soldier–class gadgets is the peacetime phenomenon known as "paper bullets." When a soldier is caught up in the life-or-death career struggle, the thing to be avoided is actions or situations that can threaten promotion. Since most soldiers today rarely see real combat, they have more to fear from paper bullets (a bad evaluation or a permanent paper reprimand for not getting with the program) than from real ones. There is a tremendous incentive for the peacetime soldier to not do anything risky. In combat, a very risky proposition, you cannot avoid risks and, as many have discovered, fortune usually favors the bold. Not so in peacetime, where fortune favors those who avoid the most paper bullets.

On the nonmilitary side, the way to get ahead is to conjure up digital soldier kinds of programs and get approval to spend huge chunks of taxpayer dollars. Allocating money to train combat soldiers gets a paper pusher nowhere. Buying a new gizmo does. Politicians also stand in fear of their own paper bullets, otherwise known as ballots. Military spending has become another way to buy votes, or lose them to an opponent if a legislator should be rash enough to vote against defense spending for his constituents.

The Bulletproof Pork Barrel

THE CURRENT POLITICAL trend is to shrink government. Ironically, a lot of people don't want to apply this to the military. But this attitude is not there to make the military more effective, but to preserve a primary source of political patronage. The money goes where it will do the most political good, not the most military good.

This is nothing new. For thousands of years there has been a close relationship between money, political corruption, and the size of the armed forces. Consider, for example, how the earliest empires came about. When the first

231

cities and "advanced" (for the time) civilizations came about it was because the society had become so productive that there was a large surplus of goods and it was concentrated in one place (the cities). Some individuals were more capable than others and they accumulated considerable wealth. Those who had more wealth had an enhanced interest in maintaining order and security so they, and their families, could hold on to their wealth. Religion and law evolved to serve this need. Religion, and the priests, hailed the powerful families (of which they were often members) as blessed by the gods. The priests were in turn blessed with contributions from the wealthy (out of gratitude) and the poor (out of fear and worship) alike. But power, as the twentieth-century quip put it, "came out of the barrel of a gun." Back then, power came at spear point. Whoever controlled the most spears was top dog. The earliest (five thousand years ago) known political leader, Gilgamesh of ancient Sumer (in Babylonia, in modern Iraq), was given a title that meant "strong man." It wasn't his physical strength the temple records were referring to, but the number of spearmen Gilgamesh controlled. In a custom that developed many times throughout history, danger to the city caused the leading families to appoint the most capable of their number to command the troops and defeat the invaders. In this case, the invaders were probably a horde of hungry soldiers looking for some easy pickings among the crops and farming villages surrounding the cities of Sumer. Gilgamesh defeated the enemy, and went on to conquer neighboring cities, thus establishing the first known empire.

But there was a catch. Warfare is expensive. Until the last few centuries, 90 percent or more of the population was farming, hunting, or fishing. People lived from crop to crop. A drought, or anything else that interrupted food production, meant a portion of the population would starve to death before the next crop could be brought in. Cities were founded partially so that a surplus of food could be accumulated as insurance against these disasters. But the surplus only went so far. If you used the surplus to cover 10 or 20 percent of the farmers being away fighting, and then got hit with a drought, you had a problem. You also had to take farmers away from their fields to make shields, spears, and other weapons, as well as to build and repair city walls and other fortifications.

There was also a constant battle with the nomads, who were fewer in number than the city people, mainly because the nomads had less food and lived closer to the edge. But often the starving nomads had nothing to lose and would fall upon the settled peoples with the fury born of desperation. The nomads would sometimes attack just to steal. But the worst attacks were the result of hunger. Fortunately, most of the nomad attacks were relatively small, compared to the much larger populations in the settled farming and city areas.

The solution to the problem of pay for the army was to make war pay for itself. This is why all the great military commanders of the past were conquerors. Stealing from one's neighbors paid for the army and the campaigning. You stole the enemy's food, weapons, and people (as slaves). When you ran out of people to conquer, you had no way to pay for the troops, and the empire would usually fall apart as the leading families fought over the shrinking pie.

Naturally, you would think that when an empire had conquered all its neighbors, it would simply tax them and maintain a reserve of weapons and conduct training in between harvests so an army could be mobilized for whatever threat arose. But it never worked out that way, at least not for long. Weapons were bought and stored in arsenals. Ancient Chinese records mention hundreds of thousands of crossbows stashed away, so as to arm farmers when an emergency arose and a large force of well-equipped troops was needed. Spears, armor, shields, ships, and even horses were also kept in readiness. But corruption is also an ancient institution. Contracts to build, or store and maintain, the weapons were eventually given out to the politically connected, not the most capable people. Ancient chronicles also speak of shock at finding defective weapons, or no weapons at all, in the arsenals. Warships were allowed to rot, while the people in charge pocketed the money allocated for their maintenance. Fortifications were not kept in repair, or were attended to in a shoddy manner. Long periods of peace led to more and more corruption. When a hostile army did appear on the frontier, the empire would often quickly collapse. No mystery here, this has happened as recently as this century (Russia, Austria-Hungary, etc.). America found itself with a hollow army when the Korean War broke out in 1950, only five years after it began demobilizing its World War II host. The Spanish-American War revealed similar shortcomings in 1898, only thirty-three years after the Civil War armies disbanded. Many smaller nations have found themselves with worse situations, although they received less attention. A good example is Kuwait in 1990. Their troops looked good on paper, but a lot of the billions Kuwait spent on defense had fattened civilian bank accounts rather than increased military strength.

Some ancient peoples struggled more successfully than others against this corruption of the military. The Romans, founders of the greatest and longest-lasting empire in European history, tried the hardest. For their efforts, the Roman state lasted, in one form or another, for two thousand years, until Constantinople (modern-day Istanbul) fell to the Turks in 1453. The Romans stressed honest government and professional troops. When Rome began its existence as a republic in the fifth century B.C., it used an army typical of contemporary city-states. All citizens with sufficient wealth to buy armor and weapons were enrolled in the army and drilled regularly. The citizens were largely farmers, with the city serving as a market and a religious and administrative center. The city also was fortified and was the last refuge in the event of enemy invasion. This form of government was a step forward from the earlier kingdoms and depended on individual farmers making a good enough living to provide a surplus to buy weapons and armor. There was always free time between sowing and harvest for drill, and campaigning. What gave the Romans their advantage was their tradition of honest government. The Romans were diligent about administration and fairness. Although only male citizens could vote, and the wealthier citizens had more votes, this was as democratic as it got until the last century. The Roman system created enormous dedication and enthusiasm among its citizens. This made it possible to create a well-trained and highly disciplined armed force with a minimum of corruption in defense spending. The citizens put up with it because they knew they would gain from the system's success. And gain they did. By 167 B.C., Roman conquests had become so lucrative that direct taxation of citizens was abolished for several centuries.

But corruption did slowly seep in. It was difficult to keep civil and military officials honest and diligent century after century. By the first century A.D., the republic had turned into a military dictatorship. Although the old traditions of honest public service were still honored, elections became less and less important as more officials were appointed by the (in modern terms) "president for life" (or "First Citizen") in Rome. By the fourth century A.D., the leader was called an emperor and more and more of the administrators were men who had bought their positions and were mainly interested in enriching themselves.

The army took longer to decline, for it was the armed forces that ultimately kept the peace internally and kept Rome's enemies at bay. But the rot in the army spread and got worse. Officers could be bribed to excuse troops from training or marching out to campaign. Shoddy weapons and equipment were bought, with the contractors and government officials keeping most of the money. Sometimes even the troops' pay was stolen, leading to mutinies. From time to time there were reforms, especially after a few disastrous defeats. But the western part of the empire, and the city of Rome, fell under barbarian control in the late fifth century A.D. The eastern part of the empire, and its capital of Constantinople, carried on until 1453. In both cases, the end came, in large part, because of corruption when spending defense money.

The experience of Rome made a big impression on succeeding European governments, and on the founding fathers of the United States. While many European governments were able to adopt Roman practices, they also found themselves making the same mistakes the Romans did. By the fourteenth century, most parts of Europe had organized governments, complete with taxes and bureaucrats. But there was also quite a lot of corruption. Dipping into the till was accepted as almost a right by the aristocrats who snagged most of the senior positions. This led to absurdities such as those in France, where the nobles feuded with each other over who should get away with stealing the most from the government. Murder and assassination was a part of this mayhem.

The army and navy were, as always, the major source of stolen money. Keep in mind that it is only in this century that military expenses have not been the largest government expense. Before that, the army and navy were usually the largest item in the government budget. Then, as now, there were always officials who saw the military spending as an opportunity to get rich. This was particularly true in peacetime, when you only had to look good. Given the general lack of auditors, or even efficient bookkeeping systems to audit, this left ample opportunity to steal.

Until the last century or so, it was common for the government to give its generals and admirals a sum of money, with the understanding that a certain amount of combat-ready troops or ships would be made available for a specified length of time. This system worked when the officers getting the money were trustworthy and capable. But all too often, the money was seen as a license to steal. And it was easy in peacetime, when all you had to do was report that you had more troops or ships than you had actually paid for. All sorts of scams were pulled off under this system (which is thousands of years old). Troops were paid less than they were supposed to be, or not paid at all. Ships were not properly equipped, manned, or kept in repair. Weapons and equipment needed were not bought. Or if this stuff was already in hand, it was sold off.

In wartime, the officers in charge of the money were rather more honest, if only because skimping on weapons when someone, and their army, was trying to kill you did not make much sense. But stealing from the troops made a lot of sense in peacetime because most nations are at peace most of the time. Moreover, this kind of racket is not as risky as it seems when all of the nations in a region are doing it. On occasion the situation gets dicey when someone doesn't play the game the way the locals do. This is what happened during the period of European expansion from the 1500s to the 1800s. As corrupt as many European officers were, their counterparts in Africa, the Middle East, and Asia were much worse. The Europeans showed up in their natty uniforms, equipped with the latest muskets, and drilled so that they were able to march (in step, of course) right over the ragged local opposition.

Now all these little scams have not disappeared. In many nations today it is big business to embezzle defense funds and sell military gear out the back door. Getting substantial "commissions" for "brokering" procurement contracts is also big business. But perhaps the most lucrative pile of defense treasure to be plundered is in the United States, where it's all done more or less legally.

The American Way

ONE OF THE MORE revealing observations corrupt foreign officers have made about how the United States handles its defense spending is that "in America, there's enough graft to go around." In other words, in America, you can afford to pay everyone off. It's a graft fantasyland where you can get rich off the military legally, and rarely worry about going to jail for it.

How this came about has to do with money, lots and lots of money, and the fear of losing it.

Big, well-equipped, and lavishly supplied armies are relatively new. Multimillion-man armies were not possible in the past because the wealth needed to equip, organize, and supply such hosts was not there. But the Industrial Revolution, the scientific method, and modern capitalism have, in the past two centuries, created unheard-of wealth for people to play with. And in a stroke of wonderfully good fortune, especially if you were an American, more than a quarter of this new wealth came from one country: the United States (which has only about 6 percent of the planet's population—you do the math on that).

America had been working itself up to being the planet's premier economic power since the early 1800s. By the early 1900s, the other industrial nations (in Europe) nervously looked across the Atlantic and double-checked their statistics. Yes, it was true, those colonial bumpkins were on their way to outproducing them all. What was to be made of this? Well, nothing at first. Europeans spent the next forty years slaughtering each other with an abandon, and ferocity, never before seen. America was involved in these world wars, but much less so than any of the European nations. World War II smashed all of the industrial nations except one—the United States.

In 1945, the majority of the manufactured goods on the planet were coming from America. Twenty years later, that share of the world's wealth came down to about 25 percent, where it has remained for the rest of the century. In 1945, America also had the world's mightiest armed forces, a monopoly on the atomic bomb, and strategic bombers to carry them. While America promptly disarmed, cutting defense spending by nearly 90 percent, the world did not become a peaceful place. The Soviet Union installed dictatorships, or fomented unrest, in Eastern Europe, and encouraged North Korea to invade South Korea in 1950. This last action was the last straw; America ended up in another war with North Korea and China. By 1953, defense spending was at about 40 percent of World War II levels. But there were only about a quarter as many troops. After the Korean War ended, defense spending stayed at about 50 percent of the World War II level. Troop strength was less than 25 percent of the World War II level.

What was going on here?

It was the cold war. This was a conflict that began in the late 1940s, as the Soviet Union resumed its support of world revolution under the Communist banner. During World War II, the Soviets had been made out to be friends of the Western democracies. After all, the Soviet Union was doing most of the fighting against the Germans. The warm glow toward the Soviet Union lasted for a few years after the war. But the Soviets were having none of it. They wanted it all and were willing to get it all any way they could. By 1950 the Soviets had nuclear weapons, Eastern Europe, and China, and more conquests seemed within their grasp.

At that point, America dug in its heels, and thus began a forty-year struggle between the two superpowers. It was a war like no other. While World War II had cost the U.S. three trillion dollars and three hundred thousand combat dead, the cold war cost twice as much. Although only half as many Americans were killed during the cold war (mainly in Korea and Vietnam), the monetary cost was what had the greatest impact.

The six-trillion-dollar cost of the cold war was the money spent on defense above the lower, pre–cold war spending levels in the late 1940s. This was 4 to 5 percent of GNP, quite a bit (three times) more than the prewar 1 or 2 percent, quite a bit (a third) less than the cold war average of 6.5 percent.

Immediately after World War II, U.S. defense spending reflected America's larger role in the world, but not the eventual superpower levels. Military strength was kept at about 1.5 million, more than three times what it had been before World War II and the highest military strength America had ever maintained in peacetime. The cold war was a popular war in the sense that most people supported it. America had become rich after World War II, and people did not want to lose this to a bunch of heavily armed socialists (the Soviets). The Great Depression of the 1930s and the rationing of World War II had quickly changed in the late 1940s with the onset of a three-decade economic boom.

In the aftermath of World War II, America had left behind occupation armies in Germany and Japan. Those armies are still there over half a century later. The American people became used to having troops overseas in peacetime, something that was rather rare until World War II. With its growing wealth (GNP doubled, even after accounting for inflation, between 1946 and 1965, then doubled again by 1991), the American people could afford to support large armed forces. And so they did. Even with a growing population, per capita GNP increased 45 percent from 1946 to 1965, and another 58 percent by 1991.

But what exactly was being bought with all this money?

A lot of well-armed troops, but also a lot of politicians. Votes and politicians.

As long as there have been government budgets, there has been a tendency to spend the money in such a way that will do the government officials, the spenders, the most good. In a democracy, the money is spent in a way that enhances the reelection prospects of the legislators who vote on how the money gets spent. This was always the case in America, but never to the degree achieved with the enormous cold war defense budgets.

Most of the money was spent on paying and maintaining the troops. This was the case even before conscription was ended in 1973. Although many nations pay their conscripts much less than volunteers, over 50 percent of American troops were always officers or NCOs, who were paid much more than the lower-ranking conscripts. In addition to the payroll, there was housing, food, medical care, and a number of fringe benefits. Procurement and research averaged about a third of the budget. But the rest was spent where the troops were. And where the troops were there were voters.

Politicians at all levels of government quickly noted that defense spending meant jobs, and profits for their corporate contributors. It wasn't long—actually, it was already the case in the 1950s—before voters and contractors realized there was a game to be played. The winners saw more defense money being spent in their area or their company. All you had to do was support the legislator who approved the defense spending. All of this was done quite openly, for in large part it was not illegal. It was obvious that legislators who voted most frequently in favor of defense spending would be rewarded. The U.S. Department of Defense (DOD) made sure that the spending was spread around to insure that the maximum number of legislators in Congress would vote yes on Defense legislation.

Table 19 / Congressional Voting Tendencies and Defense Spending

Defense Spending $ Range (millions)	CDs	Pro-Defense Voting Index	Average Defense Dollars (millions)	Total Defense Dollars (millions)
0–9	36	33.4	3.4	124
10–19	24	62.9	15.8	380
20–49	85	54.1	34.6	2,941
50–99	86	51.2	73.9	6,352

Table 19 / Congressional Voting Tendencies and Defense Spending (continued)

Defense Spending $ Range (millions)	CDs	Pro-Defense Voting Index	Average Defense Dollars (millions)	Total Defense Dollars (millions)
100–199	64	60.5	143.6	9,187
200–299	39	53.6	241.5	9,419
300–499	35	62.1	379.4	13,278
500–999	38	51.8	695.9	26,445
1,000–3,999	26	55.1	1,865.4	48,500
4,000+	2	47.0	4,588.4	9,177
ALL	**435**	**53.7**	**289.2**	**125,804**

Notes for the above table. *CDs* are congressional districts. The *Pro-Defense Voting Index* indicates the degree to which the representatives from the districts voted for pro-defense items. The higher the index number, the more pro-defense the votes. Dollar amounts are what the districts received annually in the late 1980s, at the height of the cold war arms race, by each congressional district. Only a small number (8 percent) of districts are left out of the DOD's spending list. One can't help but note that the legislators from these districts have a pro-defense voting record that is 37 percent less than the average.

For most of the cold war period, the Democratic Party dominated the United States Congress. The data above reflect this, and the generally anti-defense spending of many Democrats. The chart above represents 263 Democratic representatives and 172 Republicans. Democrats averaged a pro-defense voting record of 33.8, while the Republicans' average was 84.1. But the Democrats were not shut off from the defense goodies. Each Democratic representative brought an average of $267 million a year of defense spending to his or her district. Each Republican representative, however, brought in $324 million. The DOD political strategists knew where the votes were and what they would cost.

One thing that helped the anti-defense Democrats was the presence of military bases in their districts, for one could safely vote against defense spending safe in the knowledge that these bases were unlikely to be closed. However, if any move was made to close any of those bases, said representative quickly became quite pro–defense spending. It became so difficult to close bases, even when it was obvious that there was no possible need for the base, that a special routine had to be developed for Congress to overcome the political pitfalls of base closing. An independent commission was set up to decide which bases were to be closed. Then the Congress voted yes or no on the entire list. Such was the political pressure to not lose the jobs these bases represented, that representatives and senators often went to court to overturn the Base Closing Commission's decision.

DOD and contractor political strategists also discovered that votes could be had if the dollar value of defense procurement contracts let to local firms in a district went up. In general, the trend is that the more a representative votes for defense projects, the more likely is the district to be the beneficiary of large procurement contracts from the Department of Defense. The top ten districts in terms of procurement dollars have an average index of pro-defense spending of about 50, while the bottom ten, which get no procurement dollars whatsoever, have an average defense voting index of about 10. The chart does not show the influence of large contracts on the voting tendencies of representatives from adjacent districts. Workers in a large shipyard or aircraft plant will often live, and vote, in adjacent congressional districts, and this will bring the representatives from these districts to the defense of any threatened defense plant in a nearby area.

Contractors have enormous political clout. Part of it comes from the thousands of lobbyists they employ to constantly cover legislators' and defense bureaucrats' line of vision. But there are also millions of workers who depend on defense spending for their jobs. Aside from the two million uniformed and civilian workers in the Department of Defense, there are several million more people in defense industries and companies that serve them. In the first half of the 1990s, 740,000 defense workers lost their jobs, providing considerable incentive to those still employed to be politically active in keeping their jobs. Writing letters, making phone calls, and attending meetings and demonstrations can have an effect on the congressional budgetary process.

Defense industries have several other advantages.

• They maintain close relationships with the bureaucrats who supervise the defense-procurement projects by hiring retired military officers and appointed officials who leave the government. In both cases, the new employees are generally paid more than in their previous jobs. However, these jobs are not as secure as civil service or military ones. A contractor employee can be fired at any time for any reason, or no reason at all. Everything has its price.

• Many military items are needed in small quantities and there is not enough business for more than one manufacturer. Thus the cost is higher than it ought to be, and there is no way to easily find out how low the price could be unless there is some competition. Jacking up the price like this happens a lot, sometimes without thinking, often deliberately to make more money.

• When there is only one supplier for an item, which is quite common in the realm of military weapons and equipment, how do you determine what a "fair" price for said item is? It's not as easy as it might appear. There is a mountain of government regulations to comply with, and the defense contractor is allowed (and this is quite reasonable) to add these administration costs into his overhead. Many of the regulations are absurd, often because they are the result of laws passed to deal with problems that no longer exist. Some examples have passed into legend, as the discovery, in 1940, that the British government was still paying people to stand by the Channel coast and watch for a French invasion (a leftover law from the Napoleonic wars of the early 1800s). The military has its own standards ("mil-spec") for materials, said specifications being more exacting than comparable civilian standards to account for the more demanding battlefield environment. But most military equipment, and personnel, never come anywhere near a combat zone. Yet most items are held to the higher, and more expensive, mil-spec standard. This provides more profit opportunities, as well as more chances to cheat. It's not all that difficult to slip a lot of lower-quality (and much cheaper) nuts and bolts into a shipment of much more expensive mil-spec stuff. In many cases, this will never be found out, since it is difficult to tell, with the naked eye, the difference between common shelf brackets you can pick up in a local hardware store and those that are mil-spec. Many of these items will never see a battlefield and will be used, and recycled out of service, without ever being exposed as frauds.

• Now every company that sells something has to market its products, but defense marketing is different. You don't have one customer, although you have only one buyer for a product. While the military buys the product, Congress and the president decide what is to be bought. You can get a sale going by working on the military end *and* the government end. The president's staff is always receptive to some new military gadget or weapon that will, in some way, help the president. Senators and representatives can always be enchanted by some new defense-spending program that will bring money, and votes, to their district. There are also a few legislators and presidential officials who are seriously interested in improving defense. But mostly, it's about money.

• A long history of shady dealing and sundry procurement scandals has led to enormous amounts of government supervision and auditing. This sometimes reaches absurd proportions. For example, the government spends some two billion dollars a year on employee travel. But it costs slightly more than that to supervise spending the travel money. Even buying commonly available items costs 10 to 20 percent more for the government just to cover the cost of the paperwork. Government contractors use this situation to their advantage in two ways. First, they simply add these administrative expenses to their costs and seek to make a profit (which they usually do) on their total costs. Secondly, they use the complex government regulations to their advantage by establishing special staffs that can deal with the bureaucracy no matter how complex it becomes. Any new firms going after government work will thus face another barrier to being competitive with the existing defense suppliers. Many commercial firms do, in fact, refuse government work because of the attendant paperwork and bureaucracy.

Military bases are a particularly favored form of military spending, as these are relatively permanent. Procurement contracts might end if shifted to another manufacturer, or because the weapon became obsolete and had to be replaced. But bases tended to stay put. There was usually intense competition to bring bases into a district, for this feat would generally pay off in votes for the senator or representative who could take credit for it. If a base was closed or other military business moved out of an area, you could be certain that come the next election, the loss of this economic activity would be a campaign issue.

The system of giving out these defense-related funds eventually acquired a life of its own. Unless some powerful event, like the end of the Korean or Vietnam War, came along, there was plenty of incentive to maintain or increase defense spending. A classic example was the end of the cold war. The chief foe, the Soviet Union, was no more. The Russian armed forces were quickly reduced to about a third of their previous combat capability. And it turned out that their cold war combat capability had been overestimated at that. Yet the American defense budget only fell by about 10 percent from the cold war average. Sure, defense spending in 1995 was one-third what it was at the cold war peak in 1985. But the defense budget was still much higher than could be justified by any threat to American security. What was keeping defense spending so high? Politics was, and a political maxim of ancient provenance holds that "you can give, but you can't take away" (at least not without great difficulty).

The Value of a Soldier's Life

FEW POLITICIANS ARE willing to risk losing votes by going after defense spending. But it's not just the money. There's an emotional issue involved. The military is there to defend the nation from foreign enemies. In a democracy, there is a certain amount of affection for the troops because of their high-risk public service–type jobs. "Nothing's too good for our boys," as the saying goes. American troops getting killed in combat is always a sensitive issue with the voters and a political football that U.S. politicians have not been reluctant to put into play.

The war over Kuwait came at a fortunate time in this respect. Just as the cold war was ending, the troops got a chance to decisively trounce a truly vile foe. Such a demonstration of professionalism and efficiency caused public opinion to side even more with the soldiers. And best of all, the deed was done with an uncharacteristically small number of American casualties. Much was made, especially by defense industry publicity departments, about how U.S. weapons technology saved lives. Actually, it was superior training and leadership that was most responsible. But the hardware partisans got their point across more strongly, for training and leadership of the troops does not have nearly as many lobbyists. Even highly effective electronic training equipment loses out in the competition for money. The point made was pretty stark. High tech saves the lives of American troops. Take away the high tech, or spend less money on it, and you are sacrificing the lives of American soldiers.

As a result, the defense budget stays large, with little incentive to bring it down. The reason most often put forth is that it is still a dangerous world. And it is. But backing up that argument is the less easily attacked one that no one wants to see American troops killed because they were not properly equipped.

What is implied, and this is played subtly lest anyone be accused of bad manners, is that American combat deaths cannot be tolerated. This is something new. Until the 1991 Gulf War, a certain amount of death and mutilation was taken as an unavoidable cost of combat. But the uncharacteristically low American casualties of the Gulf War promptly enshrined in American popular thought the idea that all future wars should be equally bloodless. This gave American generals and admirals the chills. They knew better, but American public opinion and many legislators (increasingly lacking any military experience) now thought otherwise. The popular attitude has become one that assumes U.S. high tech will make American combat casualties practically nonexistent. It's been impossible to get across the point that superior training and leadership, plus the nature of desert fighting and the low quality of most Iraqi troops, was the real cause of the low casualties. Low American casualties are now associated with the possession of large quantities and qualities of high-tech weaponry and military equipment. Ironically, the push to load up on the latest combat gear often comes at the expense of training funds and pay to retain the better military leaders. America has painted itself into a corner on this issue and will only see the light in the aftermath of a major, and bloody, war where the fables will play themselves out in the form of long casualty lists.

How Much Is Enough?

THE MILITARY SPENDING of America's potential enemies (Russia, Iraq, China, North Korea, Libya, Iran, Syria, and Cuba) combined is less than what the United States spends on defense. Include America's close allies (Japan, NATO) and the "enemies" spend less than half of what the American coalition does. Although the hostile nations do maintain over six million troops, and large numbers of combat aircraft, armored vehicles, and warships, America and her allies control the world's oceans and maintain a wide margin of superiority in military technology.

What it comes down to is, how much is enough American defense spending? Sorting this out and deciding how much is a complex process that calls into play many different interest groups. The principal ones are:

• Economic interests. Countries will find a way to scrape together troops to defend their own economic interests. This was rather starkly demonstrated during the 1991 Gulf War. The Persian Gulf has about half the world's oil and the United States and other industrialized nations depend on that oil for their economic well-being. Thus Kuwait, and free access to the Gulf oil, was worth fighting for. Economic interest was the same issue that caused America to spend nearly a trillion dollars for over four decades to maintain an army in Western Europe. The Soviet Union, it was feared, would try to annex Western Europe. America could not allow its major trading powers to become Communist satellite states. For the same reason, U.S. armed forces have been, and still are, maintained in Japan. Another crucial economic interest, in the form of trade with Japan, must be defended.

• Intelligence information. While there are plenty of potential enemies of the United States, just how hostile, and how dangerous, we think they are depends a lot on the information we have about them. Cuba may be hostile to America, but it does not pose a serious military threat. How do we know that? We know because we use space satellites and other spy devices to keep track of the quantity and quality of Cuban armed forces. Of course, information gathered by the CIA and other intelligence agencies can backfire. This has been revealed in the embarrassing items that came to light after the cold war. It seems that the Soviets were much better at the spying and deception game than their American counterparts. The result was that we had a rather inaccurate picture of Soviet military strength. The Russians made themselves out to be considerably more powerful than they actually were. This is one way to make your enemies behave. But if you are not a nuclear superpower, you might find it convenient to present yourself as weaker than you are. So whom does one believe when trying to figure out what the bad guys are capable of? Good question. No one has yet found a perfect answer to this. There are as many experts as there are TV news shows with large audiences. Whom does one believe, indeed.

• Political and diplomatic interests. Throughout history, large armed forces have been maintained simply because of bad political and diplomatic relations with a neighboring country. This is still the principle reason for the existence of most nations' armed forces. The United States is one of those rare exceptions, there being no neighbors, until the Soviet Union got nuclear weapons, that posed any military threat. Of course, now Russia is a kinder and gentler neighbor than the Soviet Union. That said, the United States has cast a wider net of diplomatic interests in the last century, and acquired a world full of potential political entanglements. Most of these foreign nations, namely the ones that hold no economic interest for America, could be ignored, and often are. But politics and diplomacy don't always work that way. So America gets involved in places like Bosnia and Somalia.

• Military planning. Soldiers like to plan ahead. Theirs is a dangerous profession and good planning can lower the risk. Some of the planning takes the form of working out the details of wars not fought, or not even likely to be fought. You don't hear about some of these, like a military intervention in some European nation we are currently friends with. But these planning exercises are there not just to train the staff officers, but also to test the likelihood that this plan or that one has a chance of success. These exercises are not perfect, but they do put you in the ballpark with your estimates of how many divisions, carriers, and fighter wings will be needed to deal with any particular situation. If a potential military operation appears to require far more resources than are currently available, well, then no one is going to get too enthusiastic about getting behind it. This doesn't always stop some overseas adventure, but it is always a major obstacle.

• Popular opinion. In the age of mass media (the last hundred years or so), this has become a decisive factor in making armies larger and then sending them off to some overseas adventure. Public opinion is what it has always been, someone with a catchy idea and the means to share it with a lot of people. Popular opinion often starts wars, and less often stops them. Ever since the media frenzy that led us into the Spanish-American War a century ago, the mass media have increasingly taken the lead in shaping public opinion about where the troops should go. It's not that the mass media want to start wars, but wars are the ultimate disaster and disasters sell newspapers and attract TV viewers. Now there are always several wars going on around the world, but the media tend to follow the lead of whoever makes one particular war a conflict particularly deserving of sending "our boys" in to straighten things out. How does one war get "selected" and others not? Mostly it's a matter of access. The Spanish-American War got going because Spanish colonies like Puerto Rico and Cuba were right off U.S. shores and American reporters had easy access. Moreover, the colonial rebels knew how to work the U.S. media and did so with great success. We tend to think of this sort of thing as a recent development, but it first appeared in its full form a century ago. Today, wars that allow easy access for camera crews will get coverage, and perhaps a media campaign to "do something." The media coverage of some hellhole is usually all it takes to disgust the TV audience and bring forth a growing call for stopping the war, and its attendant horrors. This is especially true with the appearance of instant TV news. A hundred years ago, it would take at least a day for tele-graph or fast ship to get the word back to newspapers. Often a week would pass before some wartime tragedy would be reported. Television news, ini-tially, still had to wait for film to be flown back. But since the 1980s, the grow-ing use of satellite communications has made possible "instant news." This has more impact, especially on public opinion. The public now will crank up its fax machines and electronic mail, with public officials getting an outraged response from the voters before the newscast is even over. The media tend to follow the leader when someone stumbles across a story that hits a public nerve particularly hard. Everyone piles on with coverage and, before you know it, the waves of public opinion pound governments into "doing some-thing."

• What you've already got. Most of the time, there is no great debate over how much armed forces are "enough." What is already available is judged "enough" and the debates that do take place are about justifying what is al-ready there, or moving around items in the defense budget. What happened in the United States after the cold war was an example of this. The principle jus-tification for the large peacetime armed forces America had maintained since 1945, the Soviet Union, was gone. While U.S. armed forces were subsequently reduced, they did not shrink in proportion to the decline in Russian military might. New reasons for maintaining large peacetime American forces soon appeared.

Okay, so we now know how "enough" is explained, justified, and generally agreed upon. But this has historically been an imperfect arrangement, with "enough" being a compromise of sorts.

But how much is enough?

There is no perfectly logical or agreeable "enough." For one thing, the en-emy you will next face on the battlefield is not necessarily one you anticipated. In early 1950, few, if any, senior American officials thought the United States would be fighting a major war in Korea, against Chinese armies, by the end of the year. In the early 1960s, few people considered the possibility of half a million American troops battling North Vietnamese regulars and South Viet-namese guerrillas by the end of the decade. Now, when you think of it, what a scandal it would have been if the American government had been caught, in early 1950, getting ready for a major war in Korea, or in 1963 preparing to send half a million troops to Vietnam. No, the enemy you face on the battle-field is often the one you were not anticipating. The one time we did correctly anticipate our potential foes was in World War II, but in that case the Germans and Japanese were already at war when America began to get ready.

In the late 1990s, we have a large number of potential military opponents. To name just the more obvious ones:

• Iran. For thousands of years, Iran has dominated the region. Well, at least most of the time. But that's often enough, for example, to have the Persian Gulf named after them (Persians, Iranians, different names for the same people). Iran feels that all the oil in the Gulf, not to mention the people currently sitting on that oil, would be better off under Iranian control.

• Iraq. For over a thousand years, Iraq's major city, Baghdad, was a major center of Arab culture. But Iraq is a recent creation as an independent state and has been aggressive with its neighbors ever since it came into existence in the 1930s.

• China. The economy is increasingly capitalist, which makes the economy much stronger. But the government is still Communist, or, at best, dictatorial and stridently nationalist. Chinese military officials speak openly of future wars with their neighbors, and the United States.

• Russia. The transition from communism to something else has not been easy. Politicians with a nationalist and militarily aggressive policy have garnered a lot of popular support.

• North Korea. Another Communist government in decline. But well armed and noted for aggressive behavior in the past.

• An Arabian Islamic republic. Saudi Arabia has a lot of people who would be rather harshly anti-American. If the current ruling family (the Sauds) are overthrown, they could easily be replaced by a bunch of religious fanatics.

• A poverty-stricken nation in chaos. There are a lot of poor countries around the world that have fallen into murderous chaos, or could easily do so. Somalia, Bosnia, and Haiti are only a few of those that have done so. Some poor nations have nuclear weapons, or are trying hard to get them.

There's no way the American voters will foot the bill to maintain troops capable of taking on all of these situations, or even two or three at once. The more likely solution is a combination of:

• Some American forces. Ever since the early 1800s, America's navy and marines have been used to protect American interests overseas. Traditionally, the "navy belonged to the president, the army belonged to the Congress." There wasn't much for the army to do most of the time. There was guard duty on the frontier until the frontiers disappeared a century ago. But this domestic soldiering was more like police work than traditional soldiering. The navy was always doing the overseas adventure bit, until World War II anyway. All this changed somewhat after World War II, when the army and navy both became huge by traditional peacetime standards, and a separate air force was also created. All of America's armed forces were now looking overseas for work. Until the end of the cold war, there was plenty of work for everyone. The American public leans toward keeping the troops at home, but there's nothing for them to do at home as there are no hostile and heavily armed neighbors to keep an eye on. As U.S. forces are reduced, those that remain tend to be units that can be quickly dispatched to far-off trouble spots. This is about all one can expect in the next decade or so—a few divisions ready and able to fly or ship out to distant battlefields. Anything more than that would require a declaration of war and major mobilization.

• A lot of high-tech U.S. weapons. America and its allies will have an increasing number of robotic and high-tech weapons. One of the many advantages of robotic weapons is that they are easier to fly to distant trouble spots than troops and their weapons. Even with the huge cutbacks in military research, America still has the most capable weapons designers on the planet and many of them will remain at work. If the resulting equipment cannot be sold to American forces, it will be exported. France has done this for many decades, developing high-tech weapons and then paying for the development by exporting most of them. Actually, this sort of aid has been used for some time. All of the Arab-Israeli wars featured American equipment, but not American troops, going to help the Israelis. Same with the British during the 1982 Falklands War. Afghanistan featured U.S. weapons, but no U.S. troops. There have been other situations like this, and there will be more.

• Troops from nearby allies. Many American allies have been spoiled by nearly half a century of U.S. troops protecting them. Europe and Japan have been able to keep their defense spending relatively low because America maintained large forces in their parts of the world. American taxpayers no longer tolerate this and, in any number of ways, U.S. allies have been told to be ready to take care of problems in their own backyard. This doesn't always work, or only works for a while before the allies convince the United States that only the planet's only superpower can deal with Bosnia, Somalia, or whatever. This routine will lose its effect over time, and fewer U.S. troops will be fixing problems for our allies in their own neighborhood.

• American diplomacy. This, more than anything else, will determine how much American military power is enough. For decades, our allies have successfully pled insufficient resources and lack of leadership, thus leaving an opportunity for ambitious American politicians to play "leader of the Western world." This leadership has been very expensive for America, and quite beneficial for U.S. allies. But the world has changed and it's not as easy to be the leader of the Western world. For one thing, it's expensive. The cost is high and the debts were pushed under the rug for many decades. But now, the trillions of dollars of debt the United States piled up during the cold war is rather visible and the money spent defending rich allies is much harder to justify. Something has to give, and the American taxpayer wants to stop giving.

"How much is enough" has little to do with "how much is enough." The need for troops to keep the peace throughout the world is beyond what any one nation can, or is willing to, provide. What America is willing to send in the way of armed forces will consist of whatever can be agreed to by various interest groups in the United States. Sure, you can reduce opinion polls and estimated risk to American interests to numbers, and then calculate which size armed forces are the most "efficient." But that's not the way it's really done. "Enough" is always how much you are willing to put up when the crunch comes. That's enough.

14

Tested in the Media and in Combat

W HICH WEAPONS ARE worth having? No one in uniform, or the arms business, likes to dwell on this point too much. But the highest accolade a weapon or military gadget can get is "tested in combat." Without that stamp of approval, the weapon is suspect. Never mind the hoopla that accompanied the weapon's development and introduction. This is the story of the real story behind how news of military affairs is more often used for ideological grandstanding than to inform anyone about what it actually going on.

There is a lack of professionalism and responsibility in the coverage of military affairs that simply fuels the debates over military high tech. It works like this.

• Most of the time, there is little public interest in military affairs. This is not surprising, as most of what the military does in peace, or war, is very technical in nature. How much media coverage do you see of technology, especially technology that is used by very few people?

• When there is a war, people become *very* interested in military affairs. This is also quite natural. No one pays much attention to the fire department except when there's a fire. At that point, you have to call out the cops to keep the crowds back. But as a result of no interest in the military most of the time, and intense interest when there's a war, you have the media under tremendous pressure to become instant experts on a very complex subject. This generally does not work out very well. In their haste to deliver the news in a very competitive situation, a lot of misinformation gets passed around as absolute truth.

• The draft evasion of the Vietnam era, and the elimination of the draft itself in the early 1970s, has left us with a shrinking number of military correspondents and television news producers (the people who actually put the stories together) with any military experience. Without that personal experience of the military, journalists had a more difficult time determining what was significant in a military story and what wasn't. Outside experts were often called in, but these people are of variable quality and are usually not paid for appearing as talking heads. Indeed, that appearance is considered sufficient compensation and tends to attract people more intent on getting screen time than in getting the story straight.

• Another leftover of the Vietnam era was a noticeable dislike for the military by journalists who largely leaned to the liberal end of the political spectrum. This meant that many journalists were basically mistrustful of the military and inclined to believe the troops were up to no good.

• Bad news is good news. This is a basic rule for journalists everywhere and for all time. Good news does not sell, bad news does. When there's a war going on, that's bad news enough and it's considered good manners to say nice things about the troops. But in peacetime, the military is mainly a source of bad news stories.

• The news business is market driven. News directors deliver what the public wants, and the public does not want a lot of detail on military affairs, at least in peacetime (which is most of the time). In wartime, many of the details are secret anyway. In peacetime, most of the work is done that determines how well you will do in the next war. So while the media are at fault for not presenting an evenhanded and detailed story of military affairs in peacetime, it's not really their fault. They don't know, and the lack of interest among their customers (the population in general) gives them little incentive to do otherwise. So you get sound bites, a few headlines, and some exposés of uncertain provenance. Of course, people reading this book are an exception. But there aren't enough of you, at least according to my royalty statements.

• Memory does not exist. Consider several of the feel-good stories to come out of the 1991 Gulf War. Everyone was thrilled at the stories about the AWACS, the Maverick missile, the M-1 tank, and the stealth fighter. All were praised for their performance in the war. Yet ten years earlier, all of these systems had endured one negative story after another. What's going on here? It's simple. No one who wrote the bad news stories in the early 1980s expected anyone to remember them if, years later, these same weapons turned out to be pretty effective after all. This was not always done with malice or instant distrust of the military in mind; often it was done in ignorance of how weapons are developed. Whatever the case, one is in for quite a shock if one goes back to look at the stories written about these Gulf War weapons years earlier.

Bad News and Good News

TAKING A LOOK at some of the early media coverage of the hotshot weapons of the 1991 Gulf War reveals a pattern that is still with us. These earlier stories heavily accentuate the negative and show little appreciation for the realities of weapons development. Let us examine some specific examples of the news reports, and the subsequent performance of new weapons.

AWACS aircraft. The latest in a line of air-control aircraft, a type of airplane that had its origins in later World War II. The AWACS was in development from the late 1960s to the early 1980s. It finally went into service in 1982, and the negative stories in the media became more numerous in the early 1980s as the actual production of the aircraft began. These aircraft would cost some $300 million each (1996 dollars), and this always attracted press attention. Most new weapons are quite complex, especially aircraft; otherwise one could just go on building the previous, and simpler, model. AWACS-type aircraft had been in use since the 1950s, to control combat air operations, but the AWACS itself was, as new weapons are wont to do, taking advantage of the latest technology to do things in ways never done before. Journalists attacked the AWACS because it was too expensive. This is a standard critique, and is certainly not unique to AWACS. The next bunch of critiques had to do with how reliable the AWACS would be. Civilians have never come to terms with the relative unreliability of military electronics. To get peak performance from state-of-the-art equipment, the military has, for over half a century, accepted using gear that would fail every hundred hours (or less) of use. This proved workable in wartime, but many journalists never caught on to this and continued to put the reliability of military electronics in the same category as TV sets and microwave ovens. But the early 1980s criticism that was most damaging, and misleading, was that the Russians could easily jam the AWACS radar and, worse than that, sneak their jets in unseen and shoot the AWACS down. What was so absurd about this was that it was an obvious vulnerability of an AWACS-type aircraft and was dealt with during every phrase of the aircraft's development. Articles appearing in such national publications as the *Christian Science Monitor* and the *Wall Street Journal* hammered away at the "AWACS is vulnerable" theme. Trade journals like *Aviation Week* explained, for any journalist to see, how the AWACS would work and why it would work. But most editors were looking for bad news, not history lessons and technical explanations. During the 1991 Gulf War, the AWACS was universally praised for performing flawlessly in directing the massive number of aircraft movements over the battlefield. Not a single friendly aircraft was lost to collision, an unprecedented event for an operation of this type. The AWACS did what it was designed to do, despite over a decade of press criticism.

Maverick missile. The Maverick is a Vietnam-era missile that was a success in the last years of Vietnam and was, in the early 1980s, about to go into production with an improved version. As effective as the Maverick was in Vietnam, the missile was itself a redesign of an earlier weapon, the Bullpup. While the Maverick performed well in Vietnam and the Middle East (Israel used it in 1973), its principal battlefield was expected to be central Europe against Russian armies. But the misty and fogbound European climate made the 1960s-vintage Maverick sensors less effective. Critics jumped all over this, as well as suggestions as to new technology needed to overcome these problems. The critics were generally oblivious of the historical and practical facts. Central Europe has always been wooded, misty, and fogbound. Soldiers have been coping with this for thousands of years. Most importantly, the nasty climate bothers both sides, not just the side with Maverick missiles. The typically one-sided and shallow criticisms of the Maverick demonstrated an ignorance (more likely) of military history and combat operations, as well as simple headline hunting (often enough). Over five thousand Mavericks were fired in the 1991 Gulf War, with great success. The pilots loved them, the Iraqis feared them.

M-1 tank. This was the first really new American tank design since 1945, when the M-26 "heavy" tank went into action at the end of World War II. All subsequent designs had been variations (always) and improvements (most of the time) on the current model. But the M-1 was all new. Every element of the tank was redone. The results were expected to be spectacular. But before the M-1 could prove its ability to survive on the battlefield, it had to survive media scrutiny. Patrick Oster and Bruce Ingersoll of the *Chicago Sun-Times* conducted something of a crusade against the M-1. Between April of 1981 and October of 1982, these reporters had six articles in the paper slamming the M-1. The usual accusations: too complex, too expensive, too unreliable, plus a few lesser sins. All true, of course. But the ink-stained wretches missed the point that warfare, as it is wont to do, was changing. If they had taken a look at the similar situation at the start of World War II, they would have been amazed at how similar things were. The "new" weapons of 1939 were, compared to the "proven" weapons of World War I, too complex, too expensive, too unreliable. Yet by 1945, no one in his right mind would have seriously contemplated using the older weapons against the newer ones. Does anyone study history anymore? Apparently not a lot of journalists. In any event, the army got its M-1 to the troops in the 1980s, and by 1991 the U.S. Army M-1 tank battalions went on to prove they were the most effective tank units in the world.

Stealth fighter. This aircraft was developed in secrecy, with development beginning in 1978 after a year of initial design work. It was a "black" (ultra-super-secret) project, with all work done outside normal air force budgeting and procurement channels. The first aircraft flew in June 1981, although a prototype crashed in 1979 (the test pilot survived). There were two further crashes, in which the pilots died, in July 1986 and October 1987. The aircraft became operational in 1983, and was used, with mixed success, in 1989, when

Panama was invaded, and then the aircraft went to war with spectacular success in the 1991 Gulf War. The journalism that "followed" this aircraft's development was particularly entertaining because the reporters had only a vague idea about what they were criticizing. This did not slow the media down. Some details leaked out. These, mixed with journalistic speculation, resulted in a plastic model of the "stealth fighter," as well as a computer game, before the F-117 was officially revealed in 1988. The model and game got the shape all wrong, although the game was pretty accurate about the aircraft's capabilities. But by and large, journalistic efforts were all over the lot. Some stories described what would eventually become the B-2. Others described a very elaborate "stealth" aircraft that would not work. Well, at least that was familiar ground for many reporters. When in doubt, serve up a lot of bad news. There were some positive stories, but not enough to prevent most people from being shocked at how effective the F-117 was during the 1991 war.

Journalism and the Military, Now and Then

MILITARY JOURNALISM is arguably the oldest form of journalism. Wars have always been exciting and easily able to arouse wide interest among the population. In ancient times, those who could write often recorded wartime events if they happened to be in a war. Or people recorded oral sagas that were still being conveyed from generation to generation. Many of these accounts have survived to this day. Some were carved into stone, almost always by the victors, who were eager to make the record of their triumphs last as long as possible.

When mass journalism came into being (via steam-driven newspaper presses) in the early 1800s, reports from battlefields were always popular. During the American Civil War, over 130 years ago, we saw the same kind of stories, and the same kinds of tensions between press and military leaders, that we have today. So the current situation, with sensationalist, often inaccurate reporting, is nothing new. On the plus side, reporters wandering around the battlefields and with the armies kept everyone alert to the fact that whatever they did while in uniform had a chance of being reported in the mass media. But there was, even at the beginning of mass media coverage of military affairs, the risk of things being misreported. Mostly, the misreporting was unintentional. But even during the Civil War, some reporters and newspapers had political agendas that took higher priority than accurate and honest reporting. Not much has changed since. Military affairs have become one of those subjects that is tolerated, and often treated in shabby fashion, in peacetime. When there's a war, or some kind of military action going on, there's a lot more coverage. But the accuracy is no better than that accorded the latest serial killer or celebrity divorce.

We also have the problem of newly anointed (by the media) "weapons" which are described inaccurately and then used to conjure up absurd news stories. For example, in late 1995 the British newspaper the *Daily Telegraph* published an article about a U.S. Air Force captain using a PC and the Internet to enter the control system of a U.S. Navy group of ships until "the computer screen announced 'Control is complete.'" The article described, with numerous inaccuracies, an actual event in which a U.S. Air Force computer security team had tested the security of communications within a U.S. warship. The British reporter got hold of that story and turned it into a fabricated tale of how one could use a commercial E-mail service to sneak into a warship's internal communications system and take over a battleship and then all the other ships steaming along with the battleship. In fact, no such event occurred. The U.S. Navy has no more battleships in service and, while at sea, American warships do not have any contact with commercial E-mail systems. Moreover, the ships' control systems are on separate "nets" from any E-mail system on board. The two systems cannot "talk" to each other. The actual event was more concerned with testing the security of the secret coding methods used to protect messages sent out via radio. The test was planned long in advance and was mainly testing internal security, not the problems of some civilian taking over warships via E-mail. Yet this news story will no doubt enter the realm of legend, to be quoted endlessly for as long as people are arguing over the security of military messages.

Despite the unrelenting search for bad (and salable) news, the media do get on target from time to time. There have been weapons systems that were flawed from conception, through development, and, if they survived long enough, after they got into service. The problem always was, the media were never able to tell the real targets (weapons that were dogs) from the false targets (weapons that were simply going through the normal teething problems). This, in turn, had the effect of making the military, and its weapons builders, quite sensitive about any criticism. The fear of bad publicity, deserved or otherwise, caused not only cover-ups or disinformation, but also more devotion to making sure a weapon "looked good," even at the expense of it "being good." The impact of the media actually distorted the weapons-development process. Sometimes this was in the form of rigged tests; at other times it was changing the design of a weapon so that it would play better in the press.

But this brings us to another interesting angle, those periodicals where weapons were discussed with less passion and more accuracy. This branch of the media has always existed, and has always been a place where military secrets were, well, not so secret.

Where Secrets Are Not Secret

THE MILITARY TRADE press is more evenhanded, but not read by many people outside the business and not much consulted by the mainstream journalists. Publications like *Aviation Week & Space Technology, International Defense Review, Janes Defense Weekly,* and many others have, since World War II, become major sources of open discussion of current and planned weapons. These trade journals are supported by weapons manufacturers as a way to sell their stuff to military establishments worldwide. That said, it is obvious that the articles will not be as relentlessly negative as those found in the general media. As is common with trade press in any area, the article writers tend to make the advertisers look good. But, there's a major catch in this particular industry (the death and destruction business). The users of these weapons have a life-or-death interest in the weapons being as effective as possible. With that in mind, the advertisers tolerate a certain amount of critical reporting. The articles published right after a war of any size are rather scathing in their evaluation of which weapons worked, which ones didn't, and why. Few reporters in the general media catch on to these trade press articles and, apparently, may have such a slight grasp of military affairs that they cannot follow what the trade press is talking about.

Even if journalists spent more time consulting the military trade press, it wouldn't make a lot of difference, because the media are using fewer journalists. Most people now get their news from the electronic media and this sector has long been unable to provide more than "expanded headlines." CNN gets a "truth in packaging" award for calling their primary news service *CNN Headline News.* But thousands of smaller radio and TV stations have minuscule or nonexistent news staffs. The latter simply pipe the news in from a distant "news provider."

While the network newscasts reach millions of viewers each night, even more people get their news from a local TV or radio station. An "expert" brought on the air to explain some military situation has only a few minutes, at most, to deliver the information and make some sense. Even if the expert is indeed expert, there's simply not enough time to get much across. Same with the regular staff. Even if some of them are expert on military affairs, and some are, there's not enough time for much more than a few headlines.

Print journalists are more likely to read the military trade press, or at least have access to it. But only a minority of the population reads newspapers and many of those readers don't buy the paper for military news, but for sports and financial news.

Most reporting of military affairs is the blind leading the blind. Hardly a newscast is made without some serious error or another being passed off as gospel. Misidentifying weapons and equipment is common, but not as serious as not getting straight what is going on. Asking troops inane questions and then misinterpreting the answer is frequent. Looking for dirt, as if the combat troops were errant actors or rock stars, also causes amusing, but unedifying, moments.

The truth will set you free. But in an age of fast and frequent news, finding truthful military reporting is a vain quest.

15

....

What Happens Next

W ITHOUT A REAL WAR or two to provide a reality check, we get a lot of gee-whiz, gold-plated gadgets that are likely to embarrass those paper pushers concerned and kill the poor grunts who have to fight.

But What Will the Future Be Like?

W E CAN GET A glimpse by looking at the situation of infantrymen fifty and a hundred years ago. In the late 1890s, the infantryman's job had gotten easier in some ways, and more complex in others. The infantryman's weapons had become simpler. Bolt-action rifles with five or more rounds in a magazine were now standard. It was easy to use such a rifle. Aim, fire, then pull the bolt back and forth to load another round. Until the 1860s, reloading a rifle was a very complicated task, requiring a lot of drill to get it right. Even with that, the shock of combat often led troops to miss a step or two and find themselves unable to fire their muskets. But the late-1800s bolt-action rifle was no problem at all.

Things had gotten more complicated in that more and more soldiers were being trained to advance across the battlefield on their own. For thousands of years, fighting men had fought in formation, either in a tight-packed group whose overlapping shields provided protection, or in slightly looser formations where everyone marched in step according to shouted or musical commands. Even with the introduction of muskets, the marching together in groups was still standard. But now there were so many bullets and artillery shells flying around that it was not possible to march in groups. Such formations of troops were easily mowed down by all that firepower. Out on their own, the troops required a lot more training on how to advance and what to do under different circumstances. New tactics had to be invented and leaders had to learn how to control troops they often couldn't even see.

Fifty years ago, in the late 1940s, many soldiers had automatic weapons.

Miniature machine guns these were, giving an individual tremendous firepower, at least until he went through all the ammunition he could carry. But that wasn't all. Each infantryman also had grenades. For as far as you could throw this one-pound object, you could deliver your own small artillery shell. You could also attach a special device to your rifle and throw grenades even farther (one hundred to two hundred meters, versus thirty for a good throw). There were portable rocket launchers (bazookas) and flamethrowers as well as handheld radios (walkie-talkies). Well, you get the picture.

While fifty years ago there were still some illusions about advancing, under fire, in some kind of loose formation, that illusion is now gone. The troops went out in ones, twos, and small groups. The soldier was alone on the battlefield, for only one in twenty or thirty (at best) or hundred or more (more likely) had a radio. There was a lot more firepower, as the amount of artillery per thousand men had more than doubled (to nearly ten big guns per thousand men) over the previous fifty years. There were now tanks and aircraft. Troops and all the new armored vehicles and warplanes needed radios to talk to each other, a lot of radios.

Today, fifty years away from World War II, things appear quite similar: lots of folks running around with machine guns, grenades, portable weapons, and radios. But there is a lot more automation and electronics. Jobs like locating enemy artillery or directing incoming artillery and bombers are automated. Computers and radars do the artillery location. Directing artillery and bombers is done with laser designators.

Fifty years from now?

• More automation. Machines will do more of the actual work. But this does not mean that the troops can just kick back and relax. Far from it. The historical trend has been that as more automation is used, more jobs are invented to be done and the troops are busier than ever. As more weapons for the infantry were invented, it meant that the troops had more stuff to carry, more stuff to take care of, more stuff to learn how to use. Most infantry now have their own armored vehicle to carry them around, but they also have to spend hours maintaining it. And even then, they often find themselves digging trenches some distance from their armored vehicle and humping stuff up to their holes in the ground. Yup, progress.

• More robots. The concept of robots became really popular about a century ago. It's taken that long for the concept to go from speculation to something that actually works. A hundred years ago we had primitive war droids in the form of land and naval mines. Cruise missiles, and guided (by themselves) missiles of all sorts, are the warrior robots of the moment. But more are in the works. They will look like machines, machines that are out to get you.

• More communications. A century ago, soldiers began to lose one of the few battlefield comforts they had long had—the presence of their fellows. As soldiers had to spread out to avoid the increased amount of battlefield firepower, they had no one to talk to and, more importantly, depend on for emotional support. In a group, men will readily fight to the death. The primary purpose of battles before the late nineteenth century was to make these formations of soldiers break up, with each of the soldiers fleeing. At that point, the troops were no longer soldiers, but terror-stricken individuals running for their lives. Up to the present, radios have increasingly kept the commanders in touch with each other, but have not done much for the individual soldiers. But because more troops are in armored vehicles (where everyone is "plugged in," or sitting next to someone who is), the battlefield loneliness problem has been narrowed down to the infantry operating away from their vehicles. This will change in the next fifty years, as it already has for some infantry in special assault units. Each soldier will have a radio in his helmet and will be in touch most of the time. Other electronic gadgets will let the soldier know where he is and will automatically report things like physical condition and exact location to commanders. Normally, people don't like to be watched by the boss all the time. But on the battlefield this is seen as the lesser of two evils.

While there has been a tremendous growth in technology in the past century, the soldier of today, fifty years ago, and a century ago still look a lot alike and would easily learn each other's jobs. The basics have not changed much at all. You still have to find the enemy, blast him into oblivion or submission, and avoid having the same done to you first. In a century, the changes have not so much been "different" as much as "more." The rifles fire more bullets, the artillery is larger caliber and fires more deadly shells. There are now aircraft dropping all manner of bombs and helicopters either shooting at you, carrying you to the fight, or picking you up after you've been killed or wounded.

Moreover, all the high tech mainly fights the other guy's technology and brings a lot more firepower to the battlefield. A soldier and his shovel are still the best defense against the highest-tech weapons. This was true a hundred years ago, fifty years ago, and today, and will be true a half century from now. Soldiers facing death have shown themselves remarkably inventive, much to the consternation of those bright folks who developed the high-tech weapons.

The big problem is that the likely enemies come in two flavors: clones of yourself and primitives. The former are easy to understand, as they are trained, equipped, and likely to fight pretty much like you are. The latter are usually guerrillas or irregulars of some sort armed with yesterday's weapons, plus some of today's gadgets. The primitives are primitive only in the sense that they don't have all the technology you have. What the primitives do usually have is smarts, knowledge of the area they are fighting in, and a lot of determination. Because of lower post–cold war defense budgets, an increasing amount of military technology is off-the-shelf, or freely sold on the world market to whoever has the cash. This means that your "primitive" opponents are likely to have a wide array of military technology. Either they will have it, or you will have to assume they might and act accordingly. Terribly confusing this will be, but on good days you will have an easy time with your low-tech foes; on bad days they will zap you with technology you didn't expect. Best to be ready for anything, which has long been the watchword for professional soldiers.

There's going to be a lot of improvisation on the battlefield in the next decade or so.

Digital Versus Well-Trained Soldiers

TECHNOLOGY IS EASY, training is hard. This is why there are so many well-equipped troops in the world who don't know how to use their weapons very well. The enormous amount of money needed to pay for digital soldiers leads to the temptation to cut back on the money for training. This is an ancient trap, and the paper pushers keep falling for it. The temptation is very strong, because you don't get caught unless the well-equipped but ill-trained troops get sent into combat. Even then, it depends on the opposition. Well-armed but poorly trained troops can do rather well against poorly equipped and even less well trained opponents. If the enemy is more effective than your own troops, the clamor to "support the troops" will go a long way to hide the peacetime cuts in the training budgets. Moreover, you can't "see" training. You can go up and touch expensive weapons and see well-designed uniforms on soldiers who at least know how to form a straight line and march in step.

After the cold war ended, voices were raised in America warning about the dangers of cutting training budgets. This was the result of military reforms between the Vietnam and Gulf Wars. Everyone in uniform, and many legislators, was aware of the training problem. But the pressures on the American defense budget made it very difficult to resist the training cuts. There have been cuts in training, accompanied by a blizzard of press releases explaining how these are not really training cuts. Maybe, maybe not. Time, and casualties on some future battlefield, will tell.

Sensor Combat

SENSOR COMBAT is seen as the key component in warfare of the future. It's been this way for half a century.

Your eyeball is a sensor. It lets you see things. Radar is a sensor; it lets you see a lot farther and through clouds and the dark of night. In the sixty years since radar was developed in the 1930s, a lot more sensors have been developed. Camouflage and the creative use of things like smoke and dust were the first weapons in the sensor combat armory. Shortly after radar appeared, there were things like chaff and jammers to defeat it.

But decades of building countermeasures (to defeat sensors), counter-countermeasures (to defeat countermeasures), and counter-counter-counter-measures (you get the picture) have put the fear of uncertainty into all who build and use sensors. Some of this fear is justified. There are so many sensors out there, broadcasting so many exotic (and mundane) signals, that no one is quite sure what will happen the next time a major battle takes place.

When engineers and scientists sit down to sort out this situation and determine what can be done, they quickly break out in a cold sweat. To be systematic and thorough about dealing with the enormous number of electronic weapons that can be conjured up would take more money then even the most generous legislature would part with. What is one to do? Well, several groups did several interesting things to deal with the enormity of sensor combat;

• Play the percentages. Build sensors that can deal with the most likely countermeasures. Build counter-countermeasures that can deal with the most likely countermeasures. And so on. This still leaves one vulnerable to something exotic, which leads us to . . .

• Programmable devices. The first sensors and countermeasures could operate only one way, usually on only one frequency. But as computers have become cheaper and electronic gear more capable, it has become easier to field equipment that is more flexible. Sometimes much more flexible. The device can be reprogrammed, or, more likely, a new program can be loaded to reconfigure the radar, sonar, jammer, or whatever so that it will operate differently. The operator can choose any number of canned programs, or a computer can have a master program that makes the changes in response to the current situation (the "artificial intelligence" approach). Fifty years ago, bombers lumbered in at about two hundred miles an hour. Interceptors scrambled after them at about three hundred miles an hour. In the hour or two it took the antagonists to get into lethal proximity, radar and countermeasure operators had lots of time to twiddle their dials and ponder their instrument readouts. Now the bombers come in at six hundred miles an hour and missiles roar out to meet them at two or three times that speed. Reaction time is now measured in minutes. Too fast for mere humans. Time to let the computers fight each other.

• Fake it. Give it the old college try when building the sensor or countermeasure but, in fact, produce a device that is, well, not up to the task it was set to. This happens quite a lot. More so in totalitarian nations (like the Soviet Union), where there was so much lying and cheating going on, and so much enthusiastic denying of same, that you could get away with producing shoddy military equipment. After all, war was a rare event. If some foreigner bought your equipment and was unable to make a good showing with it, you could usually blame it on the operators ("Those ignorant peasants were too dumb to understand how our marvelous stuff worked."). Actually, everyone who makes military electronics equipment fakes it to one degree or another. There are too many unknowns in warfare and cutting-edge (or "bleeding-edge") technology for there not to be a certain fudge factor. You have to fake it a bit just to get the beast out the door.

The reality is that all three of the above techniques are used to build sensor warfare equipment. Testing it has become the biggest problem. Using computers to simulate the millions of possible situations helps. But a simulation is just that—a simulation, not the real thing. There's still lots of guesswork involved in setting up the simulation. Reality always finds a way of throwing you curves you didn't anticipate. But what simulation will do is prepare you for more of the potential future situations than others will be prepared who do not use simulation.

Sensor combat is warfare of technology. This is not just who can conjure up the most complex and powerful gadgets, but who can learn how to use them the way they should be used. Technology by itself is no advantage on the battlefield. Knowledge of what technology will do, and experience in using it, is what does make a difference. Nations that simply buy the best technology and store it away for a military crisis will lose to a less affluent nation that bought second-rate gear but used it and learned how to use it. It's one of the few cases where second best can be better. In sensor combat, experience, not tonnage, is king.

The Electromagnetic Pulse (EMP)

AN ELECTROMAGNETIC PULSE (or "radiation") is a surge of electrical power strong enough to cause a malfunction in electronic equipment. One disadvantage of microelectronics now found in everything from appliances to nuclear weapons is that they are vulnerable to very small charges of electromagnetic pulses commonly found in natural or man-made situations. For example, at higher altitudes, it is more likely for gamma rays (produced by the sun) to reach the ground. Normally, all gamma rays are absorbed by the atmosphere before they can reach sea level. A gamma ray, hitting a personal computer at just the right spot, can cause an electrical error and bring the system down. This can be a problem in high-altitude cities, like Denver or Mexico City. You also see signs around areas where blasting is being done, warning you not to use radio transmitters. This is because commercial and military communications and radar transmissions have been known to cause accidental firings of high-explosive detonators and malfunctions in computers and other electronic and electrical equipment. The latter effect is why you cannot use certain kinds of electronic equipment on commercial aircraft. The effects of electromagnetic radiation on military ordnance have prompted efforts to protect against it. Some measures include enclosure in material that will absorb the pulse, and avoiding the use of components that can be sensitive to electromagnetic radiation. These measures have not always been entirely successful.

The EMP has been known to exist since the late 1940s. But with the arrival of transistors (the first microelectronics) in the 1950s, the nuclear EMP became a real threat to civilization as we know it. A one-megaton nuclear weapon detonated at an altitude of one hundred thousand feet will disable electronic components thousands of kilometers away. Using smaller nukes at lower altitudes produces EMPs that cover smaller areas.

A 1995 James Bond movie, *Goldeneye,* features one EMP weapon that is theoretically possible (no one has tried to build and test one yet). What you have to do is convert the energy released by a one-kiloton nuclear explosion into electromagnetic radiation and then direct that "pulse" via a fifty-meter-diameter antenna or an equivalent microwave laser. If such a device were used from a 30,000-kilometer-high orbit, it would plaster an area of over 250 square kilometers on the earth's surface (more than enough for any large city) with an EMP capable of disrupting (certainly), damaging (in most cases), and destroying (in many cases) electrical equipment. This would include computers, electronics of all kinds, antennae, relays, and power lines. If you brought the *Goldeneye* satellite down lower, to, say, 400 kilometers, you would increase the strength of the pulse by some six times. (For you electrical engineers out there, we are talking some five million joules per square meter at this point.) This would vastly increase the portion of damaged and destroyed electrical equipment.

It wasn't long before some weapons designers (yes, there are such creatures—someone has to do it) realized that you didn't need a nuke to produce a powerful EMP. Most of these techniques involved an explosion of some sort, so the idea of an "EMP bomb" began to attract a lot of military research money. Some of these have been tested, but most of the work is kept secret. The main reason for this is because a nonnuclear EMP bomb will generate particular types of EMP which, if known to potential opponents, could be defeated. Knowing what kinds of pulses are coming at you makes it easier for you to protect your electronics.

High-power microwaves (HMPs) could be created by several nonnuclear means, including some that do not involve explosions. This would be in the form of portable HMP generators that would do many of the same things as an explosive EMP generator. This would include such militarily useful tasks as detonating ammunition fuzes, shutting down engines, and damaging military electronics in general. This could all be accomplished by using the HMP to do what is, in effect, high-powered jamming. The HMP could be pointed, like a gun, and have a range of several kilometers.

One American weapons laboratory even developed a suitcase-size device that generates a high-powered electromagnetic pulse. This item could be used by commandos, who would sneak into a foreign capital, place the EMP suitcase next to a bank or government headquarters, and set it off. The resulting pulse would burn out all electronic components in the building. Such devices could also be delivered by cruise missiles, or even ballistic missiles. A relatively small explosion would cause relatively large damage to equipment.

The reason such EMP weapons have not taken over warfare is because no one is really sure exactly how much damage they will do. You have to test real systems to understand their vulnerabilities. Getting the armed forces to turn over multimillion-dollar pieces of equipment for destructive testing is not easy to do, especially now that defense budgets are shrinking. But not only are the actual effects of EMP poorly understood, there is also the complicating factor of ongoing efforts to shield military electronics against EMP. There is even an effort to shield a lot of civilian electronics because the military uses a lot of off-the-shelf civilian gear. Also, smaller nations, like Iraq, that get into a future rumble with the United States have to worry about EMP being used against all of their facilities.

But just because EMP weapons have not been used by troops, or terrorists, yet, does not mean they do not exist. They very much do exist and it's only a matter of time before some poor wretches will hear a loud bang, followed by massive gadget failure.

Information War

INFORMATION WAR is one of those nineties buzzwords in the military and government. Basically it's a marketing scam. It's taking a lot of stuff that's been around for years and repackaging it so that it's easier to get more money from increasingly reluctant taxpayers. Hundreds of different military and government organizations are now recasting their mission in life to include information war. What information war means is doing what you've always done, but doing it faster with computers and cellular phones. In short, information warfare is nothing new. The basic ideas have been around for several thousand years, and the current high-tech version has been with us for nearly a century.

The problem with information war is that it is a bunch of old notions mixed up in a new bottle. Depending on whom you're talking to, information war is:

• Command and control warfare. Doing things that make it more difficult for your opponent to communicate with and control his combat forces. This is an ancient principle of war. And the ancients didn't call it information war. Yet this is perhaps the most potent military aspect of information war. The key here is to be able to make decisions faster than your opponent, and then act on those decisions. This is known as speeding up the decision cycle. Or, as the military likes to put it, "Getting inside the opponent's decision cycle." There should be nothing mysterious about the decision cycle—it's a fact of life. Everything we do is made up of decision cycles. The military has encapsulated the decision cycle in the acronym OODA (Observe something, Orient ourselves to what just happened, Decide how to Respond, Act). Information war can, for example, prevent us from observing. Lacking that information, we are unable to properly orient ourselves, make a decision, and, most importantly, act effectively. As an example, let us assume that some computer whiz got into one of the networks serving the U.S. intelligence-gathering operations. The enemy hacker deleted some information and changed other data, in effect creating a false view of what was going on out there on the battlefield. This done, U.S. commanders would be observing a false version of reality and would end up making disastrous decisions. Like, say, bombing areas that were supposed to contain enemy ammunition dumps or vehicles, but actually contained refugee camps. Get the picture?

• Operational security. This is keeping an eye on your own secrets at the place where they live: keeping your secret documents locked up, making sure your electronic messages are in code or otherwise not easily readable by the enemy, and training your troops to keep important information to themselves. Known as OPSEC (operational security) by people in the business, it is what generated such World War II slogans as "Loose lips sink ships" and "The enemy is listening."

• Cyberwar. This is one that's still in the process of being invented. Cyberwar is the use of all available electronic and computer tools to shut down the enemy's electronics and communications, and to keep your own going. No holds barred, anything goes. A lot of what can be done in this area is speculative, partly because new equipment is constantly appearing on the scene, and partly because it's only recently that military planners began looking at this angle as a new form of warfare. Earlier, elements of Cyberwar were found here and there, as opportunities presented themselves. But cyberwarriors see themselves ensconced in combat information centers (CICs) filled with video displays and skilled technicians feeding commanders the latest data on who's (and what's) on and who's off the screen. This is actually the over fifty-year-old story of radar and sonar operators playing with their equipment to nail the enemy. It's just writ larger with a lot more gear tied together electronically and run from the same place. The U.S. Navy introduced the use of the CIC over fifty years ago. And it just kept growing and being adopted by the other services.

• Electronic warfare. The ancient game of deception using electronic means. This sort of thing has been going on since the military began using the telegraph in the 1850s. Electronic warfare came of age in World War II and is now a standard part of any professional warrior's arsenal.

• Hardening. One of the side effects of nuclear war is the EMP. This is a wave of high energy that shorts out microelectronics. Not older technologies like vacuum tubes, but the modern stuff. Add 5 or 10 percent to a microchip's cost and you can insulate it from most EMP effects. It will not be completely EMP proof, but close enough for government work.

• Hackers. This is guerrilla war where just about anyone, anywhere in the world, can join in. All you need is a computer, a modem, and some determination. This is new, because only recently have we seen the introduction of international computer networks that just about anyone can get onto. The Internet is the best example of this. A lot of bored programmers and other people with time on their hands and malice in their hearts cruise the net looking for trouble. This has been going on for over a decade. There's also a lot of mischief on nets within companies. Some crime, but a lot of mischief. Some attempts have been made in the past decade or so to turn the hacker problem into a military weapon. It hasn't been easy. Mischief is not always a useful weapon. But the payoff can be quite spectacular if you get one of your cyberwarriors into an enemy network during wartime. This has happened only in fiction so far, but many nations are working hard to make it real next time around.

• Information blockade. This is a variation on the ancient practice of blockading enemy territory from receiving shipments of goods. With data now so important, one can shut down the satellites, cable links, and microwave towers beaming data into enemy territory. This will hurt after a while, especially in the more technical areas.

• Information-based warfare. Now we're getting onto familiar ground. During the 1960s it was noticed that the electronic mass media could have a decisive effect on public opinion and political decision making. Even before that, tyrants of all flavors (Nazis and Communists) realized how important it was to seize control of the media (print, especially) and direct them toward their own ends. As more people have become wise to the way the media work in collecting and distributing information, more people participate in shaping and influencing what passes for mass media news. Excellent examples of information-based warfare were seen during the 1991 Gulf War and, indeed, during every war in the past thirty years. News is now considered a weapon, and is used as such.

• Psychological warfare. Long used, and nothing more than spreading demoralizing or misleading information among the enemy. Still used, and still works.

But there's another aspect to information war that must be considered. Information war is largely defined by how you use information as a weapon against enemy troops. You can attack information, as you seek to keep the enemy in the dark, or defend against it, as you try to eliminate false information that the enemy is trying to feed you via computer, telephone, or camouflage. It is possible to seize control of an enemy control system with the right techniques and electronics. This is real information war. The technology needed for information war ranges from the jamming radars that have been around for decades to the high-tech network intrusion that we read about in the news, and fear will become more common in the future. Information war is not new; we just have some new gear and techniques that increase our capabilities, and the number of targets we can go after. The increase in capabilities and dependence on software and computer hardware have increased the need for commanders to consider information war targets as part of their war plans. For if they don't, it is realized, the enemy might.

The 1991 Persian Gulf War is often cited as the first information war. Well, it was and it wasn't. That war saw more use of items considered part of information war. But at the same time, there was nothing done in the Gulf War that hadn't been done before.

The air campaign opened with an air attack on headquarters, communications, and utilities. Nothing new here. Except that in the Gulf War it was done more quickly and thoroughly than in the past. Nothing new there either. Since World War II, warfare by industrialized nations has been getting faster and more thorough. Learning from experience, as it were.

The Gulf War Coalition waged a psychological warfare campaign on the Iraqis which was remarkably effective, at least if you go by the speed and extent to which the Iraqis surrendered when Coalition ground forces appeared in their vicinity. Nothing new about this. It's happened several times in this century. This was information warfare, insofar as the leaflets dropped on the Iraqi troops told them exactly how to surrender and emphasized the advantages of surrender (becoming honored guests of the Saudis).

The Gulf War also saw an enormous amount of electronic warfare, using methods, albeit with newer equipment, that were invented half a century earlier. The media were used extensively by both sides to influence public opinion. Again, this was a technique with an ancient (over four-thousand-year-old) pedigree.

Okay, so what exactly *is* information war? Was what happened in the Gulf War information war? Yes, it was. And the success of high-tech weapons and equipment in that war, plus growing anxiety over computer hackers, led to the phenomenon where organizations, particularly military ones, began using the term information war when there was an agenda or budget situation that needed a little something extra to put it over the top. Each military service and department sought a definition of information war that would serve its immediate needs and long-range goals. The current definitions of information war are militaristic in nature, but many people are beginning to realize that information war does not have to be a military event. What information war is can be described as the use of information (and equipment that handles information) as tools (weapons) against opponents.

Typical nonmilitary uses of information war are industrial and economic spies who, whether as freelancers or as government agents, attempt to gain a competitive advantage for their side by revealing the enemies' secrets and protecting those of their employer. This can have a direct military effect if your infospies are going after military technology. The Soviet Union did this big-time for decades, and was quite successful at it. It wasn't called information war then, but that's what it was.

Consider the effect of bringing personal computers and police experts into a Third World nation. You use the computers and experts to set up databases of those who oppose the local dictator. All of a sudden, the tyrant is a lot more effective in keeping dissidents under control. It's information war and it's been going on for quite a while. The competent practitioners of police state information war were the Communists, and they were the last ones to adopt the use of computers.

You don't need guns and bombs to wage information war, but you can use violent weapons. Yet most of the tools of information war are rather more nonviolent. Information is, after all, just data. But warfare has a large data component to it. Even primitive tribal warriors, armed with nothing more than bows and spears, were acutely aware of the value of data: information on where the enemy is, how he fights, and the battlefield environment in general. Primitive man may not have had a lot of technology, but he needed and used a lot of data. I mean, how many birdcalls can *you* identify?

From primitive man to high-tech man, we see one of the major differences being how much more data is available and how dependent we are on so much data we don't understand and often don't even know we have. Do you know all the data being passed between components of your car? Automobiles now have microprocessors and data-storage systems. Without these, they cannot operate. Thieves have learned that your car radio and air bag are not as valuable as your car computer. So many a driver starts his car only to find out that someone has forced the hood open, unscrewed the car computer, and left the automobile without its brain and unable to even turn over the engine. One form of information war is to use an electronic device that shorts out the circuits in a vehicle's computer, rendering the vehicle (civilian or military) useless without leaving any visible marks on it. So, whether stealing the car computer or zapping it, you are engaged in information war.

One could say that information warfare is whatever you do to preserve the integrity of your own information systems from exploitation, corruption, or destruction while at the same time exploiting, corrupting, or destroying an enemy's information systems and in the process achieving an information advantage if it comes to armed combat. Well, that's the Pentagon take on information war. You don't have to use force as a follow-on to information war.

Information, and its use in combat, is fundamental. Often the information "war" is nothing more than getting the information faster and looking it over carefully with equal swiftness.

For example, back in the 1970s, I was approached by someone from the U.S. Forest Service to help develop a manual game for fighting forest fires. It was a pretty straightforward assignment, and I helped get them started. The basic idea was that forest fires are fairly predictable if you can get a constant supply of information on things like weather conditions (wind speed and direction) and if you already know a lot about the area the fire is in (type of trees and vegetation, moisture situation, etc.). The game allows you to play "what if" with your fire-fighting resources and variations on which way the weather will go. All this is much like a war game, which was what brought the Forest Service to me, as I was one of the most prolific publishers of war games in the 1970s.

The Forest Service went on to computerize its games and use a lot of technology to fight fires. There's a lot of similarities between fighting fires and fighting human adversaries. But there is also a difference, and this can be seen in the attitude toward using high-speed computer games to predict what a fire will do, versus what a human opponent will. Fires are a force of nature and follow the laws of nature. Human adversaries are more unpredictable, and therein lies one of the potential problems with information warfare.

The Forest Service, like the military, uses aircraft and electronic sensors on the ground to collect information about its opponent. The aircraft use various types of sensors (cameras, infrared devices, etc.) to keep an eye on where the fire is and what shape it's in. Automated sensors dropped to the ground, or carried by fire crews, automatically record and transmit vital information like air temperature and humidity. Some of these sensors keep track of wind direction and velocity. Based on information on many earlier fires, computers can now take the sensor data of an ongoing fire and predict, with a high degree of probability, what the fire will do next. More importantly, applying similar knowledge about fire-fighting personnel and equipment, the computer model can provide an accurate prediction of what the fire will do if different strategies are used to fight the fire.

This approach to fighting fires has obvious appeal to military commanders. What information war means in a combat situation is the ability to gather enough information fast enough, and accurately enough, to feed the computer model. But what happens if the opponent is also practicing information war? What if the opponent knows that if he feeds you false information, your computer program can be forced to give unreliable results? What if your opponent plays games with your computerized war games? Forest fires don't think, they just go on doing what they have been doing for millions of years. Forest fires only seem unpredictable at times. If you gather enough information on a forest fire, there will be little unpredictability. And what erroneous forecasts you do make can be traced back to some bad, or late, information about the fire.

Military opponents go out of their way to prevent you from collecting information. A battlefield foe will try and feed you bad data. An armed enemy will do something off-the-wall just to confuse you. With that in mind, it makes sense that using more computers, high-speed communications (like cellular phones), and sensors (like satellites) for combat operations is called information war.

The Future of Information War

THE QUESTION IS, how well will information war work in the future? We got a preview of information war during the 1991 Gulf War. The Coalition had most of the information war weapons, but Iraq was not defenseless. Armed with access to the world media, Iraq tried, with some success, to mold public opinion to aid its cause. The Iraqi cause remained popular among the general population in many Arab and Third World countries because of the way the Iraqi leadership played the situation on CNN and in other international media. The Iraqi "media offensive" also had some effect on public opinion in nations they were fighting. Iraqi agents outside Iraqi also made attempts to sabotage military computer networks in Coalition nations. While the Iraqi military and information war efforts were unsuccessful, there is nothing more instructive, or as compelling, as defeat. Not only Iraq, but many other nations who might go to war any time soon, took the lessons of Iraq, and information war, to heart. Future wars will have the weaker side making the most of the CNN angle of information war. We've already seen quite a lot of it since the Persian Gulf War.

There was also another information war going on, or at least being prepared for. This was the one that could threaten the millions of messages that went back and forth between Coalition units inside Saudi Arabia, and between those units and their supporting organizations back home. The Iraqis were not able to cause much damage in this department, but it was not for want of trying. What was most troubling were those information war techniques that would be difficult to spot until it was too late. For example, what if a foe was able to delete some of your messages between the sender and receiver. It would take you a while to figure out that this was happening and even longer to sort out the resulting confusion. The damage would be serious. Spare parts would not be sent, leaving equipment idle. Units would not get their orders to move, or orders to change their direction.

This problem of the enemy getting into your communications network and deleting messages became a hot topic in the early 1990s, when it was realized how vulnerable the world's communications links were to this sort of attack. There are supposed to be fixes in place, or on the way. But who can be sure?

Yet another potential problem arose out of the Persian Gulf War experience. It was realized that air, land, and naval units had become much more dependent on their own local computer networks. Oh, there had been telephone networks since the first decade of this century, but now it was computer data running across those wire, and wireless, links.

The navy found that it was particularly vulnerable, for a naval task force could not quickly bring in nearby experts or resources to deal with an attack on its computer networks. Not only does each ship have several nets, but all the half dozen or more ships in the task force are linked into an even larger network so that all the task force's defenses, and offensive weapons, can be massed against the enemy. When the U.S. Navy took a close look at its network setup, it found that it was quite vulnerable. You didn't hear much of this vulnerability because no one knows who is onto these vulnerabilities, or still able to overcome the new features the navy has added to protect its communications.

The U.S. armed forces in particular, and those of other industrialized nations as well, are increasingly dependent on electronic communication. The superior weapons used by American troops work so well because they rapidly pass data around the battlefield. Interrupt this flow of information and you cripple the high-tech edge. Zapping the flow of information is difficult, but not impossible for a nation with Western-educated engineers and scientists. Jammers and receivers to examine the signals used by U.S. equipment can, in the hands of determined and technically skilled people, make wonder weapons much less wonderful. A higher percentage of missiles will miss, communications will be interrupted or intercepted, and the bad guys will take a lot longer to beat. Friendly casualties will be higher and the good guys will be less trusting of their weapons and equipment. The latter is not such a bad thing, but these disasters are unlikely to be previewed in peacetime. It's difficult to re-create the pucker factor (fear of death) of a low-tech opponent about to get pounded by a high-tech army. Self-preservation is a tremendous motivator and many low-tech nations have been so motivated by the results of the Gulf War.

The American troops closest to the fighting, namely the pilots and ground fighters, are most aware of how thin the high-tech advantage is. All the new gadgets are viewed skeptically by the combat troops, especially since the new stuff is often just given to them with orders to "use it." The troops respond with the attitude, "If it doesn't do anything for me, it's a rock." In other words, the battlefield is littered with new equipment the troops don't trust. Pilots, being officers, are in a better position to argue back about new stuff. But they usually don't get any action until several of them are lost in combat.

Information war brings a new kind of frontline soldier into action: the equipment operator. Of course, tank crews and many infantry are already operating a number of high-tech gadgets (laser designators, various kinds of radios, portable missiles, sensors), but many new gadgets require specialists who operate their gear at, or very close to, the front. Electronic warfare apparatuses are getting smaller and more portable. More of this stuff is at the front and more folks who thought they were just going to be "technicians" find themselves under fire much of the time. Aside from briefing the operators more accurately on their future working conditions, there is also a trend toward making the new electronic equipment simple enough so that most of the traditional combat specialists (infantry, tank crews) can operate it.

The Original Network and the Original Information War

WITH INFORMATION WAR, what gets the most attention, or at least an awful lot of attention, is the "hacker" aspect. This means a malicious user (a "hacker") disrupting a major network of computers by doing bad things to the programs that run the network. Now information networks are nothing new, for that is what the telephone system is, and extensive long-distance telephone systems have been with us for a century.

These telephone networks, put together in the early part of this century, originally had subscribers to local telephone companies being able to call the human operators in order to be connected to other subscribers. At the time, this was considered as amazing as computer networks are today. It was only in 1878 that the first local telephone exchange (in New Haven, Connecticut) was opened, two years after the first practical telephone device was demonstrated.

It took only five years before distant cities began to get connected. At this point, a human operator was still needed in order to connect subscribers from two distant telephone networks. For example, in 1883, the first long-distance calling between New York City and Chicago was introduced, while in 1884, calling between New York City and Boston began. In 1915, the first transcontinental telephone "net" between New York City and San Francisco opened for business. The first transoceanic telephone call was in 1926, between New York City and London. The dial telephone was not invented until the late 1890s and did not replace the "ring up the operator and make your call" system for several decades. In fact, the last hand-cranked telephone exchange did not go out of service in the United States until 1983. The telephone companies did not become sufficiently automated to allow long-distance calls without operator assistance until 1951. But telephone company automation continued, and that's what made the less resourceful telephone company robots more vulnerable to deceit then the previous human operators.

But it's only been in the past few decades that all the telephone systems have been computerized. Before that, there were a lot of people you had to go through in order to connect with someone far away. Once computers were put in charge, it was soon discovered that the computer programs could be fooled much more easily than the human operators. These hackers didn't use personal computers to attack the phone network, because personal computers hadn't been invented. Rather, the "phone phreaks" of the 1960s used hand-held, battery-powered devices that emitted the various electronic tones that the telephone company used to control the long-distance phone net. Some of the phreakers could whistle the tones, but anyone could use the various electronic boxes. All one could really do with this phreaking was make long-distance calls for free. But that was enough to attract a lot of people to phreaking. This battle between telephone companies and phreakers goes on to this day, even though the phone system attackers equipped with personal computers get most of the attention.

The century-old telephone networks were subject to information war, mainly in the form of phone taps. These were used legally and illegally to gain an advantage in commercial and military matters. Phones were also used to send misinformation. It was easier to disguise one's voice then one's person.

The Internet Wars

IN THE LATE 1970s, personal computers with modems became increasingly common, and it wasn't long before networks of computers began to form. Many were essentially private undertakings, where enterprising programmers created "bulletin board" software that allowed others to call in and share files and messages with other users. This involved nothing more than a computer with its "BBS" (bulletin board system) software running and a modem attached. Anyone who knew the phone number of that modem could call in and get connected. Some private companies also began to set up these systems, although they used more security procedures to keep out people who were not supposed to be in their system. But the system that changed everything was the Internet. This was first conceived in the late 1960s, and put into use during the 1970s. University and military computers were connected by telephone. University and commercial researchers, as well as military personnel, could now communicate more easily on technical projects where written communication was more efficient than spoken discussions. The experimental nature of the net made for rapid progress in solving a mass of technical problems. The system was set up so that anyone on the net could gain access to any other computer on the net. While this exposed all computers on the net to the possibility of someone sabotaging whatever he wanted, this rarely happened, at least in the beginning. All was pretty swell until the net got so big that the small number of "evil hackers" that had always been there became a much larger number. By the 1990s, the Internet was international and had over ten million users. The playful and energetic spirit that had made technological progress so swift on the net now came back as an Evil Twin. Many of those playful "hackers" had decided it was more entertaining to bring down the system than to expand or maintain it. While the people running the individual computers attached to the net were aware of their vulnerability, not everyone upgraded his system to keep the vandals out. Moreover, there was some question as to whether the net could be made secure at all.

The Internet had developed as a loosely organized project, and the U.S. government officials financing the work encouraged the net to be designed as a very "loose" net. That is, if large portions of the net were knocked out by, say, a nuclear war, the surviving elements would still be able to function. While the government was not silent about the "surviving the nuclear war" aspect of the Internet, it didn't play it up either. But the people building the net, many of them on a volunteer basis, also saw the advantage of a network that was free from the control of one central authority. The net was like a swarm of bees. You could kill parts of it, but not all of it. The more traditional concept of a network was an elephant, where one large bullet in the right place would bring the entire net down for keeps.

The Internet is millions of individual computers, joined by telephone lines and common software and formats for transferring information. A computer connected to the Internet can be a desktop system used by one person, or a mainframe shared by thousands of users. Each computer on the Internet has its own address, like BROWN.EDU for a university, ARMY.MIL for the U.S. Army, MOBIL.COM for a corporation, or AOL.COM for a large commercial network. While all these computers use common software to talk to each other, they still use hundreds of different operating systems on the individual machines. A declining number of Internet computers allow users to get into their guts, which is where most of the mischief occurs.

By the 1990s, the system had become so large and complex that no one really understood the entire thing. It was not known for sure all the vile things you could do to the many different types of computers attached to the Internet. Some of these computers were more vulnerable than others. All you had to do was sneak into one Internet computer and that would often reveal passwords and other information that would give you easier access to many other Internet computers. In response, many companies began to develop for themselves, or for sale to others, "firewall" software that isolated that portion of your computer connected to the Internet from the other parts of your computer system. But because just about any type of computer (from PC to mainframe) could be attached to the Internet, not all firewall systems were the same, nor were all equally effective.

To further complicate matters, local area networks (LANs) came into wider use during the 1970s. A LAN is, as the name implies, computers in the same building hooked together via wires. When one of the computers on a LAN became part of the Internet, all the other machines on the LAN were also, usually, reachable by anyone on the Internet.

The Internet had become too valuable to shut down, but too risky to use without the danger of some evildoer sneaking into your computer and, if you had one, LAN. This was a lot more dangerous than it was half a century ago, when the only networks were telephone nets.

The Internet was somewhat different from the original phone networks. For one thing, a lot more was now on telephone networks. These nets now carried more than just voice conversations and were not always carried via wires. Satellites and transmitters now carried a lot of data. Increasingly, it was robots talking to robots. Yes, robots. For over half a century, the popular conception of a robot was a vaguely human-shaped machine that could move, talk, and, to a certain extent, think. In reality, more and more things have been automated over the last few decades using robots of a rather different size and shape. The "robots" are generally found in metal boxes, large and small, often stuck in small rooms or closets. These "thinking machines" control power, communications, and a multitude of jobs in factories and anyplace where simple, repetitive jobs are found. While the jobs these robots perform are simple and repetitive, they are often vital. If one of these robots makes a mistake, or is sabotaged, power can go out in a city, phone service over a wide area can be disrupted, or a bank can be robbed. Information war has been going on to a greater degree since the robots began taking over a lot of dull, routine work. You see, as hardworking, uncomplaining, and efficient as these robots are, they are not very bright. If a human can get into contact with these robots, the human can often override the robot's decision making. Even though "police" and "guard" robots are put in place to protect the "worker" robots, a human still has the edge. So far anyway.

Now it's one thing to goose the phone robots to make free long-distance calls, or grab a few million dollars from a bank's automated money transfer system. This sort of thing isn't going to get anyone killed. But the military also uses many of these automated systems. For example, over 90 percent of military communications goes over commercial data links. You, your bank, and the Department of Defense use the same phone lines. Although much of this data is being sent from one machine to another without human intervention, humans can intervene if they can get access to the system. Sure, you can send the data in a secret code ("encrypted"), but these codes can be broken. Everyone who uses networked computers is vulnerable. Exploiting that vulnerability is largely what information war is all about.

You cannot afford not to use computer networks these days. Too many weapons, radars, supply dumps, and headquarters depend on the speed of computer networks to keep them going. Anyone who tries to run his armed forces without these nets will be at a major disadvantage against someone who is fully networked. Remember, the first thing attacked during the 1991 Gulf War was the Iraqi communications networks. Once those nets were cut up, the Iraqis never really recovered. That was information war with bombs. But you can also wage information war with a personal computer and a telephone line.

Rather than cringe in terror before the prospect of hostile personal computers and the evil hackers behind them, many in the military have begun looking for ways to outhack the hackers. This is going to be a rather unique fight. There has never been a time when war was open to anonymous individuals sitting at distant locations armed with computers and other electronic devices. Oh, there were nerds heavily engaged in other wars in this century. World War II had nerds designing, and often operating, radars and electronic countermeasures. Other geeks cracked codes and invented arcane, but quite lethal, tools like operations research. But all of these fellows (they were mostly men, then as now) were organized, if not highly disciplined, and worked under tight security. Their current counterparts, at least the feral ones, are largely unknown, and no one is sure of their loyalty. One thing is certain, the techno–rude boys are out there and have been raising hell, and blood pressures, for over a decade. Most of those that have been caught are, arguably, the usual suspects. That is, they are disaffected sons of the middle class. The former Communist nations turned out to have quite a few of these cyber-thugs, some of whom were on a government payroll. But as far as anyone can tell, it was not the organized hackers who were writing all the computer viruses and breaking into "secure" networks. No, all this mayhem was being done by free-wheeling freelancers. Some of these independents would do business with spy agencies, for ideological, monetary, or "just for the hell of it" reasons. Some were caught; uncertainty over how many were not caught is driving the current mania to acquire a commanding information war capability.

What gets lost in all the fear and desperation over information war is that most of the damage to information systems is, and always has been, caused by human error. The flubs are either by the users, or by the programmers, hardware designers, and "integrators" (who put the hardware and software together). Often it is impossible to tell if a system failure is a result of some bad programming or sloppy chip design, or the consequence of someone's information war attack. This has led to work on developing techniques for sorting out the usual systems failures from real (really real) information war attacks. What makes this angle interesting is that a clever information war attack would try to introduce failures into enemy networks that looked like failures from hardware or software problems. But the more popular information war thinking is to hit the other guy hard and fast with everything you've got. Bring down the enemy's information systems as completely as possible.

Many nations, however, see information war as a way to level the playing field. Sort of another version of "getting a nuke." Alas, it doesn't work that way. The industrialized nations have most of the computers, and most of the hackers. There are exceptions. The former Communist nations educated more people than they could put to work and this created a lot of computer specialists with time on their hands and a grudge against society. Bulgaria, for some odd reason, has been the source of a lot of the computer viruses since the 1980s. Non-Communist nations that produce educated people and no work, like Pakistan, have also produced a lot of malevolent hackers.

India, on the other hand, has put much of its programmer talent to work. While this has lowered the percentage of programmers who turn to malicious hacking, it does provide India with a pool of information warrior talent. It is also possible to hire hacker mercenaries. In fact, it has already been done. But as with any weapon, it is the nation that is the best organized and led, and has, as the saying goes, "the bigger battalions" that has the advantage. While a handful of "superhackers" working for a smaller nation might possibly inflict massive damage on, say, U.S. information systems, the likelihood of that happening is pretty remote (as is getting hit on the head by a falling meteorite). The industrialized nations have taken the information war dangers seriously, far more seriously than the opposition has been in developing information war weapons. Information war makes good copy—nothing like a frightening lead story to spice up a slow news day. But information war is nothing more than the same old use of deception against an enemy that has been with us since the first recorded battle, 3,200 years ago. There, in southern Lebanon, the Hittites successfully "compromised" the Egyptians' "information systems" with lots of bad and deceptive information. That was information war.

Making It Easier to Kill Someone

TECHNOLOGY HAS, after centuries of trying, made weapons easier to use. This is a relatively rare event in history. Better weapons have usually been more complex weapons. This is particularly the case with missile weapons, even thousands of years ago. The throwing spear took years to master. The more efficient throwing stick–type spear took even longer to master. Archery was a big advance over spears and has long been noted as something that required even more years of effort to attain proficiency, and constant practice to maintain those skills.

Not surprisingly, it was archery that was the first weapon system to be automated and simplified, and it happened nearly three thousand years ago. While it took years to train a competent archer, a few days (or hours, if you were desperate) drilling would produce a capable crossbowman. For defending a castle, that was enough. For fighting battles out in the open, it took a few more months of training. As effective as the crossbow was, it did not revolutionize warfare by itself. The crossbows were expensive, costing five to six times as much as a regular bow. The more complex crossbow had to be carefully maintained, and this required skilled technicians. As effective as the crossbow was, there were other types of bows that were more effective, even if they required a lot more training. But the crossbow was a clear-cut case of weapons automation and simplification. But until this century, something like the crossbow was seen simply as "clever," and not the forerunner of similar changes. And until the last few centuries, that's exactly what the crossbow was, a clever exception. The Chinese were major users of crossbows, the imperial arsenals often holding hundreds of thousands of these, for the time, complex machines. Thousands of skilled technicians were occupied generation after generation to maintain all these crossbows. These weapons allowed the Chinese to field large, effective armies on short notice. This kept the "northern barbarians" (Mongols and their ilk) at bay for centuries. The Chinese had a rather efficient government, and were able to manage mobilizing and demobilizing these armies without leaving a lot of troublesome troops unemployed at loose ends and banditry. Besides, without access to the imperial technicians, it was difficult to get a broken crossbow fixed.

Until recently, those in power did not want more efficient weapons so much as they wanted warriors who could be trusted. The fewer professional soldiers there were, the less trouble there would be, for a smaller number of troops could be bought off and more easily watched. A classic example of the need to control the warriors, and the fear of efficient weapons, can be found in seventeenth-century Japan. After decades of civil wars, peace finally came to Japan in the early 1600s. Japan, like Europe centuries earlier, had a social class of professional warriors. In Europe, we know them as knights, in Japan they were called samurai. Both knights and samurai dedicated their lives to training for war, and served a feudal lord to whom they pledged everlasting loyalty. There were never a lot of knights during the medieval period in Europe. For every million people, there would be fewer than a thousand knights. But these warriors were able enough fighters to keep the rest of the population under control, and have enough time left over to fight other knights for business (wars) or pleasure (tournaments).

The civil wars in Japan during the sixteenth and seventeenth centuries coincided with the introduction of muskets. Now Japan had always had archers. Indeed, one of the many skills a samurai mastered was archery. But archers took years to train, and crossbows were seen as a less effective, and overly expensive, substitute for archery. But the musket was another matter. Its projectiles did greater damage than arrows, and a musketeer could be trained in a few weeks. A few thousand musketeers could stop a charge by mounted or dismounted samurai dead, literally. The battles of this civil war were exceptionally bloody, and when they were all over the Japanese aristocrats that led the surviving factions also noted that anyone with the money to buy muskets could attract commoners to serve as musketeers. For successful armies got to pillage the losers, and this was seen as good business for a poor young rice farmer. The Japanese leaders solved the problem by banning muskets. They also deported most foreigners and put strict controls on Japanese ships. For two centuries, Japan was a closed kingdom. With the muskets gone, only the small number of well-trained samurai swordsmen-archers were available to fight. Oh, there were commoners who got out of hand during these two centuries, but the samurai troops made short work of them. Without a musket, a commoner had little chance against a samurai. All of this changed in the 1850s, when a force of American warships showed up and announced that the U.S. wanted Japan to open up for trade, or else. The Japanese quickly caught up on what they had missed during the previous two centuries of low-tech isolation.

When firearms began to appear on battlefields five hundred years ago, they were something of a step backward. For several centuries thereafter, archers were, theoretically, still more effective. But even the first muskets, which required a complicated drill to load and fire, were good enough. Most importantly, they were expensive, and only kings and princes could afford to buy them. Troops were given muskets to use, not to keep. Few men outside the royal army had a musket. What made the American colonies unique was that, because of the danger from large animals and hostile natives, it became a common necessity for most families to have one or more muskets. The American Revolution would not have been possible without all those muskets held by citizens. The subsequent French Revolution was largely a result of the royal army going over to the rebels, and emptying the royal arsenals of their muskets to arm the citizens of France. Thus for two centuries the musket in the hands of a civilian has been the symbol of revolution.

The 1800s brought forth the mass army of citizen volunteers (or conscripts) and the willingness to equip these troops with the most efficient arms possible. Arming a lot of your citizens with second-rate weapons was a sure way to lose both your army, and control of the country in the bargain. This was also when the Industrial Revolution was getting under way, so there were now the means to make more complex weapons cheaply. As it turned out, the new weapons were not only cheaper, but a lot easier to use. In the space of fifty years, from the early 1800s to the late 1800s, technology completely transformed the musket. What began as a weapon that had to be loaded via a cumbersome drill involving pouring gunpowder and a lead ball down the musket's barrel, quickly turned into what we now know as the bolt-action rifle. This was a lot easier to use. You loaded it with five or more rounds. Then, as fast as you could pull the trigger, and then move the bolt back and forth to load another round, you could fire again and again. In the next fifty years, from the late 1800s to the early 1900s, came the machine gun and assault rifle. The latter did not appear in its modern form until World War II, but less sophisticated versions were used in World War I in the form of automatic rifles (the BAR) and machine pistols ("tommy guns").

The wide availability of easy-to-use rifles and machine guns created a lot more mayhem in the world, as any small group of desperadoes could intimidate much larger groups of unarmed people. The rifle was a boon to banditry and revolutionaries. But on the battlefield, governments now had another weapon that rarely fell into private hands: artillery. Big guns had been around since the 1400s, and had become much more deadly in the 1800s. By the early 1900s, artillery dominated the battlefield, causing most of the casualties. Only governments could afford the big guns and the large amount of ammunition these weapons could fire in short periods of time. Using artillery was not as simple as using a rifle. Training and drill were required. Individuals now had their rifles, but artillery conquered all.

World War I also produced, in its last years, another new weapon: the tank. Basically machine guns and light artillery on an armored vehicle, the tank dominated artillery. Tanks were even more expensive to build and maintain. Crews required a lot of training, and private individuals did not get their hands on many tanks.

Professional soldiers and weapons designers began to wonder, if rifles could be made simpler to use, why not tanks and artillery? Technology in the latter half of the twentieth century had made all sorts of technical items easier to use. Why not the most complex ground warfare weapon, the tank?

Tanks had always been complex beasts. The first ones contained intricate, for the time, engines and mechanical systems to move the vehicle. More than one weapon was carried and everything was more difficult to do within the noisy and cramped confines of the tank. From their first use in 1915, to the end of World War II in 1945, tremendous progress was made in tank technology. But they were still complicated machines, for as soon as one item was simplified, new and more complex gadgets were added. The guns got bigger, the fire-control systems more complex, and the engines more powerful. Everything about the tank got larger and more complex, except the size of the crew. In fact, over the next three decades the crew size of Russian tanks would actually shrink (from four to three) as even more equipment was added. In the early 1970s, the Russians introduced the T-64 and T-72 type tanks. Both were similar, and the T-64 eventually faded from the scene. But these two tanks introduced the autoloader for the new 125mm gun. While this eliminated one of the four crewmen (the guy who manually loaded shells into the gun), the autoloader added a complex piece of machinery to a tank that had recently added special equipment for operating underwater (to cross shallow rivers) and dealing with chemical weapons. There was more complex radio and navigation equipment to deal with as well as a more complex engine and automotive system. The autoloader itself was a mechanical monstrosity, and very unreliable in its first ten years of service. All this extra gear, and now only three men (driver, gunner, and commander) to deal with it. Keep in mind that, for every hour a tank was operating, the crew had to perform from fifteen to sixty or more minutes of maintenance. You could put off this maintenance for a while, but eventually it caught up with you in the form of a broken-down tank.

It now took longer to train everyone, there being fewer men to deal with more items. It wasn't long before users of these Russian tanks began to notice how poorly these vehicles performed in combat because of their habitually ill-trained crews. It also became apparent that, while one could train crews to effectively handle these high-tech tanks, it took longer than the two years conscript soldiers served and cost more than Russia, or many other nations, could afford.

American tank designers had noticed the same things the Russians had, and then came up with the U.S. M-1 tank as an example of how to make the complex simple. Actually, the American tank designers first took a few wrong turns, but they avoided making many of the mistakes the Russians had. For example, in the 1960s, the United States and West Germany collaborated in developing a radically new tank, the MBT 70. It was to have many of the features that eventually showed up in the M-1, as well as an autoloader. Costs climbed, squabbles developed over how to implement new technology, and the U.S. Congress got nervous about all this. The partnership broke down in 1969 and the United States went it alone for two years. But eventually the MBT 70 was killed. This in itself was unique, as a major army project had never been killed before. But out of it came the M-1 Abrams tank project, that, ten years later, did show good results. The M-1 design team dropped a lot of fancy stuff, like the autoloader, and concentrated their high-tech attentions on fire control.

This was not an easy task, since the most complex, and crucial, element in a tank is the fire-control system. This is a complex of optical sights, computers, and links with the gun. The crew has to spot an enemy tank, bring the gun to bear on it, and get off an accurate shot as quickly as possible. As tanks became more and more powerful, it became more and more the case that whoever got the first shot off won. That is, whoever got off the first accurate shot. In the past, first-shot speed and accuracy were largely a matter of practice. But it was very expensive to practice. The gun was only good for a few hundred rounds before it had to be replaced. The tank in general could not go more than a few thousand miles before it needed a major overhaul, or replacement. The Russians used crude simulators to give their tank crews practice. But these simulators were a poor substitute for the real thing. In the West, tank crews spent more time actually using their tanks. But this made Western tanks a lot more expensive to operate, what with all the overhauls and spare parts needed to keep them going.

The solution in the M-1 was a fire-control system designed for ease of use. No matter what complex gyrations the fire-control system went through, just make it easy to learn and use. This approach worked, as could be seen by the tales of VIPs taken on the "M-1 Tour," dropped into the gunner's seat, given a minute of instruction, and then allowed to find and hit a target down range. It couldn't be much simpler than that, for most of the VIPs were politicians.

The chart below shows the results of tests conducted in the early 1980s, just before the M-1 was distributed to the troops.

Table 20 / Intelligence Levels and Tank Crew Effectiveness

Intelligence Level of Gunner and Tank Commander	Kills on Evaluation Program (24.5 Max) Type of Tank		
	M-60	M-1	% Improvement
I (highest)	10.23	12.75	25
II (above average)	9.51	12.47	31
III (average)	8.52	12.05	41
IV (below average)	7.47	11.57	55
V (lowest)	5.84	10.72	84

The armed forces administer their own intelligence test, which grades recruits on their potential ability to perform military tasks successfully. The M-60 tank is an older, more conventional model. In that tank, the gunner and tank commander (the two people who have the most to do with the tank's success, the driver and loader being less important in combat) had much lower success depending on intelligence levels. The brightest (category I) troops were nearly twice as effective as the dumbest (category V). This is a phenomenon long noted in combat. Successful warriors tend to be brighter people, as well as being stronger and more aggressive. But the M-1 not only made it easier for the dumber troops to perform well, but even made the brightest troops more lethal. In the M-1, the category I troops were still about 19 percent more effective than the category V troops.

The increased ease of use of the M-1 had many benefits.

• It didn't take as long to train tank crews. This saved money, as well as time.

• You could use a wider range of intelligence categories for tank crews. With the increasing need for technicians, there is always keen competition for the brightest recruits. With the easier-to-use tanks, you can afford to send nearly all the brightest recruits into technical jobs, and still get people who will make effective tank crews. Note the small difference in performance between categories I through IV.

• It's easier and cheaper to maintain tank-crew skills. It's always been the case that soldiers quickly lose many of their skills if they do not practice regularly. But the M-1 was so easy to use, so "intuitive," that it took longer to "forget" how to use the fire control and other systems on the tank.

• Simulators, of which the U.S. armed forces have been enthusiastic users, are more productive with the M-1, because the items to be simulated are fewer. The troops can concentrate on honing their video game–type skills and improving their tactical skills (how to outsmart other tank crews on the battlefield) and situational awareness (knowing what's likely to happen next).

All of this ease of use is costly. The weapons are more expensive to design if they are easier to use. This ease of use is the result of several different developments.

• The design of the systems must be carefully thought out with thousands of man-hours spent on observing actual tank crews operate existing systems, and then having crews work with various designs for new ones. There's a lot of trial and error with this, and it gets pretty expensive.

• A key element in the ease of use is the extensive use of computers. While the microcomputer components themselves are not that expensive, the programming is, as is making sure the computer equipment is installed so that it will not easily fail during the stress of combat.

• The software, which ties all the computers, range finders, sensors, and weapons together, is a new development in weapons design and manufacture. Software, or instructions for machines, is something that was only invented over the past two centuries (initially for weaving machinery) and only used for computers during the past half century. Software is still a developing field, and software in weapons is even more of a murky area. The software in the M-1 tank was something of a breakthrough, at least insofar as it worked quite well.

• Maintenance and repair is made easier by combining many parts into modules and then making it easier to remove and replace the module. Many vehicles now have computerized diagnostic systems that alert the crew when a module has failed, or is about to fail. The computer can advise on how to work around the failure, if possible, or how to replace the broken module. On many systems, CD-ROMs have replaced manuals, and the maintenance computers carry on a dialogue with the crew or mechanic to quickly find the problem and fix it. All of this has reduced the maintenance load on the crew, resulting in less fatigue for the troops and more readiness for the vehicles.

All these techniques to save time and effort at the front are expensive. For example, the modular repair technique (key components, especially electronic components, are in separate "black boxes") requires computerized test equipment to tell the repair people, often the crew, which black box is defective. The faulty module is unplugged and removed, and a new one is put in its place. The broken black box is shipped back for repair, although this will not always be possible on the battlefield and the defective module may just be dumped. Thus this ease of repair saves you time and lives on the battlefield, but costs you a lot more to buy and maintain these systems. Even major items like tank engines and turrets can be dealt with this way.

The Enemy Is Not Always Clueless

DESPITE THE STARTLING victory over Iraq in 1991, there were several aspects of that campaign that should give one pause. The Iraqis managed to keep their Scud missile launchings going until the very end. And after the war was over it was discovered that the Iraqis still had quite a few usable Scuds left. All this despite the considerable American effort before the war to find out what missiles the Iraqis had and the more violent efforts during the war to find and destroy the Scuds. What the Iraqis pulled off in concealing their missiles should come as no surprise. There were several other technical accomplishments of the Iraqis during the Gulf War that you don't hear much about. For example, the Iraqis were able to use their electronic-warfare equipment to figure out where Coalition aircraft were operating, and several ambushes took place. The most common victim was the low flying A-10, but all Coalition aircraft tended to be sloppy in how they used their radios, and the Iraqis were able to take advantage of that.

It could have been worse, and in future wars it may well be. The Iranians openly boast of deceiving U.S. military intelligence with their locally designed and manufactured electronic-warfare equipment. Many other nations have shown an ability to manufacture their own weapons and equipment that, while not better than U.S. gear, is different enough to give American troops a nasty shock when encountered on the battlefield. A seemingly "inferior" opponent who refuses to surrender is most likely hard at work coming up with new devices and techniques to confound you. It has always been this way, and only a fool would ignore this lesson of history.

Making the Most of Experience

COMBAT EXPERIENCE IS an extremely valuable commodity, and a very perishable one. For most of this century, the rate of technological change caused combat experience to have a very short shelf life. New weapons and equipment would come along and make last year's tactics obsolete. No one really was able to get on top of this problem. What we have ended up with is typical of military affairs. That is, when it comes to experience, it's not usually a matter of who is better, but who is worse.

But with the demise of the cold war, and our entry into the era of little wars, experience suddenly has a longer shelf life. The little wars, especially the "peacekeeping operations," rely less on technology and more on tactics and techniques that have not changed for thousands of years. Well, there have been some changes. We now have electronic media that allow the folks back home to see what kind of trouble the troops can get into overseas. Thus it's ever more important to make sure you do it right the first time.

The problems with Haiti (a U.S. ship getting chased away by a mob) and Somalia (U.S. troops in a desperate firefight) led American officers to concentrate on collecting and organizing practical experience. Much of this experience for little wars is quite the opposite of what one would do in a major war. This is particularly true with peacekeeping operations, where fighting is secondary to keeping the peace. It is in these latter operations that troops must learn new habits that are often contrary to what they have always been told. For example, tanks normally seek cover and avoid showing themselves to the enemy. But in peacekeeping operations, you want to put your tanks in plain sight where your (usually) less well equipped adversaries will be suitably awed and discouraged from any hostile actions.

When moving, combat troops must be prepared for combat, but always ready to talk their way past hostile local forces. "Shoot on sight," which is normal in conventional warfare, is the exception in peacekeeping operations. Troops have to be trained to deal with a new set of situations. How do you deal with potentially hostile troops whose language you don't speak? How do you maintain combat readiness without inciting the local armed forces?

Manning roadblocks and checkpoints are the most common activities for peacekeeping troops, and these situations often put low-ranking officers and NCOs in tricky situations for which their previous training has not prepared them. A twenty-five-year-old sergeant in charge of a roadblock could find himself in danger of causing an international incident if he's not very careful with whatever strangeness comes down the road toward him.

When there is combat in these situations, it is often of the "low-intensity" (guerrilla) type. Not all troops are trained or equipped to deal with the sniping and harassment that this form of combat entails. Because guerrilla warfare involves getting rather intimately involved with a foreign culture, it is not much studied by armed forces. Yet this form of warfare is still encountered at least once per generation, and has to be relearned each time. Technology is not much help in guerrilla operations; more useful is good old-fashioned "getting to know the locals and the lay of the land." As armed forces place more of their emphasis on technology, they become less able to deal with low-intensity warfare and dealing with guerrillas. The next decade will reveal whether or not many, or any, nations have decided to deal with this problem head-on and trained for these "little wars" ahead of time.

Making the Robots Do It for Us

ROBOT WARRIORS are among us, their number is increasing, and this is, oddly enough, not much noticed. Many types of missiles qualify for robot status. ("Just turn them on and they fight without human intervention.") The first robot weapons were mines; the modern versions began to appear in the mid-1800s. These were naval mines that exploded if a ship ran into them. Very effective. Land versions went into production just before World War I. Many would not think of these mines as robots, but they were. The first true mines had sensors that exploded the mine if something hit the mine. It was simple, and it worked. Mines were an important development because they replaced troops, or warships. At sea, you could place a string of mines where you wanted to be sure the enemy would not go, or would be slowed down if he found out about the minefield and decided to clear it. Without mines, you would have had to assign ships to the same task. On land, mines served the same purposes: replacing troops with the mine "robots." Mines were even better than troops, as they did not have morale problems, would not run away, and would fight to the death. The perfect soldiers.

During World War II, naval mines became more "intelligent," being able to detect things like noise and water pressure. From there, mines have since been fitted with microprocessors and a lot more "intelligence" about whom to attack and how to go about it.

Next came torpedoes that searched for targets on their own. During World War II torpedoes learned to chase the noise a ship makes, or the disturbances in the water caused by the ship's wake. After World War II these types of torpedoes were perfected. In effect, torpedoes became self-guiding missiles. You fired the torpedo in the general direction of a ship and the torpedo would pick up the target and run it down. These torpedoes were largely submarine weapons and, because the submarine no longer had to get in close enough to fire a "dumb" (unguided) torpedo, the robotic torpedoes made life easier, and safer, for the subs.

Guided missiles have gotten some publicity, but they are simply cousins of the mines and guided torpedoes. Cruise missiles more frequently take the place of bombers. The earliest surface-to-air missiles replaced antiaircraft artillery, but for the last decade or so the SAMs have replaced interceptor aircraft. Air-to-air missiles, especially the longer-range ones, use their own radar and computer to hunt down and destroy enemy aircraft. Antiradar missiles seek out and destroy radar transmitters. Antiship missiles have increased in range and "smartness" to the point where they often replace the usual air attack on enemy ships. Antitank missiles are increasingly of the "fire and forget" variety. In other words, you fire the missile in the general direction of an enemy tank. After the missile is launched, it uses its own sensors to seek out and destroy armored vehicles. Like most current missiles, there is no sure way to tell enemy from friendly targets. But on the battlefield, "friendly fire" is a common, if little discussed, problem.

Truly robotic aircraft, ones that return in one piece, unlike one-way missiles, are increasingly taking over the dangerous air reconnaissance work. Even during the Vietnam War, some three thousand recon sorties were flown over North Vietnam by drone aircraft (albeit remotely piloted). Today, computers are available to fly these missions without any human intervention.

Robotic ground vehicles are proving more difficult to perfect, as there is a lot more detail on the ground for the computer to sort out and deal with. But it's only a matter of time before the needed computing power becomes powerful enough and cheap enough to do the job. The first use of drone ground vehicles will probably be for reconnaissance work, which is always the most dangerous.

Even now, simulated robots are widely used in planning and training for war. The air force was an early adapter of flight simulators, borrowing from, and contributing to, the technology used for civilian flight simulators. Military simulators have since gained competition from simulators designed as games for civilian use. You can buy these in software stores, and air forces have used these same "toys" for training their own pilots. The U.S. Air Force and Navy also use powerful simulators so that pilots can fly dangerous missions on the computer before taking off to do it for real. This allows pilots to practice what might happen to them in enemy airspace before they get there. These mission-planning simulators are also being adopted by the ground forces and the navy. In these simulators, the troops use simulated robots. It's only a matter of time before they use real robots.

The future of warfare is robots. These are a better way to deal with dangerous situations, and what could be more dangerous than combat? What is amazing about this is that there has never been any conscious program to replace people with robots and machines on the battlefield. Yet that is what has been happening for the last century. The number of combat troops on the battlefield has dramatically declined in the last century. In the last years of the 1800s, you had twenty troops in the same area of the battlefield where you would find one today. But the battlefield has not become safer because there are fewer troops there. One finds far more deadly machines in the combat zone, machines that will kill man or machine indiscriminately. We'll probably never see robots in the shape of men, lurching about the battlefield firing their weapons. You will see more machines of different shapes and sizes that can find other machines by themselves and destroy them. Humans are not seen as the principal target, other machines are. It may be a while before mankind can just step back and let the machines fight it out among themselves.

Not So Much New, but Definitely Improved

THE END OF THE cold war meant the end of copious funds for new weapons systems. The only new weapons likely to show up in the next decade or so are those that were already in development in the early 1990s. The only new projects will be for upgrades and modifications of existing systems. Not only has weapons research been cut by more than half worldwide, but the purchase of new weapons has markedly decreased. For example, America bought 20 ships, 511 aircraft, 448 tanks, and 175 strategic missiles in 1990, but five years later purchased only 6 ships, 127 aircraft, 0 tanks, and 18 strategic missiles. Russian declines in purchases have been even greater.

Since new equipment will not be available, there is much opportunity to upgrade older stuff, especially the older Russian-built equipment. European and Israeli companies have been doing a lot of business providing Western-based upgrades to Soviet-made aircraft. Egyptian Mig-21s have been fitted with HUDs and Sidewinder missiles. British contractors have installed HUDWAC (HUD plus weapon-aiming computer) and a ranging radar to the Chinese F-7M fighter (a copy of the Mig-21). the F-7M has been sold to Bangladesh, Iran, Pakistan, and Zimbabwe. The Pakistani F-7Ms were equipped with British ejection seats.

This upgrading is going on worldwide and will be the common way of improving one's armed forces over the next decade or two.

Laptop Leadership

BUT THERE IS definitely a "revolution in warfare" (a popular buzzword) within the American military. As the nation that invented the personal computer (PC) enters its third decade using such machines, it should be no surprise that PCs are found throughout the military. The troops have also adopted cellular phone technology, satellite communications, and maps on CD-ROMs. The current generation of officers leading the troops grew up with PCs. These officers feel quite comfortable leading their troops with a cellular phone in one hand and a laptop computer in the other. In the early 1980s, the senior military leadership began talking of "digitization" and "battle space." For the second time in this century, a revolution in warfare was at hand. Mechanized warfare got started in World War I and matured during World War II. Ever since 1945, it was pretty much more of the same.

Until the 1980s.

Now there's a new military revolution in the wind and no one is quite sure what its final shape will be. One thing that is agreed on is that the new forms of warfare will be highly dependent on computers, lots of different kinds of computers. There will be computers in nearly every piece of equipment and many of the computers will be talking to each other. There will be lots of robots, most not looking like what we think robots should look like. Continuing a trend that has been ongoing for several centuries, there will be fewer troops per square mile on the battlefield.

This revolution does not mean that the infantryman will be replaced. He never is. When the mechanized revolution reached its peak during World War II, the infantry were still there. But in addition there were tanks and other armored vehicles, aircraft flew overhead, and radios carried orders hither and yon faster than any messenger of old.

The new form of warfare will seem almost like a parody of a science fiction movie. The commander will spend a lot of time looking for information. His troops will be spread out all over the place and all the robotic weapons lurking about will make it dangerous to go visiting in person. Taking more than a cue from the creators of computer games, the soldiers now have computer screens full of detailed and easy-to-understand images. It looks like a game, but the deaths are not simulated. Commanders play Space Invaders for keeps. The computer not only collects information on the battle situation and presents it visually, but also calculates what the best tactic would be at the moment. So, between the radio/cellular phone/satellite link and the information on the laptop, the commander will lead his troops from wherever they are to wherever they have to go.

Okay, it sounds so cool. But reality and a sense of history tell us that some of the stuff will work some of the time and you won't know exactly what stuff and what time. But that's the way it's always been. The troops will have to adapt to a new collection of weapons working only some of the time. The side that adapts the quickest will tend to survive longer.

Tough Decisions

ONE OF THE MAJOR problems in the post–cold war world is the smaller amounts of money available for defense. A major goal is to find ways to get more out of less money. There is ample opportunity to cut defense spending without leaving America, or her troops, defenseless and at risk.

Some examples:

• Accept that the cold war is over, and so is cold war–level defense spending. That means doing what is rarely done: killing weapons programs and old strength levels. Want to save $25 billion a year? Easy, cut personnel strength about 300,000. Deactivate three of the army's ten active divisions, three of the navy's twelve carrier groups, and three or four of the air force's twenty combat wings.

• Get rid of the long-range bombers, or at least all the different flavors. Currently the air force plans to field a bomber force of twenty B-2s, ninety-five B-1Bs, and sixty-six B-52Hs. Politicians (who want the money spent on their voters) and the air force (who want the money spent on other things) continue to fight over the program to develop and buy twenty more B-2s. The first twenty cost $44.4 billion. One suggestion is to immediately retire the entire fleet of B-1Bs as a way to pay for the additional twenty B-2s. This actually plays well in Congress, as building twenty more B-2s for about $15 billion gives you more pork to play with than the few billion dollars keeping the B-1Bs around would. Besides, the B-1Bs have become an embarrassment, with one aspect or another of the aircraft coming under fire for not working.

• Do more interservice consolidation. A good example of this at work is the U.S. Air Force decision to retire its EF-111A Wild Weasel and let the Navy EA-6 do the same job for both services. Although the EF-111, carrying 3.5 tons of antennae, transmitters, and computers to detect, analyze, and scramble enemy radar signals to prevent antiaircraft artillery or missiles from attacking U.S. aircraft, flew more than 1,300 sorties during the Persian Gulf War, subsequent analysis showed that the navy EA-6 was superior. Although first delivered to the air force in 1981, with the last EF-111 received in 1985, retiring the planes would save more than $1 billion in operating, maintenance, and upgrade expenses. The navy would hand over twenty EA-6 aircraft while the two services shared in the maintenance and upgrade expenses.

• Drop the new aircraft and upgrade the old. No one can afford to design and build new combat aircraft that will overpower the current American models (F-15, F-16, F-18, etc.). Upgrading rather than buying may be forced on us. The new aircraft like the B-2 bomber and F-22 fighter cost so much that, even with the current lavish defense budgets, there won't be enough money left to upgrade or buy any other aircraft. At the moment, the U.S. Air Force plans, from 2002 through 2009, to buy forty-eight F-22 fighters a year. But this leaves no money for any other combat aircraft. To have enough aircraft to keep twenty wings flying, the air force would have to keep its F-15s and F-16s in service for up to forty-five years. That is more than twice the usual limit, and it could be dangerous and expensive to keep aircraft that old maintained. Without the F-22, there would be money to improve the F-15 and F-16, building the improved models and still being able to overwhelm any other air force on the planet. Each F-22 fighter will cost $134 million, compared to $10 million to $15 million per F-16/F-15 fighter-bomber upgrade.

• Make sure you can handle what you've got. During the first two days of the Persian Gulf War, U.S. troops were bombarded by nearly two million electronic messages. Information passed through radios, computers, telephones, and fax machines. The volume of information was unexpected and overwhelming. For the rest of the war, there was a lot of scrambling to cope with what happened when everyone used all their new communications gear at once. For the previous decade or so the military had added more communications equipment—a lot of stuff. But it had never been used in a war before. Some signal officers suspected that they might be flooded with messages when the first major military emergency came around, and those suspicions proved correct. This was not a unique event—this sort of thing has happened before. But it provides ample opportunities for major-league disaster. For example, most of the current communications technology is developed commercially. Using commercially produced information and communications technology keeps costs down for the military. But anyone can buy, and examine, this commercial technology. This can create some serious security problems for the United States. Among those millions of messages coursing through the military communications system in the first days of the Gulf War were some from foreign computer hackers (Denmark, Russia, and Iraq, among others) who tried to penetrate U.S. military computer systems. The U.S. military has now created emergency-response teams to detect and react to this hacking. But new communications hardware and software is added all the time. One can only speculate on just how bad the next round will be.

• For the army, canceling its new Comanche attack helicopter would mean flying older ones longer or settling for a smaller fleet. But there is considerable momentum behind the Comanche project and no one in the army aviation crowd wants to lose it.

• The Marine Corps, as a part of the navy, has always gotten by on a relatively low budget. The marines don't have a lot of the overhead that the other services do, because they *are* a part of the navy. But they have some expensive new items of equipment in development. Their V-22, tilt-engine transport could be lost. Another loss could be their independent tactical fighter arm (which the navy would take over) and the acceptance of a modified version of the army Blackhawk to replace the marines' aging CH-46 medium-lift helicopter.

• Stop building new ICBMs for the navy's missile submarines. These new Trident missiles were designed to take out underground Russian missile silos that have been emptied by disarmament treaties.

• Stop building new nuclear submarines like the Seawolf. The Russian sub fleet, the main reason for our nuclear subs, has fallen apart. The Russians can't afford to maintain the nuclear subs they have and the production of new ones has declined (and will probably stop, due to lack of resources). If you want to maintain a force of forty-five nuclear attack submarines, you have to build one and a half a year because they wear out in thirty years. You can't afford to build one and a half Seawolf subs a year. Simple as that.

• The air force could pull F-16s (and other late-model aircraft) out of its aircraft storage (for surplus aircraft) and refurbish them or use them for spare parts. Air force generals hate to do this—it smacks too much of using second-hand goods. But when your potential opponents are doing even worse, secondhand isn't so bad. And it's affordable.

• Get realistic about weapons and equipment standards in the post–cold war world. For example, the air force got hit with charges that it installed a defective, untested radar jammer (the ALQ-135) on its F-15E bombers just before the Persian Gulf War. Technically, the ALQ-135 had not passed its tests. But the tests were unrealistic, requiring the ALQ-135 to jam twelve threats simultaneously. But it is rare for even three radar-guided missiles to be launched simultaneously. Often these unrealistically stiff requirements are written up mainly to keep the worst critics of the program at bay. ("How can you afford not to fund something this wonderful?") Jammers are heavily dependent on complex software and electronics and are very difficult to develop. The air force and navy have spent more than $9 billion on radar jammers for their aircraft since the mid-1970s. It's something of a black art testing these devices, because of the variety of conditions that can be encountered, as well as the countermeasures a potential foe can come up with. This makes it difficult to judge real successes and failures. Many of the arguments in Congress over "defective" systems have to do with how one interprets test results, or runs the tests in the first place. Testing a radar jammer is not like testing a traditional weapon system such as a bomb, which leaves an unambiguous mark upon a target. Electronic-warfare systems, including jammers, deal with invisible electrical impulses sent out against enemy radar waves, resulting in conditions that are hard to measure in testing. Part of the problem is educating the Congress on what is being tested and how.

• The U.S. Navy has a similar problem. Each new F/A-18E/F Hornet aircraft costs $81 million, compared to $36 million for each of the older F/A-18C/D. The navy wants to build a new all-weather attack aircraft that will cost more than $100 million each. The best thing to do is to scale back the number of carriers and their air wings.

• Perhaps the most far-reaching cost-cutting suggestion of all would propose that the air force again becomes the army air forces. The army and air force have remained linked since the air force was spun off in 1947. The air force still does close air support for the army, although reluctantly. The air force still provides the army's airlift. Army and air force bases are still located near each other in many cases, and they even have a joint exchange (sort of a supermarket and general store) system. Cutting duplicated command staffs at neighboring army and air force bases would result in major savings. Similar advantages would be found on the battlefield. Currently, the marine ground commanders have the advantage their army counterparts had until the air force became a separate service: complete control over air support for the ground troops. Merging the army and air force would give soldiers that same edge once more. The fact is that the army and air force are as dependent on one another as the navy and Marine Corps. Just as the marines could not go to war without the navy, the air force could not go without the army. The navy carries the marines to distant shores and provides gunfire support for the marines as they storm ashore, and continues with air support once they are ashore. The army takes ground for air force bases and protects the air force units while the aircraft assist the ground forces. Consolidating the two services once more would eliminate a lot of waste and duplication. Consider, for example, that the army, with all its helicopters, still has an enormous air force, with more aircraft than the air force. Of course, the air force has larger and more complex aircraft, including a thousand heavy transports and over five hundred four-engine jet tankers. But the main reason for folding the air force back into the army is to cut back on the squabbling over who does what. The navy has always been the force out front. This was true even before aircraft carriers came along. If heavy lifting was required, you brought up the army. Nowadays, you would also bring forward the air force, which consists largely of maintenance and supply units to keep all the aircraft armed and flying. But as a separate service, the air force has, from its inception, been going after army and navy jobs—without much success, but with a great deal of noise and expense. Thus far, the air force has argued that its missions should increase. The air force believes that it can replace navy carriers with bombers based in the United States. It also contends that it, and not the other services, should be in charge of buying and developing space technology. While it is true that bombers can reach any place in the world, it also is true that they can't provide the same degree of coverage and control that a carrier battle group or marine amphibious ready group can provide. A carrier can stay in one place for months at a time, along with sixty combat-ready aircraft. The ships in a carrier battle group can also launch cruise missiles at land and sea targets. The marine amphibious group, meanwhile, carries about two thousand marines with their own helicopters, landing craft, and Harrier jump jets. The air force can't provide that kind of presence with bombers flying in from distant bases. Moreover, while the air force has enormous experience with space technology, it's the army and navy who are the primary users of space systems for targeting, intelligence, navigation, and communications. It's time to admit that we made a mistake creating a third service. Other nations do quite well without making the air force a separate service. You can go either way, but having the air forces as part of either the army or navy is the cheaper way to go. After all, even after the air force became a separate service, the army just grew another "air branch" and the navy never considered splitting off its own considerable air force.

The Toughest Decision: Stop Voting for Pork

THIS IS THE EASIEST decision to make and the hardest to carry through with. Over the past fifty years, American taxpayers have grown used to a system where defense spending has become more important for its political than for its military impact. The defense budget has become one giant pork barrel. Just about any defense project can get money if enough congressional districts get a piece of the action. Back in those districts, there are always potential opposition candidates waiting to jump on the incumbent for "losing jobs" by not snagging a share of the defense pork.

Many have tried, and all have failed, so far, to break this cycle. But if you can stop the pork, you solve some large budget problems.

Index